Proceedings of the
Seventh European Conference on
Computer Supported Cooperative Work

T0180676

ECSCW 2001

Proceedings of the
Seventh European Conference on
Computer Supported Cooperative Work
16-20 September 2001, Bonn, Germany

Edited by

Wolfgang Prinz
GMD-FIT, Germany

Matthias Jarke
RWTH Aachen, Germany

Yvonne Rogers
University of Sussex, United Kingdom

Kjeld Schmidt
Technical University of Denmark

and

Volker Wulf
GMD-FIT, Germany

KLUWER ACADEMIC PUBLISHERS
DORDRECHT / BOSTON / LONDON

A C.I.P. Catalogue record for this book is available from the Library of Congress.

ISBN 0-7923-7162-3 (HB)
ISBN 0-7923-7163-1 (PB)

Published by Kluwer Academic Publishers,
P.O. Box 17, 3300 AA Dordrecht, The Netherlands.

Sold and distributed in North, Central and South America
by Kluwer Academic Publishers,
101 Philip Drive, Norwell, MA 02061, U.S.A.

In all other countries, sold and distributed
by Kluwer Academic Publishers,
P.O. Box 322, 3300 AH Dordrecht, The Netherlands.

Printed on acid-free paper

Cover Design by Lucia Sassen, GMD-FIT

Printed in the Netherlands.

Sponsors

ECSCW 2001 is grateful for the generous support of the following sponsors:

OrbiTeam GmbH

Sun Microsystems

T-Nova

Table of Contents

From the Organizers

This volume represents the proceedings of ECSCW 2001, the 7th European Conference on Computer Supported Cooperative Work. ECSCW is an international forum for interdisciplinary research activities from various technical and social disciplines. The conference alternates with the ACM International Conference on CSCW to provide annually a principal forum for CSCW research.

This year the German CSCW community takes pride in organizing ECSCW. The establishment of a German research community reaches back to the early 1990s. In 1991 the first German speaking CSCW conference was organized in Bremen by Jürgen Friedrich. Since then, a biannual conference series, called DCSCW, developed. It brought together researchers from Human Computer Interaction, Distributed Systems, Information Systems, Humanities and Social Sciences. While academics often acted at the edges of their home disciplines, government funds at the European, federal, and state level helped creating research groups with international reputation. Industry picked up on the results to innovate products and processes. Recently the CSCW community decided to join forces with other fields of applied Computer Science as well as industrial designers to shape a newly created conference series called *Mensch & Computer*.

The ECSCW program of technical papers presented in this volume is the result of a very selective review process. This year the conference received 109 submissions of very high quality from which 21 papers were selected. Both the number of submissions and the quality and diversity of the program presented here are testimony to the importance the CSCW community has gained. We are sure that you will enjoy the papers in this volume.

The papers in this volume are only one aspect of a diverse and dynamic event such as ECSCW. The technical paper program is complemented by a record number of 10 workshops, high quality tutorials, demonstrations from industry and academia, and posters representing research in progress. These events reflect some of the most exciting and novel aspects of CSCW research and practice. They are essential to the success of the conference and the continued growth of the community.

This conference could not have taken place without considerable enthusiasm, support, and encouragement as well as sheer hard work. Many people have earned the thanks of those who attended and organized ECSCW 2001. In particular, we would like to gratefully thank:

- All those who submitted to the conference. The standard was very high and reflects well on the research work in the community.
- All of those who contributed to the conference through workshops, tutorials, posters, demos, and paper presentations.

- All of those who contributed to the organization of the conference. Planning a major international conference is a complex endeavor and many people made significant contributions to realizing a successful conference.
- The Student Volunteers who work so tirelessly during the conference to ensure things run smoothly.
- Those members of the Conference and Program Committees who gave so freely of their time and energy to ensure that the conference was both smoothly run and of high technical quality. The many individuals we owe our thanks to are listed elsewhere in this volume.
- The many sponsors and supporters of ECSCW 2001 for their contributions to the conference and to the CSCW community generally.

We would also like to acknowledge the organizers of the ACM CSCW conference for the support and encouragement they extend to this conference. The close cooperation between ECSCW and the ACM CSCW conferences allows us to continue the growth of a truly international research community tackling the problems crucial to CSCW. Between both conferences we have been able to establish an annual international conference on CSCW for the last decade charting the development and maturity of the discipline. The future appears to hold considerable promise for us all.

Matthias Jarke, Wolfgang Prinz, Yvonne Rogers, and Volker Wulf

ECSCW 2001 Conference Committee

Conference co-chairs:
  Wolfgang Prinz, GMD-FIT, Germany
  Volker Wulf, GMD-FIT, Germany
Program co-chairs:
  Matthias Jarke, RWTH Aachen,
  Germany
  Yvonne Rogers, University of Sussex,
  UK
Proceedings chair:
  Kjeld Schmidt, Technical University of
  Denmark
Tutorials co-chairs:
  Peter Carstensen, IT University
  Copenhagen, Denmark
  Tom Gross, GMD-FIT, Germany
Workshop co-chairs:
  Jörg Haake, GMD-IPSI, Germany
  Andrew McGrath, Hutchison 3G, UK
Demonstrations chair:
  Stefan Uellner, T-Nova, Germany
Video chair:
  Johannes Bumiller, Daimler Chrysler
  Research, Germany
  Jean Schweitzer, Siemens, Germany
Posters chair:
  Markus Rohde, Agenda Consult,
  Germany
Student volunteer co-chairs:
  Michael Koch, TU Munich, Germany
  Volkmar Pipek, University of Bonn,
  Germany
Doctoral colloquium co-chairs:
  Liam Bannon, University of Limerick,
  Ireland
  Tom Rodden, University of
  Nottingham, UK
Electronic media support:
  Wolfgang Gräther, GMD-FIT, Germany
  Leonie Schäfer, GMD-FIT, Germany
Local arrangements:
  Helge Kahler, University of Bonn,
  Germany
Conference office
  Christine Harms, ccHa, Germany

Liaisons

North America:
  Wendy Kellogg, IBM, USA
Australia:
  Geraldine Fitzpatrick, University of
  Queensland, Australia
Japan:
  Ken-ichi Okada, Keio University, Japan
South America:
  Jacques Wainer, Universita de
  Campinas, Brasil

ECSCW 2001 Program Committee

Program co-chairs:
   Matthias Jarke, RWTH Aachen
   Yvonne Rogers, University of Sussex
Mark Ackerman, MIT Lab for Computer Science, USA
Liam Bannon, University of Limerick, Ireland
Steve Benford, University of Nottingham, UK
Tora Bikson, RAND Corporation, USA
Janette Blomberg, Sapient, USA
John Bowers, University of Manchester, UK
Susanne Bødker, University of Aarhus, Denmark
Peter Carstensen, IT University, Denmark
Elisabeth Churchill, FX-PAL, USA
Giorgio De Michelis, University of Milano, Italy
Prasun Dewan, University of North Carolina, USA
Paul Dourish, University of California, Irvine, USA
Geraldine Fitzpatrick, University of Queensland, Australia
Saul Greenberg, University of Calgary, Canada
Beki Grinter, Xerox PARC, USA
Tom Gross, GMD-FIT, Germany
Jonathan Grudin, Microsoft Research, USA
Christine Halverson, IBM T.J. Watson & Almaden Research Centers, USA
Christian Heath, University of London, UK
Thomas Herrmann, University of Dortmund, Germany
Simon Kaplan, University of Queensland, Australia
Laurent Karsenty, AHRAMIS, France
Reinhard Keil-Slawik, University of Paderborn, Germany
Wendy Kellogg, IBM, USA
Finn Kensing, Roskilde University, Denmark
John King, University of Michigan, USA
Michael Koch, Technical University of Munich, Germany

Helmut Krcmar, University of Hohenheim, Germany
Kari Kuutti, University of Oulu, Finland
Hideaki Kuzuoka, University of Tsukuba, Japan
Morton Kyng, Danish National Centre for IT Research, Denmark
Wendy Mackay, INRIA, France
Gloria Mark, UC Irvine, USA
Anders Mørch, University of Bergen, Norway
Horst Oberquelle, University of Hamburg, Germany
Kenichi Okada, Keio University, Japan
Steven Poltrock, Boeing Company, Seattle, USA
Atul Prakash, University of Michigan, USA
Wolfgang Prinz, GMD-FIT, Germany
Ralf Reichwald, Technical University of Munich, Germany
Toni Robertson, University of New South Wales, Australia
Mike Robinson, University of Jyväskylä, Finland
Tom Rodden, University of Nottingham, UK
Kjeld Schmidt, Technical University of Denmark, Denmark
Gerhard Schwabe, University of Koblenz, Germany
Carla Simone, University of Torino, Italy
Norbert Streitz, GMD-IPSI, Germany
Lucy Suchman, Xerox PARC, USA
Yngve Sundblad, Royal Institute of Technology, Sweden
Ina Wagner, Technical University of Vienna, Austria
Alexander Wolf, University of Colorado at Boulder, USA
Volker Wulf, GMD-FIT, Germany

W. Prinz, M. Jarke, Y. Rogers, K. Schmidt, and V. Wulf (eds.), *Proceedings of the Seventh European Conference on Computer-Supported Cooperative Work, 16-20 September 2001, Bonn, Germany*, pp. 1-17.
© 2001 Kluwer Academic Publishers. Printed in the Netherlands.

Cooperation in massively distributed information spaces

Olav W. Bertelsen & Susanne Bødker
Department of Computer Science, University of Aarhus, Denmark
olavb@daimi.au.dk, bodker@intermedia.au.dk

Abstract. Common information spaces are often, implicitly or explicitly, viewed as something that can be accessed *in toto* from one (of many) location. Our studies of wastewater treatment plants show how such massively distributed spaces challenge many of the ways that CSCW view common information spaces. The studies fundamentally challenge the idea that common information spaces are about access to everything, everywhere. Participation in optimisation is introduced as an important feature of work tied to the moving around in physical space. In the CSCW literature, peripheral awareness and at a glance overview are mostly connected with the coordination of activities within a control room or in similar co-located circumstances. It is concluded that this focus on shoulder to shoulder cooperation has to be supplemented with studies of cooperation through massively distributed information spaces.

Introduction

This paper discusses the massively distributed information space of a large industrial artefact, a wastewater plant. Common information spaces are often, implicitly or explicitly, viewed as something that can be accessed *in toto* from one (of many) location. Our studies of wastewater treatment plants show how such massively distributed spaces challenge many of the ways that CSCW view common information spaces. The studies fundamentally challenge the idea that common information spaces are about access to *everything, everywhere*. The paper looks at the distribution and geographical spreading of the information paper looks at the distribution and geographical spreading of the information space, and the ways that workers organise their activity around this. As pointed out by Schmidt & Bannon (1992), providing a common information space is not a matter of providing overview and uniform access independent of physical location to a shared database. Nevertheless, many recent technical solutions are based on this assumption - e.g. that users want to access the same web pages from their mobile phone as they do from their office PC. This assumption is, however, contradicted by several authors, primarily from the perspective of technological diversity, arguing that it is better to utilise the particular capabilities of a particular device (screen size, etc. when accessing the information space from a particular device e.g. Nielsen & Søndergård, 2000).

Bannon & Bødker (1997) discuss some of the many problems of the general, idealised assumptions made about common information spaces. In the present study, we illustrate how workers actively construct the common information space that is necessary for them in order to run and not least to optimise the running of a wastewater plant. This active construction requires cooperation while moving about in the geographically dispersed plant, exploring and experimenting with optimisation of the plant, while being more or less peripheral to this experimentation process.

Re-placing the term space with the notion of place, is the key concern for Harrison & Dourish (1996). The argue that what we should be looking for are ".. sets of mutually-held and mutually available, cultural understandings about behaviour and action", their definition of place.

In the CSCW literature, peripheral awareness and at a glance overview are important concepts for understanding cooperation and transitions between cooperative work activities. However, these concepts are mostly connected with the coordination of activities within a control room or in similar co-located circumstances. In the wastewater plant we see a somewhat different version of peripheral awareness and at a glance overview; one that is connected to moving around and physically orienting oneself in the plant. The wastewater plant is not controlled and operated from one central control room and there is no single place where at a glance overview can be obtained. From this perspective the 'standard' CSCW concepts such as overview and peripheral awareness are given new meaning, contrasted with the situations of co-located cooperation. Furthermore, mobility is given a new meaning because workers move about in a well-known terrain where their information needs depend on their particular physical location. They zoom with their feet, not with their information appliance. Bellotti & Bly (1996) studied how designers have a high degree of local mobility in their design work so as to communicate with one another. They point out that these same designers, accordingly, do not cooperate from their desk. In a similar way, the wastewater workers are highly mobile and rarely placed in front of their computer. The difference between the two studies, however, is that the designer moves about to find people, whereas the wastewater workers primarily move about to control the plant.

The wastewater study

During the past year we have been engaged in a study of a wastewater treatment plant. We have conducted workplace studies, and we apply an interventionist approach through the construction of prototypes for new computer support for the running and optimisation of the wastewater plant. The project is part of an ongoing study of common information spaces. Furthermore, we use examples from one plant even though the research is part of a set of coordinated studies in three plants, carried out in cooperation with other research and industrial partners.

Our prototyping experiment has been focussing on how to get and maintain a local overview of parts of the plant while moving about, and on compiling and interpreting information that is massively distributed on meters and dials. For a more detailed description of the project and the study, see (Bertelsen & Nielsen 1999).

In the context of CSCW, a wastewater plant like the one we focus on is interesting because it challenges some of the central conceptions in CSCW.

While one might think that providing cleaned wastewater is the overall objective of wastewater cleaning, it turns out that clean water is but one of many parameters that have to do with optimisation of the running of the plant. The cost of running the plant can be reduced by producing as much electricity as possible, using gas turbines running on biogasses. Taxes are high on sludge, and can be reduced by proper fermentation and water extraction (pressing). The plant is built for a much smaller daily production of waste than what is processed today, and must handle a continuous overload of 25-50 pct. Accordingly, the plant is the scene of an ongoing experimental optimisation process.

At the plant, 8 people do their daily work in a large physical area. But for the water basins, well known from wastewater plants, most machinery and water processing take place in-doors in buildings that are spread out on the land so as to support the flow of water through the plant. The division of work is structured around this process, and hence, also geographically. One pair of workers is responsible for the inlet water and the initial filtering of this, one pair for the fermentation and gas production, and one pair for the removal of the sludge. Added to these three pairs are a foreman and a plant manager. The plant manager has his office in the main building where the remaining staff meets as well for breaks etc. It is characteristic of the plant, that there is no central control room from which it is operated, and where coordination of the activity takes place. There are two places in the plant where somewhat traditional control room overviews of the plant can be obtained through computers, networked with the central process automation and control system, but neither of these are places where people spend much time.

Fig 1: The fermentation towers.

We describe the work at the plant through four characters based on our studies at the plant:

Andy is the manager of the plant. Together with the leading biologist at the municipal wastewater office he develops and optimises the running of the plant by introduction of new machinery.

Bob is primarily working in the gas and electricity production area. Furthermore, he checks machinery in the plant in general, he does minor repair work etc. In contrast to his colleagues, Bob is sharing the managers overall motive of optimising the overall running of the plant.

Dan, together with his work-mate, is working with the sludge press. Their two main tasks are to monitor the press as sludge is filled in and pressed, and to scrape down the pressed sludge from between the slats of the press. In addition they move containers with pressed sludge, and they tidy the sludge press building. Dan is an old-timer at the plant, he knows how to run the sludge press so that it requires the least effort. The main objective for Dan is to maintain the smooth running of the press, i.e. to avoid too sticky sludge, and to avoid machine breakdowns.

Joe is responsible for testing inlet and outlet water and the water at different stages of the process. These tests are used for calculating taxes, and for monitoring the process in order to be able to optimise it. The tests are made with standardised test kits, with water from automatic test samplers. Joe uses mornings to collect the samples in the plant, check the samples, and make the tests. Joe and his work-mate are also responsible for the inlet area, mechanical filtering, and reception of trucks delivering wastewater.

The remainder of this paper is structured around themes introduced by means examples from our study of the wastewater plant.

Geography and participation

A basic tenet of our analysis of wastewater work is that geographical radius and action radius are closely related. Moving about is a basic feature of everyday problem solving. Participation in optimisation is related to how workers move in and through regions of the plant.

The first two examples are related to dis-colouring of water. Each of the situations shows how one worker observes the water and interprets it as a potential problem. Though the ways they deal with the situation are quite different, it is characteristic to both situations that *the workers are moving about to examine the problem and to deal with it.*

THE WATER IS BROWN

As part of his daily round, Bob checks the sludge tanks and notices that the surface water in the tanks is brownish. He immediately proceeds to where the water comes from to check a filter. This turns out to be in dire need of a rinse. This way of proceeding illustrates how he moves about in "his" part of the plant in non-routine ways so as to solve the problem. He explains that in normal circumstances he would have checked the filter anyway because it is part of his area of responsibility, but that he would not have done so until much later.

THE WATER IS GRAY

While Joe is out collecting the daily test samples, his work-mate calls him over to tell that the water in the inlet looks strange, "almost as gray as cement". They briefly discuss possible explanations, but decide that the best thing to do is to wait for the test results. Joe finishes his water sampling and goes back to the lab to make the analysis. After an hour and a half and a coffee break, the tests are ready, showing nothing out of the normal. Joe and his work-mate decide that there is no reason to take extraordinary action.

The two situations belong to the ordinary day to day routine and show how workers have to move about and orient themselves to various parts of the plant to deal with the everyday problem solving.

In Joe's round he moves in his region of the inlet water. His primary activities are here, and he primarily co-operates with one work-mate who also has duties here. Their focus is on the filtering and initial preparation of the inlet water, the machines involved in this filtering and some of the sensors etc. connected to the water basins. On top of this, Joe does the lab work. The lab is centrally placed so that he can monitor various pieces of machinery and basins as he passes by, and so that he can utilise spare time between lab work for other kinds of supervision and maintenance, e.g. cleaning of primary filters. This leads him to take several rounds out into the open space of the water basins every day. Joe's rounds take him through much of the plant in order to pick up one of his samples. Our empirical material shows that these other regions do not belong to him: he passes ringing telephones that he does not answer, and on one particular day he had to use a computer in Bob's region. This was obviously not part of the daily routine to the extent that Joe had to ask Bob for permission to do so.

As exemplified above, all workers have a region of the plant as their main area. However, there are differences in how much they move about in the region, how large the region is, how it intersects with others, and how much they move out of the region. Furthermore, there are differences in how varied their ways of moving about are. At one end of the spectrum, Dan is mainly handling the sludge press and his main territory is the sludge press building. Joe, as described above, moves about more: his route takes him through a substantial part of the plant, including visits to two sites that are somebody else's main territory. However, his route is very much the same from one day to the next and variation is mainly a matter of what special monitoring is needed and how that may be fitted in between the lab work. Bob works in a different region of the plant, the part where most of the heavy machinery is placed. His daily rounds are more varied, he plans on varying the rounds, e.g. in order to maintain particular machinery, and suspends the routines entirely when he feels that this is needed. The manager, Andy, has no fixed rounds, he moves out from his office where computers provide overview of the running of the plant whenever he finds it necessary, and he has made a habit out of moving about the plant a lot.

In moving about the plant there is a large variety in how the workers are orientating towards others and cooperating. As described the overall coordination takes place in the coffee breaks where the workers and the foreman, Ed, meet in the lunch room. More detailed cooperation happens as illustrated by the following example.

ADDING POLYMER 1

Bob on one of his rounds passes a temporary polymer tank and observes that it is less than half full. Later he passes by a storeroom and sees that there is a couple of leftover sacks of polymer powder that could perhaps be used in the tank. He proceeds with his work, and much later he meets Andy. Bob asks if he should add the polymer. Andy acknowledges Bob's idea, but explains that for this specific optimisation experiment the polymer needs to be of another kind. They discuss this, and Bob proceeds with his work.

Workers collaborate in rather different ways beyond sheer coordination. In the one end, Dan and Joe primarily do their jobs as they have been told to and are expected to report back to management if there are problems that need to be dealt with. Andy is very dependent on Joe to report back if he finds problems with the water quality, because Joe is the first to know if a problem occurs. At the same time there is very little Joe can do on his own. Decisions to mend the problems have consequences to the entire water process and needs to be made with an overview of all of this. Dan and his work-mate in the sludge press building, however, deal with a variety of issues and problems that relates to the sludge. Bob solves some problems on his own and he engages in cooperative problem definition and solving with Andy and the foreman, Ed. Andy masterminds the optimisation process in an ongoing dialogue with Ed, Bob (as illustrated by the ADDING POLYMER 1 example) and the consulting biologist at the municipal water office. As described in Bertelsen & Nielsen (1999), he continuously modifies the purification and sludge processes with their help. They help him identify problems as well as they participate in finding and implementing the experimental solutions.

The mobility and flexibility of the movement of workers, along with their possibilities for action, contribute to their participation in the optimisation and to their orientation in the distributed information space that constitute the plant. They retrieve information as they move about, and their information needs depend on where they are, who they are, as well as on what they are doing. *They do not need access to the entire information space independent of location and purpose, on the contrary.* This is what we have called zooming with the feet.

Participation and learning

The perspective of the workers on the plant and their contribution to the optimisation is illustrated by the "position" from which they view, talk about and take responsibility for the plant. At one end of the spectrum, Dan is firmly located in the sludge press building and his perspective is anchored there. He is concerned mainly with optimisation from the perspective of what makes the sludge most suitable for pressing and for being removed from the press. Bob and Andy at the other extreme, are seeing things from the perspective of the plant *in toto.*

This difference can be illustrated by the basic difference between the way Joe and Bob act in the 'water colour' examples (THE WATER IS BROWN, THE WATER IS GRAY). Joe and his work-mate discuss the strange situation, but they take no immediate action. An important reason for not taking action in THE WATER IS GRAY is that there is no action to take at the inlet, if not related to the measurable parameters. In THE WATER IS BROWN, however, the strange colour is a result of malfunction of the machinery which can be corrected immediately. The two situations, however, point to a regular difference between the jobs of Bob and Joe. Joe is working primarily with standardised tests, monitoring the state of the plant for the purposes of both running the plant and reporting to the authorities. Bob is working with the later stages of the process, including the production of electricity, maintaining the equipment and optimising the process.

Such differences can be further illustrated by the difference between ADDING POLYMER 1 and the following:

ADDING POLYMER 2

A typical situation in Dan's work is that the plant manager, Andy, calls on the phone and asks Dan to adjust the amount of polymer added to the sludge before it is pressed. The right amount of polymer gives an optimal reduction of water in the pressed sludge. For Andy, this is a matter of the costs of getting rid of the sludge. From Dan's point of view, adjusting the polymer may lead to more sticky sludge, and hence more work when removing the sludge. Accordingly, he perceives Andy's request as an annoying intervention in the smooth running of the press. As Dan maintains a somewhat peripheral role in the overall optimisation, his judgement call is more closely coupled to what is immediately more optimal to the work in his region.

The two situations of addition of polymer (ADDING POLYMER 1, ADDING POLYMER 2) illustrate the differences in optimisation and learning horizons between Dan and Bob. Bob's role in this situation is that of the apprentice where Andy's the master. In general, Bob does not take action independently, but he is aligned with the optimisation efforts and other concerns of the manager. Dan has more autonomy over the part of the plant that he deals with, but is far less involved in Andy's process of optimisation. Lave and Wenger (1991) use the notion of legitimate peripheral participation to describe how apprentices move from the periphery of a community of practice towards the centre, as they become more and more skilful participants. The central purpose of optimising the running of the plant is in itself an exploratory purpose, or we might say, a continuous learning process. If we look at the above patterns of looking at and moving about the plant from this perspective, we see that some people are indeed in the centre of the activity whereas others are more peripheral participants. They may be peripheral in several ways: either they are peripheral because they conduct a work where they don't have to orient as much to the central exploratory purpose, they can very much stay in their part and master that activity independently of the rest. Or because they move about, but do not take responsibility for the optimisation of the plant. All of these participants are indeed legitimate. What we find interesting in relation to Lave & Wenger's (ibid.) notion of legitimate peripheral participation is that in work at the wastewater plant some participants stay peripheral to optimisation, and may never fully move to the centre, even though all workers appreciate that optimisation is what it is all about. And even more interesting from the perspective of exploration is that the people who are concerned with optimisation move about a lot in the rather distributed space of the plant.

As a common information space the wastewater plant supports not one, but several kinds of learning and exploration. Learningwise people may end up at many different places in relation to the centre and periphery of the optimisation purpose of wastewater purification. At the same time they may thoroughly master their own more limited purpose and space.

Holding in common

Running the wastewater plant is a common endeavour taken on by the people working there. They are continuously recreating an overview enabling them to locate each other, and they are continuously rendering the status of the plant visible through the process of moving about.

Despite the varying degree of centrality in relation to optimising the running of the plant, all workers share a surprising sense of where to find each other when they need to talk to each other, as illustrated in the following.

THE BROKEN WIRE

One morning before dawn, Andy asks Bob to go and look at one of the secondary clarifier basins when he can see the details. The basin has been automatically shut down, probably because a wire pulling the sludge scraper is broken. Andy needs to know where the wire is broken to determine which preparations are needed before the blacksmith can do the repair. Bob goes about his normal routines and makes sure that he passes by the sludge scraper after daybreak. Later in the day, Andy has placed himself on Bobs "route" to hear his conclusions regarding the broken wire. Despite Bob's rather varied route, Andy has a clear idea about Bob's moving about, and he is able to locate himself so as to have the brief meeting.

The workers all contribute to rendering visible the status and history of the plant in the various distributed locations of the plant, as illustrated by the following examples from Bob's and from Joe's work (figures 2 and 3).

READING THE GAS METERS

The daily report for the gas generators is represented by a row in the monthly report table, one for each gas generator. This report is left in the room where the relevant meters are located. The report contains readings of e.g. oil temperature, oil pressure, errors and the power produced (in kW). When he has calculated the result, Bob furthermore brings them to the control room and confirms with computer readings. Only then are they entered into a paper protocol left on the table in this room.

PRODUCING THE LAB REPORT

In the lab, Joe enters all lab test results into a form that is stationary on the desk. While entering the numbers, he compares them with the results from the past month, and he is expected to let the manager know if there are any major discrepancies. The lab results are furthermore transported to the manager's office where Joe types them into the computer.

Fig 2: Bob's Gas protocol

Fig 3: Joe's Lab report

In these studies we see a variety of ways of cooperating, from sheer coordination of separate activities over coffee and coordination caused by changes in the state of the plant, to systematic, continued discussions of the optimisation process between Andy and Bob. Within the various regions there is much everyday coordination and cooperative solving of a variety of problems such as in THE WATER IS GRAY example. However, very much of what takes place is to render visible the status and history of the plant for future problem solving and for optimising.

We have observed that wastewater workers create an overview of the wastewater process and the status of the plant by walking around in the physically distributed plant. Joe samples water for lab testing in the various corners of the plant, similarly Bob routinely checks up on machinery at locations around the plant. While performing these tasks they walk by the water basins, inspect the wastewater by looking, Joe looks at the incoming water and sludge when cleaning the filters, etc. The smell, together with the look at the water and sludge sampled along the way, allow the workers to form an overview of relevant parts of the plant and the waste processing. This overview is supported as well by meters, alarms (on components and in the central automation control system), and other kinds of support technology distributed in the plant.

The overview created by the wastewater workers cannot be retrieved from any central position in the plant; neither can it be separated from being physically present in particular parts of the plant. The information necessary for the creation of overview is irreducible; it cannot be obtained from pure measurements alone. The wastewater workers need to see and smell the actual water and they need to touch and look at the actual components to create the overview. Otherwise they would risk letting totally strange water pass by, or risk not replacing worn down components in time. In many ways the distributed sampling and looking as one passes by serve as distributed windows into the purification process. What is seen through each of these windows are often not very important in isolation. It is through the physical and geographical location of the "windows" and through the juxtaposition of the information created by the workers when walking about, that the overview is created. The need for information cannot be separated from specific action, which in turn is tied to specific places. This is what zooming with the feet is about: the purposeful "reading of information" placed according to physical arrangement, systematic context, routines, responsibility and action. Thus, enhanced information in the wastewater treatment plant is not a matter of providing universal access to huge amounts of data — "everything, everywhere, for everybody".

How information reception and handling was dependent on action, location and responsibility was evaluated in a series of experimental prototypes, where we explored the possibilities of walking about without e.g. reading and recording values, or of not walking about at all. The experiments pointed to the importance, in the work we have studied, of creating overview through acts such as rewriting numbers in columns with the numbers from previous days, in the various dispersed locations. However, it also became clear through the studies that rewriting alone does not guarantee that the numbers are digested. Actual responsibility and possibility to act on the state reflected by the numbers seemed to be a better guarantee for thorough digestion. In the case of the wastewater plants we have studied, overview is about the state and history (optimisation) of the plant/process. It varies very much how much of such overview each person has, what the person has an overview of, and what this overview is used for. In our examples we have seen that the kind of overview needed by Dan is very different from that needed by Andy or Bob, and similarly that the work they do to maintain the overview differs.

Common artefacts

To further explore the matter of artifacts that are held in common by several cooperating uses, we turn to Robinson's (1993) notion of common artefact. According to Robinson (ibid.), *overview* is one important dimension of a common artefact. The common artefact is an elaboration of the dimensions of communication that takes place through and is supported by a computer application/an artefact. Any specific artefact with the requisite dimensionality is considered a common artefact. A common artefact is an effective tool for getting a job done. It helps people see at a glance what others are doing. It enables actions and changes made by others to be understandable, and appropriate changes to be made. It provides a focus for discussion of difficulties and negotiation of compromises; it offers an overview over the work process that would not otherwise be available. As such we make the hypothesis that *if common artifacts exist, the wastewater plant is one.*

Fig 4: The meter panels

Robinson mentions *predictability* as an important dimension of common artifacts. Predictability is covering issues like dependability, functionality (including consistency of, compatibility of), and appropriate interface (including comprehensibility) as an important dimension. All our experiments and studies point out that predictability is a very local thing in the wastewater plant. Bob handles a large number of dials and meters (see fig 4) every time he calculates the amount of produced electricity: All the instruments/meters that need to be read are visible (i.e. not behind panels or doors). The meters are read differently: some of the meters are just counters/numbers where others have a needle pointing at a scale or are lightbulb-buttons. Some values are read instantly while others need to be focused on for several seconds before the values are written down. For the calculation of the electricity produced in a day Bob uses 4 protocol pages, which he has piled up on the table, a pocket calculator, an A5-pad and a pen. He reads numbers from the protocol page, makes calculations on the pocket calculator, transfers the result to the pad where he makes the final calculation when all 4 numbers needed have been calculated. This pad already has other columns with similar calculations. When the result has been calculated, Bob transfers the numbers to a small personal notepad he always carries. These numbers are carried to the control room and confirmed with the computer before they are entered into a paper protocol. This illustrates how the wastewater workers are able to handle a wide variety of different interfaces, functionality etc., depending on where they are and what kind of purpose they are facing. In the wastewater treatment plant, predictability is bound to location and purpose so much that consistence and coherence seem to be unimportant aspects of the big artefact.

Peripheral awareness is conceived as local and immediate ("at a glance"). We have on several occasions observed how the workers are very able to identify the location of each other in the plant. This is despite the fact that they cannot see and hear each other in the manners most often discussed in studies of peripheral awareness (e.g. Robinson 1993). This is illustrated by the following example:

LOCATING JOE

After completing the daily tests Joe finds his work-mate in a small room used for hanging around during shorter breaks. A couple of minutes later, Dan comes to talk to Joe and his work-mate about some possible later problems resulting from repair work of the sludge press. Dan knows when it is time to find Joe in a more or less idle state.

A general example of peripheral awareness at the plant is that we have called on the phone many times to arrange meetings, field trips, etc. Very often the person we needed to talk to has not been available. However, the person answering the phone (one of the 8 persons working on the plant) has always been able to tell where the person we tried to reach was.

Peripheral awareness in the wastewater plant is a product of the way people are moving about in physical space. It is not the side by side positioning, but rather the passing by and talking occasionally and during breaks that is the basis for being peripherally aware; the shared rhythm of work, the shared objective of optimal running, the shared domain.

The dimension of *double level language* includes conventionalised implicit communication through the artefact ("shared material") and the role of artefact as "indexical focus" for dialogue. In the wastewater plant a very particular double level language is unfolding, that of the "optimisation debate". From our studies we find that a prerequisite for keeping this exploratory discussion going is that the workers each know when they need to report problems to Andy. This means that they carefully digest the numbers that they read off meters and off measuring equipment and write these into the reports. The experimentation also benefits from the master-apprentice relation between Andy and Bob. Bob knows what optimisation is about and has ideas about how to optimise. He is, however, not able to undertake the overall optimisation himself. In this he is clearly the helper of Andy.

If common artifacts exist, the wastewater plant is one. Indeed, Robinson's definition (ibid.) has helped shed light on important features of the wastewater plant as a common artefact. Two aspects stand out as interesting, the first being that the notion of a common artefact is indeed seen as something that is tied to a place. Whereas the wastewater plant is also located in one place, our research shows that it is exactly the moving about and the purposeful action in a variety of places that makes possible the juxtaposition of information, and hence the running and optimisation of the plant. Overview, predictability and peripheral awareness are all related to how people move about in the plant, and not to a particular location. Whereas many examples of common artifacts and coordination mechanisms (Schmidt & Simone, 1996) that we have come across are separate artifacts that serve the purpose of cooperation and coordination, the wastewater plant as such serves this purpose, and the additional artifacts used cannot be separated from this.

Common information places

Our findings regarding the constitution of information in the wastewater treatment plant, emphasise that information is always located according to what Harrison & Dourish (1996) refer to as place; not necessarily geographically fixed but well defined according to some social orderliness. Unfortunately, in most of the CSCW literature place is taken to be geographically fixed. The constitution of shared workspaces has been the focus of Suchman and colleagues, with inspiration from the studies of Lynch and others of scientific practices and cooperation. Suchman (1993, 1996) brings their view on space out of the science lab and into such distributed work settings as an airline operations room (and surroundings). She states that the operations room "is not so much a locale as a complex but habitual field of equipment and action, involving intimate relations of technology and practice, body and person, place and activity" (Suchman 1996 p. 36). This description fits well with the wastewater plant as well. Suchman goes on to analyse a number of cooperative situations that all, in ways similar to those of Heath & Luff (1992), deal with situations where people, while dealing with their own activities, can perform surreptitious monitoring of the activities of others by (primarily) overhearing what is happening. The wastewater plant is different in this respect. As we have pointed out it is possible for the workers to maintain a peripheral awareness of others in the large geographical area, even when they cannot see and hear each other. And more noteworthy, perhaps, this peripheral awareness does not involve the creation of what Suchman calls centres of coordination, geographic places that people set up to assure that they can meet other people in distributed settings. It could be argued that the place where Andy meets Bob in the BROKEN WIRE example is a centre of co-ordination, but that would be to accept very ephemeral and transient phenomena as being centres.

Our conclusion is that the wastewater plant, in contrast to many cases described in the CSCW literature, and in contrast to such ideal cooperation devises as common artifacts, reveals a continuum of places of which many are geographically fluent. With reference to Harrison & Dourish (op. cit.), we might call such continuums "spaces of understood reality". Spaces that are dealt with through movement, and movement as a precondition for learning, participation and experimentation.

The way in which peripheral awareness is a product of movement rather than location may not be specific for wastewater treatment. We suspect that the focus on co-locatedness in the literature comes from the methodical convenience of being able to capture the object of study within one scene.

Our study of wastewater treatment work feeds into the design of (and for) common information spaces by pointing to the intertwining of physical and virtual space in a sort of wired wilderness. Constitution, ordering, juxtaposition and interpretation of information are mixed with and depending on the continuous rearrangement and reinterpretation of the technical installation. Interestingly in the case of the wastewater plant, action radius in the information space is correlated with action radius in physical space. Computer applications aiming at supporting overview, awareness, etc. should not do so by providing uniform access to information across geography and purpose, but rather by supplement the implicit information space already present through the technical arrangement of basins, pipes, pumps, etc. Furthermore, we have seen strong indications that overview is not isolated from purposeful action. There is no technical solution that can yield overview to anybody beyond his horizon of action.

We have, however, also seen that very experienced and competent workers may have a very local horizon of optimisation and exploration, thus staying in the periphery (of the general optimisation of the plant) forever, in a perfectly legitimate way. The very different activities in the wastewater treatment plant, with their varying optimisation horizons are over-layered and mutually dependent. These activities "take place" as they are all supported in the common information space, but not all actors are on the way to become part of the total optimisation activity. Common information spaces, as well as wastewater plants, have centres and peripheries, and they are composed of overlapping regions. With this perspective, learning takes place in parallel with the ongoing juxtaposition of information in the intertwined physical and virtual common information space.

Conclusion

Our studies of wastewater treatment plants show how such massively distributed spaces challenge many of the ways that CSCW view common information spaces. Furthermore, the studies support the idea that common information spaces is not merely about access to everything, everywhere. Participation in optimisation is introduced as an important feature of work tied to the moving around in physical space. In the CSCW literature, peripheral awareness and at a glance overview are mostly connected with the co-ordination of activities within a control room or in similar co-located circumstances. Whereas the wastewater plant is also located in one place, our research shows that it is exactly the moving about and the purposeful action in a variety of places that make possible the juxtaposition of information, and hence the running and optimisation of the plant. Overview, predictability and peripheral awareness are all related to how people move about in the plant and not to a particular location. The wastewater plant reveals a true focus on common spaces, rather than common places. Spaces are dealt with through movement, and movement as a precondition for learning, participation and experimentation. Common information spaces have several centres and peripheries, and are composed of overlapping regions. Learning takes place in relation to the ongoing movement and juxtaposition of information in the massively distributed common information space.

Acknowledgements

We owe a special thank to Christina Nielsen who has been cooperating closely with us in developing some of the ideas on which this paper is based. Wendy Mackay, Astrid Søndergaard and Christian Yndigegn have all contributed to the work and discussions that this paper builds on. We appreciate the time and effort put into the project by the guys from the plant, as well as by the people from three other plants and our colleagues at Danfoss and Malmö University College. The work has been sponsored by CIT/CMT grant #23 and by Centre for Human-Machine Interaction (the Danish Research Foundation). Ann Eg Mølhave has helped correcting our English.

References

Bannon, L. & Bødker, S. (1997). Constructing Common Information Spaces. In Hughes, J., Prinz, W., Rodden, T. & Schmidt, K. (Eds.). *Proceedings of ECSCW97*, Dordrecht: Kluwer, pp. 81-96.

Bellotti, V. & Bly. S. (1996). Walking Away from the Desktop Computer: Distributed Collaboration and Mobility in a Product Design Team Work Practices. *Proceedings of ACM CSCW'96 Conference on Computer-Supported Cooperative Work*, pp. 209-218.

Bertelsen, O. W. & Nielsen, C. (1999). Dynamics in Wastewater Treatment: A Framework for Understanding Formal Constructs in Complex Technical Settings. In *Proceedings of ECSCW99*.

Harrison, S. & Dourish, P. (1996). Re-Place-ing Space: The role of place and space in collaborative systems, *Proceedings of ACM CSCW'96 Conference on Computer-Supported Cooperative Work*, pp. 67-76.

Heath, C. & Luff, P. (1992). Collaboration and control: Crisis management and multimedia technology in London underground control rooms. In *Computer Supported Cooperative Work: The Journal of Collaborative Computing*, 1, nos. 1-2, pp.69-94.

Lave, J., & Wenger, E. (1991). *Situated learning: Legitimate peripheral participation.* Cambridge: Cambridge University Press.

Nielsen, C. & Søndergaard, A. (2000). Designing for mobility: an integration approach to support mobile technologies. *NordiCHI 2000 Proceedings*, CD-ROM.

Robinson, M. (1993). Design for Unanticipated Use. In G. deMichaelis & C. Simone (eds.), *Proceedings of the Third European Conference on Computer-Supported Cooperative Work* (ECSCW '93). Dordrecht, Boston, London: Kluwer, pp. 187-202.

Schmidt, K., & L. Bannon (1992). Taking CSCW Seriously: Supporting Articulation Work. In *Computer Supported Cooperative Work (CSCW): An International Journal*, vol. 1, no. 1-2, pp. 7-40.

Schmidt, K. & C. Simone (1996). Coordination mechanisms: Towards a conceptual foundation of CSCW systems design. In *Computer Supported Cooperative Work: The Journal of Collaborative Computing*, vol. 5, no. 2-3, 1996, pp. 155-200.

Suchman, L. A. (1996). Constituting shared workspaces. In Engeström, Y. & Middleton, D. (eds.). *Cognition and Communication at Work.* Cambridge: Cambridge University Press. pp. 35-60.

Suchman, L. A. (1993). Centers of Coordination: A Case and Some Themes. Presented at the *NATO Advanced Research Workshop on Discourse, Tools and Reasoning, Lucca, Italy, November 2-7.*

W. Prinz, M. Jarke, Y. Rogers, K. Schmidt, and V. Wulf (eds.), *Proceedings of the Seventh European Conference on Computer-Supported Cooperative Work, 16-20 September 2001, Bonn, Germany*, pp. 19-38.

Adaptability of Classification Schemes in Cooperation: what does it mean?

Carla Simone, Marcello Sarini

Dipartimento di Informatica - Universita' di Torino

e-mail: {simone,sarini}@di.unito.it

Abstract The overview of a set of field studies highlights how different are the scenarios in which classification schemes (CS) play a role in cooperation. In all cases, adaptability is claimed as a fundamental requirement for their usability and effective usage. What adaptability means for CS is not an easy question. The paper tries to articulate this requirement and derive implications on the design of a supportive technology.

1. Motivations and goal

Classification Schemes (CS) are artifacts people widely use to organize entities of various kinds. For example, consider the large-scale CS used in publishing (e.g., ACM, IEEE, ISI), or used in specific disciplines like biology, medicine, and in libraries. CS organize information in smaller setting too: for example, CS can take the form of artifacts like Bills of Materials in specific manufacturing organizations. CS are used also by individuals in order to organize their private working space, their desktop or files. In all situations, CS do not serve the only purpose of organizing entities: in so doing, they contribute to the definition and the coordination of individual and collective actions around the classified entities.

CS have been mainly studied within humanistic disciplines dealing with the theory and application of classification and within technological disciplines oriented to knowledge representation and engineering, typically in the framework of Artificial Intelligence. In both cases, "the social life of information" (Brown and Duguid, 2000) is not taken into account. Classification is considered as a rational decontextualization of work practices and is often produced outside the cooperative work it supports. CS are part of CSCW research agenda from the very beginning (Schmidt and Bannon, 1992). They were listed among the mechanisms of interaction devoted to help the effective articulation of cooperative work. Despite this fact, in CSCW CS have been considered as part of the background where cooperation happens. How CS are defined, used and maintained is not recognized as a fundamental reason why cooperation happens or is hindered, as it was the case for other aspects of cooperation considered so far: typically, for mechanisms of interaction more oriented to the definition of control. Recent empirical investigations highlighted how pervasive and differentiated is the role of CS in cooperation. Although presently limited in number and scope, these studies show how profitable is to look at work from this specific point of view in order to better understand how knowledge is managed in cooperative ensembles. This is especially needed since on the one hand Knowledge Management is one of the keywords used by companies to state that knowledge is one of their basic assets, and on the other hand CSCW can significantly contribute to define mechanisms to preserve and improve it.

As in the case of other mechanisms of interaction, adaptability is claimed to be the key requirement of CS to guarantee their usability and effective usage. However, what adaptability means in this case is not an easy question since the scenarios where they operate are very different. This paper aims to be a contribution in answering this question. It is not about new empirical studies, methods or technological proposals. More modestly, it is an effort to learn from existing empirical studies, lessons learned in CSCW and our research experience, and to identify a research path to deal with this new challenge from the point of view of the design of a supportive technology. This research is rooted in our work on Coordination Mechanisms (Schmidt and Simone, 1996) and inspired by (Bowker and Star, 1999). Moreover, it takes advantage from the presentations and discussions that took place last year during two workshops focused on the role of CS in Common Information Spaces and in Cooperative Work, respectively.

The paper is organized as follows. First, the relation between CS, Knowledge Management and CSCW is discussed. Then, a selection of reference case studies is presented and a simple conceptual framework is used to highlight their similarities and differences. The framework guides the identification of requirements whose implications on design highlight open problems. Their solution is, in our opinion, an unavoidable passage to answer the new challenge in an innovative way.

2. Learning from CSCW history

The increasing emphasis on how knowledge is organized and used by actors to improve their cooperation brings into CSCW an increasing attention on the themes that are typical of Knowledge Management. The latter became quite popular in the last decade in organizational disciplines (see, e.g., (Nonaka and Takeuchi, 1995)) and in disciplines having 'knowledge' as main focus, as knowledge representation and engineering (Dieng et al., 1999). Basically, it became a buzz word, a sort of umbrella under which companies frame problems and solutions of the emerging need to recognize and preserve the knowledge used in the accomplishment of tasks and characterizing the tasks themselves. Unfortunately, a poor analysis of the real mechanisms governing the management of knowledge by cooperating actors together with the obvious need of a technology as part of any solution to manage the related complexity, led in almost all cases to base solutions on the idea that knowledge can be stored in a repository from which it can be retrieved later on. How simplistic is this view has been widely discussed in (Bannon and Kutti, 1996). The current technological proposals for Knowledge Management have been produced in the framework of knowledge representation, acquisition and engineering where the storing capabilities of Information System technologies have been augmented by Artificial Intelligence techniques. In these disciplines concepts like CS (e.g., taxonomies, ontologies) are widely and explicitly used and technologically supported (Dieng et al., 1999). The various approaches share the common characteristic to delegate to a 'domain expert' or 'knowledge engineer' the duty to define the CS, possibly in cooperation with a selection of 'knowledge workers', while other actors are supposed to accept and use it. The existence of such CS, capturing the ontology of the company, is not only *not questioned* but constitutes the *basic hypothesis* on which both analysis of the reality and design of the technological support are based.

Years ago, CSCW considered Knowledge Management from the point of view of argumentation structures as a basis to construct Organizational Memory (Conklin, 1988). Recently, starting from the deconstruction of this concept (Bannon and Kutti, 1996), a few authors propose a more articulated and dynamic connotation: e.g., as a distributed structure of local memories (Ackerman and Halverson, 1998) or as an artifact mediated process (Kovalainen et al., 1998). In (De Michelis et al., 2000), the relation between knowledge creation and cooperation, and the fundamental role of context for interpreting collections of documents are widely discussed along the criticism of memory as a pure repository. In this proposal, a document and its context entail *general information*; *content* and its *representation*; *knowledge information* and finally, *context information*. This is a nice example of the relation between context and CS. The constituents of the context are classified and the content of each constituent will be classified in turn.

Irrespective of the specific classification, every time we propose an *explicit or implicit* classification, we support Kwansky's statement (reported in (Star, 1998)):

> Like theories, classification schemes can provide an explanatory shell for looking at the world from a contextually determined perspective.

Now, the problem of supporting the definition and use of CS looks like a problem CSCW encountered time ago. Classification plays in relation to knowledge what control mechanisms did play in relation to work processes. We refer to the evolution from rigid and exhaustively represented control mechanisms to fully unspecified ones, in the path to reach a more realistic view of mechanisms that can range within the limits of the two above extremes in order to *adapt* to the needs of the current situation (Schmidt and Simone, 2000). In this view, adaptability is the less constraining approach since it does not claim for any dogmatic or ideological or fixed once and forever choice of the solution.

The empirically based research method characterizing CSCW, corroborated by the experience of designing tools supporting control mechanisms, suggests to put CS under the spot to avoid the problems generated by implicit, but sometimes silently constraining, representations. As the observation of the control mechanisms in the field and the evolution of the related technologies defined a research path improving the existing proposals and determined a space where to look for still better solutions, in the same way, we have to understand from a variety of field studies *what adaptability means in the case of classification* (schemes) so as to orient our empirical research and technological design accordingly. The field studies reported in the next section show that *answering the above question is not straightforward.*

3. Classification Schemes at work

This section presents a selection of case studies which sustains the claim that CS are ubiquitous in cooperation, serve different purposes and are about different entities. Moreover, they point to the need of further investigations, since the nature and role of CS in cooperation is far from being univocal and fully understood. The considered settings are characterized by well recognized business processes (like in engineering and manufacturing) as well as by emerging processes (like cooperative problem solving and planning in front of emergencies). In addition, the use of CS occurs in cooperative settings whose actors are linked by organizational ties of different strength: from structured (distributed) organization, through customer-service provider relationships, up to virtual communities and communities of practice possibly acting in non-working environments. In these diversified scenarios, CS are used to support different needs of cooperation. We take this point of view in presenting them: what follows should not be read neither as a systematic survey of the literature nor as a detailed description of the selected cases.

The aim is to create an interpretation context for our subsequent reflections, by making explicit which aspects of the field cases triggered them.

3.1 Retrieving past behavior and experience

We refer to the cases where CS are about the classification of documents produced during projects lasting for a long time in quite well structured organizations.

PVE II archive (Carstensen, 1997): This case concerns a large engineering project whose aim is to design a complex mechanical controller (PVE II) and plan its production, both evolving from a previous product and project. Different kinds of information are collected in a centralized (PVE II-) archive which is organized according to a unique CS and maintained by an engineer of the project team, the PVE file manager. The users are all engineers and members of the project team too: therefore quite experts of the domain. They considered the PVE II archive very successful. This success seems to be strongly related to the simple structure of the archive and to individual capabilities of the file manager, who knows about the domain, the project and its history. The possible weaknesses of the "explicit" CS were overcome by some "non-explicit hidden structure of his mind" and by the possibility to clarify questions through the verbal interaction with the engineers asking for factual information concerning the specification of the product and the project. These interactions allow the PVE file manager to take into consideration the needs users elicit in searching for information, or in re-using it, when he has to file and retrieve information for them.

Danish Medical (Christensen and Schmidt, 2000): This case concerns the use of CS in a large pharmaceutical company: it shows a combination of centralized and local, material and digital archives. During the tests of new drugs the Laboratory Unit produces a documentation of paramount relevance, since it records information about the product and the production process that play a fundamental role in the approval of new drugs by internal and external authorities. This peculiar usage makes it easier to identify classification schemes that can be adopted locally and combined in a more comprehensive one: the latter supports the mediation among the different sources and the users. The purpose of allowing quality assurance and auditing by external departments pushes people to use the scheme when such documents are produced as well as when they are used to support the above control functions. Other less 'formal' usages seem to raise problems and solutions similar to the previous case. For example, also in this case there is a relevant role of mediation performed by the units devoted to manage the material and digital archives. The Legal Unit uses the documentation for supporting attorneys in lawsuits. Its requests are in general not adequately supported by the various CS since the pieces of information the Legal Unit is looking for and how they should be grouped do not always make sense to the other departments. Typically, what they need is the history of the document in all its diverse facets (people involved, annotations, and so on). To overcome this difficulty, the Legal Unit members use their capability to traverse the human network "to understand what they really need", possibly starting from the information gathered from some retrieved document. Consequently, the Legal Unit uses a local classification scheme to organize copies of the retrieved documents that can hardly be reconciled with the central one organizing their originals.

Uniform File System This case describes the usage of an organizational filing system (the UFS) adopted by an engineering company to improve the flux of information across different project stages and the retrieval of project documentation. The analysis showed that the centralized approach made the coding and retrieval activities quite problematic since the 'uniform' solution wasn't able to take into consideration local needs. The pressure of the management forced the engineers to use the UFS, but actually its adoption looks like as a partial failure since the system was often circumvented or used in disagreement with the 'imposed' scheme: manual annotations, local conventions, fictitious categories and the like contrasted the initial goal to reach uniformity across groups of specialists. Unlike the previous cases, the role of a human mediator (the project engineer) is formally established but does not really succeed in avoiding problems. Two more flexible classification support tools were experimentally designed: the first one (Trigg et al., 1999) is based on the enrichment of the original documents with meta-data containing, among the others, user defined keywords, free text and obviously the UFS code(s); the second one is based on layered views of the scheme to obtain a more direct customization of the UFS itself (Dourish et al., 1999).

3.2 Improving coordination and communication

We refer here to situations where CS are about the classification of information in coordinative artifacts used for short term cooperation to solve emerging problems. Their material support is paper, but they are not documents in the more traditional sense. Here the relevant organizational aspect is that cooperation involves different roles or different actors playing the same role.

Rush Cheat Sheet (Halverson, 2000): This case concerns the creation of a classifying structure used in Traffic Management. This process was motivated by the FAA's decision to 'take a more proactive role in keeping the traffic moving smoothly', especially to handle periods of concentrated traffic. At Dallas airport a new job, the traffic manager, was created. Moreover, in order to overcome the partial knowledge of each controller about the overall traffic at the suitable level of detail, a document was created with all the relevant information about the traffic composition and schedule. In order to make it more usable, the information was concentrated in a single sheet. The traffic manager used and displayed this artifact to the other members of the community who began to use it for various purposes. Hence, the Rush Cheat Sheet was created and evolved over time as the community evolved. In this process, it supported a common language that the community derived from the information provided by the airlines and used to improve coordination in critical situations.

NASA (O'Neill, 2000): This case is in the domain of air traffic control too and is about the management of delays. The problem was managed in the opposite direction: the CS to handle delays was proposed by the airlines management as an evolution of routine classification systems. In so doing, some fundamental time aspects generating the delays were totally disregarded (e.g., frequent critical load and work cycles of different length in the departments) as well as some considerations about the difficulty to assign delays to the departments and to report on their motivations. The crucial point is that, despite the above difficulty, the airline management considered the delay data as objective information to be used for sake of process improvement and cross-airlines comparison. The analysis showed that the really needed artifact should be based more on real work, to be linked to real-time data, to be oriented to the causes of the delays instead of their side-effects, and finally to be proactive by prompting workers to start activities. Moreover, this new artifact should come together with a realistic assessment of the consequences of the surrounding airline strategies (typically, overbooking) that could undermine its effectiveness.

3.3 Improving services

We refer here to situations where CS are about the classification for sake of retrieval of various kind of items contained in a structured repository. Here the relevant organizational aspect is that cooperation involves the roles of 'librarian' and 'customer', possibly belonging to a community (of practice).

Book House and **Database2001** (Albrechtsen and Jacob, 1998): This case concerns two interrelated projects in the domain of digital libraries. The goal was to build systems and related interfaces responding to the needs of sets of user communities. This goal was achieved by a collaborative effort of librarians, users, researchers and technicians. The solution was a combination of different modalities to access the desired information, depending on the type of users. This experience is imported into a new European project (Collate) whose aim is the development of collaborative methods and tools for the coordination and maintenance of classification, indexing and meta-data of digitized historical archive material. These experiences show how the traditional Library and Information Science (LIS)-approach leading to one-size-fits-all classifying structures, based on a centralized consensus model and oriented to the construction and preservation of collections, is currently questioned in the view of libraries as open, service-oriented agencies targeted to particular user groups. This case can be taken as representative of a range of similar situations implying the management of teaching or bibliographical materials. Teachers, students and researchers can easily recognize in the above description their own experience of frustration in using any type of official classification of scientific publications, e.g. in the field of Information and Communication Technology!

3.4 Triggering learning and participation

We refer here to situations where the organizational structure is almost absent. They can be considered as sub-cases of the ones described in section 3.3 since CS serve similar purposes. However, one of the main goals is to increase the sense of belonging of the participants to the considered community (of practice).

TeachDiver (Guy, 2000): This case concerns the evolution of a single open mailing list for the discussion of technical diving into a network of more local mailing lists. The latter serve as infrastructure for the groups of super-expert divers and as a tool for recreation divers to learn about "the collective development of technical diving practice as it has been articulated through the on-line discussions of the list". Irrespective of this evolution, the list is still not administrated or moderated and provides very elemental searching tools. A very simple CS organizes messages by Date, Author and Subject. The implicit convention underlying the list usage is that newbies have to spend some effort in order to acquire the necessary knowledge (e.g., terminology, names of authoritative authors) to perform searching. If this it not the case, they are "gently admonished". Searching can be based on Subject and Author in order to retrieve threads of messages constituting discussions on particular topics. Again, silent conventions push people to use meaningful Subjects, to keep them if the message belongs to the same thread, and to declare a change of focus through the pattern: **new heading (Was: old heading)**. Classification of messages by subject headings identifies a thread also when it is closed and becomes part of the community 'memory'. The same double use was recognized in a completely different setting where messages were used to provide information within and across work-shifts (Kovalainen et al., 1998). Classification by author realizes the transformation of *resources* into *sources* since it allows the searcher to discriminate between valuable and misleading contributions. The kind of support provided by the very simple CS was oriented to stimulate learning and create participation with the final goal to improve the safety of the community members, not simply to distribute information. The overhead required to the users didn't prevent the archive to be highly valuated and used by TeachDiver participants.

4. Requirements from the case studies

The considered case studies raise contrasting issues. When the cases are about the *use* of CS, the experiences are perceived as a (partial) success or failure, irrespective of the fact that they share the same, or adopt alternative, strategies. When the cases are about the *need* of a CS to solve problems, CS seem to be overloaded with requirements enlarging their 'natural' scope of usage. This not surprising outcome is problematic for the identification of the requirements for a technology supporting CS.

4.1 A simple conceptual framework

In order to facilitate the identification of the requirements in the above complex scenario we derived from the cases a very simple conceptual framework for sake of comparing, or simply better understanding them. The framework is based on some orthogonal dimensions (Table 1) which define a logical space where the various cases can be positioned. In any case, these dimensions are not to be considered as exhaustive, definitive or as an attempt to build an ontology: this goal does not belong to our research goals.

dimensions	possible values		Case Study
expertise of Consumer	low		Book House and Database2001, TeachDiver
	high		PVEII, Danish Medical, UFS, Rush Cheat Sheet, NASA, Book House and Database2001, TeachDiver
distance	endogenous		Rush Cheat Sheet, Book House and Database2001
	exogenous		PVEII, Danish Medical, UFS, NASA, TeachDiver
purposes	accountability/auditing		Danish Medical
	re-use		PVEII, UFS
	comm. /coordination		Rush Cheat Sheet, NASA
	dialogue with clients		Book House and Database2001
	learning /participation		TeachDiver
entities	processes		PVEII, Danish Medical, UFS, Rush Cheat Sheet, NASA
	products	information	PVEII, Danish Medical, UFS, Book House and Database2001, TeachDiver
		collection of artifacts	Bill of Materials
domains	all the reported cases use languages with a balanced mix of formalization		

Table 1

The first two dimensions are related to the (sets of) people who define/maintain and use the CS. We distinguish between *Producers* who define the CS and *Consumers* who organize and use the entities of the target domain accordingly. The first dimension accounts for the fact that Producers necessarily hold a quite sophisticated expertise, while this is not always the case for Consumers. The second dimension focuses on the degree of overlapping, that we metaphorically call distance, between Producers and Consumers. Common situations, among the many that constitute a continuum, are when they intersect in various ways, are disjoint but cooperate in the 'information space' where the CS applies and finally, are disjoint and their activities are independent as far as this space is concerned. These situations show different distances between definition and use of a CS: we will use the terms *endogenous* and *exogenous* (in relation to the common practices) to characterize an irrelevant or relevant distance, respectively. The various combinations of values for these two dimensions may help in making explicit the problems associated with the definition/maintenance and use of the CS when they related to the act of *making sense* of the CS itself.

The third dimension refers to the `purpose` of the CS. The cases highlighted purposes that are quite specific and related to concrete actions: namely, *accountability/auditing* (as discussed in (Bowers et al., 1995) for control mechanisms); *re-use* in the sense of Knowledge Management; improving *communication* and *coordination* within and across distributed teams; supporting the *dialogue with clients* in order to propose goods/services; improving *learning* and *participation* in communities (of practice). Notice that purpose implicitly incorporates a notion of duration of a CS and characterizes different degrees of *social pressure* or *individual needs* in adopting the scheme. Although there are often multiple purposes to be supported by a single classification scheme, in the considered cases it was natural to identify a predominant one: hence, the framework was nevertheless usable and useful. However, we recognize that this dimension has to be worked out more precisely to be applicable in more general cases.

The last dimensions refers to the `entities` to be classified and their `domain` . We make a distinction between entities describing *processes* through templates, forms or graphical representations; and entities being *products*: 1) *information* in terms of books, library material, source references, messages with their attachments, physical and electronic documents or 2) *collections of artifacts* like elemental or compound components, structured descriptions. Often, products can be characterized by categories that are grounded in sound scientific disciplines, as in the case reported in (Bandini and Manzoni, 2000). Physics and chemistry were the two main reference disciplines to "formalize" the properties of ("the knowledge about") the product. They provided the involved engineers with the language to communicate and to recompose different views by "isolating" the crucial properties of the products and constructing suitable "hinges" that allow for local flexibility while keeping cooperation possible. On the contrary, the categorization of processes is generally less consolidated (Malone et al., 1998). These aspects can influence the existence of a *pre-existing language* from which CS are derived and which makes their use more natural.

4.2 Requirements as difficult trade-offs

The dimensions proposed in the previous section are used to ground on the previous cases the requirements of a technology supporting CS. The first immediate consideration is that there are good reasons for exogenous and endogenous CS to exist and co-exist in the same reality. Since they differ in how they are generated, both processes have to be suitably supported. Let us consider them in turn.

Exogenous CS find their main motivations in the purpose of accountability (see Danish Medical and, more generally, any application of Quality Assurance standards) or compliance to some recognized standardization in production (as Bill of Materials (Schmidt, 1994)) or finally, as a precise choice to use categories 'ready at hand' (e.g., implicit in a technology, as in the case of TeachDiver). More specifically, in the two former cases the scheme reflects the needs of the external agency defining it, in terms of information contents or product/process characteristics. Exogenous CS are also proposed when the purpose apparently does not require them as such. Here, their usage is strongly influenced by the organizational structure surrounding them, typically the role of a mediating agency, and/or by their structure. The main problem raised by exogenous CS is understandability as a basis for their usage. For example, in (Hinrichs, 2000), the classification scheme (based on bare numbers) wasn't able to reflect the semantics of the products (basically, drawings) as well as the production process. Simplicity is often claimed as a fundamental property to obtain understandability: see PVE II and TeachDiver. However, simplicity is used in different ways in the two cases. As the core of a communication language across different departments whose limits are overcome by the mediating agency in the first case, or as a stimulus for an individual/collective learning process in the second one. At the same time, unless in special cases, the domains involved in cooperation are too complex to be classified by simple CS. In this case, simplicity becomes a drawback, and richness is claimed. There is a third aspect playing a role in this conflict: namely, the learning process that takes place at the individual as well as at the collaborative level in front of a new artifact like a CS. Both types of learning can make a simple CS useful enough and a rich CS understandable enough, since users can rely on the contextual information implied by both types of learning.

Hence, simplicity, richness and a support to individual and collaborative learning process are three requirements to be balanced according to the local needs and culture of the target setting and to be considered by the adaptative technological support to exogenous CS. In addition, the learning process has to adapt to the properties of the Consumers, that is on their level of skill in the domain (see e.g., (Adar et al., 1999) for the case of individual learning).

Endogenous CS find their main motivations in the purpose of improving communication, coordination and services (see Section 3.2 and 3.3). Their genesis can be described as a process making the 'structure' *emerge from practice*, from the problems it highlights, since no external agency or recognized standard can play as a reference starting point. Moreover, Producers and Consumers often overlap considerably and none of them is the only 'expert'. *Negotiation* among people with different, and all needed, skills is the core of the genesis of the resulting structure. Its usefulness and effective usage depend on how the CS fits the problems it contributes to solve. Therefore the learning process is heavily *a by product* of the negotiation needed to construct and use the CS: it is based on both positive and negative examples and on the improvements they generate. When exogenous CS are proposed in these situations, on the hypothesis that it is possible to achieve uniformity and without relying on a mediating agency, the reaction of the users is typical: either they use all the possible means to circumvent or bend the imposed CS or simply they do not use it, if they can. Again, a nice analogy with the history of control mechanisms (Bowers et al., 1995).

Hence, the main requirement for a technology supporting endogenous CS is to facilitate the `integration of articulation` (Schmidt and Simone, 1996) and `categorical work` (Bowker and Star, 1999). In other words, the CS is just one of the many artifacts people use to achieve their goals and the boundary between them is often fuzzy, in terms of structure and functionality so that any sharp separation between them looks quite artificial.

Of course, there are requirements that apply to both kinds of CS and can be derived from almost all the considered cases. In the line of (Bannon and Bødker, 1997), they articulate the observation that classification schemes are effective because of their locally immutable structure but at the same time they have to be open and flexible. First, both kinds of CS live in dynamic contexts and therefore have to be `malleable` in relation to the `context evolution`, at the functional and organizational levels. Second, they have to be interpreted in these contexts. `Historical information` about the joint evolution of CS and their context is a fundamental resource for interpretation, especially when construction and usage are separated in time and/or space. Last but not least, different endogenous and/or exogenous CS coexist in the same setting as autonomous and interconnected artifacts (since autonomous and interconnected are the activities generating them). A degree of `interoperability` has to be guaranteed across CS, especially when they support communication and coordination.

5. Implications on design

The requirements listed in the previous section show many similarities with the requirements identified earlier for control mechanisms. A lesson we learned from our experience in control mechanisms (Divitini and Simone, 2000) was that malleability in relation to the context evolution has to interpreted not only as a way to adapt the mechanism to the *current situation*, but also as a way to support its *continuous co-evolution with its context*. In the case of CS, malleability to the current situation is heavily related to the possibility to support multiple views of the same reality. We consider multiple views again in relation to endogenous and exogenous CS. The latter are typically proposed as a CS from which other CS can be derived to fulfill *local* needs. This can be done by a selection of attributes/keywords among a set of predefined possibilities so as to create the desired structure on the fly: examples of this type are the first solution in the UFS case (Trigg et al., 1999) or the proposal contained in (Lindstaedt and Schneider,

1997) or in the case of the commercial product Autonomy™ by Autonomy Ltd. An alternative solution is to allow for the manipulation of the structure itself together with the reallocation of the classified entities (like the second solution in the UFS case (Dourish et al., 1999)).

An important distinction is the motivation of such a dynamic construction: either individual search for information, or communication and coordination. In fact, in the first case, there is a single point of view to be taken into account, that is, the one of the searcher. The less the CS imposes a point of view the more the support provides an adequate locality. On the contrary, if the motivation is communication/coordination, two (or more) are the points of view to be considered, namely the ones of the two (or more) interacting actors. Communication and coordination require a great degree of mutual understanding by the interacting actors: understanding the received requests/responses in communication and increase the awareness of the other's situation in coordination. Contextual awareness is a fundamental means to support any collaborative learning process (Mark et al., 1997). Consequently, a valuable support should help people in 'transforming' a representation into the other ones, in both directions. The UFS case proposes a nice solution to this problem (Dourish et al., 1999). Local views are obtained through local transformations that are stratified in layers. In this way they can be constructed incrementally to answer individual or collective needs. The transformations can be undone up to the reference (exogenous) CS and re-done to define a continuous path of transformations between the two contexts achieving a sort of translation between local CS at the various levels. In the case of communication and coordination, on-the fly constructions are of little help, as they do not carry the contextual information incorporated in the CS, as discussed in Section 2. This can be a drawback in the case of individual search too, because the contextual information needed to re-interpret the retrieved information is reduced, by definition, unless additional remedies are provided, e.g., by recording some useful classifications (Adar et al., 1999).

Endogenous CS are, by their very nature, generated by 'local groups' as part of the solution to 'local problems'. Here locality has to interpreted in a broad sense, that is, parametrically in relation to the scope of the organization where the local problems arise. Two are the typical situations. As in the case of the Rush Cheat Sheet, the scope of locality crosses the borders of several departments, the resulting CS is the outcome of the negotiation among them and solves their mutual communication problems. In other cases, the endogenous CS solves the communication/coordination problems inside a group and in so doing it makes the inter-group communication more difficult: in this case translation is again a valuable support. Unlike the case of exogenous CS, here translation cannot rely on a unique reference CS since the locally generated ones cannot, in general, be unified in a single CS. The translation should be based on other means, typically on correspondences between categories and relations linking them in the two CS.

These correspondences can be derived in a more or less automatic way from the source schemes.

The theme of inter-group communication and coordination naturally links the issue of multiple views to the issue of the interoperability of endogenous CS (i.e., generated inside those groups). Interoperability can be dealt with at different levels and deserved the attention of many research efforts. Here, we want to deal it 'at the semantic level of categorical work', that is, at the semantic level that makes sense to the human actors. This point of view has been taken also by other disciplines (e.g., Cooperative Information Systems and Knowledge Representation) in order to deal with the interoperability of the pertinent technologies. Irrespective of the detailed solutions, the approaches they propose are based on techniques which aim at deriving the above mentioned correspondences in an automatic way on the basis of predefined sets of rules, possibly interacting with a domain expert who defines the rules or adapts them when unforeseen conflicts emerge. The aim is to make the translation process fully transparent to the users. These solutions cannot be directly adopted in approaches which take a CSCW perspective which emphasizes the role of mutual learning when interoperability is considered at the user semantic level. Mutual leaning is achieved through a direct involvement of the various groups in the definition of the above mentioned correspondences. A solution of this type is proposed in (Simone et al., 1999). Whatever is the means by which it is achieved, mutual learning is fundamental not only to use in a effective way the technology supporting the translation but especially to overcome its inherent limits, also in the case when there is an invisible human mediator.

Malleability in relation to the continuous co-evolution of a CS with its context has additional implications. The context can evolve both in terms of organizational structure and in terms of the domain (entities to be classified and/or classification criteria). Moreover, this can lead to temporary or permanent changes. In any case, beside modifying the CS structure, the main problem is in the need to re-classify the entities accordingly. Here, computer supported CS show some advantages in flexibility, especially if the underlying technological infrastructure is designed by applying innovative approaches (Dourish, 2000). A more subtle source of changes is connected with the evolution of the human actors using the CS in terms of skill about the domain and its classification. We mentioned this phenomenon in discussing simple versus rich CS in section 4.2. However, the situation can be more complex as reported in (Wulf, 1997). Since we are about dealing with every single problem by proposing initial solutions, there is the risk to improve each of them without taking into account their interoperability and to meet again the fragmentation we formerly encountered with technologies supporting communication and control mechanisms. This fragmentation was recognized as one of the main factors hindering their usability and effective use. If this is true, the integration of functionalities solving single problems has to be taken into account from the very beginning, by considering any partial solution as an incremental effort toward integration. This view has a strong impact on the way in which this functionality is conceived and implemented.

An additional set of considerations can be derived from the requirement of a tight integration of articulation and categorical work, when CS emerge from (local) practices. In fact, for sake of articulating their activities, users define which *entities* are worthwhile to be brought in the common working space and where they have to be 'positioned' to make the accomplishment of a cooperative task possible. Positions define, in a more or less explicit way, the semantic *relations* linking those entities. The same holds in the case of the construction of *artifacts* making visible (the state of) the flow of work that characterizes the specific cooperation. In this case, the artifact links actions, roles, actors, resources, processes in a direct way, and supports the existence of indirect (or derived) relations among the same entities. The structure of this common working space naturally becomes the framework where categorical work can be based with the guarantee of preserving the local culture (what really matters) and/or to avoid the conflicts generated by the superimposition of a newly conceived (if not external) structure. In order to support this bottom-up construction of CS the related tools have to be integrated in the tools supporting articulation work.

6. Issues towards innovation

The integration of functionalities supporting CS with those supporting articulation work requires innovative conceptual tools at the categorical work level as well as the level of the underlying technical infrastructure. We fully agree with (Dourish, 2000) that the two levels should progress in parallel to exploit the full capability of the infrastructure and to avoid undue constraints of the latter to the upper level. However, we concentrate only on the categorical work level.

Our experience in the design of a technology supporting control mechanisms shows the crucial role of linguistic tools in achieving integration. Hence, also in the case of CS we need a *powerful language* actors, with different skills and roles, can use to define, manipulate, use and finally link together CS. To keep the language general enough we can consider a CS as a set of *entities* to be linked according to some *relations*. The considered cases and our everyday experience show that CS are based on different kinds of relations: is-a and part-of relations are the most usual ones but cause-effect, version-of, depends-on are possibilities that are equally reasonable, among the others. Moreover, although several cases propose CS with a hierarchical structure, a hierarchical view of entities is not always needed. For example, classification can be made in terms of the state or type of the entities or can involve a rich cross-reference of attributes characterizing them. Hence, CS can take the form of simple *linear structures up to articulated networks* of entities and relations, depending on how and where they are used in cooperation. To complete the picture, the same cases show the need to consider *heterogeneous* CS both in terms of involved entities and relations to obtain the expressivity required by the real situations.

We conjecture that the more articulation and categorical work are integrated, the less a hierarchical and homogeneous structure is adequate for representing CS. This conjecture is sustained by both empirical evidences (Subrahmanian et al., 2000) and the outcomes of our current attempt to derive from the definition of a Coordination Mechanism in Ariadne (Divitini and Simone, 2000), the space of possibility where users can define classification schemes meaningful for them. This is our first step towards the integration in a technology of articulation and categorical work.

Giving users a tool to manipulate CS conceptualized as heterogeneous networks requires a deep understanding of these manipulations in terms of manipulations of the meaning (for sake of classification) of their constitutive elements. This calls for the definition of a pragmatically based 'algebra of relations' (Gerson, 2000) to understand which manipulations preserve both meaning for the users and internal consistency of the CS. In fact, heterogeneity implies that not all relations apply to all entities and not all relations can be freely composed. A formal treatment of relations is not new in computer science. However, is this theory enough to deal with classification in CSCW? At least, the purposes are different. In computer science the goal is the optimization of the representation to improve performances at the computational level; in CSCW, the goal is giving users manipulation tools preserving both meaning and consistency. Our claim to treat CS as formal objects does not contrast with the observation of the *value of ambiguity* emphasized in (Bowker and Star, 1999). On the contrary, this claim is coherent with the design requirement of "protecting [zones of ambiguity] where necessary to leave free play for the schemes to do their organizational work" (pages 324-325). Ambiguity can have different causes ranging from partial knowledge to implicit conventions. Here again, the co-evolution of the CS with its context implies that both partiality and implicitness can be at different degrees at various steps of the evolution, and can be useful and used in different ways by different actors. To take this variety of situations into account, the algebra of relations should support *powerful abstractions*, since this is the only way to reduce the explicit informational content without loosing trace of what is abstracted from.

Presently, abstractions are proposed for CS that are hierarchies constructed on is-a or part-of relations. Since this is not the general case, abstraction has to be provided for other types of relations too. For example, in (Donatelli et al., 2000), abstractions in the case of causal relation linking activities is proposed to support the promotion and use of awareness within and across groups and to the distributed modification of the protocols incorporated in Coordination Mechanisms. This kind of abstraction works on a network of actions and is able to combine a very detailed view of a portion of the behavior (namely, a single action) with abstractions that disregard any possible combination of uninteresting (technically, unobservable) actions surrounding it. The nice property is that the abstracted behavior can be automatically constructed on the fly just by letting users mark on the network or specify independently of it, which actions they want to observe without any additional engineering activity (Figure 1). The latter, beside imposing an undue overhead to the users, introduces arbitrary elements to the structure (as the arbitrary intermediate nodes required in the case of inheritance or refinement) which can hinder mutual understanding in cooperation.

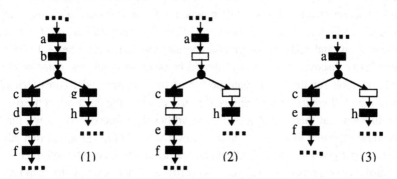

Figure 1. (1) A fragment of protocol with all information explicit; links express causality between actions; the bullet means choice among alternative behaviors (OR); (2) The user selects the actions to be abstracted from (white boxes loosing their label); (3) The reduction algorithm eliminates the white boxes that are not necessary for preserving the communicative behavior in any communicative context (Milner, 1980).

Moreover, this manipulation preserves meaning and consistency, since the abstracted behavior contains the minimum of additional information about causality links that makes this behavior indistinguishable from the detailed one in any context of components communicating with it. To our knowledge, a similar notion does not exist in 'knowledge' representation. As in the case of causality, we believe that it could help in supporting local multiple views, in defining what is worthwhile to be recorded in histories, in characterizing boundary entities and relations, and finally in supporting the translation and reconciliation that are required by interoperability of CS with different degrees of granularity. For example, this new abstraction could make it conceivable to extend to heterogeneous CS the technique applied in the UFS case (Dourish et al., 1999). The discovery of new abstraction techniques for CS, of which the proposed one is just an example, encompasses the definition of correspondingly innovative means to support them at the infrastructural level as well as the level of their representation at the user interface.

7. Conclusions

Since we looked at CS in cooperation as designers of a supportive technology, it is appropriate to read the effort reported in this paper as an activity that in (Schön and Bennet, 1996) is called *reflection on practice* . The goal was to put order and make sense of existing contributions, coming from various perspectives, to the theme of CS in cooperation. Obviously, the outcomes are neither systematic nor complete. They are an artifact typically used in design: a scaffold to sustain the work oriented to build something else. As any scaffold, they are not designed to last for a long period: their main value is to help the work to progress. Indeed, they play this role for us since they help us to orient our future efforts toward the mentioned open problems. Specifically, we believe that the outline provided by the referenced experiences shows the complexity inherent in the situated, distributed and evolving nature of cooperation when CS are considered. This complexity deserves additional investigations to discover new facets of CS's role in cooperation, and make more precise the already uncovered ones. However, the complexity discovered up to now should be taken as a *starting point in design* in order to look for the appropriate power of the (present and future) technological solutions, and *not as a surprising re-discovery* when the latter are conceived under the illusion that this complexity can be artificially reduced and show limits that could be supposed in advance. In this view, the need of integration often advocated in the paper gives us a framework where partial solutions can be interpreted as step towards a comprehensive support, powerful and rich enough to respond to the needs implied, all at the same time, by the situated, distributed and evolving nature of cooperation. In this path we will surely need new scaffolds that we hope to be able to build with the help of the community.

Acknowledgments

The authors want to thank the participants of the two mentioned workshops (organized with the support of the Danish National Research Councils under the Distributed Multimedia Project-Task 1.2) for the rich discussions about CS, and the reviewers for their very constructive criticisms.

References

Ackerman, M.S. and C. Halverson (1998): Considering an Organizational Memory. In *CSCW98, Seattle, Wa*, ed. J. Grudin and S. Poltrock. ACM Press, pp. 39-48.

Adar, E. , D. R. Karger, and L. A. Stein (1999): Haystack: Per-User Information Environments. In *CIKM , November 2-6-1999, Kansas City*. ACM Press, pp. 413-422.

Albrechtsen, H. and E.K. Jacob (1998): The dynamics of Classification Systems as Boundary Objects in Electronic Library. *Library Trends*, vol. 47, no. 2, pp. 293-312.

Bandini, S. and S. Manzoni (2000): A support based on CBR for the design of rubber compounds in motor racing. In *5th European Workshop on Case Based Reasoning, Trento - Italy*. Springer Verlag, Berlin, vol. LNAI 1898, pp. 348-357.

Bannon, L. and S. Bødker (1997): Constructing Common Information Spaces. In *ECSCW97, Lancaster*, ed. J. Hugues, W. Prinz, T. Rodden, and K. Schmidt. Kluwer Academic, pp. 81-96.

Bannon, L. and K. Kutti (1996): Shifting Perspectives on Organizational Memory: From storage to Active Remembering. In *Proceedings of the 29th IEEE HICSS, vol. III,* Washington: IEEE Computer Society Press, pp. 156-167.

Bowers, J., G. Button, and W. Sharrock (1995): Workflow from Within and Without: Technology and Cooperative Work on the Print Industry Shopfloor. In *Proceedings of ECSCW95k,* ed. H. Marmolin, Y. Sundblad, and K. Schmidt. Kluwer, pp. 51-66.

Bowker, G. C. and S. L. Star (1999): *Sorting things out: classification and its consequences.* Inside Technology, ed. W.E. Bijeker, W. B. Carlson, and T. Pinch. Cambridge, MA: The MIT Press.

Brown, J. S. and P. Duguid (2000): *The social life of information.* Boston (MA): Harvard Business Press.

Carstensen, P.H. (1997): Towards information exploration support for engineering designers. In *Advances in Concurrent Engineering (CE97), Oakland (Mi),* ed. S. Ganesman, pp. 26-33.

Christensen, U. and K. Schmidt (2000): Using Classification in Common Information Spaces. In *Workshop on Classification Schemes in Common Information Spaces, Copenhagen,* ed. K. Schmidt. - (to appear).

Conklin, J. (1988): gIBIS: A hypertext tool for exploratory policy discussion. In *Proceedings of CSCW '88, Portland, Oregon, 26-28 September 1988.* ACM Press, pp. 140-152.

De Michelis, G., F. De Paoli, C. Pluchinotta, and M. Susani (2000): Weakly augmented reality: observing and designing the work-place of creative designers. In *Designing Augmented Reality Environments (DARE2000), Helsinore, DK.*

Dieng, R. , O. Corby, A. Giboin, and M. Ribiere (1999): Methods and tools for corporate knowledge management. *Human Computer Studies,* vol. 51, no. 3, pp. 567-598.

Divitini, M. and C. Simone (2000): Supporting different dimensions of adaptability in workflow modeling. *CSCW Journal- Special Issue on 'Adaptive Worflow Systems',* vol. 9, no. 3-4, pp. 365-397.

Donatelli, S., M. Sarini, and C. Simone (2000): Towards a Contextual Information Service supporting adaptability and awareness in CSCW systems. In *COOP 2000, Sophia-Antipolis (Fr),* ed. R. Dieng, A. Giboin, G. De Michelis, and L. Karsenty, IOS Press, pp. 83-98.

Dourish, P. (2000): Technical and social features of categorization schemes. In *Worshop on Classification Schemes in Cooperative Work held at CSCW2000, Philadelphia,* ed. K. Schmidt, C. Simone, and S. L. Star.

Dourish, P., J. Lamping, and T. Rodden (1999): Building bridges: customization and intelligibility in shared category management. In *ACM-Group99, Phoenis AZ,* ed. S. C. Haynes. ACM Press, pp. 11- 20.

Gerson, E. (2000): Different parts for different smarts: partonomies and the organization of work. In *Workshop on Classification Schemes in Common Information Spaces, Copenhagen,* ed. K. Schmidt. - (to appear).

Guy, E.. (2000): Classification and participation: issues in a study of an internet mailing list. In *Worshop on Classification Schemes in Cooperative Work held at CSCW2000, Philadelphia,* ed. K. Schmidt, C. Simone, and S. L. Star. - (partial information can be found at www.nwls.com/list-archive).

Halverson, C.A. (2000): Instances in the lifecycle of Classification Schemes in Cooperative Work. In *Worshop on Classification Schemes in Cooperative Work held at CSCW2000, Philadelphia,* ed. K. Schmidt, C. Simone, and S. L. Star. - (more information in: Halverson, C. A. Cognitive Adaptation: the Effects of Introducing New Technology on Air Traffic Control. -Dissertation,1995).

38

Hinrichs, J. (2000): Telecooperation in engineering offices - The problem of archiving. In *COOP 2000, Sophia-Antipolis (Fr)*, ed. R. Dieng, A. Giboin, G. De Michelis, and L. Karsenty, IOS Press, pp. 259-274.

Kovalainen, M., M. Robinson, and E. Auramäki (1998): Diaries at work. In *CSCW98, Seattle, Wa*, ed. J. Grudin and S. Poltrock. ACM, pp. 49-58.

Lindstaedt, S.N. and K. Schneider (1997): Bridging the gap between face-to-face communication and long-term collaboration. In *ACM-GROUP'97, Phoenix (AZ)*, ed. S. C. Hayne and W. Prinz. ACM Press, pp. 331-340.

Malone, T., et al. (1998): *Tools for inventing organizations: Toward a handbook of organizational processes*. Center for Coordination Science, MIT.

Mark, G., L. Fuchs, and M. Sohlenkamp (1997): Supporting groupware conventions through contextual awareness. In *ECSCW97, Lancaster*, ed. J. Hugues, W. Prinz, T. Rodden, and K. Schmidt. Kluwer Academic, pp. 253-268.

Milner, Robin (1980): A Calculus of Communicating Systems. In *Lecture Notes in Computer Science, LNCS 92*. Berlin: Springer-Verlag.

Nonaka, I. and H. Takeuchi (1995): *The knowledge creating company*, Oxford University Press.

O'Neill, J. (2000): Creating Classification Schemes that support the "real work" of large organizations. In *Worshop on Classification Schemes in Cooperative Work held at CSCW2000, Philadelphia*, ed. K. Schmidt, C. Simone, and S. L. Star.

Schmidt, K. and L. Bannon (1992): Taking CSCW Seriously: Supporting Articulation Work. *CSCW*, vol. 1, no. 1-2, pp. 7-40.

Schmidt, K. and C. Simone (1996): Coordination Mechanisms: Towards a conceptual foundation for CSCW systems design. *Computer Supported Cooperative Work (CSCW). An International Journal*, vol. 5, no. 2-3.

Schmidt, K. and C. Simone (2000): Mind the gap! Towards a unified view of CSCW. In *COOP 2000, Sophia-Antipolis (Fr)*, ed. R. Dieng, A. Giboin, G. De Michelis, and L. Karsenty, IOS Press, pp. 205-221.

Schmidt, K. (ed) (1994): *Social Mechanisms of Interaction*. COMIC (#6225) – Deliverable 3.2. (ftp.comp.lancs.ac.uk/pu/comic).

Schön, D. and J. Bennet (1996): Reflective conversation with materials. In *Bringing Design to Software*, ed. T. Winograd. New York: Addison Wesley.

Simone, C., G. Mark, and D. Giubbilei (1999): Interoperability as a means of articulation work. In *WACC'99, San Francisco*. ACM Press, pp. 39-48.

Star, S.L. (1998): Grounded Classification: grounded Theory and faceted Classification. *Library Trends*, vol. 47, no. 2, pp. 218-232.

Subrahmanian, E., et al. (2000): Classification for communication and communication for classification in engineering design. In *Worshop on Classification Schemes in Cooperative Work held at CSCW2000, Philadelphia*, ed. K. Schmidt, C. Simone, and S. L. Star.

Trigg, R. H., J. Blomberg, and L. Suchman (1999): Moving documents collections online: the evolution of a shared repository. In *ECSCW99, Copenhagen*, ed. S. Bødker, M. King, and K. Schmidt. Kluwer Academic, pp. 331-350.

Wulf, V. (1997): Storing and retrieving documents in a shared workspace: experiences from the political administration. In *INTERACT'97*, ed. S. Howard, J. Hammond, and G. Lindgaard. Chapman & Hall, pp. 469-476.

W. Prinz, M. Jarke, Y. Rogers, K. Schmidt, and V. Wulf (eds.), *Proceedings of the Seventh European Conference on Computer-Supported Cooperative Work, 16-20 September 2001, Bonn, Germany*, pp. 39-58.
© 2001 Kluwer Academic Publishers. Printed in the Netherlands.

Finding Patterns in the Fieldwork

David Martin, Tom Rodden, Mark Rouncefield, Ian Sommerville, & Stephen Viller

Computing Department, Lancaster University, Lancaster LA1 4YR, UK

{D.B.Martin@lancaster.ac.uk, tam@comp.lancs.ac.uk, M.Rouncefield@lancaster.ac.uk, is@comp.lancs.ac.uk, viller@comp.lancs.ac.uk}

Abstract. This paper considers the potential of using *patterns of cooperative interaction* to support the development of general design principles drawn from a range of work settings. It reports on the development of patterns from ethnographic studies in a number of work environments. Our particular interest is in the possibilities surrounding the use of *patterns* as a means of organising, presenting and representing this growing corpus of ethnographic material and in the contribution this might make to CSCW design. In this paper we focus on outlining some of our experiences and difficulties in developing patterns from ethnographic studies and present some initial ideas towards the development of a pattern language to exploit the experience gained from a decade of field studies.

The use of ethnographic studies, from a variety of perspectives (Ackerman & Halverson, 1998; Bardram, 1998; Bowers & Martin, 1999; Hughes et al., 1992), has been a regular and routine feature of CSCW research for a number of years as research has attempted to inform the requirements and design of cooperative systems through studies of 'real world real time' work (Hughes et al., 1997). Despite being strong advocates and supporters of the method (Hughes et al., 1994) we also acknowledge persistent problems in meeting the needs of developers and deploying the results of ethnographic studies in design. To some considerable extent the arguments about ethnography and workplace studies have moved on from 'what are workplace studies for?' (Anderson, 1994; Plowman et al., 1995) to how these studies can best be utilised for design. As Bannon argues;

".. a critical issue for research lies in determining ways of transforming the ethnographic material in such a way that remains sensitive to the practices of designers themselves and thus can readily be used by them in the design process." (Bannon, 2000, p.250).

Many ethnographers would add, *"while still remaining faithful to these rich descriptions of real-time situated work"* to this statement. The tension between the need for designers to develop the abstract structures underpinning computer systems while being informed of the rich everyday character of work has become one of a number of central issues of CSCW research. This issue has emerged against a backdrop of alternative approaches to the development of CSCW systems including participative approaches (Schuler & Namioka, 1993) and those from a more theoretical design orientation (Nardi, 1996) where theory is often seen as having a much more central role. The tension between study and design has sometimes been characterised as simply one of communication between fieldworkers and designers. Subsequently, researchers including ourselves have developed variations in methods (Beyer & Holtzblatt, 1998; Viller & Sommerville, 1999); presentation mechanisms, frameworks and notations (Hughes et al., 1997; Hughes et al., 1995; Twidale et al., 1993) in attempts to bridge this apparent divide.

While efforts have been made to ensure that field studies are better communicated to developers and designers the community has also amassed a substantial corpus of fieldwork material. Studies of work have routinely been reported at CSCW conferences and many projects currently undertake an ethnographic study as part of their development. However, what has been learnt from all of these studies is less clear and very little *systematic* consideration has been afforded to the thorny problem of developing a corpus of good design practice and experience drawn across this growing body of research. This, in turn, touches on the fundamental question of the more general role of ethnography in design as well as difficult academic and practical issues regarding the generalisation of ethnographic findings (Hughes et al., 1994). Over the years a considerable corpus of workplace studies has been generated. As this corpus continues to develop the issue becomes one of how the, to this date little discussed, 're-examination of previous studies' (Hughes et al., 1994) can be facilitated productively. While researchers may be exploring the development of general design principles and guidelines the extent to which ethnographic studies can contribute to the formation of general concepts and principles of systems design remains an open question (Pycock, 1999).

Developing useful and applicable general guidelines for systems design is a thorny issue, as it requires a balance to be struck between the need for the emergence of *general* principles and the central importance in ethnographic studies of *detailing* everyday situated practice. If we are to provide more general design principles, techniques need to be uncovered that facilitate generalisation from ethnographic studies and that allow the results of such studies to be married with more general statements of design. This paper seeks to address this problem by presenting our experiences of exploring the potential offered by *patterns* as a means of presenting ethnographic work. We do so firstly by exploring the discovery and construction of *patterns of cooperative interaction*—patterns of cooperation and IT use that recur across a number of settings.

In this paper the patterns we develop and present focus on our ongoing ethnographic research and draw from a number of ethnographic studies of different work environments (Bentley et al., 1992; Blythin et al., 1997; Bowers et al., 1996; O'Brien & Rodden, 1997; Rodden et al., 1994). It is not the intention behind either the notion of patterns or the development of a pattern language that these should guide *fieldwork* in any way[1]. The patterns we document are drawn from the fieldwork as grossly observable patterns of activity and interaction. The intent behind the construction of these patterns is that they will serve both as a means of *documenting* and *describing* common interactions, and as a vehicle for *communicating* the results of a specific analysis to designers—to be drawn upon and used as a resource for design. The presentation of different patterns of interaction seeks to allow different *general principles* and issues to be presented alongside *specific* material drawn from empirical studies. Thus rather than seek a simple translation from the specific of the empirical work to the general of the design principle we are seeking to explore mechanisms that allow both to be present and available to designers and developers.

Patterns and Pattern Languages

The origin of patterns lies in the work of the architect Christopher Alexander, outlined in two books, *A Timeless Way of Building* and *A Pattern Language* (Alexander, 1979; Alexander et al., 1977). Patterns are attempts to marry the relevant aspects of the physical and social characteristics of a setting into a design; they provide a facility to share knowledge about design solutions and the setting in which such a solution is applied:

"..every pattern we define must be formulated in the form of a rule which establishes a relationship between a context, a system of forces which arises in that context, and a configuration which allows these forces to resolve themselves in that context" (Alexander et al., 1977)

Patterns are then a way of conveying to designers some sense of the application domain. They are,

"..ways of allowing the results of workplace studies to be reused in new and different situations. .. ways of representing knowledge about the workplace so that it is accessible to the increasingly diverse set of people involved in design.." (Erickson, 2000b)

---

[1] This is not to say that, after a period of time, patterns that are found to be more robust should not be used to focus requirements gathering activities. Indeed, this use of patterns may prove of high utility to those with less experience of conducting fieldwork.

There are, however, a number of rather different conceptualisations of patterns. Perhaps the most notable usage of these is patterns within the software engineering community where design patterns (Gamma et al., 1994) and pattern code books (e.g. Cooper, 2000) are increasingly popular. While inspired from Alexander's original work the notion of patterns has moved from the original conception suggested by Alexander. In fact, within the use of patterns suggested by this community, patterns tend to be prescriptive in nature offering template solutions to problems. These "reuse templates" tend to be less flexible than those originally suggested by Alexander where the patterns were intended to be used as a resource to be drawn upon.

We wish to exploit patterns in the much looser spirit suggested by Alexander's original work where familiar situations were used to convey potential architectural solutions. In fact, the observed reoccurrence of familiar situations lies at the core of our argument for patterns. Designers often encounter situations that are similar to previous ones and one justification for this focus on patterns is a particular take on notions of re-use—where the emphasis is on drawing from previous experience to support the collection and generalisation of successful solutions to common problems. As Alexander suggests;

> "each pattern describes a problem which occurs over and over again in our environment, and then describes the core of the solution to that problem, in such a way that you can use this solution a million times over, without ever doing it the same way twice".

Another rationale behind patterns - and one that perhaps both attracts and repels designers - is Alexander's notion of 'quality' ('The Quality Without A Name') and the idea that "a pattern is a solution to a problem in a context". Here 'quality' refers not to some mystical characteristic but to features of systems that ensure that they 'really work', that they fit with the social circumstances of use. Interestingly this is also part of the rationale for the turn to ethnography in systems design. (Crabtree et al., 2000).

The appeal of patterns for interactive systems is that they provide a flexible means of presenting design solutions and in recent years the notion of patterns and pattern language has become increasingly popular and influential in a number of disciplines related to system design. Patterns have been examined in software design (Gamma et al., 1994) and in the HCI community (Erickson, 2000b) as a means of recording design solutions. A number of researchers (Coplien, 1998) have also suggested the application of pattern techniques to convey different forms of organisational structure.

In the following sections we outline our own efforts to uncover and present *patterns of cooperative interaction* derived from a corpus of ethnographic studies. The main body of work consists of ethnographic studies of work and technology undertaken in the last ten years by researchers from Lancaster, for example in air traffic control (e.g. Bentley et al., 1992), small (Rouncefield et al., 1994) and banking (e.g. Randall et al., 1995). However, the corpus also includes well known studies undertaken by other researchers at other institutions, for example in

London Underground Control (Heath & Luff, 1992), the accountancy department of a catering firm (Anderson et al., 1989), ambulance control (Martin et al., 1997; Whalen, 1995), and the fashion industry (Pycock & Bowers, 1996).

Within the HCI/CSCW communities there is no single definition of what patterns are, how they should be presented, what their purpose should be and how they should be used. We started by considering that in finding patterns we were looking for examples of repeated, grossly observable phenomena in ethnographic studies, describing them with reference to their context of production and seeking a way to present them using a standard framework. The program to find patterns of cooperative interaction can be seen as one way in which the *'re-examination of previous studies'* can serve to provide a resource for systems design. The discovery and presentation of patterns hopefully may be a way through which the important findings of different studies are highlighted and presented in a manner that is more accessible to the CSCW community at large.

Developing Patterns in Practice

While considerable literature exists documenting patterns of different types little is said in the pattern community about the genesis of patterns. It is unclear how patterns come into existence and how these should be generated. The core of most descriptions is that a series of "pattern workshops" are held where patterns are identified and expressed using some form of pattern language. In this paper we wish to explicitly document our experiences in uncovering patterns and the development of a pattern language to express patterns to designers.

When seeking to outline patterns of cooperative interaction much of our early work focused towards the discovery of potential patterns based on the illustrative vignettes often used in the reporting of ethnographic studies of work. The earliest work centred on whether the major findings, in terms of grossly observable phenomena, from ethnographic studies could be presented as sets of problems and solutions according to a template based on the presentation format used by Alexander for presenting his architecture patterns.

Although every search for patterns means beginning with looking for specific examples in context it is also equally clear that a pattern gains increasing credibility through being found to be present in more than one setting. This led us to search for patterns and repeated patterns firstly within particular domains. For example, the domain of control rooms was selected due to its prominence in particularly the early field studies of work and technology. The technique was to identify one example of a grossly observable phenomenon within one control room study and to examine the others to see whether similar examples of the same phenomena could be identified in these. While it became clear that while recurrent examples might be found within a domain it was equally clear that there were a number of examples of similar patterns to be found in studies of banking, or hospitals or small offices and so on.

In the following section we document our experience in developing a language to express our patterns. Before we develop a pattern language it is worth reflecting on the role we anticipated the pattern language playing within the overall process of design.

Patterns as a lingua franca of design

In seeking to uncover patterns we began by looking at how the major results from ethnographic studies could be presented as problems and solutions according to a template very similar to that employed by Alexander. Alexander's original pattern languages focused on presenting patterns as solutions to design problems. The broad structuring principle was that each pattern responded to a particular design problem. The pattern language presented the problem addressed, the solution suggested and provided links to other problem-solution structures within the pattern language.

However, even on the crudest of initial inspections it is not clear that the problems to be solved are routinely observable as part of a field study. While it is easy to envisage designers developing solutions to problems informed from studies of work it is not clear that the problem to be solved will always be the same or that these problems are an inherent part of the current setting. However, pattern languages do more than provide a template of ready made solutions and much of the popularity of Alexander's patterns is that they provide a ready resource for others to draw upon. In fact, the pattern language's principle role is often that of a communication device. Indeed Erickson (Erickson, 2000a) suggests that the principle role of a pattern language is as a *lingua franca* to be used by a number of designers, within a project.

In his paper *"Supporting Interdisciplinary Design: Towards Pattern Languages For Workplaces"* Erickson (2000b) outlines and discusses some patterns he has derived from an ethnographic study of a consulting firm as reported by Belotti and Bly (1996). Erickson describes a number of patterns, most notably focusing on three: *Maintaining Mutual Awareness*, *Locally Mobile Workers* and *Receptionist as Hub*. He draws attention to the fact that this is just the beginning of such work. Most notably, he does not present these patterns according to a format which approximates to that employed by Alexander. Instead, he simply provides a paragraph of description for each pattern. These outline the basic details of the phenomenon in question and sketch out the relationships with other patterns in that setting.

Taking Maintaining Mutual Awareness as an example, Erickson describes how it is crucially important that the workers in the consulting firm maintain an awareness of what one another are doing even if their projects are different. This allows for the range of expertise to spread across different projects and help and advice to be shared. Erickson describes how mutual awareness is maintained by *"activity patterns"* such as *"Doing A Walkabout"*, where a worker has a stroll round the office looking at what others are doing. Furthermore, how it is supported by *"spatial patterns"* such as a *"Central Scanning Station"* where people bump into one another and may instigate useful conversations about their work.

Erickson's work is clearly more oriented to the description of workplace phenomena rather than to providing design solutions. Although, it must be conceded, the patterns he describes are meant to represent things that *work* in that setting. This appeared to be a good model to follow, at least in the initial discovery of patterns. However, importantly, Erickson provides little treatment of the question of generalisation. Rather, he considers how these patterns might be useful as broad design themes. Our challenge was to consider how we may provide more structure to allow patterns to be more generally used but maintain the commitment to their use as a descriptive device.

Moving from Design Patterns to Descriptive Patterns

Our first attempt at using patterns exploited a series of ethnographic studies of the use of technology in people's homes. Although agreeing with the broad motivation suggested by Erickson our aim was to outline a vehicle for presenting the major findings of these studies. We took the structure used by Alexander in his architectural patterns as our starting point. Our aim was to see if this could be used as a uniform style for presentation. These patterns followed Alexander's structure in that a recurrent problem is presented with a solution to that problem. The format used was an HTML presentation to make it accessible (figure 1).

However, although these patterns provided support for the representation of the setting a number of key observations emerged that were a result of the problem orientation of Alexander's original patterns.

- *Expressive power was limited.* The attachment of the pattern with a problem meant that features of the study needed to be presented in terms of the problems they addressed or solved. While the vocabulary of problems and solutions made sense for designers it was felt that large parts of the study could not readily be expressed in this way.
- *The application domain was limited.* The utility beyond a study undertaken as part of a particular design project became problematic. As a consequence of the strong orientation to problems and designed solutions we noticed that once we sought to apply the pattern language outside a project we were familiar with our ability to capture the essence of the setting reduced significantly.

These two limitations required us to seriously reconsider how we may want to use patterns and the sort of patterns and pattern language we wished to develop.

46

While the focus on problem-solution as a central structuring concept had immediate appeal to our target audience of designers we strongly felt that its limitations prohibited the presentation of studies to such an extent that the use of Alexander's patterns and indeed of the design patterns suggested by the software engineering community would not meet our purpose in presenting ethnographic studies of work.

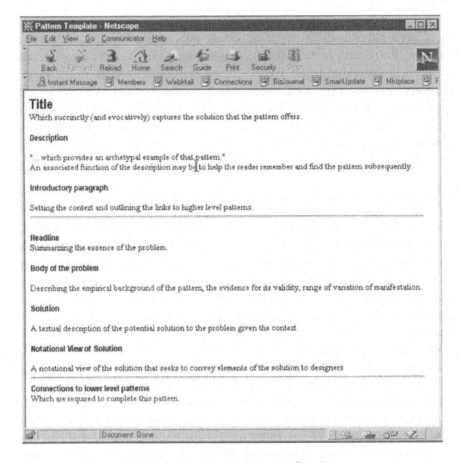

Figure 1. A problem oriented pattern Template.

The development of patterns presented in this paper represents a rather different focus than in this initial work. It also represents a turn away from the current approach to design patterns. In order to break free of the current limitations of patterns we sought to move away from problems as the defining characteristic of patterns. While the concept of problems has a resonance for design patterns and makes sense in terms of the overall process of design it is less clear that a pattern language oriented around problems would be of utility in presenting studies. Consequently we have focused on the development of descriptive patterns that convey the nature of settings to those who may seek to develop technologies that are sensitive to the nature of work settings. The aim of these patterns is to act as a general resource for developers to be drawn upon when they are seeking to build systems for a particular setting rather than to suggest a particular working arrangement as being more appropriate than others.

In order to meet the needs of patterns for presentation we shifted our consideration to finding patterns as recurrent phenomena in ethnographic fieldwork without necessarily making judgements as to the 'success' of the arrangement of people and artefacts undertaking some activity in the given context. Sometimes it may be appropriate to contrast similar examples where one case seems to work better than the other, however at this stage this is not to be taken as a prerequisite for including an example as a pattern. The idea is to firstly discover patterns as recurrent phenomena and to make these patterns available to designers. The arrangement of patterns according to a particular framework and outlining their implications for design is deliberately postponed until some point after this initial process has been completed to a satisfactory extent.

Identifying Descriptive Patterns

Given that we had abandoned the notion of problems as central structuring mechanisms the identification of appropriate descriptive patterns raised a challenge for us. How might we identify particular patterns from the large corpus of fieldwork available to us? What sort of pattern language might we develop to convey these patterns and how might we present these to users? In order to address this issue we decided to focus on an exploration of not only previous studies undertaken at Lancaster but also a collection of other studies reported in the literature. Our aim in considering a wide range of studies was to directly tackle the issues of generalisation by seeking to uncover *generally recurrent phenomena* that can form the basis of a descriptive pattern language.

As a starting point for uncovering patterns we focused on control room studies. This combined studies such as the London Underground Study (Heath and Luff, 1992) with other control room studies (ATC, Ambulance control) some of which we were directly involved in. This cross examination of studies suggested that there was a certain degree of cross-over in terms of similar major findings in the different control rooms studied. For example, Hughes et al. (1993) draw attention to the use and display of flight strips as a public artefact, Martin et al. (1997) also discuss co-ordination around public screens showing the state of ambulance deployment, and Heath and Luff (Heath & Luff, 1992) point to the use of shared artefacts as a means of coordination in the London Underground. Furthermore, these studies are concerned with such features as the ecology of the settings studied and how co-workers achieve and maintain an awareness of one another's work.

From Domains of Study to Principles of generation

Our success in the examination of studies drawn from control rooms initially suggested that one way in which patterns might be arranged was according to domain, and it appeared sensible to begin with control room patterns. This also suggested a solution to how the question of generalisation might be tackled. Here we had similar situations where similar types of phenomena were reported. For example, we could extract the *use of a public artefact* as a basic pattern and describe three similar but different examples of it from three control room studies. Common domains of study offered a good initial candidate as a means of generating potential descriptive patterns.

However, it also became clear that adopting a rigid idea of domain as a manner of organising sets of patterns might not be altogether satisfactory. For example, studies of call centres (e.g. Martin, 2000) have drawn attention to the public display of various call waiting and answering statistics for a group of operators to clearly see. Furthermore, it was clear that other potential patterns we were discovering and extracting fell across domains. For example, we described a pattern, *Artefact as an Audit Trail* (discussed later), which related to the observation that in certain studies researchers noted that paper-based artefacts acted as stratified records of the work that had been completed in relation to them. They would attract amendments, signatures, date stamps and other attachments that indicated who had done what work on them, why and at what point in their life-cycle. This record of work incorporated in the artefact was readily accessible to workers in the given setting. Our examples of this potential pattern however came from the disparate settings of Air Traffic Control, with the flight strips displaying this property but also from observations about invoices in an accountancy department of a catering firm (Anderson et al., 1989) and had potential in describing the use of documents in hospitals (Fitzpatrick, 2000).

Due to the fact that as we attempted to discover and delineate patterns we were beginning to find potential patterns that had instances that were clearly cross-domain it appeared sensible to abandon the notion of organisation around domain. We had always acknowledged that organisation around domain brought with it inherent difficulties of definition. Control rooms seemed attractive as a single domain because there had been a number of studies of these, however we were aware that, for example, a nuclear power plant control room might be rather different to control rooms that managed the deployment of vehicles or transport. And when we looked at other domains, we were ending up with categories like *offices*, which we readily acknowledged covered a very large range of settings. While abandoning this type of organisation around domains it is worth noting that we were open to the possibility that certain patterns might be more representative of certain settings, groups of studies, user groups and so forth, however we considered that similarities or groupings of patterns might be derived from the collection of patterns rather than being an organising principle from the start. At this stage we wanted to pursue a different type of organisation that could apply across a range of patterns.

Outlining Principles of Generation.

Trying to uncover descriptive patterns within the fieldstudies under examination soon highlighted the need for some set of guidance. Although we were focusing on grossly observable features as the core of the genesis of the patterns it was unclear what sorts of features provided a set of readily understood patterns and what features were of most significance. In order to provide a focus on the issues of importance to designers (our eventual target audience) we turned to our previous work in outlining a framework of presentation in order to develop a set of generative principles. These principles broadly divided into two main sets.

- *Spatially oriented features* that focus on the physical nature of the work and the observable arrangements within the workplace.
- *Work oriented features* that focus on the principles of social organisation used to structure and manage the cooperative work.

The purpose of a focus on these features is to seed potential patterns and to use this as a means of highlighting the grossly observable features of work.

Spatially oriented features

These principles seek to foreground the observable arrangement of work and physical nature of the work setting.Three key features are of particular importance and can be expressed as key questions

- Resources- what are the various resources in the setting used to support the work taking place and how are they shared.
- Actors – who is involved in the cooperative work taking place and how do they orientate to each other.
- Activities – what are the main observable techniques for structuring activities and how are these represented.

Work oriented features

These principles seek to foreground the socially organised nature of work and how these are manifest in practice within particular settings. For simplicity we have again focused on three key features drawn from previous work on a framework for presenting fieldwork.

- Awareness of work—how and through what means are those involved in work aware of the work of others, how do they exploit this awareness and how do they make others aware of their own work?
- Distributed Coordination—how do those involved in the work coordinate their activities and what practical techniques do they use to do this?

- Plans and procedures—what techniques do those involved in the workplace use to orient their work in practice to the formal plans, procedures, representations and artefacts of work?

Developing a Descriptive Pattern Language

The basic principles underpinning the generation of patterns were now agreed in terms of the spatial principles (actors, resources, activities) and the social organisational principles (Awareness of work, Distributed coordination, Plans and procedures). These basic principles provide a key set of concepts to drive the identification and highlighting of descriptive patterns. In seeking to identify descriptive patterns by looking for evidence of these core principles within the field study provides a means of starting the development of patterns. However, these basic generative principles are not necessarily the best way of presenting patterns to potential developers and allowing comparison across them.

The identification of descriptive patterns progressed through one more stage of evolution to the development of a basic descriptive pattern language that allows patterns to be conveyed to potential designers. The basic ways in which patterns were to be described and presented took the principles of generation as a starting point. However, there was a desire to re-cast and even extend the framework to capture the main aspects of the proposed patterns in a manner that allowed designers to make sense of the patterns as quickly as possible. What was needed was a structure that represented a common demonimator for describing and presenting the identified patterns.

To develop an agreed pattern language all members of the research group independently produced a list of all the features that were required to describe a pattern. Through the presentation and discussion of these individual frameworks a set of potential pattern languages were proposed and then refined as different patterns were presented from the fieldwork. After some discussion the following framework was settled upon. This pattern language combines the different features of the principles of generation to allow different features of the identified descriptive patterns to be described. The identified fields within the agreed pattern language are:

- **Cooperative Arrangement:** The cooperative arrangement details in very basic terms the *actors* and *resources* that are constituent of the pattern of interaction: the people, the number and type of computers and artefacts, the communication medium(s) employed and the basic *activity*.
- **Representation of Activity:** This describes how the activity is represented, for example, in technology or as a plan and may address the relationship between the activity and the representation. This is related to *plans and procedures*.
- **Ecological Arrangement:** This has the form of one or more pictorial representations of the pattern. For example this may include *abstract*

representations, plan views, information flows, copies of paper forms, screen shots or photographs. There may be good reason for these to be fairly abstract as the real detail may be found in the referenced studies themselves if this is desired. This explicitly addresses the *spatial* characteristics.

- **Coordination Techniques:** This details the type of practices, procedures and techniques employed in carrying out the activity/interaction and how and in what way coordination is achieved. This is related to *awareness* and *distributed co-ordination.*

- **Population of Use:** This is related to an idea of domain, but instead seeks to capture something about the user group. For example, is it organisation-customer or a small team of co-workers in a control room.

It should be noted that, whilst the above fields are intended to highlight different characteristics of a pattern, they are not intended to be orthogonal, and indeed in some cases will be very strongly related. Further, whilst we have identified a common framework for describing patterns, depending on the primary focus of a particular pattern, more attention may be devoted to particular fields, as appropriate.

For each identified pattern a set of illustrative examples drawn from the field studies is presented. This arrangement is designed to promote comparison across pattern examples drawn from different fieldsites. A further challenge is to at some point derive generic overviews for patterns, however as discussed later we do not feel that it is appropriate to attempt this at this stage. This basic descriptive structure is outlined in figure 2. The reader should note that the table is presented for summary pusposes while the vignettes are presented in HTML as web pages.

Pattern Name

	Fieldwork vignette # 1	....	Fieldwork vignette # N	Generic overview?
Cooperative Arrangement				
Representation of Activity				
Ecological Arrangement				
Coordination Techniques				
Population Of Use				

Figure 2. The pattern language descriptive structure

The pattern Language in use

The identified pattern language held considerable promise but how might it be used to present different field studies? This section briefly presents examples drawn from a range of field studies. The aim of this section is to convey the potential utility of the pattern language to emerge from the process described in the previous sections. This section illustrates how the pattern language can be used to present generally observable features to emerge from a set of field studies.

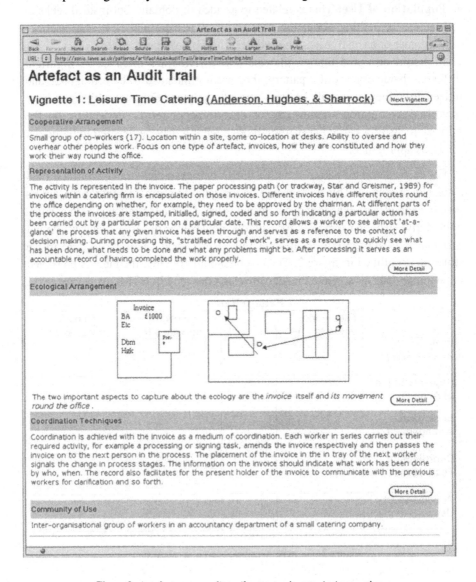

Figure 3: *Artefact as an audit trail* pattern, vignette 1: Accounting.

Pattern 1 - Artefact As An Audit Trail

This pattern is presented based on two different field studies. As indicated when it was introduced earlier we believe that other instances occur in the literature, however for economy of space we provide only the two examples here. The pattern is concerned with how artefacts gather annotations, etc. that are representative of the process of work completed in relation to them. Vignette 1 is drawn from a field study of an accounting department of a small catering company (Anderson et al., 1989) (figure 3). Vignette 2 for this pattern is drawn from a study of air traffic controllers (Hughes et al., 1992) (figure 4). The patterns have been developed and presented here as web pages, allowing access to further detail to be provided via hyperlinks. The further detail may take the form of the original study report, fieldwork notes, video clips, photographs, etc.

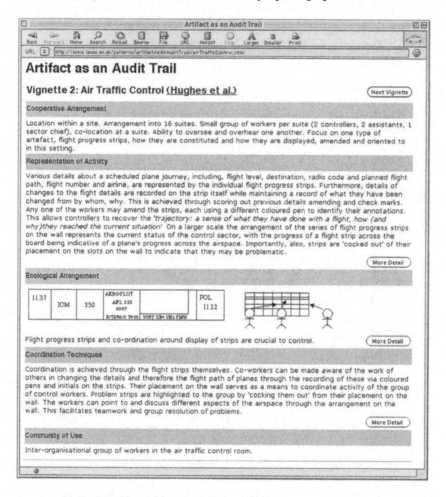

Figure 4: *Artefact as an audit trail* pattern, vignette 2: Air traffic control.

Pattern 2 – Multiple Representations of Information

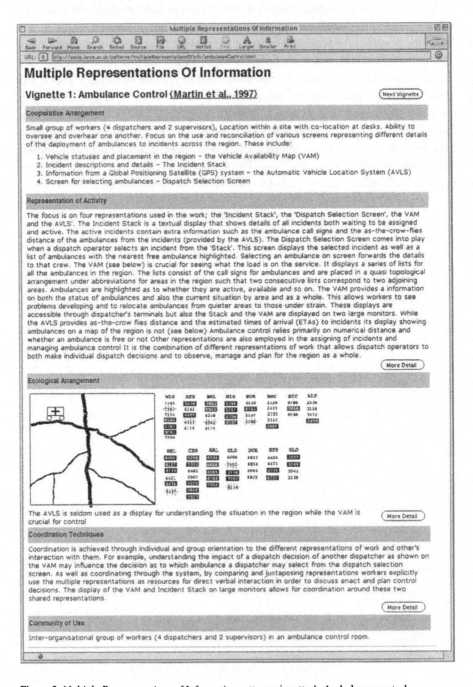

Figure 5: *Multiple Representations of Information* pattern, vignette 1: Ambulance control.

This pattern is presented based again on two different field studies. It is concerned with how multiple views onto information are used in different settings to support the understanding of often complex and dynamic data. Vignette 1 (figure 5) is drawn from a study of ambulance controllers (Martin et al., 1997), and vignette 2 (figure 6) once more from air traffic control (Hughes et al., 1992).

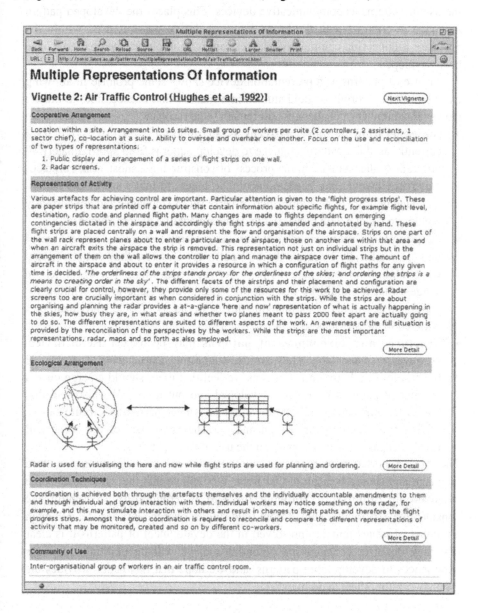

Figure 6: *Multiple Representations of Information* pattern, vignette 2: Air traffic control.

Conclusions

This paper has presented our experiences of developing a pattern language that can be used to present field studies. The focus of this work has been on a move away from the problem orientation within Alexander's original work to consider the use of patterns as communicative devices. This places the developed pattern language in contrast with the broad range of design patterns used within the Software Engineering community where strongly solution-oriented patterns have been developed.

Our use of patterns as a presentation device shows some promise in allowing us to represent a corpus of field studies in a manner that is accessible to others. However, a number of challenges still remain to be resolved:

- **The generation of more patterns** is an important next step. We have currently used the pattern language to develop patterns from approximately 10 different studies and are in the process of constructing a substantial corpus of patterns. However, we need to encourage others to make use of the pattern language in order to develop a more diverse set of languages and are currently seeking to engage with others in the development of a pattern database.

- **Handling large numbers of patterns**. As patterns emerge and are generated how do we handle large numbers of patterns? How are they structured and what relationship will patterns have between each other. For example, we suggest that it should be possible to write a more generic description for patterns that will act as an indexing device to the set of field study examples outlined in the previous section.

- **Structures and taxonomies of patterns** may become a useful device. However, we have deliberately avoided suggesting a structuring of patterns or the relationship between patterns as we feel that these should emerge once a number of patterns have been developed and put to use. We also feel that these structures may well be developed to meet particular circumstances arising from their use in design and that the next stage of our work will involve engaging with designers in the use of these patterns.

The work reported here represents our initial steps in developing a pattern language and should be seen in that light. We believe that the work holds some considerable promise in allowing the CSCW community to exploit the considerable experiences gained from field studies over the last decade. Although a number of issues remain unresolved in the development of patterns it is clear that they do offer considerable potential and we will be building upon our experiences to develop more patterns, and we hope that this paper provides the groundwork for others to do likewise.

Acknowledgements

We would like to thank John Hughes, Wes Sharrock, and Tom Erickson for their comments and contributions to the research reported in this paper. The research was supported by grants from the UK Engineering and Physical Sciences Research Council.

References

Ackerman, M.S. & Halverson, C. (1998): 'Considering an organization's memory', in: *Proc. CSCW'98*, Seattle, WA USA, ACM Press, pp. 39-48.

Alexander, C. (1979): *A Timeless Way of Building*, Oxford University Press, Oxford.

Alexander, C., Ishikawa, S. & Silverstein, M. (1977): *A Pattern Language*, Oxford University Press, Oxford.

Anderson, R., Hughes, J. & Sharrock, W. (1989): *Working for profit: The Social Organisation of Calculation in an Entrepreneurial Firm*, Avebury, Aldershot.

Anderson, R.J. (1994): 'Representations and requirements: the value of ethnography in system design', *Human–Computer Interaction*, vol. 9, pp. 151-182.

Bannon, L. (2000): 'Situating workplace studies within the human–computer interaction field', in Luff et al. (eds.): *Workplace Studies: Recovering Work Practice and Informing System Design*, Cambridge University Press, Cambridge, pp. 230-241.

Bardram, J. (1998): 'Designing for the dynamics of cooperative work activities', in: *Proc. CSCW'98*, Seattle, WA USA, ACM Press, pp. 89-98.

Bellotti, V. & Bly, S. (1996): 'Walking away from the desktop computer: distributed collaboration and mobility in a product design team', in: *Proc. CSCW'96*, Boston, MA, ACM Press, pp. 209-218.

Bentley, R., Hughes, J.A., Randall, D., Rodden, T., Sawyer, P., Shapiro, D. & Sommerville, I. (1992): 'Ethnographically-Informed Systems Design for Air Traffic Control', in: *Proc. CSCW'92*, Toronto, Canada, ACM Press, pp. 123-129.

Beyer, H. & Holtzblatt, K. (1998): *Contextual Design: Defining Customer-Centered Systems*, Morgan Kaufmann, San Francisco, CA.

Blythin, S., Rouncefield, M. & Hughes, J.A. (1997): 'Never mind the ethno stuff—what does all this mean and what do we do now?: Ethnography in the commercial world', *Interactions*, vol. 4, no. 3, pp. 38-47.

Bowers, J. & Martin, D. (1999): 'Informing collaborative information visualisation through an ethnography of ambulance control', in: *Proc. ECSCW'99*, Copenhagen, Denmark, Kluwer Academic Publishers, pp. 311-330.

Bowers, J., O'Brien, J. & Pycock, J. (1996): 'Practically accomplishing immersion: Cooperation in and for virtual environments', in: *Proc. CSCW'96*, Boston, MA, ACM Press, pp. 380-389.

Cooper, J.W. (2000): *Java Design Patterns*, Longman, .

Coplien, J. (1998): 'A Development Process Generative Pattern Language', in Coplien & Schmidt (eds.): *Pattern Languages of Program Design*, Addison Wesley, Reading, MA.

Crabtree, A., Nichols, D.M., O'Brien, J., Rouncefield, M. & Twidale, M.B. (2000): 'Ethnomethodologically-informed ethnography and information system design', *Journal of the American Society for Information Science*, vol. 51, no. 7, pp. 666-682.

Erickson, T. (2000a): 'Lingua Francas for design: sacred places and pattern languages', in: *Proc. DIS'00*, Brooklyn, NY, ACM Press, pp. 357-368.

Erickson, T. (2000b): 'Supporting interdisciplinary design: toward pattern languages for workplaces', in Luff et al. (eds.): *Workplace Studies: Recovering Work Practice and Informing System Design*, Cambridge University Press, Cambridge, pp. 252-261.

Fitzpatrick, G. (2000): 'Understanding the paper record in practice: Implications for EHRs', in: *HIC2000 Proc. Australian Health Informatics Conference*, , .

Gamma, E., Helm, R., Johnson, R. & Vlissides, J. (1994): *Design Patterns: Elements of Reusable Object-Oriented Software*, Addison-Wesley, Reading, MA.

Heath, C. & Luff, P. (1992): 'Collaboration and control: crisis management and multimedia technology in London Underground control rooms', *CSCW Journal*, vol. 1, no. 1, pp. 69-94.

Hughes, J., King, V., Rodden, T. & Andersen, H. (1994): 'Moving out from the control room: ethnography in system design', in: *Proc. CSCW'94*, Chapel Hill, NC, ACM Press, pp. 429-439.

Hughes, J.A., O'Brien, J., Rodden, T., Rouncefield, M. & Blythin, S. (1997): 'Designing with Ethnography: A Presentation Framework for Design', in: *Proc. DIS'97*, Amsterdam, Netherlands, ACM Press, pp. 147-159.

Hughes, J.A., O'Brien, J., Rodden, T., Rouncefield, M. & Sommerville, I. (1995): 'Presenting ethnography in the requirements process', in: *Proc. RE'95*, York, UK, IEEE Computer Society Press, pp. 27-34.

Hughes, J.A., Randall, D. & Shapiro, D. (1992): 'Faltering from Ethnography to Design', in : *Proc. CSCW'92*, ACM Press, Toronto, Canada, pp. 115-122.

Hughes, J.A., Randall, D. & Shapiro, D. (1993): 'From ethnographic record to system design: some experiences from the field.', *CSCW Journal*, vol. 1, no. 3, pp. 123-141.

Martin, D. (2000): *Ethnomethodology and Systems Design: Interaction at the boundaries of organisations*, Unpublished PhD thesis, University of Manchester, Manchester, UK.

Martin, D., Bowers, J. & Wastell, D. (1997): 'The interactional affordances of technology: an ethnography of human–computer interaction in an ambulance control centre', in: *People and Computers XII: Proc. HCI'97*, London, Springer-Verlag, pp. 263-281.

Nardi, B.A. (1996): *Context and Consciousness: Activity Theory and Human–Computer Interaction*, MIT Press, Cambridge, MA.

O'Brien, J. & Rodden, T. (1997): 'Interactive systems in domestic environments', in: *Proc. DIS'97*, Amsterdam, NL, ACM Press, pp. 247-259.

Plowman, L., Rogers, Y. & Ramage, M. (1995): 'What are workplace studies for?', in: *Proc. ECSCW'95*, Stockholm, Sweden, Kluwer, pp. 309-324.

Pycock, J. (1999): *Designing Systems: Studies of Design Practice*, Unpublished PhD thesis, University of Manchester, Manchester, UK.

Pycock, J. & Bowers, J. (1996): 'Getting others to get it right: an ethnography of design work in the fashion industry', in: *Proc. CSCW'96*, Boston, MA, ACM Press, pp. 219-228.

Randall, D., Rouncefield, M. & Hughes, J.A. (1995): 'Chalk and cheese: BPR and ethnomethodologically informed ethnography in CSCW', in: *Proc. ECSCW'95*, Stockholm, Sweden, Kluwer, pp. 325-240.

Rodden, T., King, V., Hughes, J. & Sommerville, I. (1994): 'Process modelling and development practice', in Warboys (ed.): *Proc. EWSPT'94*, , Berlin: Springer-Verlag, pp. 59-64.

Rouncefield, M., Hughes, J.A., Rodden, T. & Viller, S. (1994): 'Working with "constant interruption": CSCW and the small office', in: *Proc. CSCW'94*, Chapel Hill, NC, ACM Press, pp. 275-286.

Schuler, D. & Namioka, A. (eds.) (1993): *Participatory Design: Principles and Practices*, Lawrence Erlbaum Associates, Hillsdale, NJ.

Twidale, M., Rodden, T. & Sommerville, I. (1993): 'The Designers' Notepad: supporting and understanding cooperative design', in: *Proc. ECSCW'93*, Milan, Italy, Kluwer, pp. 93-108.

Viller, S. & Sommerville, I. (1999): 'Coherence: an approach to representing ethnographic analyses in systems design', *Human–Computer Interaction*, vol. 14, no. 1 & 2, pp. 9-41.

Whalen, J. (1995): 'A technology of order production: Computer-aided dispatch in 9-1-1 communications', in Psathas & Have (eds.): *Situated Order: Studies in the Social Organization of Talk and Embodied Activities*, University Press of America, Washington, DC, pp. 187-230.

W. Prinz, M. Jarke, Y. Rogers, K. Schmidt, and V. Wulf (eds.), *Proceedings of the Seventh European Conference on Computer-Supported Cooperative Work, 16-20 September 2001, Bonn, Germany*, pp. 59-77.

Team Automata for Spatial Access Control

Maurice H. ter Beek
LIACS, Universiteit Leiden, The Netherlands

Clarence A. Ellis
Department of Computer Science, University of Colorado, U.S.A.

Jetty Kleijn
LIACS, Universiteit Leiden, The Netherlands

Grzegorz Rozenberg
LIACS, Universiteit Leiden, The Netherlands
and
Department of Computer Science, University of Colorado, U.S.A.

Abstract. Team automata provide a framework for capturing notions like coordination, collaboration, and cooperation in distributed systems. They consist of an abstract specification of components of a system and allow one to describe different interconnection mechanisms based upon the concept of "shared actions". This document considers access control mechanisms in the context of the team automata model. It demonstrates the model usage and utility for capturing information security and protection structures, and critical coordinations between these structures. On the basis of a spatial access metaphor, various known access control strategies are given a rigorous formal description in terms of synchronizations in team automata.

Introduction

As the complexity of technical systems continues to increase, abstractions tend to be especially useful. For this reason, computer science often introduces and studies various models of computation that allow enhanced understanding and analysis. Computer science has also created a number of interesting metaphors (e.g., the desktop metaphor) that aid in end user understanding of computing phenomena. This document is concerned with a model and a metaphor. The model is team automata, which were created explicitly for the specification and analysis of CSCW phenomena and collaborative systems (Ellis, 1997). The metaphor is spatial access control, which is based upon current notions of virtual reality, and helps demystify concepts of access control matrices and capability structures for the end user (Bullock et al., 1999).

Many of the concepts and techniques of computer science, such as concurrency control, user interfaces, and distributed databases, need to be rethought in the groupware domain. Team automata are helpful for this rethinking. The framework provided by the team automata model allows one to separately specify the components of a collaborative system and to describe their interactions. It is neither a message passing model nor a shared memory model, but a shared action model. It has been proposed as a formal framework for modeling both the conceptual and the architectural level of groupware systems (Ellis, 1997). Components can be combined in a loose or more tight fashion depending on which actions are to be shared, and when. Such aggregates of components can then in turn be used as components in a higher-level team. Thus team automata fit nicely with the needs and the philosophy of groupware (Ellis, 1997) and thanks to the formal setup, theorems and methodologies from automata theory can be applied. Team automata are an extension of Input/Output automata (Lynch, 1996) and are related to, but different from Vector Controlled Concurrent Systems (Keesmaat, 1996), Petri nets (Reisig et al., 1998), and other models of concurrent and collaborative systems (Nutt, 1997).

Our spatial access control metaphor piggy-backs upon the virtual reality metaphors of places and spaces (Bullock, 1998). Different places are conducive to different activities, and different rooms and different buildings have different affordances. The metaphor of virtual rooms and virtual buildings can help to guide the user through a complex computer system to find the resources needed for a particular task. In need of a certain document, e.g., the user would naturally think of entering a virtual library, where he or she would have read access.

In the following sections we first discuss the spatial access control metaphor by means of an example and subsequently gently present the team automata model by applying it to this example. In the core of the document we then show how certain spatial access control mechanisms can be made precise and given a formal description using team automata. First we introduce information access modeling by granting and revoking access rights, and show how immediate versus delayed revocation can be formulated. In the subsequent section we extend our study to the more complex issue of meta access control, and consequently we show how team automata can deal with deep versus shallow revocation.

The style of this document is relatively informal. Full formal definitions, observations, and results relating to team automata can be found in (ter Beek et al., 1999). Our aim here is to connect the metaphor of spatial access control to the framework of team automata, and to show through examples how this combination facilitates the identification and unambiguous description of some key issues of access control. The rigorous setup of the framework of team automata allows one to formulate, verify, and analyze general and specific logical properties of various control mechanisms in a mathematically precise way. In realistically large systems, security is a big issue, and team automata allow formal proofs of correctness of its design. Moreover, a formal approach as provided by the team automata framework forces one to unambiguously describe control policies and it may suggest new approaches not seen otherwise. There is a large body of literature concerning topics like security, protection, and awareness in CSCW systems. Although team automata are potentially applicable also to these areas, this paper is not concerned with issues outside of spatial access control. In the final section we discuss some variations and extensions of our setup.

Access Control

A vital component of any system or environment is security and information access control, but this is sometimes done in a rather ad hoc or inadequate fashion with no underlying rigorous, formal model. In typical electronic file systems, access rights such as read-access and write-access are allocated to users on some basis such as "need to know", ownership, or ad hoc lists of accessors. Within groupware systems, there are typically needs for more refined access rights, such as the right to scroll a document that is being synchronously edited by a group in real time. Furthermore, the granularity of access must sometimes be more fine-grained and flexible, as within a software development team. Moreover, it is important to control access meta-rights. For example, it may be useful for an author to grant another team member the right to grant document access to other non-team members (i.e. delegation). Various models have been proposed to meet such requirements (see, e.g., (Shen et al., 1992), (Rodden, 1996), and (Sikkel, 1997)).

We use a spatial access metaphor based upon recent work of Bullock and colleagues in (Bullock et al., 1997) and (Bullock et al., 1999). There, access control is governed by the rooms, or spaces, in which subjects and objects reside, and the ability of a subject to traverse space in order to get close to an object. Bullock also implemented a system called SPACE to test out some of these ideas (Bullock, 1998). A basic tenet of the SPACE access model is that a fundamental component of any collaborative environment is the environment itself (i.e. the space). It is the shared territory within which information is accessed and interaction takes place. Often this shared space is divided into numerous regions that segment the space. This allows decomposition of a very large space into smaller ones for manageability. It also allows cognitive differentiation (i.e. different concerns, memories, and thoughts associated with different regions), and distributed implementation (i.e. different servers for different regions).

By adopting a spatial approach to access control, the SPACE metaphor exploits a natural part of the environment, making it possible to hide explicit technical security mechanisms from end users through the natural spatial makeup of the environment. These users can then make use of their knowledge of the environment to understand the implicit security policies. Users can thus avoid understanding technical concepts such as so-called access matrices, which helps to avoid misunderstandings.

We consider here a virtual reality, in which a user can traverse from room to room by using keyboard keys, the mouse, or fancier devices. It is a natural and simple extension to assume that access control checking happens at the boundaries (doors) between spaces (rooms) when a user attempts to move from one room to another. If the access is OK, then the user can enter and use the resources associated with the newly entered room.

To illustrate the various concepts throughout this document, we present a simple running example which is concerned with read and write access to a file F by a user Kwaku. This file might be any data or document that is stored electronically within a typical file system. The file system keeps track of which users have which access rights to the file F. Three types of access rights are possible for a file F: null access (implying the user can neither read nor write the file), read access (implying the user cannot write the file), and full access (implying the user can read and write — i.e. edit — the file).

In security literature, authentication deals with verification that the user is truly the person represented, whereas authorization deals with validation that the user has access to the given resource. Assume that when Kwaku logs into the system, there is an authentication check. Then whenever he tries to read or write F, authorization checking occurs, and Kwaku is either allowed the access, or not. Using the SPACE metaphor, the above three types of access rights can be associated with three rooms as shown in Figure 1.

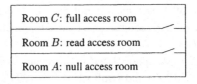

Room C: full access room

Room B: read access room

Room A: null access room

Figure 1: A rooms metaphor for access control.

Room A is associated with no access to the document, room B is associated with read access, and room C models full access. Suppose Kwaku is in room B, the reading room. Presence in this room means that any time Kwaku decides to read F, he can do so. However, if he attempts to make changes to F, then he will fail because he does not have write access in room B. There are doors between rooms, implying that user access rights can be dynamically changed by changing rooms. We discuss this dynamic change in more detail in a later section of this document.

This access mechanism satisfies a number of end user friendly properties: it is simple, understandable by non-computer people, relatively natural and unobtrusive, and elegant. In the next sections we show how modeling this type of access metaphor via team automata adds precision, mathematical rigor, and analytic capabilities.

Team Automata

In this section we introduce component automata and team automata as formally defined in (ter Beek et al., 1999) by using the example of the previous section.

A team automaton consists of component automata, combined in a coordinated way such that they can perform shared actions. Component automata within a team automaton can during each clock tick simultaneously participate in one instantaneous action (i.e. synchronize on this action), or remain idle. The team automata model forms a mathematical automata theoretic specification, rather than a high-level language specification such as Hoare's CSP (Brookes et al., 1984), Forman's Raddle (Evangelist et al., 1988), or the n-party interaction mechanism (Attie et al., 1990). Team automata, like I/O automata, are adequate for specifying shared memory systems and message passing systems, although they are neither of the two. While inappropriate for capturing aspects of group activity such as social aspects and informal unstructured activity, the model has proved useful in various CSCW modeling areas (Ellis, 1997). A spectrum from hardware components to interacting groups of people can be modeled by team automata.

The component automata are rather ordinary, but their interconnection strategy is intriguing because, as we mentioned, it is neither shared variable nor message passing. We classify the actions which take an automaton from one state to another into two main categories, one of which is subdivided into two more categories. *Internal* actions have strictly local visibility and can thus not be observed by other components, whereas *external* actions are observable by other components. These external actions are used for communication between components and consist of *input* actions and *output* actions. Composing component automata into team automata is based on an interconnection strategy of shared actions, in which one or more automata participate in the execution of the same external action (which may be input to some components and output to other components). The choice for a specific interconnection strategy is based on what one wants to model, and this possibility to choose is the main feature of the team automata framework.

We now return to our access control example by showing how to model it in the team automata framework. The component automaton M^C depicted in Figure 2(a) corresponds to room C of Figure 1, as it models full access to file F. The states of M^C are C_e modeling an empty room, C_n modeling F is not accessed, C_r modeling F is being read, and C_w modeling F is being written (edited). The wavy arc in Figure 2(a) denotes the initial state C_e. The actions of M^C are e_{BC} (enter room), e_{CB} (exit room), r^C (begin reading), $\underline{r}^C$ (end reading), w^C (begin writing), and $\underline{w}^C$ (end writing).

A component automaton thus consists of *states*, *actions*, and (labeled) *transitions* which describe state changes caused by actions. We distinguish a set of *initial states* and the set of actions is further partitioned into *input*, *output*, and *internal* actions. Hence a component automaton is a labeled transition diagram with three distinguished types of labels (actions).

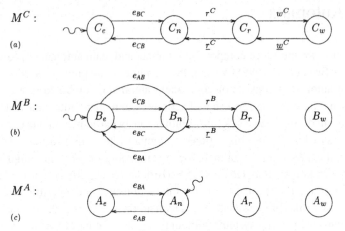

Figure 2: Automata M^C, M^B, and M^A: rooms C, B, and A.

Returning to M^C we have the transitions (C_e, e_{BC}, C_n), (C_n, e_{CB}, C_e), (C_n, r^C, C_r), $(C_r, \underline{r}^C, C_n)$, (C_r, w^C, C_w), and $(C_w, \underline{w}^C, C_r)$. Now the transition (C_e, e_{BC}, C_n), e.g., shows that in M^C we can go from state C_e to C_n by executing action e_{BC}. We also see that transitioning directly from C_n to C_w is not possible. Furthermore, entering and exiting room C may only occur via state C_n. We choose to specify actions r^C, $\underline{r}^C$, w^C, and $\underline{w}^C$ as internal actions of M^C, and e_{BC} and e_{CB} as external actions of M^C. Both e_{BC} and e_{CB} clearly should be externally visible and therefore cannot be internal. For the moment we choose them to be output actions. These two external actions are candidates for being synchronized with actions of the same name in other component automata when we form a team automaton over M^C and the two component automata as described next.

Component automata M^B and M^A corresponding to rooms B and A, respectively, are somewhat similar to M^C. However, write access is denied in rooms B and A and read access is denied in room A. Automata M^B and M^A are depicted in Figure 2(b,c). Note that M^A has initial state A_n (hence initially room A is not empty) and that both M^B and M^A have states unreachable from the initial state. Actions r^B and $\underline{r}^B$ are internal, while the rest of the actions of M^B and M^A are external (output) actions.

Now suppose that we want to combine M^C, M^B, and M^A into one (team) automaton reflecting a given access policy. Then, first of all, the internal actions of each of these components should be private, i.e. uniquely associated to one component automaton. This is formally expressed by stating that when composing a team from a collection $\mathcal{S}$ of component automata, no internal action of any component automaton from $\mathcal{S}$ may appear as an action in any of the other component automata in $\mathcal{S}$. If this is the case, then $\mathcal{S}$ is called a *composable system*.

The three automata in our example clearly form a composable system and we combine them into a team automaton T^{CBA} as follows. Each state of T^{CBA} is a combination of a state from M^C, a state from M^B, and a state from M^A (hence T^{CBA} has upto $4^3 = 64$ states). Initially T^{CBA} is in state (A_n, B_e, C_e), a combination of initial states from the three component automata. This means one starts in room A, while room B and C are empty.

Assuming that one can have only one kind of access rights at a time, two of the rooms should be empty at any moment in time. This means that T^{CBA} should be defined in such a way that in each of its reachable states two of the three automata are always in state "empty". We let the automata synchronize on the external actions e_{AB}, e_{BA}, e_{BC}, and e_{CB}. Each such synchronized external action of T^{CBA} corresponds to exiting a room while entering another. Synchronization of action e_{AB}, e.g., models a move from room A to room B. This move is represented by the transition $((A_n, B_e, C_e), e_{AB}, (A_e, B_n, C_e))$ showing that in automaton M^A we exit room A, in automaton M^B we enter room B, and in automaton M^C we do nothing (i.e. remain idle). This represents a change in access rights from null access (in room A) to read access (in room B). We do not include, e.g., the transition $((A_n, B_e, C_e), e_{AB}, (A_e, B_e, C_e))$ which would let the user exit room A but never enter room B. Furthermore, the user could be in more than one room at a time if we would allow transitions like $((A_n, B_e, C_e), e_{AB}, (A_n, B_n, C_e))$. In T^{CBA} we include only the four transitions representing the synchronized changing of rooms. In each of these transitions, one automaton is idle. All internal (read and write related) actions are maintained. In each of these only that component is involved to which such an action belongs.

The reachable part of the thus defined T^{CBA} is depicted in Figure 3.

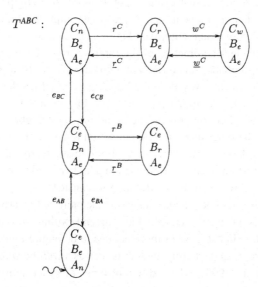

Figure 3: Team automaton T^{CBA} over M^C, M^B, and M^A.

At this moment it is important to stress that T^{CBA} is not the only team automaton over M^C, M^B, and M^A. In general, there is no *unique* team automaton over a composable system S, but a framework is provided within which one can construct a variety of team automata over S. The flexibility lies in the choice of the transition relation for a team automaton over S, which is based on but not fixed by the transition relations of the component automata in S. The requirements the transition relation of a team automaton has to satisfy are as follows.

The *complete transition space* of action a in S consists of all transitions on a from a state q to a state q' of the team such that at least one component automaton is active, i.e. performs a. Moreover, each of the component automata either also executes a (i.e. joins in executing a) or remains idle (thus does not change state). Consequently, the transformation of the state of the team automaton is defined by the local state changes of the components involved in the action that is executed. The transitions in the complete transition space (of a) are referred to as *synchronizations* (on a). For each action a a specific subset of its complete transition space is chosen. In the case of an internal action however, each component retains all its possibilities to execute that action and change state. Note that since S is a composable system, synchronizations on internal actions never involve more than one component.

Any choice of a transition relation satisfying these requirements defines a team automaton over S. Its states, initial states, as well as a partition of its actions are fixed (and the same for all team automata over S). The state space of any team automaton T over S is the product of the state spaces of the component automata of S, with the products of their initial states forming the initial states of T. The internal actions of the components are the internal actions of the team automaton. Each action which is output for one or more of the component automata is an output action of the team automaton. Hence an action that is an output action of one component and also an input action of another component, is considered an output action of the team. The input actions of the component automata that do not occur at all as an output action of any of the component automata, are the input actions of the team. The reason for constructing the alphabet sets of a team automaton from the alphabet sets of the component automata in the way described above, is based on the intuitive idea of (Ellis, 1997) that when relating an input action a of a component automaton to an output action a of another component, the input may be thought of as being caused by the output. On the other hand, the output action remains observable as output to other automata. As shown in (ter Beek et al., 1999), every team automaton is again a component automaton and hence can be used in a higher-level team.

In T^{CBA}, as mentioned before, the decision to consider e_{AB}, e_{BA}, e_{BC}, and e_{CB} as output actions in all component automata was made more or less arbitrarily. In fact, it depends on how one views the action of entering and exiting a room within the team automaton T^{CBA}. By choosing all of those actions to be output (and thus of the same type), exiting one room and entering another is seen as a *collaboration* between peers.

In (ter Beek et al., 1999), where different types of synchronizations on actions shared between components of a team are classified, this synchronization of external actions of the same type is called a *peer-to-peer synchronization*. On the other hand, *master-slave synchronization* occurs when input actions *cooperate* with output actions. In that case, input can only occur as a response (slave) to output.

In our example, assume that one views the changing of rooms as an action initiated by leaving a room and forcing the room that is entered to accept the entrance. Then one would name, e.g., e_{AB} an output action of M^A and an input action of M^B, and e_{BA} an output action of M^B and an input action of M^A. This causes e_{AB} to be a master-slave synchronization between master M^A and slave M^B and e_{BA} to be a master-slave synchronization between master M^B and slave M^A. Likewise for the other actions.

In addition, (ter Beek et al., 1999) defines strategies that lead specifically to uniquely defined peer-to-peer and master-slave combinations within team automata. The team automata framework allows one to model many other features useful in virtual reality environments. A door, e.g., can be extended to join more than two rooms since any number of automata can participate in an output action. Furthermore, as said before, a user could be in more than one room at a time.

Authorization and Revocation

We continue our example of the previous section by adding Kwaku, a user whose access rights to file F will be checked by the access control system T^{CBA} of Figure 3. Kwaku is represented by automaton M^U, depicted in Figure 4. This extension complicates our example in the sense that Kwaku's read and write access rights can be changed independently of his whereabouts. Only to enter a room he has to be authorized. Thus access rights are no longer equivalent with being in a room, but rather with the possibility to enter a room. To add this to the team automaton formalization, we will use the feature of iteratively constructing teams with teams as components.

M^U :

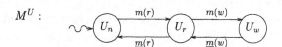

Figure 4: Automaton M^U: user Kwaku.

Kwaku starts in state U_n with no access rights. The actions $m(r)$, $\underline{m}(r)$, $m(w)$, and $\underline{m}(w)$ model the (meta) operations of "being granted read access", "being revoked read access", "being granted write access", and "being revoked write access", respectively. Since these clearly are passive actions from Kwaku's point of view, we choose all of them to be input actions. Note that Kwaku can end up in state U_w if and only if he was granted access rights to read and to write, i.e. actions $m(r)$ and $m(w)$ have taken place. When Kwaku's write access is consequently revoked by transition $(U_w, \underline{m}(w), U_r)$, he ends up in state U_r.

Now suppose that we want to model Kwaku's options for editing file F, which is protected by the access control system T^{CBA}. Then we would like to compose a team automaton over T^{CBA} and M^U. To do so, first note that T^{CBA} and M^U form a composable system. Next we choose a transition relation, i.e. for each action a subset from its complete transition space in T^{CBA} and M^U is selected, thereby formally fixing an access control policy for Kwaku under the constraints imposed by T^{CBA}.

The initial state of any team over T^{CBA} and M^U is (A_n, B_e, C_e, U_n), i.e. Kwaku is not yet editing F and is in the virtual room A without access rights. Now imagine the access rights to be keys. Hence Kwaku needs the right key to enter reading room B, i.e. action $m(r)$ must take place before action e_{AB} becomes enabled. This action $m(r)$ leads us from the initial state to (A_n, B_e, C_e, U_r). Now Kwaku has the key to enter room B by $((A_n, B_e, C_e, U_r), e_{AB}, (A_e, B_n, C_e, U_r))$. This transition models the acceptance of Kwaku's entrance of room B, i.e. this action is the authorization activity mentioned earlier. Hence our choice of the transition relation fixes the way we deal with authorization. Including, e.g., $((A_n, B_e, C_e, U_n), e_{AB}, (A_e, B_n, C_e, U_n))$ in the transition relation would mean that Kwaku can enter room B without having read access rights for F. Note however that since transitions involving internal actions of either T^{CBA} or M^U by definition cannot be pre-empted in any team over T^{CBA} and M^U, our transition relation necessarily contains $((A_e, B_n, C_e, U_n), r^B, (A_e, B_r, C_e, U_n))$. Hence Kwaku, once in room B, can always begin reading file F. By not including $((A_n, B_e, C_e, U_n), e_{AB}, (A_e, B_n, C_e, U_n))$ in our transition relation we avoid that Kwaku can read F without ever having been granted read access. This leads to the question of the revocation of access rights.

As argued, (A_e, B_n, C_e, U_r) meaning that Kwaku is in room B with reading rights, will be a reachable state. Now imagine that while in this state Kwaku's reading rights are revoked by $\underline{m}(r)$. To which state should this action lead, i.e. in what way do we handle revocation of access rights? We could opt for modeling *immediate revocation* or *delayed revocation*. The latter is what we have chosen to model first. Thus our answer to the question above is to include $((A_e, B_n, C_e, U_r), \underline{m}(r), (A_e, B_n, C_e, U_n))$ in $\mathcal{T}$. The result is that Kwaku can pursue his activities in room B, but cannot re-enter the room once he has left it (unless his read access has been restored). He is thus still able to read (browse) F, but the moment he decides to re-open the file this fails. Likewise, if Kwaku is writing F when his writing right is revoked, then he can continue editing (typing in) F, but he cannot re-enter room C as long as his write access right has not been restored. On this side of the revocation spectrum, the user can thus continue his current activity even when his rights have been revoked. He can do so until he wants to restart this activity, at which moment an authorization check is done to decide if he has the right to restart this activity. In some applications, this may be an intolerable delay.

Immediate revocation, on the other hand, means the following. If a user is reading when his or her reading right is revoked, then the file immediately disappears from view, while if a user is writing when his or her writing right is revoked, then the edit is interrupted and writing is terminated in the middle of the current activity. In some applications, this is overly disruptive and unfriendly. If we would want to incorporate immediate revocation into our example we would have to adapt our distribution of actions a bit. As said before, since r^B is an internal action we cannot disallow action r^B to take place after $((A_e, B_n, C_e, U_r), \underline{m}(r), (A_e, B_n, C_e, U_n))$ has revoked Kwaku's reading rights. If we instead choose r^B to be an external action, we are given the freedom not to include $((A_e, B_n, C_e, U_n), r^B, (A_e, B_r, C_e, U_n))$ in our transition relation. The result is that as long as Kwaku is not being granted read access by action $m(r)$, the only way left to proceed for Kwaku in state (A_e, B_n, C_e, U_n) is to exit room B by $((A_e, B_n, C_e, U_n), e_{BA}, (A_n, B_e, C_e, U_n))$. Modeling immediate revocation thus requires that actions such as r^B are visible, since in that way we can choose them not to be enabled in certain states. Immediate revocation also implies that we still want Kwaku to be able to stop reading and leave state (A_e, B_r, C_e, U_n) by $((A_e, B_r, C_e, U_n), \underline{r}^B, (A_e, B_n, C_e, U_n))$. Action $\underline{r}^B$ can thus remain internal.

This finishes the description of part of a team automaton $\mathcal{T}$ over T^{CBA} and M^U. In Figure 5 the full reachable part of $\mathcal{T}$ (for delayed revocation) is depicted.

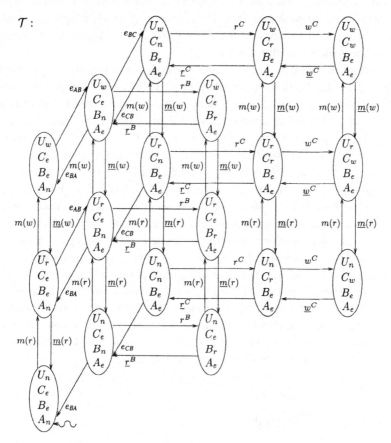

Figure 5: Team automaton $\mathcal{T}$ over T^{CBA} and M^U.

Note that team automata as dicussed here are used to model logical design issues. An action can take place provided (local) preconditions hold, and affects only states of those components involved in that action. Hence at this level there is no notion of time and no means are provided to give one action priority over another. A result of the lack of a notion of time is, e.g., that nothing can be said about how long it takes before Kwaku has left reading room B after his reading access right has been revoked. However, time and priorities may be added to the basic model as extra features.

Again, $\mathcal{T}$ is not the unique team automaton over T^{CBA} and M^U, but it is a team automaton one obtains by choosing a specific transition relation with a specific protocol in mind. In (ter Beek et al., 1999) certain fixed strategies for choosing transition relations in a predetermined way are described, which lead to uniquely defined team automata. One of these fixed strategies prescribes one to include for all actions a, all and only transitions on a in which all component automata participate that have a as one of their actions. This leaves no choice for the transition relation, and thus leads to a unique team automaton. Constructing the transition relation according to this particular strategy is very natural and often presupposed implicitly in the literature. Note that the freedom of the team automata model to choose transition relations offers the flexibility to distinguish even the smallest nuances in the meaning of one's model. Leaving the set of transitions of a team automaton as a modeling choice is perhaps the most important feature of team automata.

Another interesting feature of the framework is shown by the following application of a result proved in Section 4 of (ter Beek et al., 1999) to our example. In whatever order one chooses to construct a team automaton over the component automata M^U, M^C, M^B, and M^A, it will always be possible to construct the team $\mathcal{T}$ discussed above. This means that instead of first constructing T^{CBA} over M^C, M^B, and M^A, and then adding M^U, we could just as well have constructed what we call an *iterated team* in (ter Beek et al., 1999) by, e.g., starting from the user automaton M^U and adding successively the component automata M^C, M^B, and M^A modeling the access rights that can be exercised. Moreover, independent of the way the team over M^U, M^C, M^B, and M^A was constructed, more components can be added. As an example, suppose that Kwaku has other interests than the file F. Hence imagine an automaton T^{NBA} in which he can transition into a state in which he plays some basketball. Then we may construct a team over the team automaton $\mathcal{T}$ just described and the automaton T^{NBA} modeling when Kwaku is entitled — or perhaps even forced — to have a break (which is of some importance in these times of RSI). In general, new components can be added to a given team automaton at any moment of time, without affecting the possibilities of any new additions. The team automata framework thus scores high on scalability. In the next section we will come back to this.

Meta Access Control

In the previous sections we have seen how team automata can be used to describe the control of a user's access to a file depending on his or her rights. In this section we further elaborate on the granting and revoking of access rights and we consider *meta access control*. This means that privileges such as granting and revoking of rights can themselves be granted and revoked. The complicated (recursive) situations that may arise in this fashion depend on the chosen (meta) access control policy and we demonstrate how they can unambiguously and concisely be defined in terms of team automata.

Figure 6 shows an automaton M^0 that models a building with three levels — A, B, and C — corresponding to null access, read access, and full access, respectively.

This automaton shows the same access structure as the three rooms of Figure 2. Now, however, the status of the user directly determines the level he or she operates on and the granting and revoking of access rights is identified with changing levels. This differs from the previous example where the status of the user only determined his or her rights to enter a room.

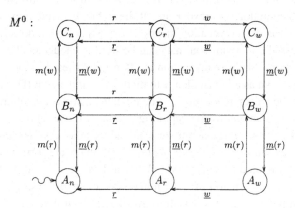

Figure 6: Automaton M^0: the access building.

Consequently, in M^0 the user moves in two dimensions: vertically between levels A, B, and C — indicating the dynamic change in access rights Kwaku has for F — and horizontally between the states "null", "reading", and "writing" — indicating the current activities of Kwaku with respect to F. Notice that in M^0, e.g., the state B_w meaning that Kwaku is writing while having read access but no write access, can only be reached from C_w by an action $\underline{m}(w)$ or from A_w by an action $m(r)$. Hence this state B_w can be entered only when Kwaku is writing while his status changes. There is no transition to B_w at level B. A similar remark holds for states A_r and A_w, which can be entered only from level B by the read access revocation action $\underline{m}(r)$. States such as A_r, A_w, and B_w are called *irregular states* because they are not reachable at their own level.

To model meta access control, we assume the existence of a system administrator, Abena, who can change Kwaku's rights. Hence Abena has the right to grant and revoke access by Kwaku to F. For this reason we have chosen all actions of granting and revoking access rights in M^0 to be input actions, while all actions of reading and writing are output actions. The right to grant and revoke are legitimate rights, but they are not directly applied to F. They are in fact meta operations — hence $m(r)$ and $m(w)$ — and the rights to apply these meta operations are meta rights. Similarly, if there is a creator, Kwesi, who can allow (and disallow) Abena to grant and revoke, then Kwesi has meta meta rights. Kwesi has the meta meta right to grant and revoke Abena's meta rights to grant and revoke Kwaku's access rights to F. A typical action of Kwesi is $\underline{m}^2(w)$, which revokes Abena's right to grant and revoke write access to Kwaku.

The notion of meta clearly extends to arbitrary layers. An example of such a multi-layered structure of meta can be seen in the journal refereeing process. The

72

creator of a document may delegate publication responsibilities to co-authors who may select a journal and grant $m^2(r)$ rights to the editor-in-chief. The editor-in-chief may grant $m(r)$ rights to assistant editors who can then grant and revoke read access to reviewers. An interesting question now arises as to the effect of revocation: should revocation of a meta right also revoke the rights that were passed on to others? This is the issue of *shallow revocation* versus *deep revocation*. Shallow revocation means that a revoke action does not revoke any of the rights that were previously passed on to others, whereas deep revocation means that a revoke action does revoke all rights previously passed on. Team automata can be used to model shallow, deep, or even hybrid revocation. Shallow revocation is often the easiest to model, whereas deep revocation is known as a big challenge to model and implement (Dewan et al., 1998). We now show how deep revocation can be modeled using team automata.

Figure 7 shows an automaton capturing one layer (layer k) of a multi-layer meta access specification for our example of read and write access. We have already seen layer 0, viz. automaton M^0. For each value of $k \geq 1$ there are corresponding automata that are directly related to layer k (viz. M^{k-1} at layer $k - 1$ and M^{k+1} at layer $k + 1$). For each such automaton M^k, the horizontal actions $m^k(r)$, $\underline{m}^k(r)$, $m^k(w)$, and $\underline{m}^k(w)$ are output actions, whereas the vertical actions $m^{k+1}(r)$, $\underline{m}^{k+1}(r)$, $m^{k+1}(w)$, and $\underline{m}^{k+1}(w)$ are input actions. For $k = 0$ we identify r with $m^0(r)$, $\underline{r}$ with $\underline{m}^0(r)$, w with $m^0(w)$, and $\underline{w}$ with $\underline{m}^0(w)$. Similarly, $m(r) = m^1(r)$, $\underline{m}(r) = \underline{m}^1(r)$, $m(w) = m^1(w)$, and $\underline{m}(w) = \underline{m}^1(w)$.

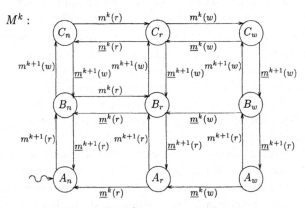

Figure 7: Automaton M^k: meta access at layer k.

We can now define a multi-layered structure by recursively composing a team automaton over M^0, M^1, ..., and M^n, for some $n \geq k$. Note that this is a composable system. As mentioned before we can also build this team automaton in an iterated way starting from, e.g., a team over any two automata M^k and M^{k+1}. In Figure 8, the reachable part of a team automaton T_{k-1}^k over M^{k-1} and M^k, representing layer $k - 1$ and layer k of this layered structure, is depicted. The transition relation of this team T_{k-1}^k is chosen with the modeling of deep revocation in mind. Finally, note that in Figure 8 we have added superscripts to distinguish the states in M^k from the states

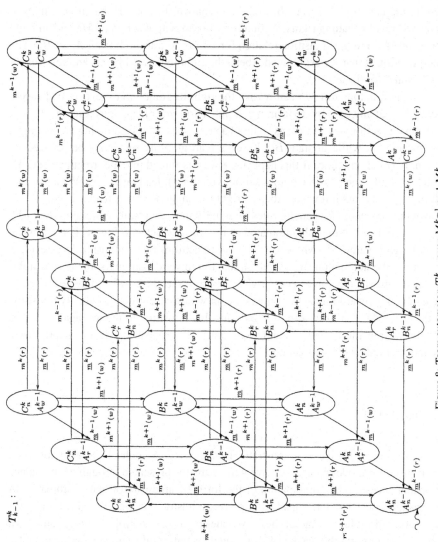

Figure 8: Team automaton T_{k-1}^k over M^{k-1} and M^k.

in M^{k-1}, e.g., state B_r of M^k from state B_r of M^{k-1}.

In our example, M^2 represents the actions of the supervisor Kwesi and M^1 those of Abena. Now consider Kwesi in state B_r^2. Then Figure 8 tells us that Abena must be in one of the three states B_n^1, B_r^1, or B_w^1. Assume that Kwesi reached this state B_r^2 by performing action $m^2(r)$ from B_n^2, while Abena was in state A_n^1 having no rights to grant and revoke reading rights. Action $m^2(r)$ is an output action of M^2 and an input action of M^1, and our transition relation forces M^1 to transition from A_n^1 to B_n^1. The interpretation is that Kwesi granted Abena the right to do read grants and revokes (to user Kwaku for file F).

Similarly, automaton M^k can revoke the right to grant and to revoke read access from M^{k-1} at any time by performing output action $\underline{m}^k(r)$, and thus forcing M^{k-1} to perform this action — this time as an input action — as well. Continuing our example, this means that while in state B_r^2, Kwesi's read granting right may be revoked by action $\underline{m}^3(r)$ at any time. If this happens, Kwesi is forced into the irregular state A_r^2, which has only one possible output action, viz. $\underline{m}^2(r)$, leading to A_n^2. Whenever that action $\underline{m}^2(r)$ occurs it revokes Abena's right to change Kwaku's read access.

We thus observe two general rules of activity in such a team automaton over M^0, $M^1, \ldots$, and M^n with each automaton of the form depicted in Figure 7. First, when a master automaton M^k where $1 \le k \le n$, transitions right (grant) or left (revoke), then the slave automaton M^{k-1} must transition upward (gaining some access right) or downward (losing some access right). Second, the slave M^{k-1} may be forced to transition downward into an irregular state, in which case it will eventually transition to the left. M^{k-1} is itself a master and thus this transition to the left again forces a downward transition of M^{k-2}, and so on until M^0 on layer 0. Hence, as promised, we indeed model deep revocation.

Conclusion

In this document we have demonstrated by means of examples how team automata can be used for modeling access control mechanisms presented through the metaphor of spatial access. The combination of the formal framework of team automata and the spatial access metaphor leads to a powerful abstraction well suited for a precise description of (at least some of the) key issues of access control. The team automata framework supports the design of distributed systems and protocols, by making explicit the role of actions and the choice of transitions governing the coordination (e.g., in the form of peer-to-peer or master-slave synchronizations, or combinations thereof). Moreover, the formal setup and the possibility of a modular design provide analytic tools for the verification of desired properties of complex systems. Team automata are thus a fitting companion to the virtual spaces metaphor used in virtual reality systems that supports notions of rooms and buildings. Each space is represented by a component automaton, dynamic access changes are represented by joint external actions, while resource accesses within a space can be represented by internal actions. For reasons of readability, we have chosen for a presentation by examples without definitions and proofs. Obviously there are numerous other possible examples as well as variations of the examples we have considered.

For one, the assumption that write access can only be granted if read access has been granted can easily be dropped. Similarly, grant and revoke rights can be coupled more loosely. Read and write operations are specified here at the file level, but could also have been specified at the page level, object level, or record level, to name but a few. This might mean that delayed revocation is precisely the right choice. At the file level, the r and $\underline{r}$ actions might be seen at the user interface as open and close file. The w and $\underline{w}$ actions might be edit and save operations. When dealing with a transaction system, combinations of these operations might correspond to begin transaction and end transaction.

The team automata framework handles group decision making well and therefore allows convenient implementations of *distributed access control*. Distributed access control means that the supervisory work of granting and revoking access rights is administered by multiple agents. Thus Kwaku could have two administrative supervisors who must agree on any change of access rights. This can be modeled as an action of two masters and one slave: the actions would be output for both supervisors, requiring both to participate, and input for the slave. Alternatively, by including transitions with one supervisor being inactive, we can model the case of approval being required by either one of the two supervisors. Hybrids between pure master-slave and pure peer-to-peer are easy to define, and useful. All these variations are due to the fact that the choice of a transition relation is the crucial modeling issue of the team automata framework.

Note that team automata model the logical architecture of a design. They abstract from concrete data, configurations, and actions, and only describe behavior in terms of a state-action diagram (structure), the role of actions (input, output, or internal), and synchronizations. It is not feasible (nor necessary) to have a distinct automaton for each individual, and for each file in an organization. In many situations, categories and roles are used rather than individuals. Any implementation would have the team automaton as a class entity, and an activation record for each person, containing their current state. Similarly, by keeping a status of the files one can model the criterion "only one person can write a file at a time, but many readers is OK". The model cast in the spirit of automata depicting roles rather than individuals becomes much more useful and general, and avoids some notational problems of exponential growth. Note that because of the product construction, a state space explosion lurks. However, the resulting automata are not difficult to process. The iterative approach to composition (forming teams with teams as components) forms an automatic and mechanizable abbreviation methodology (van der Aalst et al., 2000). In general, however, the state space explosion problem itself cannot be avoided when dealing with systems with many components that can interact or can assume many different values. See (Clarke et al., 1999) for a presentation of techniques and tools for dealing with this problem when verifying large systems. (Müller, 1998) demonstrates how to deal with the computer-assisted verification of embedded systems described as I/O automata.

As observed earlier, time and priorities are not incorporated in neither the spatial access metaphor nor the team automata model as discussed here. However, similar to the Petri net model — which is also based on local state changes — one may consider to extend team automata with time and priorities (see, e.g., (Ajmone Marson et al., 1995), which focuses on performance analysis). When time and/or priorities are part of access control this would allow the designer to control the sojourn times in the local states and to control the resolution of conflicting actions.

Using team automata for modeling (spatial) access control forces one to make explicit and unambiguous design choices and at the same time provides the possibility of mathematically precise analysis tools for proving crucial design properties, without first having to implement one's design.

To conclude we stress that (spatial) access control is only one of many CSCW concerns that can be addressed via team automata. The higher goal of this document is to demonstrate the applicability of a formal framework that was conceived specifically as a model for the specification and analysis of CSCW systems. We believe that this may be a significant step toward a better understanding of the ways in which people and systems cooperate and collaborate.

Acknowledgments

We are grateful to the anonymous referees for their suggestions to improve an earlier version of this document.

References

van der Aalst, W., Barthelmess, P., and Ellis, C.A. (2000): 'Workflow Modeling using Proclets'. Technical Report CU-CS-900-00, Computer Science Department, University of Colorado.

Ajmone Marson, M., Balbo, G., Conte, G., Donatelli, S., and Franceschinis, G. (1995): *Modelling with generalized stochastic Petri nets*, John Wiley & Sons, Chichester.

Attie, P.C., Francez, N., and Grumberg, O. (1990): 'Fairness and hyperfairness in multi-party interactions', in *Proceedings of the POPL'90 ACM Symposium on Principles of Programming Languages, San Francisco, California*, ACM Press, pp. 292-305.

ter Beek, M.H., Ellis, C.A., Kleijn, J., and Rozenberg, G. (1999): 'Synchronizations in Team Automata for Groupware Systems'. Technical Report TR-99-12, Leiden Institute of Advanced Computer Science, Universiteit Leiden.

Brookes, S.D., Hoare, C.A.R., and Roscoe, A.W. (1984): 'A theory of communicating sequential processes', *Journal of the ACM*, vol. 31, no. 3, pp. 560-599.

Bullock, A. and Benford, S. (1997): 'Access Control in Virtual Environments', in D. Thalmann, S. Feiner, and G. Singh (eds.): *Proceedings of the VRST'97 ACM Symposium on Virtual Reality Software and Technology, Lausanne, Switzerland*, ACM Press, pp. 29-35.

Bullock, A. (1998): *SPACE: Spatial Access Control in Collaborative Virtual Environments*. Ph.D. thesis. Department of Computer Science, University of Nottingham.

Bullock, A. and Benford, S. (1999): 'An access control framework for multi-user collaborative environments', in *Proceedings of the GROUP'99 International ACM SIGGROUP Conference on Supporting Group Work, Phoenix, Arizona*, ACM Press, pp. 140-149.

Clarke Jr., E.M., Grumberg, O., and Peled, D.A. (1999): *Model Checking*, MIT Press, Cambridge, Massachusetts.

Dewan, P. and Shen, H. (1998): 'Flexible Meta Access-Control for Collaborative Applications', in E. Churchill, D. Snowdon, and G. Golovchinsky (eds.): *Proceedings of the CSCW'98 ACM Conference on Computer Supported Cooperative Work, Seattle, Washington*, ACM Press, pp. 247-256.

Ellis, C.A. (1997): 'Team Automata for Groupware Systems', in J. Clifford, B. Lindsday and D. Maier (eds.): *Proceedings of the GROUP'97 International ACM SIGGROUP Conference on Supporting Group Work: The Integration Challenge, Phoenix, Arizona*, ACM Press, pp. 415-424.

Evangelist, M., Shen, V.Y., Forman, I.R., and Graf, M. (1988): 'Using Raddle to design distributed systems', in *Proceedings of the ICSE'88 International Conference on Software Engineering, Singapore*, IEEE Computer Society Press, pp. 102-111.

Keesmaat, N.W. (1996): *Vector Controlled Concurrent Systems*. Ph.D. thesis, Leiden University.

Lynch, N.A. (1996): *Distributed Algorithms*, Morgan Kaufmann Publishers, San Mateo, California.

Müller, O. (1998): *A Verification Environment for I/O Automata Based on Formalized Meta-Theory*. Ph.D. thesis, Technische Universität München.

Nutt, G.J. (1997): *Operating Systems: A Modern Perspective*, Addison-Wesley Publishers, Reading, Massachusetts.

Reisig, W., and Rozenberg, G. (eds.) (1998): *Lectures on Petri Nets I: Basic Models, Lecture Notes in Computer Science*, vol. 1491, Springer-Verlag, Berlin.

Rodden, T. (1996): 'Populating the Application: A Model of Awareness for Cooperative Applications', in M. Ackerman (ed.): *Proceedings of the CSCW'96 ACM Conference on Computer Supported Cooperative Work, Boston, Massachusetts*, ACM Press, pp. 87-96.

Shen, H. and Dewan, P. (1992): 'Access Control for Collaborative Environments', in J. Turner and R. Kraut (eds.): *Proceedings of the CSCW'92 ACM Conference on Computer Supported Cooperative Work, Toronto, Canada*, ACM Press, pp. 51-58.

Sikkel, K. (1997): 'A Group-based Authorization Model for Cooperative Systems', in J. Hughes, W. Prinz, T. Rodden, and K. Schmidt (eds.): *Proceedings of the ECSCW'97 European conference on Computer Supported Cooperative Work, Lancaster, UK*, Kluwer Academic Publishers, pp. 345-360.

W. Prinz, M. Jarke, Y. Rogers, K. Schmidt, and V. Wulf (eds.), *Proceedings of the Seventh European Conference on Computer-Supported Cooperative Work, 16-20 September 2001, Bonn, Germany*, pp. 79-98.

Supporting distributed software development by modes of collaboration

Till Schümmer, Jörg M. Haake

GMD – German National Research Center for Information Technology

IPSI – Integrated Publication and Information Systems Institute

{Till.Schuemmer\Joerg.Haake}@darmstadt.gmd.de

Abstract. Work processes in team based software development need to be structured to minimise and resolve conflicting or divergent work. Current software development methodologies propose ways for dividing the whole task of software development between team members. This paper suggests a different way of working by introducing modes of collaboration (MoCs), which support concurrent and collaborative work. A MoC defines how tight two people can work together and how much the rest of the group can demand to know about a programmer. Different MoCs are ordered in a spectrum from single user's offline usage up to concurrent editing of the same source code. Special emphasis is put on balancing gains and efforts that are related to a specific MoC. The second part of the paper presents how MoCs are implemented in the distributed co-operative software development environment TUKAN. TUKAN includes synchronous co-operative tools and awareness widgets, which operate on a spatial representation of the software under construction. TUKAN provides tools for each MoC and allows programmers to switch between MoCs.

Introduction

Nowadays, software development is usually carried out in teams. Many modern software development methodologies emphasise this fact by introducing special forms of collaboration. For instance, the eXtreme Programming methodology (XP) (Beck, 1999) introduces pair programming sessions, where two programmers share one computer and solve the programming task together. The adaptive software development process (ASD) (Highsmith, 1999) is another methodology that focuses on collaboration within the team.

Anyhow, besides the collaborative aspects, programming is implicitly an activity performed by (many) individual users, as writing a book or composing a piece of music (Weinberg, 1971). The discrepancy between isolated work and group work is therefore inherent to software development. Even within XP's pair programming sessions the participants frequently select one of two possible roles: One is coding (driving) and has the keyboard while the other person observes, comments and corrects the programming activity of the first. Environments that want to support programmers in their job of programming should therefore provide different modes of collaboration matching the roles and phases within the software development process and should ease the transitions between them.

When programming in medium sized to large teams, these teams are frequently distributed across many locations. Even small teams are often composed of experts who work at different locations. This introduces new challenges to the organisation of the programming work. Version management tools and conference systems can be used in these settings, but these tools fail to provide awareness on each other's work. Conflicting changes and the fact of solving the same problem over and over again are consequences of this lack of awareness.

To assist programmers in programming as a team we propose a new tool called TUKAN. TUKAN provides different modes of collaboration and awareness, which meet the different needs of the programming team at different phases of the collaboration.

In a previous publication on TUKAN, we first identified different points of collaboration during the process of software development (Schümmer and Schümmer, 2001). These points of collaboration (PoCs) will serve as a basis to define different modes of collaboration (MoCs) for software development in this paper. After this, the latter part of the paper describes transitions between the different MoCs and how these transitions and the MoCs were implemented in TUKAN. We will then present some experiences that we gained from first experiments with the usage of TUKAN in programming groups. A section on related and future work concludes this paper.

Different Modes of Collaboration

Based on the PoCs that we found in Schümmer and Schümmer (2001), we identified different collaboration modes that are used during distributed team programming. Following the abbreviation *PoC* for "point of collaboration", we call the mode of collaboration *MoC*. A MoC is a lightweight mode, which defines possible collaborative activities. Changing MoCs can therefore be considered as a lightweight activity (comparable to the effort of changing different modes of operation by selecting different windows). MoCs range from single user's offline usage up to concurrent editing of the same source code. In fact, MoCs can be ordered in a spectrum from isolated work to completely (tightly coupled) collaborative work (cf. cooperative modes defined by Haake and Wilson (1992)). We will now discuss each MoC in a separate paragraph following the ordering of the spectrum.

Offline mode. When programmers have to solve hard problems, they often demand to be undisturbed. They want to work on the specific problem either alone or in a co-located two person team, without being interrupted. Thus, it is important that the system provides isolation for a single or a pair of programmers during the session. If the user's work raises questions, he can use asynchronous communication tools (e.g. e-mail) to send these questions to his colleagues. He may always be contacted by e-mail, but the point of time, where he reads his mail is self-determined (and therefore, also the time for receiving the answer is unpredictable). In the case where synchronous communication is indispensable, he may decide to change his MoC to a mode that allows synchronous communication (manually or automatically, as we will describe it in the next main section).

Process level mode. Planning the software project is essential to every software development process. XP introduces a lightweight planning strategy (the planning game (Beck, 1999)): the XP project is planned by stories that are constructed together with the customer. Stories describe the behaviour of the system under development (one might thus see the stories as kind of use cases). Each story is rated by the customer concerning the stories' importance, which allows the team to implement the most important stories first.

Stories are realised by a set of tasks. Tasks transform the content of a story into a mission for the programmer. Every programming activity is related to a task and a task should be fulfilled during one session (lasting about half a day).

When collaborating in process-level mode, the programmers interact with a planning tool and take responsibilities for their current task. Other programmers can see the current task of the programmer. This helps them to get at least a feeling of what the programmer is doing. They can retrieve meta-information, but they do not know which concrete artefacts the programmer currently manipulates.

Change level mode. If a programmer works in the change-level mode, the system logs all his manipulations of the source code. Logged changes can help to understand the work afterwards, or to detect conflicts. If the programmer wants to be informed about other programmers' changes, he may change to the change aware mode.

Change aware mode. Concurrent changes are always sources for possible conflicts. If for instance two programmers change the same unit of source code (e.g. a "method" in the object-oriented programming paradigm), these changes have to be integrated by including the intentions of both programmers in the source code. The change aware mode helps to avoid parallel changes at related or same artefacts of the software project by telling all other programmers that the artefact has been changed. Unlike traditional version management systems (e.g. CVS (Price, 2000)), this notification is done at the time of change and not at the time of reintegration. In the change aware mode, programmers are thus aware of the artefacts that are currently modified by other developers.

Presence level mode. The change level mode records only the modifications that programmers do to the project's artefacts. In addition to this, the presence level mode also tracks activities that do not modify artefacts. Viewing artefacts is such an activity that can be very important for understanding the programmer's changes, because it reveals what knowledge led her to the change.

Presence aware mode. If the non-modifying activities are recorded, it is possible to display this information to all other programmers using a small presence indicator in front of the artefact (if the artefact is visible to them). The presence indicator tells the programmer that there is someone else around and thus helps to find a colleague with a comparable focus on the software system. By focus we mean the set of artefacts, which a programmer is currently inspecting or modifying. If another programmer is viewing the same or a related artefact (i.e. he has the same or a comparable focus), it is likely that he tries to solve a related problem. When detecting another person, there are two possible reactions: The programmer who detected another developer nearby moves away from this person so that he can act alone, or the two people start tighter collaboration by switching to communication mode.

Communication mode. Tighter collaboration starts mainly by discussing the circumstances that brought the participants together. In this phase, each of the participants tells the group about their aims and the group tries to formulate a common goal. Without a common goal the group will hardly be able to act as a group. So, this is an important phase when switching to a tighter mode of collaboration. Communication tools, such as a chat tool or electronic mail, assist the participants in this phase. If a common goal is found, or if the group had a common goal even without discussing it (because it was discussed in a previous session), the group might switch to the tightly-coupled collaboration mode.

Tightly-coupled collaboration mode. When programmers work in the tightly-coupled collaboration mode, they allow others to share their workspaces. One example is a collaborative class browser, where programmers can browse the code and write new units of source code together, as if they would sit in front of the same screen.

The reader should note that only the information indicated above is recorded in a specific MoC. Information that is not captured in a MoC is therefore not available for future usage. On the other hand, additional monitoring can be performed by underlying tools (such as a version management system) to ensure that results can be merged after periods of work in the offline mode or the process level mode.

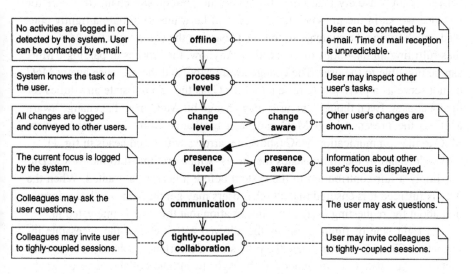

Figure 1: Constraints and transitions between different MoCs

Transitions between Modes of Collaboration

With each of the MoCs, as they were described in the former section, the pro-grammer reveals a part of her privacy and she has to provide information to the system. This causes additional work-load for the programmer or her computer system. If seen from this perspective, revealing information provides no direct benefit for the programmer. Allowing others to interrupt the own work is also regrettable, if no personal advantage can be achieved with this action.

Evaluations of other groupware systems (e.g. Grudin, 1988) have shown that one important factor for the acceptance of a groupware system is the balance be-tween efforts and gains for each individual user that are implied by the system.

TUKAN tries to address this problem by introducing rules that define how much a user has to contribute to the system, if he wants to benefit from it. Simply spoken, a user only gets as much information from the system as he is willing to provide to others. On the other hand, the user may decide to reveal more informa-tion than he is consuming. If he, for instance, works in the presence level mode, he decided to inform all other users about his present activities and about the arte-facts he is currently interested in. But this does not necessarily mean that he is interested in the focus of his colleagues or the changes that they performed.

Figure 1 illustrates the rules. The middle part shows the possible MoCs. Each MoC (except the change aware, the presence aware, and the tightly-coupled col-laboration mode) serves as a prerequisite for another MoC, which is indicated by the thin headed arrows in figure 1. If a user works in a specific MoC, he auto-matically provides all the information of all its prerequisite MoCs. Transitions between MoCs usually take place following the prerequisite chain. If a user for instance works in the presence level MoC and he wants to initiate a tightly coupled collaboration, he switches to this MoC passing the communication MoC (and thus fulfilling all the duties for this MoC). Anyhow, the process of passing a MoC can be invisible to the user. The change aware MoC and the presence aware MoC do not serve as a prerequisite for another MoC, as they do not state any duties for the local user. Even though, the user may change his MoC from the change aware MoC to the presence level MoC and he may change from the presence aware MoC to the communication MoC (shown by arrows with filled heads in fig. 1).

The left part of the figure states the duties, which are linked to the MoCs. Duties imply a fair contribution to the system before a benefit is granted. When the duty is fulfilled it is ensured that all other users may get the same kind of information about the requesting user, as the information that this user is interested in.

The right side of figure 1 shows the allowed activities and the accessible information. These are for instance the provision of information about possible conflicts (in the change aware mode) or the right to initiate collaborative programming sessions (when working in the tightly-coupled collaboration mode).

If a user, for instance, wants to be informed about other users' presence, he selects to work in the presence aware mode. This implies that he has to provide all information demanded by the presence level mode to the system. He thus has to inform the system about his current focus, the artefacts that he is modifying, and the task, which is the context for his activities. He may also browse other user's tasks or activate the change aware mode, although the change aware mode is not a prerequisite for the activation of the presence aware mode.

While all MoCs up to the presence level mode (resp. the presence aware mode) primarily provide awareness on other team members' activities, the communication mode and the tightly-coupled collaboration mode provide means for negotiation future changes and resolving conflicts or exploiting synergies. This improves the collaborative processes since coordination is facilitated. The reader should note that the MoCs do not prescribe any negotiation or coordination procedure.

It is possible that different users select different MoCs. For instance, one user can work in the presence level mode, while a second user works in the tightly-coupled collaboration mode. If the second user detects the presence of the first, he might want to initiate communication or tightly-coupled collaboration with the other user. But this is not possible, since the other user decided not to communicate or collaborate in a tightly-coupled way. The system tries to meet both users needs by detecting the highest possible degree of collaboration between both users. In the case of the above example, there is no synchronous communication channel available in the first user's profile. Thus, the only way to get in contact would be asynchronous e-mail communication. If the second user, who works in the tightly-coupled collaboration mode, tries to initiate a chat session, the system

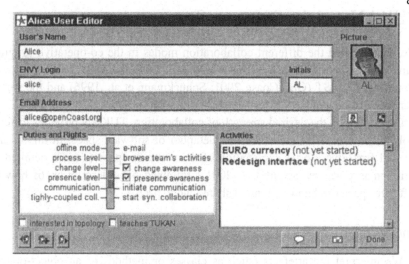

Figure 2: The user dialog

states that this MoC is not available for the first user and comes up with a mail client interface, where the second user can enter his question.

Switching between MoCs can be done automatically or manually. The first alternative eases tool usage because it does not require any explicit user action, whereas the second possibility ensures that the user always knows his current MoC. In this case, he explicitly controls the way that he wants to collaborate.

Changing MoCs automatically: Within each MoC user interface elements exist that allow a strengthening of the collaboration. For example, if a programmer works in the presence aware mode, she can easily establish a chat connection to other users. Therefore, she activates a collaboration info dialog that informs her about other the other users who work next to her. She then selects the other user and presses a 'chat'-button.

Changing MoCs manually: The user may adjust her MoC using her user dialog (as it is shown in figure 2). The slider control on the left side of the window is used to adjust the amount of information provided by this user (they correspond to the elements that appeared in the left column of figure 1). The amount of information that is displayed about other user's activities can be controlled by the two checkboxes right to the slider. Other users can always inspect their colleagues state by looking at the colleague's profile in the user dialog.

If the user decides to change her MoC from a tight mode to a more loose mode, the system will close all tools that are not allowed in the new mode. One user might for example change from communication mode to presence aware mode. All open chat connections would then be closed automatically.

TUKAN and the Software Space

We implemented the different collaboration modes in the co-operative programming environment TUKAN. TUKAN was built using the open source groupware framework COAST (OpenCoast, 2001; Schuckmann et al., 1996) and the version management system ENVY for VISUALWORKS SMALLTALK (Cincom, 2001).

Depending on the desired strength of collaboration, TUKAN provides different tools to the user. All tools share the metaphor of software space. In this section, we will first give a brief explanation of the software space (a more detailed description is given by Schümmer (2001)) followed by a description of how the software space can be turned into a shared workspace.

The Software Space

We interpret the artefacts (such as classes or methods of an object-oriented program), which are produced in the software project as semantic networks, which form a hyperspace. Each artefact is mapped to a node of a graph. Whenever a programmer creates an artefact, this is added to the graph and the system scans the artefact for possible relations to other artefacts, which are already known in the graph. The relations are then represented as weighted edges in the graph. A spatial layout is determined by the presence of an edge with a specific weight between the two nodes, which controls the distance in the space. Two semantically related artefacts are thus nearer together in the software space, as it would be the case if they were not related.

The Collaborative Software Space

During software development, the programmers work with a set of artefacts. This set forms the programmer's current focus. In a collaborative scenario, the focus can be of importance for other users and overlapping foci are important awareness clues for possible tightly-coupled collaboration.

Benford and Fahlen (1993) have analysed the application of awareness in 3D environments. In the MASSIVE system, these ideas were realised and refined Greenhalgh and Benford (1997), where worlds form spaces for communication. For each observing object (each user), they define a *focus* as the set of the object's current interests. The *nimbus* "represents an observed object's interests to be seen in a given medium." (Greenhalgh and Benford (1997)) In general, the nimbus contains all objects within a geometric area around the focused objects. By combining two user's foci and nimbi, MASSIVE calculates the awareness strength that they have of one another.

Rodden (1996) has proposed a generalisation of this awareness model for the work on artefacts, which are arranged in a spatial graph structure . He defined the

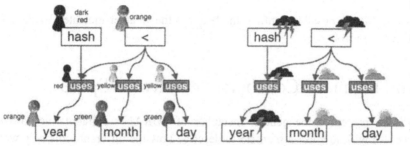

Figure 3: Presence awareness and change awareness in the software space

focus as the set of currently focused nodes and calculated the nimbus as the combination of all focused nodes' adjacent nodes within a well-defined distance.

The software space is such a graph. We define the focus as the set of artefacts (the methods, classes or applications) that a programmer is currently looking at. The nimbus consists of all artefacts in the software space, which are semantically related to the focused artefacts (i.e. they are nearby).

If the user works in the presence aware mode and the artefact, which is shown on his screen, is part of another user's nimbus, the system displays a presence indicator in front of this artefact. It is a small coloured figure with a colour ranging from red to green. The nearer the artefact is to the user's focus, the more red colour is used to display the figure.

The left part of figure 3 shows an example for the calculation of presence indicators. Another user is working on the method *hash*. The method *year* is directly related to *hash*, since it is used by *hash*. On the other hand, the method < uses *year*, *month*, and *day*. These semantic relations form the basis for the layout of the software space. The calculation of the colours for the presence indicators leads to the example shown on the left side of figure 3 (note that the figure only shows a small part of the software space and its relations).

Besides the presence aware mode, TUKAN has a second MoC where awareness information is calculated using the concepts of focus and nimbus: the change aware mode. We introduced a second definition of focus for this mode. The *change focus* is defined by the set of artefacts for which a newer version was created by another user. Artefacts, which are part of a change focus, are interpreted as sources for possible conflicts. The nimbus of a change focus is calculated in the same way as it was presented for the calculation of the presence indicators. If an artefact is part of the nimbus of a change focus, this artefact may be affected by the change.

An example for the calculation of conflict indicators is shown in the right part of figure 3. We use a weather metaphor to indicate possible conflicts. In the example, another user has modified the method *hash*. A heavy lightning symbol is used to indicate this fact. The methods *year* and < are very near to this changed artefact, thus a lightning symbol is shown in front of them. The further away artefacts are from a possible conflict, the better is the weather indicated by the symbol shown in front of it.

Working in the Collaborative Software Space

After we presented the general metaphor of TUKAN's collaborative software space, we will now use a scenario to describe how the different tools help working in the software space. For reasons of simplicity, we will describe all uses of collaborative tools for the case of two users. Of course, the tools work also for larger groups.

Assume that there are three users, who are currently working with the system: Alice, Bob and Charlie. Alice and Bob are working on an accounting application, which has two stories to solve: it has to be adapted to the new European currency (the Euro), and it has to be checked against any bugs that might occur at the beginning of the new millennium (Y3K-bugs). The project manager has identified these two stories and entered them in the planning tool.

Charlie has decided to do some optimisations of the hash functions in the class library. This is a task, which is not planned by the management. Thus, he decides to work in the offline mode.

Planning the Work

Alice and Bob both logged on to the system and look at the stories in the planning tool (Alice's display is shown in figure 4). They start their work in the process level mode. Alice modifies the tasks, which are associated with the Euro-story. At one point, she does not know how to name a new subtask. She thus decides to invite Bob to the planning tool. Therefore, she changes her MoC to the tightly-coupled collaboration mode and invites Bob. But unfortunately, Bob is currently working in the planning level mode and the system proposes to invite Bob by e-mail.

After Bob received the mail, he changes his MoC to the tightly-coupled mode. The system detects that Bob is now willing to co-operate and adds Bob to the user's of Alice's planning tool. They now share the selection of the planned tasks and can modify the tasks and stories co-operatively (cf. figure 4, showing Bob and Alice as co-operating users).

After they finished describing the tasks, they end their tightly coupled session (Bob closes the shared browser and returns to his private browser again). They have a look at the tasks and both select the task they want to work on. This is expressed by adding their user representation to the task (they press the 'add user'-button and select their name). When they start actual work, they have to choose one of the tasks, where they contribute and do the work to reach the task's goal. They launch this task by pressing the 'start task'-button.

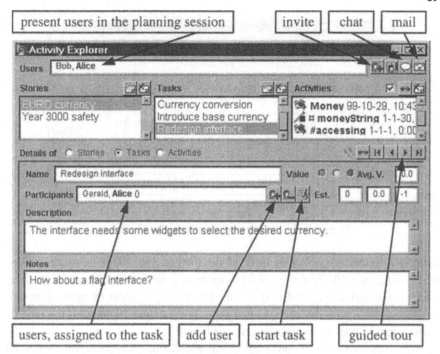

Figure 4: The planning tool.

If the user works in the change level mode, all accesses to artefacts of the software space are recorded in this task (they appear in the activities list in figure 4). The name of the selected task is also displayed in the active browsers (cf. figure 5). Programmers are thus always aware of their own task, which helps them to keep their work focused.

Alice chooses the task 'Redesign interface', and Bob decides to work on the task 'Currency conversion'. Since Alice and Bob noticed in their discussion that they work on related tasks, they decide to do their work in the presence aware mode. This keeps them informed, if they do some work with mutual consequences.

Doing the Work

Alice and Bob select the co-operation aware class browser to do the implementation, as it is shown in figure 5. This browser is a slightly adapted REFACTORING BROWSER (Roberts, 1999). In addition to the programming source code, it shows the local user's current task and awareness icons in front of the method list, which provide information about other user's activities (depending on the MoC).

The first awareness information is the visualisation of possible conflicts (provided by the change aware mode). The calculation follows the algorithm as it was explained in the section 'The Collaborative Software Space'. In the screenshot,

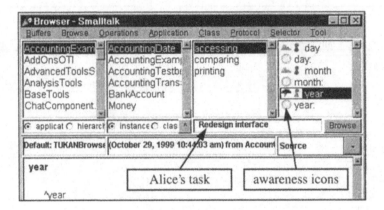

Figure 5: The co-operation aware class browser.

there is a lightning symbol in front of the method *year*. This demands caution when using or modifying this method, because another user changed a method, which is semantically related to the method *year*. Any changes on *year* might thus be incompatible with the changes that other programmers applied to the method *hash* (actually, this was the method changed by Bob).

Alice does not like this uncertainty and decides to load the newer version of the method *hash* into her workspace. This has the effect that all related methods are now up to date and only sun symbols are shown in front of the methods.

Whenever Alice selects a method, the system monitors a change of focus. This change of focus triggers a re-computation of the awareness indicators. In figure 5, Bob is working at the method *hash*. Therefore, *year*, *month*, and *day* are shown with little figures in front of it indicating that there is another user nearby.

When Alice notices that there is another user nearby, she may continue working, as if nobody was nearby. She may also feel the need to coordinate her activities and therefore she may decide to communicate with Bob about her concerns using the communication level MoC. As a result they may decide to switch to a tighter collaboration mode and meet in a tightly-coupled collaborative class browser. The next section will provide more details about how they actually meet.

Switching to the tightly-coupled mode of collaboration

The artefact that will form the focus of the collaborative session may differ according to the Alice's intention. If she is more interested in the work of her colleague, she will prefer to join him in his current work context (open a browser on the method *hash*). On the other hand, if she wants to inform Bob about her current work, she will prefer to invite him to her browser. Bob will then receive an invitation stating the person, who invited him (Alice), her current task, and the artefact, on which the collaborative session will focus.

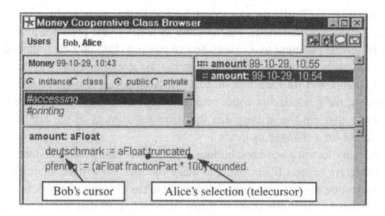

Figure 6: The collaborative class browser.

When accepting the invitation, Alice and Bob can choose how to reach one another. The fastest way is to directly meet at the artefact. Because of the rapid movement, we call this possibility *warping* to the collaboration. This will open a collaborative class browser (cf. figure 6), where the participants share the selection of the current artefact and can manipulate this artefact using a collaborative text editor widget. Each user has a personal cursor, which is used to manipulate the source code. The personalised text cursors can also be used to point at specific parts of the text and thus serve as a telecursor (Hayne et al., 1993) to focus communication.

The second way of reaching the artefact for collaboration is by following the relations of the software space from the current focus to the new focus. In contrast to warping, we call this movement *walking* to the collaboration. Walking is done by first opening a browser on the currently focused artefact. A small window (which is not shown in Figure 6) informs the user that this is not yet the artefact of collaboration, but an artefact, which is on the way from the current focus to the desired focus. This window contains a control, which navigates the browser one step further on the path to the desired artefact. Upon reaching the artefact for collaboration, the other user joins his browser and they start to collaborate.

The idea of walking to the collaboration helps the person who was currently working on a different focus to understand how the two focuses are related and what they have in common. Both users will then share a common focus, not just in the browser, but also (hopefully) in their minds.

Understanding previous work

Walking to the artefact of collaboration lets the programmer know the shared context between the two programmer's work. Another kind of walkthrough can help a programmer to understand work, which took place during his absence.

In the scenario, Charlie decides to catch up with the group again, after he finished his work in offline mode. He therefore switches to the presence level mode and activates the planning tool, where he can select a story and get a guided tour through this story (cf. figure 4). A *guide* shows the stories and tasks in their logical relationship, and for each task all touched artefacts are shown. In addition to the artefacts, the guide shows some context information, such as the name of the programmer that did the activity and the structural context of the artefact itself (e.g. the class for a changed method).

By pressing forward and back buttons, Charlie can easily navigate through the tasks. There are several filters that can make the tour even more interesting: He can focus just on the changed artefacts or include the viewing of artefacts as well. He could also let the guide show him just those activities that took place during his absence.

Compared to other modes of collaboration in figure 1, the guided tour is positioned between the presence level mode and the presence aware mode. Anyhow, it has a different quality, since it provide asynchronous history awareness to the programmers. The guide provides as much information on the tour as it can find. Thus it accumulates all available information, which was provided by users working in the process level mode, the change level mode, or the presence level mode. A guided tour therefore needs at least one user who did some work in the process level mode.

Experiences

Up to now, we used TUKAN in two settings for a period of one week: in our research group for the development of groupware prototypes, and in a company that develops groupware for knowledge management. In this section, we will present the settings and our first findings of the usage of TUKAN in an anecdotal way.

The group in our institute consisted of two full time researchers and one student, who is currently learning how to enhance the TUKAN environment. They used the planning tool for the specification of tasks (about 30 different tasks grouped into 5 stories). The full time researchers did the specifications of the tasks, while the student browsed the tasks and looked for one in which he was interested. At this time, they all worked at the process level mode. When the student decided what task he would like to solve, he switched to the tightly coupled MoC and invited one of the researchers. They discussed the suitability of the selected task and other tasks. At the end of the planning session they had sorted the tasks according their importance and the student started doing the work.

By convention, they decided all to work at least in the presence level MoC. They were working at very diverse parts of the project. This led them to the decision to switch the awareness icons off. At one point of work the student did not know how to get on with the code of a specific method. Therefore, he contacted one of his colleagues and asked him if he wanted to work in a tightly-coupled session. They both switched their MoCs to the tightly-coupled collaboration mode and started to browse through the class of the method. They discussed different alternatives and made heavy use of telepointers and communication tools (actually, they used a separate audio-connection). After the problem was solved, the student started to work alone again.

Meanwhile, the second researcher finished his task and chose a new one, which was related to the task of the other researcher. The researchers thus decided to turn the awareness indicators on. After turning on the indicators, one of the programmers saw immediately that there were some newer versions of the methods, which he was going to work on. He therefore integrated these methods and used the new versions as the basis of his work. After about 20 minutes of work they reached related points in the software space and decided to continue in tightly-coupled co-operation mode. They figured out that the two problems had the same reasons and found a solution together. This group found TUKAN very useful (especially the student liked the way of learning by contacting experts).

The second setting involved a company that develops knowledge management groupware. They tested TUKAN during the development of a large commercial application. They used it for small stories within the overall development process. The company used the planning game before and they had created a large set of story and task cards. For their use of TUKAN, they transferred only the card's title to the planning tool. The observed subgroup consisted of 4 people. They chose to work on a set of tasks that were highly related. They divided themselves into pairs that were each responsible for one task.

For programming, they worked in the presence aware mode. Each pair worked together in front of one screen using one users name (doing traditional pair programming). There were frequent occurrences of overlapping foci, which were indicated by the presence indicators. In most of the cases of overlapping foci, the two pairs decided to join for a short session and did some programming together (leading to quartet programming).

Most frequently, they used the conflict indicators. Whenever a conflict was detected, the system helped them to detect the conflict and they compared their version with the newer version. In fact, the group was used to search for conflicts manually before, thus they appreciated this feature very much.

Finally, they discovered the guide and used it to reason in front of the other programmers about the work that they did. In their setting, every programmer was sitting in front of his screen (the screens were arranged in a way that allows eye contact between all the programmers) and one programmer controlled the guide. With every displayed change, he provided some comments why he did this. This usually started a vivid discussion.

Both groups scathed the system's performance, regarding its speed. Since the calculation of focus and nimbus was done on the fly, it took about 3 seconds until the whole awareness information was refreshed. We have analysed the performance lacks and found some ways to significantly speed up the system. The resolution was to reduce the size of the user's nimbus and add some filters that remove some of the most ambiguous relations from the software space (e.g. the usage of the methods 'new' or '+' is spread around the system, but does not necessarily imply semantic nearness of clients and suppliers). An evaluation of this faster prototype will be part of our future work.

Both groups felt that their performance was improved by the usage of TUKAN and they could imagine to use it in future projects.

As for all systems, which trace users' activities, the fear of being monitored is a crucial point for TUKAN's acceptance. A social protocol and trust needs to be established to exploit the benefits of TUKAN. In our observations, the groups were working together for a long time. Thus, these social protocols already existed and trust was no problem for them.

Related Work

Related work includes general support for collaboration in shared workspace systems and group awareness as well as more software development specific support. We will first cover the groupware specific issues. The latter part of this section will compare TUKAN with synchronous software development tools.

Group awareness (Dourish and Bellotti, 1992) facilitates the assessment of the present state (who is doing what) in a shared workspace. It is usually a concept that is applied to help synchronously co-operating users to co-ordinate their activities. It also supports – to some degree – making informed decisions about what to do next (based on knowledge about who is working in which part of the shared workspace, thus showing some opportunities for synergy or conflict). However, it does not support finding out about past activities (i.e. the history of the work), and it does not explicitly address current tasks and plans of the group. Most systems in this area provide what is called local awareness by Haake (1999). Local awareness relates to information about ongoing activities in the current workspace. Examples for local awareness are applications implemented in GROUPKIT (Roseman and Greenberg, 1992) and SUITE (Dewan and Choudhary, 1991) as well as SEPIA (Haake and Wilson 1992; Streitz et al., 1992), TEAMROOMS (Roseman and Greenberg 96). Some other systems also provided tools for global awareness (i.e. giving information about the general activities in a complete shared workspace). Examples include task lists as in workflow management systems, radar views as in SEPIA, or history logs as in NOTECARDS (Trigg et al., 1986). BSCW (Bentley et al., 1997) provides workspace awareness through a user presence and activity monitor since version 3.2. ORBIT (Mansfield et al., 1997) organizes a shared workspace using the locales concept (as a means to communicate tailored awareness) and supports global awareness on other locales through a "navigator". Another interesting approach is to provide activity awareness between different individual workspaces as in the INTERLOCUS system (Nomura et al., 1998). Here, notifications and awareness functions provide asynchronous workspace awareness. However, synchronous awareness and assessment of future activities are not supported. In summary it can be said that with the exception of SEPIA no shared workspace system explicitly supported different modes of collaboration and transitions among them. Even in the SEPIA system, only three modes of collaboration were explicitly supported (and these were aimed on collaborative writing). Most systems do offer different forms of awareness, but none aims explicitly at providing awareness tailored to software development. In addition, asynchronous and synchronous collaboration are rarely equally well supported.

Coordination systems help a group in the definition and enactment of the group process. For instance, XCHIPS (Wang et al., 2001) is a shared workspace for creation and execution of emerging work process descriptions. Several programming environments followed the basic approach of guiding the programmers through the process. Weinreich and Altmann (1997) presented an environment, in which the programmers can define work packages and see the related software artefacts. It provides communication tools and change notifications. SPADE (Bandinelli et al., 1996) helps the programmers to model the software process and define when synchronous co-operation should take place. The actual co-operation took place using simple shared editing and communication tools. While all the process centred environments focus on the explicit definition process, TUKAN handles the process in a more implicit way, because collaboration is not process driven, but artefact driven.

There are some systems, which bring the artefacts and the process together in a virtual environment. Promo (Doppke et al., 1998) maps tasks of software development to rooms of a MOO (Curtis, 1997). The rooms contain the artefacts that have to be manipulated in the rooms task. Rooms can be connected and thus guide the programmers in the execution of the software development process. The mentioned ORBIT system allows a programmer to have more than one presence position in different 'locales'. Artefacts can be placed in (possibly multiple) locales, where the locales' inhabitants can edit them. Awareness clues show what artefacts other users currently work on.

Christensen (1998) presented the RAGNAROK environment that maps software design to landmarks of shared design landscapes. Users interact with the artefacts by opening them on the design landscape. A colour coding approach shows where other users are working. Within CHIME (Dossik and Kaiser 1999), programmers can walk through a graphical virtual environment that consists out of the projects artefacts and meet other programmers to communicate via a chat tool. Users can specify how the artefacts are related. CHIME places the software artefacts in a three-dimensional environment depending on the relations between them. All discussed systems that are based on the metaphor of virtual worlds provide no or just synchronous awareness. None of the systems has a conflict awareness mode, or explicit control of the mode of collaboration. Except of the virtual worlds in CHIME, all the virtual worlds require the user to design their layout manually.

Marshall and Irish (1989) presented the idea of guided tours as a means for guiding the reader through a hypermedia graph. These tours had to be created manually and were static at the time. Riedl (2001) presented the TRAILGUIDE system, which monitors browsing activities and allows authors to publish the recorded trails as guided tours. An avatar accompanies the user and provides additional comments on the visited pages. We do not know of a system that generates guided tours based on the navigation activities of other users, as was presented in this paper to aid comprehension of activities of other developers.

Conclusions and Future Work

In this paper, we presented a set of different modes of collaboration (MoCs) that support the cooperative development of software systems. We introduced constraints and transitions between the MoCs that ensure a fair balance between efforts and gains that are implied by the system.

TUKAN is our first environment that supports the different MoCs and eases the transition between them. It combines different aspects of shared workspaces with a spatial awareness model and provides collaboration tools for each MoC. Collaboration ranges from offline (asynchronous) collaboration up to tightly coupled code editing. First users rated TUKAN to be very supportive for their software development.

First experiences encouraged us to enhance the system regarding its performance and the automatic transition between MoCs. Another issue of future work is the generalisation of the concept of MoCs. One could for instance interpret a hypertext as a graph in the sense of TUKAN. Browsing the hypertext would then be matched to activities in the graph. We will examine if and how the concept can be applied to other artefact based collaborative activities (e.g. collaborative shopping in the WWW or collaborative work in virtual enterprises).

Acknowledgments

We thank our colleagues at CONCERT, especially the COAST development team. Special thanks are due to Alejandro Fernandez, Shirley Holst, Holger Kleinsorgen, Christian Schuckmann, and Jan Schümmer for the discussion of TUKAN's concepts and comments on this paper. Torsten Holmer, Ruediger Pfister, and Martin Wessner came up with the concept of a PoC. We also thank the reviewers for providing constructive comments, which helped to improve the paper.

The DFG supported the work of Till Schümmer as part of the PhD program „Enabling Technologies for Electronic Commerce" at Darmstadt University of Technology.

Bibliography

Beck, K. (1999): "Extreme Programming Explained", Addison Wessley, Reading, MA, 1999.

Benford, S. and Fahlen, L. (1993): "A spartial Model of Interaction in Large virtual Environments" in: ECSCW'93. Proc. of the third European Conf. on CSCW, Mailano, Italy, 1993, pp. 109-124.

Bentley, R.; Horstmann, T.; Trevor, J. (1997): "The World Wide Web as enabling technology for CSCW: The case of BSCW" in: *Computer-Supported Cooperative Work*: Special issue on CSCW and the Web, Vol. 6 (1997), Kluwer Academic Press.

Bandinelli, S.; DiNitto, E.; Fuggetta, A. (1996): "Supporting cooperation in the SPADE-1 environment" in: IEEE Trans. on Software Engineering, vol. 22, no. 12, 1996, pp. 841-865.

Christensen, H. (1998): "Utilising a Geographic Space Metaphor in a Software Development Environment" in Proceedings of EHCI'98, IFIP Working Conference on Engineering for Human-Computer Interaction, Crete, Greece, 1998.

Cincom (2001): Cincom Smalltalk homepage, www.cincom.com/smalltalk, accessed Jan. 2001.

Curtis, P. (1997): "LambdaMOO programmers manual", ftp.lambda.moo.mud.org/pub/MOO/ProgrammersManual.html, 1997.

Dewan, P. and Choudhary, R. (1991): "Flexible User-Interface Coupling in Collaborative Systems" in: *Proc. of ACM CHI'91 Conference*, April 1991, pp. 41-49.

Doppke, J.; Heimbigner, D.; Wolf, A. (1998): "Software process modeling and execution within virtual environments" in: ACM Transactions on Software Engineering and Method-ology, Volume 7, Issue 1, 1998, pp. 1-40.

Dossick S. and Kaiser G. (1999): "Distributed Software Development with CHIME" in: Proceedings of ICSE-99 2nd Workshop on Software Engineering over the Internet, 1999.

Dourish, P. and Bellotti, V. (1992): "Awareness and coordination in shared workspaces" in: CSCW '92. Conf. Proceedings on Computer-supported cooperative work, 1992, pp. 107-114.

Greenhalgh, C. and Steve Benford, S. (1997): "Boundaries, Awareness and Interaction in Collaborative Virtual Environments", in: Proc. of the 6th Int. Workshop on Enabling Technologies: Infrastructure for Collaborative Enterprises (WETICE), Cambridge, Mass., 1997, pp. 18-20.

Grudin, J. (1988): "Why CSCW applications fail: Problems in the design and evaluation of organizational interfaces". In: Proc. of the Conference on Computer-Supported Cooperative Work (CSCW88) (Portland, Oregon, 1988), ACM Press, New York, 1988, pp. 85-93.

Haake, J. and Wilson, B. (1992): "Supporting collaborative writing of hyperdocuments in SEPIA." in: Proc. of the 1992 ACM Conf. on Computer Supported Cooperative Work (CSCW92), Nov. 1992, pp. 138-146.

Haake, J. (1999): "Facilitating Orientation in Shared Hypermedia Workspaces" in: Group'99. Proc. of the Int. ACM SIGGROUP Conf. on Supporting Group Work, 1999, pp. 365-374.

Hayne, S.; Pendergast, M.; and Greenberg, S. (1993): "Gesturing through cursors: Implementing multiple pointers in group supports systems." in: Proceedings of the HICSS Hawaii International Conference on System Sciences, Hawaii, January 1993, IEEE Press.

Highsmith, J. (1999): "Adaptive Software Development: A Collaborative Approach to Managing Complex Systems", Dorset House, 1999.

Mansfield, T.; Kaplan, S.; Fitzpatrick, G.; Phelps, T.; Fitzpatrick, M.; Taylor. R. (1997): "Evolving Orbit: a progress report on building locales" in: *Proc. of Group'97*, ACM Press, Phoenix, AZ, Nov 1997, pp. 241-250.

Marshall, C. and Irish, P. (1989): "Guided tours and online presentations: How authors make existing hypertext intelligible for readers" in: Proc. of ACM Hypertext'89, 1989, pp. 15-26.

98

Nomura, T.; Hayashi, K.; Hazama, T.; Gudmundson, S. (1998): "Interlocus: Workspace Configuration Mechanisms for Activity Awareness" in: Proc. of the ACM 1998 *Conf. on Computer Supported Cooperative Work* (CSCW'98), Seattle, Washington, 1998, pp. 19-28.

OpenCoast (2001): "OpenCoast website", www.openCoast.org as accessed in January 2001.

Price, D. (2000): "CVS - Concurrent Versions System v1.11", online manual available at http://www.cvshome.org/docs/manual/, 2000.

Riedl, M. (2001): "A computational model and classification framework for social navigation", Intelligent User Interfaces '01, 2001.

Roberts, D. (1999): "Practical Analysis for Refactoring", PhD thesis at the University of Illinois at Urbana-Champaign, 1999.

Rodden, T. (1996): "Populating the Application: A Model of Awareness for Cooperative Applications" in: Proceedings of the ACM 1996 conference on CSCW'96, 1996, pp. 87-96.

Roseman, M. and Greenberg, S. (1996): "TeamRooms: Network Places for Collaboration" in: *Proceedings of the ACM CSCW '96*, Boston, November 1996, pp. 325-333.

Roseman, M. and Greenberg, S. (1992): "GroupKit: A Groupware Toolkit for Building Real-Time Conferencing Applications" in: *Proc. of the ACM 1992 Conference on Computer Supported Cooperative Work* (CSCW'92), Toronto, October 31-November 4, pp. 43-50.

Schuckmann, C.; Kirchner, L.; Schümmer, J.; Haake, J. M. (1996): "Designing object-oriented synchronous groupware with COAST" in: Proceedings of ACM CSCW'96 Conference on Supported Cooperative Work, Boston, Mass., 1996, pp. 30-38.

Schümmer, T. and Schümmer, J. (2001): "Support for Distributed Teams in eXtreme Programming" in: Succi, G. and Marchesi, M. (eds.) "eXtreme Programming Examined", Addison Wesley, 2001, pp. 355-377.

Schümmer, T. (2001): "Lost and Found in Software Space" in Proceedings of the 34th Hawaii International Conference on System Sciences (HICSS-34), Collaboration Systems and Technology, HI, January 3-7, 2001, IEEE-Press 2001.

Streitz, N.; Haake, J.; Hannemann, J.; Lemke, A.; Schuler, W.; Schütt, H.; Thüring, M. (1992): "SEPIA: a cooperative hypermedia authoring environment" in: *Proceedings of ACM Hypertext'92*, 1992, pp. 11-22.

Trigg, R.; Suchman, L.; Halasz, F. (1986): "Supporting Collaboration in NoteCards" in: *Proc. of the ACM Conference on Computer Supported Cooperative Work* (CSCW'86), Austin, December 3-5, 1986, pp. 153-162.

Wang, W.; Haake, J.; Rubart, J.; Tietze, D. (2001): „Hypermedia-based Support for Cooperative Learning of Process Knowledge" in: Journal of Network and Computer Applications, Vol. 23, Academic Press, 2001, pp. 357-379

Weinberg, G. (1971): "The psychology of computer programming", New York, 1971.

W. Prinz, M. Jarke, Y. Rogers, K. Schmidt, and V. Wulf (eds.), *Proceedings of the Seventh European Conference on Computer-Supported Cooperative Work, 16-20 September 2001, Bonn, Germany*, pp. 99-118.

Flexible Support for Application-Sharing Architecture

Goopeel Chung & Prasun Dewan

Department of Computer Science
University of North Carolina at Chapel Hill, USA
{chungg,dewan}@cs.unc.edu

Abstract. Current application-sharing systems support a single architecture for all collaborations, though different systems support different architectures. We have developed a system that supports a wide range of architectural mappings, which include, to the best of our knowledge, all of the existing architectures defined so far including the centralized, replicated, and hybrid architectures. Instead of being bound to a specific I/O protocol such as the X protocol, it is based on a simple abstract I/O protocol to which specific I/O protocols must be mapped by client-supplied code. We have used the system to perform experiments that compare the performance of the centralized and replicated architectures. Our experiments show that the choice of the architecture depends on the computers used by the collaborators, the speed of the connections between the computers, and the cost of the operations performed by the shared application. Under some conditions the centralized architecture gives better performance, while under others the replicated architecture gives better performance. Our results contradict the popular belief that the replicated architecture always gives better performance, and show the need for supporting both architectures in a system.

Introduction

A variety of systems have been developed to allow multiple users to share an application, that is, concurrently provide input to and view output of an application (Dewan, 1993). These systems may also provide other collaboration functions such as concurrency control, access control, undo, and merging (Dewan, Choudhary et al., 1994). However, these functions go beyond the basic capability

100

to share the I/O of applications among multiple users and, thus, will be ignored in this paper. Several, if not most, systems allow sharing of applications without any support for such high-level functions, or with support for very primitive forms of the functions.

Application-sharing systems differ in the architectures they offer to share the application. In general, users' actions are processed by multiple application layers such as the kernel, window system, toolkit, user-interface management systems, and application semantics. An example of the actual layers is given later. Each layer receives output from the layer above it and input from the layer below it. Different architectures differ in:

- the way in which they replicate these layers. Some systems completely replicate the application (Abdel-Wahab, Kim et al., 1999; Lantz, 1986; Chabert, Grossman et al., 1998), some completely centralize it (Ishii and Ohkubo; Li, Stafford-Fraser et al., 2000), some centralize the window client but replicate the window system (Abdel-Wahab and Feit, 1991), while still others centralize the top-level (semantics) layer but replicate the layers below it (Dewan and Choudhary, 1992; Hill, Brinck et al., 1994).
- the layer whose input and output is shared by the users. Architectures have been developed to support sharing of frame-buffer events (Li, Stafford-Fraser et al., 2000), window events(Abdel-Wahab and Feit, 1991; Lantz, 1986), and higher-level events (Dewan and Choudhary, 1992; Hill, Brinck et al., 1994).

These architectures can be described using the generalized zipper model (Dewan, 1998). The model assumes that if a layer is replicated, all layers below it are also replicated. Differences in architectures can result from differences in the top-most layer that is replicated. The higher this layer, the more the replication degree of the architecture. This degree is thus increased by "opening the zipper" until we reach the fully replicated architecture. Figure 1 and 2 show the zipper opened to different degrees for the same set of layers.

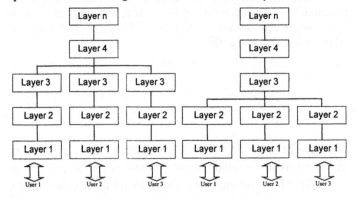

Figure 1. Varying the Sharing and Replication Degree.

Differences in architecture can also result from the level of the layer whose I/O is shared. The higher the level of this layer, the lower the sharing degree supported by the architecture. In the left architectures of Figure 1 and Figure 2, the I/O of layer 4 is shared, while in the right architectures of the two figures, the I/O of layer 3 is shared. Sharing of I/O of layer n implies sharing of the I/O of layer n+1. Thus, the right architectures offer a higher sharing degree.

The centralized and replicated architectures differ in how they support sharing of the I/O of a layer. If the layer is centralized, then its output is broadcast to all layers below it (Figure 1). If the layer is replicated, then it receives the input of all of the replicas of the layer below it. For instance, in the left architecture of Figure 2, the middle replica of layer 4 receives the input of the replicas of all layer 3. To avoid cluttering the diagram, we have not shown that other replicas of layer 4 also receive the same input to ensure that they are synchronized with each other.

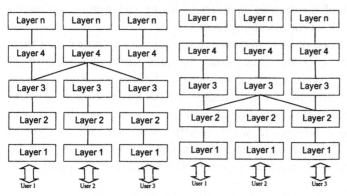

Figure 2. Varying the Sharing Degree in Replicated Architectures.

There are pros and cons of choosing a particular sharing degree (Dewan and Choudhary, 1995; Stefik, Bobrow et al., 1987). In a very tightly coupled collaboration, users may wish sharing of I/O at the frame-buffer level so that all users see a common screen. In another collaboration, users may wish sharing of I/O at the window level so that they can share some windows but not others. In a collaboration that is even more loosely coupled, they may wish sharing of I/O at the toolkit level so that they can scroll to different parts of a window.

There are also pros and cons of replicating the layer whose I/O is shared. The main advantage is that it requires lower communication bandwidth because input, rather than output, must be distributed among the application-sharing site. Thus, response times are less sensitive to network latency. This is important when the collaborators are connected by slow networks.

However, there are many disadvantages of replicating a layer. Performing computationally-expensive operation multiple times in different replicas (a) wastes computing resources, (b) in an application-sharing session involving lightweight computers (such as mobile computers), does not allow this processing to be offloaded to a heavyweight computer connected by a fast network to the lightweight computers, (c) creates bottlenecks when the operation accesses a shared (non-replicated) resource such as a file (since all replicas tend to access the resource at the same time); and (d) causes undesired semantics when the operation is a non-idempotent action such as sending a mail message. Moreover, good response times can be achieved only if input events are given to the local site first, and then distributed to other sites. This can result in different copies of the application receiving different sequences of input events, though some application-specific techniques such as operation transformation (Sun and Ellis, 1998) can be used to correctly synchronize the replicas.

Thus, the ideal architecture of an application-sharing session depends on several factors such as the layers and semantics of the shared application, the network connections and computers of the users, and the degree of sharing desired. Yet, each of the existing application-sharing architectures supports a single architecture for all collaboration sessions.

In this paper, we describe an infrastructure that supports a whole design space of application-sharing architectures, which includes the architectures of all application-sharing systems known to us. Instead of being bound to a specific layer, such as the VNC frame buffer (Richardson, Stafford-Fraser et al., 1998) or the X window system (Scheifler and Gettys, 1983), it is bound to an abstract inter-layer communication protocol to which specific inter-layer protocols can be mapped. A client of the infrastructure is responsible for translating between the specific and abstract communication protocols. The infrastructure is implemented in Java.

The infrastructure we describe does not allow the architecture to dynamically change during a collaboration session. But it does allow different collaboration sessions to use different architectures based on the application and other factors mentioned above.

By building such an infrastructure we make three contributions:
(1) We provide an application-sharing system that is not bound to a specific layer.
(2) We allow the architecture of an application-sharing session to be tailored to the application, users, computers, networks, and the task.
(3) We provide a basis for comparing the performance of different architectures under the same conditions. Such a comparison cannot currently be done because different architectures are implemented by different systems, which have differences other than the architecture supported. Architecture comparisons are much more meaningful when the compared architectures are created by configuring a single system.

The rest of the paper is organized as follows. We first describe the inter-layer communication protocol and the role of the translator. Next, we formally identify the range of architectures we can support. We then describe how our infrastructure supports this range. The next two sections describe our experience with writing translators for existing systems and the results of experiments we have done comparing the performance of different architectures. Finally, we present conclusions and directions for future work.

Layer-Independent Sharing

Current application-sharing infrastructures are bound to I/O protocols defined by specific user-interface layers. They intercept the input and output of an application using this protocol, distributing the input of all users to the application and the output of the application to all users. The key to developing a layer-independent application-sharing protocol is to recognize that this distribution task is independent of the specifics of an I/O protocol. Thus, an application-sharing infrastructure can be defined in terms of an abstract I/O protocol. If the specific I/O protocol defined by some layer can be translated to this abstract protocol, then the infrastructure can support automatic sharing of the layers above it, as shown in Figure 3.

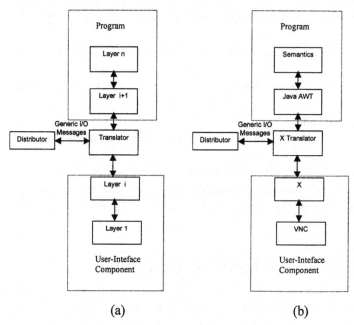

Figure 3. Translating and Distributing Messages.

If an application has n layers, and if the I/O protocol defined by the layer at level i is translated to the abstract protocol, then layers 1..i are referred to as the user-interface component, and layers i+1..n are referred to as the program component (Figure 3(a)). A layer-specific translator module translates between the abstract and concrete module while a layer-independent distributor is responsible for the actual distribution task. Thus, for each user-interface component, we build, not a complete application sharing system, but simply a module translating between the generic I/O messages understood by the distributor and the specific I/O messages understood by the component. For example, for X, we build a module translating between the X and distributor protocols (Figure 3(b)).

As we shall see later, an instance of the distributor and translator is created for each computer participating in a collaborative session. However, we will sometimes refer to all the translators (distributors) involved in supporting the sharing of an application as a single translator (distributor).

The idea of basing collaboration support on a generic protocol to which specific protocols are converted has been used earlier in the design of the DistEdit (Krasner, G. E. and S. T. Pope, 1988) collaborative replicated editor. DistEdit allows users editing a common document to use different editors. It defines an abstract editor protocol to which specific editor protocols must be converted. The DistEdit protocol defines only input editor events because it is designed to support only replicated editors. Our protocol defines arbitrary input and output events because it is designed to support arbitrary centralized and replicated applications.

The abstract I/O protocol is defined in Java and consists of the following output call:

- output (Object *object*) sends an arbitrary object specifying an output value.

and the following input call:

- input (Object *object*) sends an arbitrary object specifying an input value.

Both the distributor and translator define and use methods in this protocol, as shown in Figure 3. Before we discuss how exactly the input and output calls are processed, let us first define the range of architectures we support based on this protocol.

Range of Application-Sharing Architectures

Given n users sharing an application, we can define a set U of user interface components:

$U = \{u_i \mid 1 \leq i \leq n, n$ is the number of users, and u_i is the user interface component running on user$_i$'s computer.$\}$

and a set P of program replicas that can run on the computers:

$P = \{p_i \mid 1 \leq i \leq n, n$ is the number of users, and p_i is the program replica that can run on user$_i$'s computer.$\}$

In a particular architectural mode, each user interface component is mapped to one of the program replicas in **P**. Therefore, there is a many-to-one mapping f from **U** to **P**,

$f:\mathbf{U}\rightarrow\mathbf{P}$, such that $f(u_i)=p_j$, $u_i\in\mathbf{U}$, $p_j\in\mathbf{P}$ if p_j generates output messages for u_i in response to u_i's input messages.

In order to synchronize all of the program replicas in $f(\mathbf{U})$, input messages from a user interface component u_i are broadcast to all program replicas in $f(\mathbf{U})$. In order to synchronize all of the user interface components in **U**, output messages from a program replica p_j in $f(\mathbf{U})$ are broadcast to all user interface components u_i such that $f(u_i)=p_j$. We shall see how exactly this is done in the next section.

According to the most general definition of f, it is possible that $p_j\in f(\mathbf{U})$ and $f(u_j)\neq p_j$ – i.e. a user interface component is not mapped to the local program replica when some other user interface components are mapped to the latter. One of our major goals for supporting a range of architectures is to allow each user interface component to be mapped to a program replica that provides the best average response time for it. As we prove below, a mapping f, where $p_j\in f(\mathbf{U})$ and $f(u_j)\neq p_j$, violates the goal. In other words, if the goal is to be true, it must be the case that $f(u_j)=p_j$ if $p_j\in f(\mathbf{U})$. Therefore, our system supports only supports mappings f, where $f(u_j)=p_j$ if $p_j\in f(\mathbf{U})$.

Before giving the proof, let us first define what we mean by response time. We assume a simple model of interaction between a user interface component and the program replica to which it is mapped. In this model, the user interface component initiates the interaction by sending a single input message to the program replica, and the program replica responds with a single output message. Given that $output_h$ is the output message a program replica produces in response to an input message $input_h$, and that a user interface component u_i is mapped to a program replica p_j, we define the response time $rt_{i,j}(h)$ as follows.

$rt_{i,j}(h) = rtt_{i,j}(h) + proc_j(h)$, where

$rtt_{i,j}(h)$ is the *round trip time* associated with the exchange of $input_h$ and $output_h$ between u_i and p_j: i.e. the time it takes for $input_h$ to travel from u_i's computer to p_j's, plus the time it takes for $output_h$ to travel from p_j's computer to u_i's. If $i=j$, $rtt_{i,j}(h) = 0$.

$proc_j(h)$ is the time it takes for p_j to process $input_h$ and produce $output_h$.

We also make a simplifying assumption that $input_h$ and $output_h$ represent respectively all of the input and output messages of each of the user interface components – i.e. $rt_{i,j}(h)$ is the average response time that u_i gets from p_j for each of its input messages.

Given these assumptions, we now prove the following.

If there exists a mapping f, where $p_j\in f(\mathbf{U})$ and $f(u_j)\neq p_j$, then there must exist at least one user interface component that does not receive the best average response time available from one of the program replicas in **P**.

Proof: Suppose that $f(u_j)=p_k$, where $j\neq k$. If p_k does not provide the best average response time for u_j, the proof is trivial. Now, suppose that p_k provides the best average response time for u_j. Then, it must be the case that $proc_j(h) > rtt_{j,k}(h) + proc_k(h)$. Because $p_j \in f(U)$, there must exist u_i such that $f(u_i)=p_j$ and $i\neq j$. If we look at the make-up of the response time for u_i, it is $rt_{i,j}(h) = rtt_{i,j}(h) + proc_j(h)$. We can improve response time of u_i by mapping it to p_k, and sending its input and output messages through u_j's computer. In this case, $rt_{i,k}(h) = rtt_{i,j}(h) + rtt_{j,k}(h) + proc_k(h)$, and hence, $rt_{i,k}(h) < rt_{i,j}(h) = rtt_{i,j}(h) + proc_j(h)$ because $rtt_{j,k}(h) + proc_k(h) < proc_j(h)$. Therefore, u_i cannot receive the best average response time available by being mapped to p_j, violating our assumption.

Therefore, if we are to provide the best average response time for all of the user interface components, it must be the case that the inverse of $(p_j \in f(U)$ and $f(u_j)\neq p_j)$ is true – i.e. $f(u_j)=p_j$ if $p_j \in f(U)$.

Thus, given a user-interface component whose I/O protocol can be translated to the abstract protocol, our system will support any of the architectural mappings defined by the function above. The I/O protocols on which current application-sharing systems are based can be mapped to this protocol. Moreover, the architectural mappings supported by these systems are a subset of those we can support. As a result, the range of architectures we can support includes all of the application-sharing architectures we know of. Consider how some example architectures can be supported by our system:

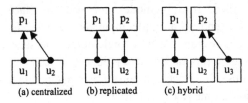

(a) centralized   (b) replicated   (c) hybrid

Figure 4. Examples of the Architectural Mappings Supported.

(1) Shared VNC (Li, Stafford-Fraser et al., 2000): The user-interface component here is the VNC layer, and the program component consists of all of the layers above the user-interface component. The user-interface component of each user is mapped to a central program component.

(2) XTV (Abdel-Wahab and Feit, 1991)/ Shared X (Garfinkel, Welti et al., 1994): Same as above except that the user-interface component consists of X and all layers (such as VNC) below it.

(3) Multiuser Suite (Dewan and Choudhary, 1992): Same as above except that the user-interface component consists of the Suite user-interface management system and all layers (such as Motif, X, and VNC) below it.

(4) JCE (Abdel-Wahab, Kim et al., 1999)/ Habanero (Chabert, Grossman et al., 1998): The user-interface component consists of the Java AWT layer

and all layers below it, and the program component consists of all layers above the user-interface component. Each user-interface component is mapped to a local replica of the program component.

(5) DistView (Prakash and Shim, 1994): Same as above except that the user-interface component consists of all layers involved in implementing DistView interface objects.

(6) GroupKit (Roseman and Greenberg, 1996): Same as above except that the "user-interface" component consists of GroupKit shared environments.

(7) Hybrid Architecture: The examples (1)-(3) above are centralized architectures (Figure 4(a)) while (4)-(6) are replicated architectures (Figure 4(b)). Keith Lantz proposed (Lantz, 1986) (but as far as we know, never implemented) a hybrid architecture in which, as in the replicated architecture, there are multiple program replicas, and as in the centralized architecture, multiple user-interface components are mapped to a replica (Figure 4(c)). This kind of architecture is also allowed by the mapping function defined above.

In general, our system can support any architecture defined by the layered zipper model (Dewan, 1998) as long as the communication protocols used by the layers are special cases of our abstract protocol. In addition, we can support hybrid architectures of the kind shown in Figure 4(c), which were not included in the zipper model.

Input/Output Distribution

We now describe how input and output are processed to support the architectural mappings defined above. As mentioned earlier, we replicate the distributor and the translator on all of the users' computers, and have the replicated distributors carry out the input/output distribution tasks for the client system. Figure 5 shows the distributor-translator replication for the mapping $f_i: U_i \rightarrow P_i$ shown in Figure 4(c). As we can see, there are two different sets of distributors – a set M of distributors that have program replicas in $f_i(U_i)$ running on respective computers, and a set S of the remaining distributors that do not. The mapping f_i forces a dependency relationship from a distributor s in S to a distributor m in M, in that s's local user interface component depends on m's local program replica for producing its output messages. For this reason, we refer to s as a slave distributor, and m as s's master distributor. A master distributor m does not depend on any other distributor in the sense that its local user interface component does not depend on a remote program replica for processing its input messages. Like distributor$_1$ in Figure 5, a master distributor may not have a slave distributor.

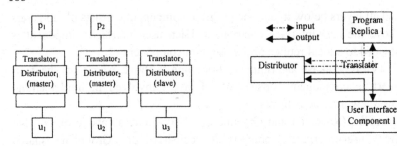

Figure 5. Master and Slave Distributors.   Figure 6. Distributor-Translator Interaction.

Supporting a mapping f_i requires both the distributors and the translators to work together to distribute input/output messages to correct destinations. As mentioned before, the part that each translator has to play to enable correct distribution is simple. As Figure 6 shows, each translator works as an intermediary between the local distributor, the local program replica and the local user interface component – it simply translates and relays input/output messages from one party to another. In particular, the translator translates generic input/output messages from the local distributor into translator-specific messages, and relays the translated input and output messages to the local program replica and the local user interface component respectively. In response to translator-specific input and output messages respectively from the local program replica and the local user interface component, the translator translates them into generic messages, and relays the translated messages to the local distributor.

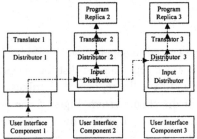

Figure 7. Input Distribution.

Given an input message sent from a translator, the distributors must cooperate to distribute the input message to all of the program replicas in $f_i(\mathbf{U}_i)$. In order to see how we have implemented the distribution, we follow an input message as it travels through different distributor modules. When a distributor receives an input message from the local translator, it must distribute the message to all of the master distributors.

In order to facilitate the distribution, we can consider having a centralized input distributor, to which each distributor passes the incoming input messages for the distribution. The input distributor would need to keep track of all of the master distributors in the current mapping. The major drawback of having a single input distributor is that it forces each input message to go through the input distributor's computer regardless of the locations of the input message's origin distributor and its master distributor, thereby causing poor response time.

We can improve the response time by making a distributor send each input message directly to its master distributor. Thus, we can consider installing input distributors on all of the computers, and having each distributor send input messages to the local input distributor. However, with this approach, any change to the composition of master distributors must be synchronously broadcast to all of the computers to guarantee that an input message is distributed to the same set of master distributors regardless of which input distributor distributes it. With asynchronous broadcast, an input message can be distributed to a different set of master distributors depending on which input distributor performs the distribution. This means that a new master distributor may miss some input messages from an input distributor that is notified about the new distributor belatedly. In order for the update to be synchronous, we must make sure that all of the current master distributors have received the same sequence of input messages before we begin the update. Moreover, we must make sure that no input distributor distributes an input message until the update ends. Therefore, the more input distributors we have, the more expensive the synchronous updates are.

As Figure 7 shows, we resolve this conflict by installing input distributors only on computers with master distributors. When a distributor receives an input message from the local translator, it passes the input message to the master distributor's input distributor (local input distributor if the master distributor happens to be itself). This approach supports direct input message delivery from slave distributors to their master distributors, and limits the range of master distributor composition updates to master distributors only.

Once a program replica receives an input message, it processes the message, and responds with an output message. The output message has to be distributed to all of the user interface components mapped to the program replica. Because only master distributors have program replicas running on their respective computers, they are the only distributors receiving output messages directly from their local translators. Each master distributor has a module called output distributor, which keeps track of all of the distributors with user interface components mapped to the local program replica. On receiving an output message from the local master distributor, the output distributor broadcasts the message to all such distributors, each of which sends the output message to the local translator. Figure 8 shows the itinerary of an output message, completing our discussion of input/output distribution in our system.

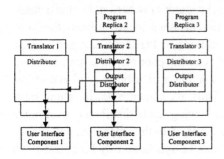

Figure 8. Output Distribution.

Translator

As we have seen in the discussion above, the client of the distributor is responsible for translating between the specific and abstract I/O protocols. If the specific I/O protocol is defined by a user-interface tool such as X, VNC, or JCE, then the translator must be implemented once for the tool (Figure 3(b)) – all clients of the tool can then be shared without making them collaboration aware. On the other hand, if the I/O protocol is specific to an application, then a special translator for the application must be implemented. Moreover, it may not be possible to translate all application-specific protocols to the generic protocols. The range of I/O protocols that can be translated measures the composability of our system, and the effort required to translate the (composable) protocols measures the automation of our system.

A translator must implement the I/O protocol defined earlier to receive input and output from the distributor. In addition, it must implement:

- `startProgram()`, which is responsible for starting the program component on the local computer.
- `startUIComponent()`, which is responsible for starting the user-interface component on the local computer.

These two methods are used to create the various architectural mappings supported by our system. The mapping of a user-interface component to a program component is done by the distributors based on the mapping defined by the user.

Composability & Automation Experiments

To evaluate the composability and automation of our system, we used it to share four applications: a text field editor, an outline editor, an object-based drawing editor, and a design pattern editor. We developed the text field and outline editors for the particular purpose of this evaluation, while the drawing editor and the pattern editor had been built before. The drawing editor was implemented at our university while the pattern editor was implemented elsewhere.

The text, outline and pattern editors are divided into program and user-interface components that communicate using special cases of the abstract protocol defined by us. Thus, implementing translators for them was straightforward. The drawing editor, on the other hand, is not based on the layered framework assumed in our design. Instead, it is based on the MVC (Model-View-Controller) framework (Krasner and Pope, 1988), in which input and output processing are separated into controller and view objects, and the semantics are implemented in a model object. A controller invokes methods in the model in response to user input, which change the state of the model. The model responds to a state change by notifying the view that it has changed. The view responds to the notification by querying the model for its new state and updating the display appropriately. A model can be composed with more than one view-controller pairs, each implementing a different user-interface.

We can map this architecture to the layering framework we have assumed in our framework by mapping the model to the program component and the controller and view, together, to the user-interface component. However, there is a fundamental difference between the assumed and MVC framework. The program component does not push output information to the user-interface component by sending output messages, instead the latter pulls this information from the latter in query requests.

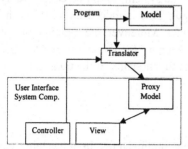

Figure 9. Mapping MVC to Layered Model.

Despite this problem, we managed to map the MVC framework to the layered framework, by adding an extra component to the architecture. Figure 9 shows how we did the mapping. The model maps to the program component, and the controller, view, and a "local proxy" of the model together form the user-interface component. The controller serves as the source of the input messages sent by a user-interface component. As mentioned earlier, the view cannot serve as the sink of output messages. Therefore, we created a local proxy model that serves as this sink. In order to synchronize the real model and the proxy model, we make sure that a user input message (generated by the controller) is sent to both objects. The translator and distributor treat the copy sent to the real model as an input message, and the copy sent to the proxy model as an output message.

This mapping is clearly clumsy, creating an additional copy of the model on each computer, which can reduce both the time and space efficiency of the system, and cause undesired semantics if the model implements non-idempotent operations. Thus, with this mapping, the "centralized" architecture creates one copy of the real model in the program component but multiple copies of the proxy model in the user-interface components, incurring some of the disadvantages of the replicated architecture. One good side effect, though, is that the proxy model serves as a local cache for the object, giving some of the benefits of caching described in (Graham, Urnes et al., 1996). This example was presented here to show the limitations rather than the strengths of our approach. The technique does show that if replicating a model does not cause any performance or semantic problems, the MVC framework can be mapped to the layered framework assumed in our design.

To evaluate the automation of our approach, we counted the lines of Java code added to clients to compose with our distributors. Table 1 shows our results.

text field	outline	drawing	pattern
74	135	115	220

Table 1. Lines of Java Code for composing with the Distributor.

Ideally, the effort required to compose with the system should be considerably less than manually distributing input and output. This is indeed the case, as the size of our distributor is several thousands of lines. Moreover, the functionality of the distributor can be increased (by adding support for dynamic architectural adaptations, for instance) without increasing the functionality of the translator.

Performance Experiments

As mentioned earlier, by supporting multiple architectures in a system, we provide a basis for evaluating the performance of different architectures – in particular, the centralized and replicated architectures. We performed a number of experiments to compare the two architectures. In these experiments we varied the application, its location in the centralized architecture, processing powers of the computers used in the collaboration, and network delays.

As the basis of our comparison, we measured, for each architecture, the fastest time in which two users finished the same task. Instead of the error-prone method of using live users to provide input, we used an actual collaboration log we acquired from MITRE. It is a sequence of n <$user_i$, $input_i$> tuples, where $input_i$ is entered by user$_i$. Two input provider modules, each representing the two users, sequentially execute the tuples - the input provider module of user$_i$ provides input$_i$ after user$_i$'s user interface component receives the program's output in response to input$_{i-1}$. This log-based method is more realistic than the approach of using synthetic workloads, which has been used so far for evaluating the performance of collaborative application (Chung and Dewan, 1996; Graham, Urnes et al., 1996; Bhola, Banavar et al., 1998).

computer assignment	Desktop (500 MHz) Desktop (500 MHz)		Desktop (500 MHz) Laptop (133 MHz)	
delay	LAN	Germany	Germany +modem	India
	0ms	72ms	162ms	370ms
client	shapes (small operation cost)		knapsack (large operation cost)	
architecture	centralized		replicated	

Table 2. Parameters Varied in the Experiments.

Table 2 shows the parameters we varied in our experiments and the values we used for them. Each entry in the first row of the table shows a computer assignment to user$_1$ and user$_2$ respectively. The two assignments allowed us to test collaborations involving computers with similar and significantly different processing power.

The second row of the table shows the three different network conditions we simulated (or used in the LAN case) and corresponding delays we imposed on the communication between the two users' computers. To base the delays on reality, we measured the average ping round trip times to actual sites for WAN and modem cases. For all experiments, we used the 10 Mbps LAN facility in the Computer Science Department in UNC-Chapel Hill. In the LAN case, we imposed no extra delays on the messages exchanges between the two users. In the Germany case, we assumed the first user was directly connected to the LAN and the second was in Germany, and we added 72ms to each message sent between the two users. The Germany and modem case was the same as the Germany case except that we assumed that the first user was connected to the UNC LAN using a modem. Therefore we added the modem delay to the Germany delay. The India case was the same as the Germany case except that the second user was assumed to be in India.

Row three shows the actual client systems we used. They were chosen to represent two classes of client systems - one with moderate operation cost per input and the other with a high operation cost. For moderate operation cost, we used the object-based drawing editor, which we call shapes. For high operation cost, we used a program implementing a solution to the knapsack problem. Though, to the best of our knowledge, such a program has not been used so far for a real collaboration, we believe it is a realistic example since we can expect that two users, especially students, would find it useful to understand the properties of the knapsack problem collaboratively. For each of the programs, we created a task with an input sequence appropriate for the program while trying not to violate the order among input events in the original MITRE log.

The last row of the table shows the two architectures used in the experiments.

	LAN	Germany
Centralized	2123	2904
Replicated	1823	2623

Table 3. Desktop-Desktop running Shapes.

	LAN	Germany
Centralized	147132	149545
Replicated	147492	154112

Table 4. Desktop-Desktop running knapsack.

Table 3 and 4 show the task completion times when we used the two desktop computers. Our hypothesis was that the replicated architecture would always provide the better performance when the computers are of equal power. Table 3 shows that this is true when the users share the drawing editor. However, Table 4 shows that it is not true when the users share the knapsack program. We do not know the exact cause of this result, but conjecture that the knapsack program's long operations (which run on both computers) hamper efficient communication between the two computers.

	LAN	Germany	Germany +modem	India
Centralized	3365	4466	6780	11156
Replicated	5408	6990	7180	8181

Table 5. Desktop-Laptop running Shapes.

Table 5 shows the results when the two users share the drawing editor using a desktop and a laptop computer, and in the central case, the program runs on the more powerful computer. In the LAN case, because the communication cost is low, the better performance is given by a central program running on the desktop machine. As the network delay gets larger, the replicated architecture gives better performance. Interestingly, it is only in the India case that the replicated architecture gives better performance than the central architecture.

	LAN	Germany	Germany +modem	India
Centralized	8460	10980	14770	16320
Replicated	8070	7960	7470	8630

Table 6. Laptop-Desktop running Shapes.

Table 6 shows the results of the same experiments we did for Table 5 except that this time, in the central case, the program runs on the less powerful computer. As expected, the central case always gives worse performance than the replicated case. The difference between the performance of the two architectures is not that significant in the LAN case. This is probably because the replica on the less powerful computer slows down the collaboration for both users.

	LAN	Germany	Germany +modem
Centralized	153891	154302	150566
Replicated	808743	816023	812969

Table 7. Desktop-Laptop running knapsack.

Table 7 shows the results of the same experiments we did for Table 5 except that this time we used the knapsack program, which has a much higher operation cost than the drawing editor. As expected, the relative performance of the centralized architecture is much better. We did not try to run the central program on the less powerful computer because of the high operation cost.

It is generally believed that the replicated architecture always gives better performance than the central architecture. It is because of this belief that many researchers have implemented replicated systems, either living with the synchronization and other problems of this architecture or providing complex solutions to these problems. Our experiments show that the replicated architecture does indeed give better performance in some cases. However, there are also realistic cases where it gives worse performance if we consider task completion times. In many of the latter cases, the replicated architecture will probably give better response times. However, task completion times are more important because they take into consideration the fact that a replica on a slow computer can slow the group's progress.

Our results also suggest that it may be useful to dynamically change the architecture mapping as users join or leave the collaboration. Typically, the central component is run on the computer of the first user who joins a collaborative session. As can be seen by comparing tables 5 and 6, if later a user with a significantly more powerful computer joins the session, it may be useful to dynamically migrate the central program to this computer. Similarly, as Table 5 shows, it may be useful to dynamically replicate and centralize an application as new users connected to others through slow connections join and leave the collaboration. Whether dynamic architectural adaptations actually improve task completion times would depend on their cost.

Conclusions and Future Work

This paper makes the following contributions:

- Layer-Independent Application-Sharing: It describes novel mechanisms for supporting a layer-independent application-sharing system. The mechanisms include the abstract I/O protocol and the division of the application-sharing responsibility into a client-specific translator and a client-independent distributor. It presents the results of composability experiments that evaluate the mechanisms, showing that a client-specific translator is easier to write than a complete, client-specific application-sharing system.

- Multiple architectural mappings: It formally defines a range of architectural mappings and describes novel distributed mechanisms to implement this range.

- Architecture Experiments: It experimentally shows that the performance of an application-sharing architecture depends on the computers used by the collaborators, the speed of the connections between them, the cost of the operations performed by them, and the location of the central component in a centralized architecture. As far as we know, results of experiments comparing the performance of different architectures have not been reported so far, though the performance of different techniques for implementing the same architecture have been reported (Graham, Urnes et al., 1996). Moreover, it is generally believed that the replicated architecture always gives better performance. Our experimental results show that, in many realistic situations, the centralized architecture gives better performance.

This work is only a first cut at providing flexible support for the application-sharing architecture. There are several possible directions for extending it:

- More Flexible I/O Protocol: It would be useful to extend the abstract I/O protocol so that it can support a greater variety of concrete I/O protocols such as the one supported by the MVC framework.

- More experiments: It would be useful to perform composability and performance experiments using a wider range of clients. Moreover, it would be useful to measure the cost (such as translation cost) client systems pay for genericity. Furthermore, it would be useful to create and use additional logs in performance experiments. Finally, it would be useful to see if it is possible to devise experiments involving live users that can be used to correctly compare the performance of different architectures. Other kinds of systems such as databases and compilers have relied on benchmarks, but these are not interactive systems. As we understand better the functionality and architecture of application-sharing systems, it is important to make evaluation of their performance a first-class issue.

- Architecture Policy: It would be useful to develop techniques for automatically determining the architecture to be used for an application-sharing session based on properties of the network connections, the computers of the collaborators, and the application.

- Dynamic Architecture Adaptation: It would be useful to explore and evaluate techniques for dynamically migrating, replicating, and centralizing a program component. The idea of dynamically migrating a program component has been explored earlier. Our previous work has extended an X-specific application-sharing system with the capability to dynamically migrate the X client (Chung and Dewan, 1996). Similarly, general distribution systems such as DACIA (Little and Prakash, 2000) support migration of arbitrary objects, but do not provide application sharing. It would be useful to extend these works to provide a client-independent application-sharing system that supports dynamic architecture adaptations. Finally, it would be useful to separate mechanisms to support architectural adaptations from those that distribute I/O so that the adaptation mechanisms can be used in existing application-sharing systems.

- Pervasive Application-Sharing: As the idea of a world populated with a wide-variety of computers ranging from palmtops to live boards is realized, the idea of supporting uninterrupted collaborations among mobile users becomes a possibility. In this world, the collaborators may use computers with varying processing power, and particular collaborators may change computers based on their location. Our experiments hint that flexible support for application-sharing architecture would aid pervasive collaborations. For example, if two users are using desktop computers, then the application should probably be replicated, but if one is using a handheld and the other a desktop, then the application should probably be centralized on the desktop. It would be useful to port our approach to lightweight computers to see how well it works for supporting mobile collaboration.

Acknowledgments

This work was supported in part by U.S. National Science Foundation Grant Nos. IRI-9508514, IRI-9627619, CDA-9624662, and IIS-997362.

References

Abdel-Wahab, H., O. Kim, et al. (1999): 'Java-based Multimedia Collaboration and Application Sharing Environment', *Colloque Francophone sur l"Ingeniere des Protocoles*, April 1999

Abdel-Wahab, H. M. and M. A. Feit (1991): 'XTV: A Framework for Sharing X Window Clients in Remote Synchronous Collaboration', *Proceedings IEEE Conference on Communications Software: Communications for Distributed Applications & Systems*, April 1991.

Bhola, S., G. Banavar, et al. (1998): 'Responsiveness and Consistency Tradeoffs in Interactive Groupware', Proceedings of ACM Computer Supported Cooperative Work, 1998.

Chabert, A., E. Grossman, et al. (1998): 'Java Object-Sharing in Habanero', *Communications of the ACM*, vol. 41, no. 6, June 1998, pp. 69-76.

Chung, G. and P. Dewan (1996): 'A Mechanism for Supporting Client Migration in a Shared Window System', *Proceedings of the Ninth Conference on User Interface Software and Technology*, October 1996.

Dewan, P. and R. Choudhary (1992): 'A High-Level and Flexible Framework for Implementing Multiuser User Interfaces', *ACM Transactions on Information Systems*, vol. 10, no. 4, October 1992, pp. 345-380.

Dewan, P. (1993): 'Tools for Implementing Multiuser User Interfaces', *Trends in Software: Issue on User Interface Software*, vol. 1, 1993, pp. 149-172.

Dewan, P., R. Choudhary, et al. (1994): 'An Editing-based Characterization of the Design Space of Collaborative Applications', *Journal of Organizational Computing*, vol. 4, no. 3, 1994, pp. 219-240.

Dewan, P. and R. Choudhary (1995): 'Coupling the User Interfaces of a Multiuser Program', *ACM Transactions on Computer Human Interaction*, vol. 2, no. 1, March 1995, pp. 1-39.

Dewan, P. (1998): 'Architectures for Collaborative Applications', *Trends in Software: Computer Supported Co-operative Work*, vol. 7, 1998, pp. 165-194.

Garfinkel, D., B. Welti, et al. (1994): 'HP Shared X: A Tool for Real-Time Collaboration', *Hewlett-Packard Journal*, April 1994.

Graham, T. C. N., T. Urnes, et al. (1996): 'Efficient Distributed Implementation of Semi-Replicated Synchronous Groupware', *Proceedings of the Ninth Conference on User Interface Software and Technology*, October 1996.

Hill, R., T. Brinck, et al. (1994): 'The Rendezvous Architecture and Language for Constructing Multiuser Applications', *ACM Transactions on Computer Human Interaction*, vol. 1, no. 2, June 1994.

Ishii, H. and M. 'Ohkubo Design of a Team Workstation', *Multi-User Interfaces and Applications*, North Holland.

Krasner, G. E. and S. T. Pope (1988): 'A Cookbook for Using the Model-View-Controller User Interface Paradigm in Smalltalk-80', *Journal of Object-Oriented Programming*, vol. 1, no. 3, August/September 1988, pp. 26-49.

Lantz, K. A. (1986): 'An Experiment in Integrated Multimedia Conferencing', *Proceedings of Conference on Computer-Supported Cooperative Work*, December 1986.

Li, S. F., Q. Stafford-Fraser, et al. (2000): 'Integrating Synchronous and Asynchronous Collaboration with Virtual Networking Computing', *Proceedings of the First International Workshop on Intelligent Multimedia Computing and Networking*, Atlantic City, USA, vol. 2, , March 2000, pp. 717-721.

Little, R. and A. Prakash (2000): 'Developing Adaptive Groupware Applications Using a Mobile Component Framework', *Proceedings of ACM Computer Supported Cooperative Work*, 2000

Prakash, A. and H. S. Shim (1994): 'DistView: Support for Building Efficient Collaborative Applications using Replicated Active Objects', *Proceedings of the ACM Conference on Computer Supported Cooperative Work*, October 1994.

Richardson, T., Q. Stafford-Fraser, et al. (1998): 'Virtual Network Computing', *IEEE Internet Computing*, vol. 2, no. 1, January/February 1998.

Roseman, M. and S. Greenberg (1996): 'Building Real-Time Groupware with GroupKit, A Groupware Toolkit', *ACM Transactions on Computer-Human Interaction*, vol. 3, no. 1, 1996.

Scheifler, R. W. and J. Gettys (1983): 'The X Window System', *ACM Transactions on Graphics*, vol. 16, no. 8, August 1983, pp. 57-69.

Stefik, M., D. G. Bobrow, et al. (1987): 'WYSIWIS Revised: Early Experiences with Multiuser Interfaces', *ACM Transactions on Office Information Systems*, vol. 5, no. 2, April 1983, pp. 147-167.

Sun, C. and C. Ellis (1998): 'Operational Transformation in Real-Time Group Editors: Issues, Algorithms, and Achievements', *Proceedings of the ACM Conference on Computer Supported Cooperative Work*, November 1998.

W. Prinz, M. Jarke, Y. Rogers, K. Schmidt, and V. Wulf (eds.), *Proceedings of the Seventh European Conference on Computer-Supported Cooperative Work*, 16-20 September 2001, Bonn, Germany, pp. 119-138.
© 2001 Kluwer Academic Publishers. Printed in the Netherlands.

Creating Coherent Environments for Collaboration

Christian Heath, Paul Luff, Hideaki Kuzuoka, Keiichi Yamazaki, Shinya Oyama
King's College London, University of Tsukuba, University of Saitama
christian.heath}@kcl.ac.uk, paul.luff@kcl.ac.uk, kuzuoka@esys.tsukuba.ac.jp,
yamakei@post.saitama-u.ac.jp, oyama@esys.tsukuba.ac.jp

Abstract. Drawing on studies of experimental systems and everyday settings we explore the relationship between social interaction and its environment. We show how interaction is inextricably embedded within its environment and discuss the ways in which innovative systems designed to support remote collaboration inadvertently fracture conduct from its setting, and undermine the participants abilities to produce, interpret and coordinate activities. We discuss the implications of these issues for the design of future systems, and, more critically, for studies of work and collaboration.

Introduction

A long-standing problem for those involved in the design and development of systems to support remote, synchronous collaboration, is how to provide users with a coherent environment in which to accomplish action and interaction. It has proved difficult to ensure that participants have compatible views of their respective domains, or even that through interaction they are able to establish, for all practical purposes, common standpoints to enable cooperative activities to be coordinated and accomplished. These problems become increasingly exacerbated if one attempts to provide participants with resources with which to undertake seemingly simple actions such as pointing, reference, or manipulating objects and artefacts within the remote location.

In this paper, we wish to explore some generic problems which arise in creating coherent environments for distributed collaborative work. In particular, we examine the use of a technology that has been developed in order to enhance the ways individuals interact with each other, orient to and manipulate objects in a video-mediated environment called GESTUREMAN (Kuzuoka, et al., 2000). Through a combination of technologies, including a mobile robot, wireless video communication and a remotely controlled laser pointer, GESTUREMAN is meant to provide resources for a remote participant to refer, point to and distinguish objects from each other in a remote domain. By examining how it is used by participants performing a quasi-naturalistic task we see how they make use of these resources. We consider the use of GESTUREMAN in the light of other systems aimed at enhancing distributed collaboration and participation, particularly recent attempts at augmenting video-mediated environments and collaborative virtual environments (CVEs). As with other systems which endeavour to provide a coherent environment for remote collaboration, we suggest that this system, though in quite a different way, fractures the environment(s) of action, and inadvertently undermines the participants' ability to produce, interpret and co-ordinate their actions. We then draw upon examples from everyday settings to show the ways in which actions and social interactions are inextricably embedded in their immediate environment. In particular, we consider how both the production of action and its recognition by others are dependent on relevant and occasioned features of the setting. We conclude by discussing the implications of the analysis for creating coherent environments for collaboration, and for our understanding of collaborative action and interpersonal communication.

Embodying Actions in Remote Domains

It has long been suggested that system designers might benefit from a more thorough understanding of what is known about groups and interpersonal communication. Unfortunately however, the dominant models and theories of interpretation and communication still tend to emphasise talk and non-verbal communication and largely disregard the ways in which action is embedded within its immediate environment. In recent years, there has been a growing emphasis on both the body and embodiment (e.g. Robertson, 1997), and on objects and material artefacts (e.g. Latour, 1992), and yet to a large extent the ways in which communication and interaction are embedded in, and constitute, 'material realities' remain under-explored (despite important exceptions, e.g. Goodwin, 1995; Hutchins, 1995).

In part, the predominant theories of communication which pervade the social and cognitive sciences may well have influenced the 'face-to-face model' which still pervades technical developments in CSCW and more generally computer systems designed to support synchronous, remote collaboration (Heath, et al., 1995). Whilst capabilities have been introduced to allow participants to refer and point to objects, in particular documents, the principle emphasis on both basic and complex systems, is to provide remote participants with face-to-face views of each other and to largely disregard the local environments in which conduct is produced. We believe that this tendency has been unfortunate for CSCW, since collaborative work, and more generally social interaction, is largely accomplished in and through objects and artefacts, tools and technologies – be they documents, diagrams, models, on paper, screen, through keyboards, pen, mouse and the like. These material resources not only feature in how people produce actions, but also, and critically, in the ways in which they recognise or make sense of the actions of others.

In this regard, for some years we have been involved in successive projects concerned with developing support for synchronous, remote collaboration. These projects are primarily concerned with exploring and developing ways in which we can provide remote participants with the ability to invoke, use, discuss, and manipulate, objects and artefacts. These projects emerged from our earlier studies of the disembodied character of conventional media space (Heath and Luff, 1992b) and led to the Multiple Target Video (MTV) experiments (with Gaver and Sellen) (Heath, et al., 1995) and more recently to develop very different 'solutions' through CVEs (Hindmarsh, et al., 1998). As we have discussed elsewhere, neither expanding media space to include features of the remote participants' environments, nor CVEs in which a seemingly compatible, pseudo-worldly environment is provided to the participants, provides satisfactory support for 'object-focused' collaboration. Indeed, in both solutions and their various iterations, participants encounter difficulties in making sense of each other's conduct even when undertaking seemingly simple actions such as pointing to objects within a particular environment.

In this paper we wish to address the more generic difficulties which arise in building coherent environments to support remote collaboration. To do this we will discuss our recent attempts to build technologies to support object focused collaboration amongst remote participants, and continue by discussing some instances drawn from everyday settings.

These concerns are also reflected by a series of technical innovations developed in a collaboration between engineers and social scientists at the Universities of Tsukuba and Saitama in Japan. In these, a number of systems to support remote collaboration with and around objects and artefacts have been developed; for example, extending media spaces to include cameras which can move when operated by remote participants and laser pointers which can indicate locations of interest in a remote space (Kuzuoka, et al., 1994; Yamazaki, et al., 1999). These techniques have been deployed in a series of evolving systems: GESTURECAM, GESTURELASER and GESTUREMAN. Such developments provide an invaluable opportunity for considering how to establish coherent distributed environments in which to undertake collaborative activities.

GESTUREMAN, for example, is the latest of these developments. It was constructed and configured at the University of Tsukuba and consists of a small robot that can move around a remote domain (see Fig. 1). In different configurations it has 2 or 3 cameras and a laser pointer. Images from these cameras and commands to the robot are transmitted through a high bandwidth wireless channel so that the remote participant is provided with high quality, real-time video.

Fig. 1: The GESTUREMAN with a 'local' participant

In the remote domain a participant sits in front of 2 projection screens displaying the images from the cameras (see Fig. 2) The participant moves the robot by use of a joystick. The laser pointer is controlled by a mouse and pressing the mouse button makes the laser dot brighter. This is a way of distinguishing movement of the laser dot from pointing with it. The participants speak to each other via wireless headsets and microphones.

In order to examine GESTUREMAN we undertook a variation of the FurnitureWorld Task which has been given to participants using the MTV configurations of video spaces and CVEs (Heath, et al., 1995; Hindmarsh, et al., 1998). In each case the task though similar had to be re-configured to match the technology under investigation. For the

Fig. 2: the 'remote' participant. The screen in front displays the image from the right camera, the display on the left is from the left camera

GESTUREMAN task, one of the participants (the 'local' participant) was in a room with real furniture. We carried out the task with 5 pairs (2 Japanese and 3 English speaking pairs) and collected data for each from 6 cameras. The objects in FurnitureWorld included examples of both Japanese and Western furniture.

The task provided us with data where the participants: referred and pointed to different objects; distinguished different objects for each other; were mobile around the domain and could move objects around the space; and allowed them to make different uses of the space. It also provided us with materials with which to assess the different capabilities of the system for pointing and referring to objects with respect to media spaces and CVEs, as well as allowing us to collect some novel data which could inform our understanding of the interactions with tangible artefacts and in mixed realities.

Locating an object for another

The laser pointer of GESTUREMAN did provide a way for the remote participant to identify objects and distinguish locations for the local participant. In the following fragment Dave (the local participant in the room) and Candy (the remote participant) are discussing the space on the left hand side of the room and how to lay out the furniture. Candy has positioned the robot in the doorway of the room and it and Dave are oriented to one corner on the left hand side. In the course of this discussion Candy utters 'let me>let me look over here' and moves the robot so that it is oriented to the right hand side.

C: let me>let me look over here to see how much room
   (.)
C: oh theres not so much room over here↓-------
D:  where where you looking –

As the right hand side of the room (behind Dave) comes into view she says 'oh theres not so much room over here↓'. Whilst Candy is speaking Dave maintains his orientation to the left hand side but glances back and forth to the robot and then asks 'where, where are you looking'.

C: I'm (.) looking over to your>behind you theres you ca n(t)   yep there see>can you
D: 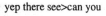 over over here

Whilst Candy responds with 'I'm (.) looking over to your...' Dave continues looking in front and even takes a small step forward. As she starts to reformulate her description of where she is looking ('>behind you theres') Candy moves her hand to the mouse and starts to manipulate the laser pointer. Only as Candy utters 'theres' does Doug spin around. On doing this he finds the faint laser dot on the wall on the right hand side and points to it down to the left whilst uttering 'over over there'. Candy replies with 'yep there see>can you see that little red light thing' whilst brightening the dot with the mouse pointer and moving it around the wall.

C: see that little red light thing=   theres not really any room over there-----so::

                 =yeah yeah-

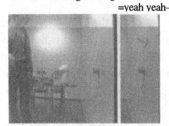

Dave follows the red dot on the wall and Candy utters 'theres not really any room over there'. They then reorient back to the left hand side of the room.

In this simple instance the remote participant uses the system to identify a location in the physical space, a location related to the matter the co-interacts are discussing. She manages to get Dave to re-orient to the location that she is talking about by moving the laser dot, brightening it and then moving it around the space.

The accomplishment of this shift in orientation is not entirely unproblematic. The talk through which it is accomplished involves various perturbations, restarts and reformulations. Candy has some difficulty identifying the location for Dave, it being 'over here', 'over to your...' and 'behind you'. In part, this is because Dave is also engaged in trying to identify the location, and even when standing still, he shifts the direction of his glance. Such utterances have therefore to be coordinated with the shifting orientation and participation of the co-interactant.

For Dave, being co-located with a little robot also presents various difficulties. Even though the cameras are visible and it is possible to see (and hear) the robot moving, it is not clear where the remote participant is looking. Some sense of this can be obtained by glancing at the orientation of the robot in relation to the environment, as Dave does in the fragment above. But, as for the remote participant, this can be problematic if the robot is itself moving. Hence it is difficult to coordinate one's own activities with another when mediated by the robot and its pointing devices. However, the participants do manage to orient to a common object or location. In this and other instances, they do this by talking about the pointing, 'the laser light', the 'little dot' or the 'red thing', thus the pointing often becomes a topic of the discussion rather than a resource for collaboration. In this instance what initially seems to be a passing remark about another area of the room ('theres not so much room over here') requires a number of activities before they can achieve a common orientation to that passing location ('theres not really any room over there') and then continue their discussion about the layout in the original area.

These difficulties and their solution resonate with conduct found in other technologically mediated environments, such as media spaces and conventional collaborative virtual environments. The laser pointer is a way of relating the talk and activities of a remote participant to the ongoing activities and environment of another, much as the extending arm does on the avatar in Fraser's augmentation of the MASSIVE CVE (see Hindmarsh, et al., 1998). In the case of GESTUREMAN the pointer can be used to mark particular locations and general areas in a physical space and, in the above instance and others, the participants do use the device in this way. However, as in a CVE a device to support pointing and achieving a common orientation with another itself becomes a subject of explicit talk and interaction and the operation of the device requires work on behalf of the participants to get the pointing done.

Securing a common orientation to an object

It is not only the remote participant who may face difficulties in attempting to have the other discover an object within their domain. The individual who is with GESTUREMAN may also have to undertake successive actions in order to have the robot, and the remote participant, locate a relevant object. The individual located in the furnished room has limited resources with which to identify the orientation and perspective of the other and in consequence may have to make various attempts to have an object seen and recognised. Consider the following fragment. As she tidies the books on the table, Jemima says 'we have a (.) we have a (.) we have a bookcase in he:re↑'. She then starts to locate the bookcase for Darren who is operating the robot. As she says 'so maybe I should (0.3) if you turn over that way↑ (0.3) to the left↑' she points in front of the cameras on the top of the robot.

J: so maybe I should---if you turn over that way↑ --- to the left↑ - yeah↑

Jemima's initial pointing gesture first appears for Darren in the centre screen, but as she says 'turn' in 'you turn over that way↑' her hand moves into the left screen, the gesture thus occupying most of the two large screens in front of Darren. Jemima then pauses briefly and brings her arm back slightly. She then extends her arm fully again and reformulates the location 'to the left↑'. Darren then starts to move the robot to the left and as he starts this movement Jemima utters 'yeah↑'. As Darren spins the robot around, Jemima continues to hold out her hand saying 'do do you see it↑(0.3) do you see the book shelf'. Her hand now appearing just on the centre screen.

J: do do you see it↑--- do you see the book shelf------   yeah yes alright
D: oh right here - okay↓okay↓

Only when Darren appears to identify the bookcase with 'oh right here (.) okay↓okay↓' does Jemima withdraw her hand and start to discuss where to put the bookcase, moving around the robot as she does so.

Jemima manages to get Darren, through his use of the robot, to see the bookcase in the far corner of the room. She does this by accompanying her spoken directions with an extended pointing gesture. But this is not a straightforward gesture. Jemima reshapes it in the course of its production and through its animation successfully secures the appropriate reorientation from Darren (mediated by the robot). This initial movement of the robot is accompanied by a 'yeah' from Jemima, but whilst the robot is in motion Jemima continues to point towards the bookcase. In all she maintains this point for some 6 seconds and tries to secure some further response from Darren that he can see the target of the point ('do do you see it↑ (0.3) do you see the book shelf'). Only when she says 'oh right here (.) okay↓okay↓' does Jemima withdraw her hand and her talk about the bookcase can continue. The robot does provide resources for Jemima to make sense of Darren's participation in the ongoing event. From its orientation it is possible to have some sense of the 'field of view' of the remote participant and by its movement whether the remote participation is transforming his or her participation in an ongoing activity, that a particular trajectory has commenced. However, these capabilities provide a limited and fragmentary set of resources. Jemima cannot get a sense of how her conduct is seen by the other and the nature of the movement once again foregrounds the means by which a common orientation is accomplished rather than the object and locale towards which the orientation is being established.

Making sense of disembodied gestures

In the following fragment Candy (the remote participant) has positioned the robot in the doorway angled so it can see into the corridor outside the room with the left hand camera and into the room with the right. She is trying to identify the object that is underneath some cushions and asks Dave: 'is that another table under those cushions'. As she says this

Dave is standing in the corridor just visible on the left hand side of the left image. Dave pauses and then points into the room as he says 'ah:::::: (0.6) you mean right right here↑'.

D: ah:::::::------you mean right
  right here↑--

Unfortunately, there are a number of cushions in the room and the corridor and the laser light just happens to have been positioned near to a cushion that has been placed on top of another and both are on top of a chair in the room (see arrow). Dave takes the location of the laser light as relevant to Candy's talk and draws on this to locate what Candy is referring to and points to those cushions. Candy then moves the laser light accompanied by some perturbations in her talk: 'huh>errm-- like oh'.

C: huh>errm--like oh   =errm no I'm not over there yet hold on------err
D: oh yeah right there↓=

In the first of the mouse movements the pointer comes temporarily to rest on the bottom cushion. Dave again takes this as relevant and says 'oh yeah right there↓='. Candy then accompanies her next movements of the laser pointer along the wall and out into the corridor with an explicit account of what she is doing with the laser pointer '=errm no I'm not over there yet hold on'. Only when the laser light comes to rest near the cushions on the chairs in the corridor can Candy ask 'out here in the hallway↑ these things?' to which Dave replies 'errm no it is another one of these chairs↓ we've got a whole mess of these (0.2) these black chairs↑'.

The laser pointer does provide a resource for a remote participant to locate objects and locations in the environment of another. It is invaluable in relating one's own actions to features in the remote environment. This simple mechanism, a visible dot operated with a mouse, allows remote participants to tie their talk and actions to particular objects and locales. It also provides individuals in one locale with a way of identifying what a participant located elsewhere is referring to and thus enables them to establish a common orientation to objects and places in the environment.

The laser does however have shortcomings. Perhaps most critically, unlike a gesture, the light of the laser lies on the surface of the landscape of the remote environment. So for example, as in the instance above, the participant in the furnished room may assume a relationship between the laser light and the actions of the remote participant, even when it is not relevant, leading the participants on occasions to have to address these misunderstandings. Lying on the surface, the laser light inevitably has a potential relationship with objects in the world, and can lead participants to assume a connection where no relevant relationship exists. Moreover, unlike gestures which can be shaped in the course of their production, and the co-participant's conduct, the laser light lies largely undifferentiated in the furnished domain. What then appears to be a obvious solution to relating talk to particular objects in a remote environment, by providing a simple tie between the activities of a remote participant and the local environment of another, renders activities such as pointing highly problematic and invokes potential relationships where none are relevant.

As mentioned above, in previous studies of media spaces, enhanced video-mediated interaction and CVEs, participants of these quite different technologies appear to face parallel difficulties. Despite efforts to provide 'common spaces', 'symmetric environments' or resources for pointing and reference, these technologies can be seen to inadvertently fracture the relationship between conduct and the environment in which it is produced and understood. Ironically, the more we attempt to enhance the environment to provide participants with a range of abilities and resources, the more we may exacerbate difficulties in the production and coordination of action.

Given these difficulties faced by individuals in these technologically-mediated environments, perhaps it is worth briefly considering the resources on which participants rely to coordinate their actions in more conventional settings, and in particular the ways in which interaction is inextricably embedded within the immediate environment. We will draw examples from various settings including control rooms, medical consultations and museums. Considering examples drawn from everyday environments illustrates the ways in which the production and intelligibility of conduct is dependent upon the participants' mutual access to the immediate environment and can suggest why the use of a simple remote-controlled pointing device may lead to difficulties.

Embedded Action in Everyday Settings

Invoking the environment

As part of their daily activities personnel frequently refer to objects and artefacts within their immediate environment. These objects and artefacts may range from diagrams in paper documents, through to complex multimedia displays, they can be presented on screens or projected onto the walls of the work setting. To a large extent these occasioned references to features of the local environment, even where they themselves are changing or in flux, rarely engender serious difficulties or problems. The smooth and unproblematic ways in which participants invoke, discover, discuss, and respond to features of the immediate environment, becomes more impressive when one considers the complexity of contemporary workplaces; environments such as control centres are littered with an array of objects and artefacts, in different media, with variable rates and quality of change.

Consider the following fragment in which one participant simply asks another where a particular object is to be found within the immediate environment. The fragment is drawn from a control centre on London Underground in which participants are provided with numerous tools and technologies to oversee traffic and passenger movement. The setting, a site of previous research (Heath and Luff 1992a) is currently being re-studied as part of a project concerned with the design and deployment of image recognition systems. We join the action as John receives a phone call asking him where the train number 225, is currently positioned.

```
J:      Hello there (3.2) Two Two Fi:ve:: Let me have a look for it. (0.4)
→  J:      Two Two Fi:ve:::? (.) He's around here somewhere
   G:      Two Two Five:s at er: (0.6) It's up there?
           (0.3)
   J:      Oh he's in the shed<he's in Queen's Park (.) °hh Sou:th Sheds:.
```

Whilst John utters 'Two Two Fi:ve:::? (.) He's around here somewhere', into the handset, he simultaneously looks at various screens along the console. During the utterance, John turns and looks at the monitor to the left of Graham; a monitor which shows the timing of the trains over the section of line for which Graham is responsible (south of Piccadilly Circus). As John turns towards the monitor to his left, Graham follows his

J Two Two Fi:ve:: me have a look   ...   G: It's up there?

gaze and they look at the screen together. John has not only encouraged Graham to help him look for something that moments ago was not explicitly relevant, but encouraged him to look at, and momentarily inspect, the information on a specific screen, in a certain way. As John turns away, failing to find the train, and uttering the word 'around', Graham continues the search by first looking at the fixed line diagram and then to the monitor directly in front of John. Uttering 'Two Two Five:s at er: (0.6) It's up there', Graham points to the image on the screen directly in front of John, and at which John is now looking.

In pointing to the object, Graham is sensitive to where John has already looked and to his current orientation. The point is designed to contrast the particular monitor with the others, and to enable John to follow the trajectory of the pointing finger to the screen which displays a complex array of trains and traffic information.

As John turns towards the screen, Graham moves the pointing finger closer to the monitor to enable John to discriminate the information displayed on the screen. The focal object is made progressively and increasingly visible, with regard to the ways in which Graham aligns his gesture and talk with the shifting orientation of his colleague. John is able to locate the object and responds with 'Oh he's in the shed<he's in Queen's Park (.) °hh Sou:th Sheds:' John finds the object in question, train 225, by virtue of Graham's search and point. He informs the caller where the train is, and simultaneously displays to Graham that he has both found the object and located its 'exact' position.

Simply encouraging a co-participant to look at and discover a particular object within a common domain therefore is a complex and emerging event. It is sensitive to the reason for finding the object, the orientation of the co-participant, the preceding actions, which in this case visibly fail to locate the object. The gesture and the accompanying talk is highly sensitive to the individual's standpoint *vis-a-vis* the object and the co-participant. As the gesture emerges it is fashioned with regard to the shifting orientation of the other, initially demarcating the region in which the object may be found, and then more specifically, the actual location of the object with regard to other objects within the surrounding area. Without access to the co-participant's immediately preceding conduct, and the relationship of that conduct to its surrounding environment, and without access to the recipient's conduct as he is beginning to discover the referent, it would be difficult for the person pointing to produce the activity in a relevant way. Just as the recipient relies upon his access to the other, and the other's progressively emerging actions *vis-a-vis* visible features of the ecology to determine the sense and intelligibility of the action, in a nutshell, to 'get the point'.

One can see why participants may encounter difficulties in referring and pointing to objects using a laser. For the remote participant, it is difficult to determine the orientation of the other with regard to the furnished world and to be able to keep track of how the shifting orientation is sensitive to that world and the actions of the other. More critically perhaps, as the remote participants refer and point to objects, they are often unaware of how the other's conduct emerges during the course of that action, so that they are unable to reshape their talk and pointing with regard to the emerging actions of the recipient. For the individual in the furnished room, it is often difficult to determine the orientation of the remote participant (for whom their referent is designed), more difficult still to determine how the other sees them in the furnished world. It is not surprising therefore that even relatively simple actions such as reference and pointing involve the participants in relatively extended sequences of action though which they render visible their own orientation and attempt to reconcile their respective views on the world.

Entailing action and animating objects

Encouraging co-participants to notice or examine something within the immediate environment is often accomplished in a less explicit and obtrusive fashion. People happen to find themselves looking at particular documents or noticing screen changes, and in consequence dealing with events which might otherwise have passed unnoticed. Colleagues encourage each other to notice particular phenomena or events, and as we and others have discussed elsewhere are highly sensitive to the concurrent activities of colleagues even though they may engaged distinct and seemingly unrelated tasks (e.g. Heath and Luff, 1992a).

In control centres, as in other environments, the participants abilities to maintain a sense of what others are doing, and to encourage them to notice changes that might otherwise pass unnoticed, derives in part from the familiarity with the local environment. Despite the seeming complexity of the settings, displays, tools and artefacts remain in stable locations. Particular phenomena, such as alarms, incoming information and other events are revealed by screens or documents that remain in the same relative location, such that particular types of activity rely on particular tools and technologies (the use of which may well be visible to others in the same domain). In consequence, the use of a particular keyboard or document, may provide resources to enable people both to discover and make sense of what others are doing within the immediate environment, and form the basis to coordination and collaboration. In a sense therefore, despite their complexity, and the changing character of materials on-screen and the like, the immediate environment provides resources to enable people to discover or make sense of the actions in which others may be engaged.

For the matters at hand, it is important to note that participants have a complex array of resources for having others notice, and react, to actions, objects and the like which may happen to arise within a particular setting. Pointing and showing are the most explicit way of establishing co-orientation to some potentially relevant feature within the local milieu. In interaction and collaboration individuals are highly sensitive to the ways in which co-participants may notice, and encourage others to notice, objects and events within the local milieu. Where the critical aspects of such noticings is for the other to examine and determine for themselves the potential relevance and significance of the object in question. In a sense therefore participants embed potential action within the local milieu, and rely upon others to make sense of those noticings by virtue of the ability to scrutinise the environment for potentially relevant objects and events. In GESTUREMAN, as in others forms of media space, these noticings, embedded actions, largely pass unnoticed, since the remote participant is unable to 'connect' the participant's action to the relevant feature of the domain. Conduct becomes disembodied.

In many cases, participants do not simply have someone look or notice something within the local milieu, but fashion, or even transform the object or artefact. In turn, these transformations serve to encourage particular actions, facilitate certain experiences, and form a foundation to subsequent collaboration. It is worthwhile considering an example from a rather different type of setting, in this case a museum. It is drawn from the Materials Gallery in the Science Museum London and in particular an exhibit which is designed to provide visitors with a sense of the form and consistency of different types of liquid. This exhibit consists of a large glass structure which contains a series of tubes which hold different forms of liquid. At each corner of the exhibit is a pole. On the top of three of the poles are buttons which when pressed cause the liquids to rise. As a young boy (B) begins to press one of the buttons he is joined by his sister (G). As she joins him, he tells her 'I'm making it go up'. She turns and looks at the relevant tube in the exhibit. As she turns, her brother

begins to gesture upwards in line with the rising liquid and at the same time goes 'Oooh:::::::::::↑' rising to a crescendo, and as the liquid falls continues with 'Oooh::::::↓' and allows the gesture to fall downwards. His sister, watching the liquid, and trying to wrestle the button off her younger brother, delivers an appreciation of the liquid's motion by producing a falling sound 'Mmmmmm↓'. The boy's gestures and accompanying sound do not simply draw attention to part of the exhibit, but exaggerate the liquid's movement, transforming it momentarily into a spectacle, a moments drama that the children experience and appreciate together. A feature of the environment is given a flavour and significance through the ways in which their actions reflexively animate its movement and function.

The ability of the young boy to invoke and animate features of the rise and fall of the liquid, relies upon his access to his sister and her emerging orientation towards the exhibit. Once again we can see how the shifting relationship between a participant and (relevant) features of the ecology is critical to the ways in which an individual is able to highlight an object and engender particular forms of experience. Moreover, the gesture and the accompanying sounds are shaped, within the course of their articulation, not only with regard to the object, the rise and fall of the liquid, but to the sister's emerging orientation towards the exhibit. The exhibit's sense and significance therefore, at this moment within the interaction, arises through the moment-to-moment co-participation of the children; the exhibit itself is critical to the production, intelligibility and coordination of their conduct.

In different ways therefore, we can see how the participants' actions give particular sense and significance to features of the immediate environment, and how various objects and artefacts provide resources for the production and intelligibility of conduct and interaction. The participants do not simply draw attention to features of the environment, but entail actions in particular objects or artefacts. In these cases we can see how participants respond to the object or the artefact, rather than the activities of the other, even though the object has been given its determinate and occasioned sense through the other's conduct. Action is *transposed* and embedded within the immediate environment; the participant's talk and gestures, their interaction and collaboration are inseparable from particular objects and artefacts, and the ways in which they, at some particular moment, are constituted as relevant. The reflexive relationship between action and the environment is a critical feature of the participants' conduct and collaboration.

Emerging material relevancies in the environment

The relevance of the local environment to action and interaction is not limited however to occasions in which the participants refer to or invoke a particular object or artefact. The local environment pervades the ways in which people make sense of each other's conduct and produce their own actions and activities. The environment provides resources for rendering the actions of others intelligible or sensible. Without access to the environment in which the actions and activities are produced the relevant sense of the conduct can be irretrievable. So for example, someone's activities like standing and walking across a room is intelligible by virtue of the fact that you are familiar with the setting and can interconnect the movement with the physical features of the environment. These actions are intelligible through their occurrence within a commonly accessible and available world. To consider these actions independently of their local environment would be to undermine the sense of significance for the participants and of course to disregard the resources which feature in their production.

For example, consider the following instance from the beginning of a medical consultation in general practice.

Dr: What's up?   (4.2)   Pt: I've had a bad eye::: in there

The patient enters the room and walks towards the chair to one side of the doctor's desk. The doctor is glancing at the medical record and as the patient crosses the room, the doctor utters 'what's up'; a euphemism for 'what can I do for you'. The patient withholds a response for four seconds or so and then, pointing to his eye, replies with 'I have got a bad eye::: in there.'

Just as the doctor times his query to the patient's pattern of movement and prospective arrival at the chair, so the patient is sensitive to the doctor's conduct in producing his response. The doctor's use of the record, his shifting gaze up and down the page provides resources not only to account for his seeming disinterest in the patient, but in anticipating the upcoming completion of the activity. At one point, soon after the patient sits down, the doctor smoothes the page and takes hold of a date stamp; the patient then glances up, opens his mouth, and finding his co-participant once more looking back towards the document, licks his lips, looks away and closes his mouth. A second or so later, the doctor turns from the record to the patient, and patient begins to speak, pointing to the blister on his eye.

The sense and significance of the doctor's conduct does not simply derive from his visual orientation, but rather from the emerging relationship between his bodily orientation and features of the immediate physical environment. The doctor's delay in aligning towards the patient is legitimised by virtue of the record's use, and his manipulation and looking at the document provides the patient with the resources to make sense of the conduct and attempt to coordinate his action. The bodily communication, non-verbal behaviour, of the doctor, is only intelligible for the patient (and of course the researcher) by virtue of how he can interweave the document, the object, with the participants' conduct; just as the patient's conduct for the doctor is recoverable by virtue of his own looking at and manipulating the record. To dissociate the talk and bodily conduct of the participants from relevant features of the environment, renders the action 'absurd', that is 'inharmonious; out of harmony with reason or propriety'. Surprisingly however, research on interpersonal communication, some of which has had an important influence on systems to support synchronous distributed working, disregards conduct and interaction from the environment in which it is produced and made sensible.

Discussion: embedded action

In the light of the materials presented here and a range of related studies of the workplace (e.g. Harper, et al., 1989; Suchman, 1996), we can begin to see ways in which the local environment features in the production, intelligibility and coordination of action and interaction. It is perhaps worthwhile outlining a few of these issues:

- participants reference features of the local environment, and encourage others to inspect, examine and look at objects and artefacts; the orientation and standpoint of the co-participant(s) and their emerging action and activity is critical to reference, and the discovery and perception of the objects;
- participants animate, and in other ways transform features of the environment for another, through gesture, touch and talk; the interplay of action and the environment giving the occasioned sense and significance of an object;
- actions can be entailed or embedded in particular features of the local environment; the object can serve to encourage and engender particular action and activities and serve as a 'centre of coordination';
- participants 'read' or make sense of the actions of others through the ways in which they interweave conduct with particular features of the immediate

environment; the embeddedness of action in the environment allows participants to discover why and what others are doing;

- the environment consists of a constellation of objects, artefacts, tools and the like; participants make sense of the actions of others, and produce their own actions with regard to each others access to and perspective on the 'occasioned' configuration of features.

The interdependence of action and the environment is critical to the ways in which participants are able to make sense of, and coordinate their actions with others. These foci are continually emerging moment-by-moment within the course of the participants' action and interaction. They are reflexively constituted in and through the participants' conduct.

The relationship between action, coordination and the local environment has profound relevance for our attempts to support synchronous collaboration amongst individuals based in different locations. In developing systems to support remote collaboration we attempt to interweave and/or create new environments, in which participants can produce actions within a setting which, in part, is accessible and intelligible to each other. However, once we begin to create new environments to enable people to interact and collaborate with each other, we fracture the relationship between action and the relevant environment, and thereby engender difficulties, which may render even the most seemingly simple form of activity problematic.

Media spaces and CVEs vividly demonstrate the significance of environment to action and point to the shortcomings of certain approaches to interpersonal communication, language use and social interaction. They powerfully demonstrate how the very intelligibility of another's conduct relies upon participants' abilities to interweave environmental features with occasioned courses of action, just those features that are reflexively constituted in and through the participants' conduct. They reveal, for example, how the most seemingly trivial action, such as pointing to an object, involves the complex and occasioned interdependence of the participants' bodies, bodily orientation, bodily conduct, talk, and visible and material properties of a scene. They demonstrate how spatial and temporal features of conduct are so easily ruptured when attempting to interweave different scenes, scenes which fracture the production and receipt of action, and environments in which conduct is 'placed'. Small scale, naturalistic experiments with a number of technologies reveal how even such an apparently straightforward activity, like a point, can be problematic when access to particular features of the environment is either unavailable or transformed in some way. The experiments with GESTUREMAN, for example, reveal how a technology can be used for such an activity, but how it fractures the participants' conduct from its setting, and hence reveals the work required in getting such apparently simple activities done.

The significance of such small scale experiments can lie beyond the observations concerning a particular system or technology. Whilst not rigorous or generative as in a conventional experiment, they provide resources for what Garfinkel (1967), borrowing from Spiegelberg, once characterised as 'aids to sluggish imagination'. By placing participants within unfamiliar environments and asking them to undertake seemingly simple activities, the experiments can serve to powerfully illustrate the resources on which they ordinarily rely in the practical accomplishment of action and interaction in more conventional environments. Garfinkel suggests that "I have found that they produce reflections through which the strangeness of an obstinately familiar world can be detected" (p. 38).

These naturalistic experiments provide important resources to recognise the importance of a range of phenomena, competencies, resources and the like, which to some extent have been treated as epiphenomenal in social science research. In turn, we believe that such resources are critical to both the understanding and design of systems to support distributed collaboration. The development of experimental systems in CSCW to support synchronous collaborative working, throw into relief not only how little we know about the ways in which action and interaction is ecologically dependent and embedded, but how predominant orientations within the disciplines largely direct analytic attention away from the material, from the object, and in particular the reflexive constitution of the physical world in human conduct. Those concerned with developing technologies in CSCW have every right to question whether contemporary social science delivers on just the issues that they face when building systems to support synchronous, distributed collaborative work.

We are currently engaged in exploring ways in which the observations and findings discussed here can be drawn upon to inform the design and development of future systems to support synchronous collaborative work, particularly amongst distributed participants. The interdependence of action and environment suggests a number of concerns and considerations which, in the light of social and technical research, we believe are relevant to the design and development of future systems. For example, consideration could be given to how to:

- provide participants with the ability to determine the location, orientation and frame of reference of others ;
- provide resources for participants to determine their standpoint with regard to other participants and the space(s) in which they and others are located;
- provide resources through which participants can discriminate the actions of others which involve shifts in orientation and reference to the space and a range of objects, artefacts and features;
- consider ways in which participants can refer to, invoke, grasp, manipulate, address, discuss, and in various ways animate properties of the space, and coordinate such actions with the real-time conduct of others;
- consider how participants can be provided with, and themselves preserve a stable constellation of relevant objects, artefacts and scenes within the space(s), so that they can produce and interpret actions and activities with respect to a presupposed coherent and stable environment.

As well as being of relevance to designers endeavouring to build new environments rendered through video, computer graphics and projection technologies, the issues raised in this paper may also be of interest to those developing collaborative systems by other means; whether these are standard shared applications presented on conventional displays or enhanced forms of remote collaboration supported by novel techniques. Considering how actions are embedded in the environment both in the production and for the intelligibility of actions may suggest a rethinking of the resources which co-participants can utilise to establish common frames of reference. Indeed, the problem of providing adequate support for users to determine common standpoints, foci or points of reference has been an incessant problem for designers of collaborative technologies (e.g. Tatar, et al., 1991). This may in part be due to a limited conception of how such activities are accomplished with respect to the local environment and the emerging and ongoing actions of co-participants. The support for establishing a 'common referent', for example, being principally considered with regard to the individual undertaking the action and the particular object of concern, rather than with respect to the ongoing activities of other participants whilst it is being accomplished and how features of the environment are utilised in its production.

These considerations pose complex problems for those of us involved in the design and development of systems to support distributed collaborative work, more complex than merely providing participants with the ability to establish common foci and points of reference. Through a consideration of the use of GESTUREMAN and of more mundane everyday examples we can begin to see that providing the participants with the ability to point at and refer to particular (shared) objects within a domain is one aspect of a more fundamental and critical problem. The problem as we have demonstrated is not simply how people can detect and identify particular objects, but rather how they can establish and maintain a relevant 'connection', 'relationship' between the co-participant (even an avatar) and the environment in which that person (or representation) is located. The reflexive relationship between conduct and ecology, poses a critical problem both for the participants, in producing, making sense of and coordinating their conduct, and for those of us engaged in the design and development of novel collaborative environments. In this regard, we have recently begun a new programme of work in which we are attempting to develop media spaces in which participants have mutually compatible access to both each other and the respective domains and ecologies of objects and artefacts. This programme of work also involves extensive studies of more conventional environments in order to begin to understand a little more about the ways in which participants reflexively coordinate their perspectives on particular domains during the course of social interaction.

Acknowledgements

The research in Japan was supported by Telecommunications Advancement Organization of Japan, Japan Society for the Promotion of Science, Grant-in-Aid for Scientific Research (B), 2000, 12558009, Oki Electric Industry Co. Ltd., and Venture Business Laboratory (VBL) of Ministry of Education, Culture, Sports Science and Technology. We should thank the Communications Research Laboratory for supporting development of the GESTUREMAN. The research in the UK was supported by the EU's Disappearing Computer Paper++ (IST 2000-26130) and Shape projects.The Anglo-Japanese collaboration, including Paul Luff's visit to Tsukuba, was supported by the VBL program and the University of Tsukuba. We would also like to thank Jon Hindmarsh, Dirk vom Lehn and other members of the WIT Group for invaluable comments on earlier drafts of this paper.

References

Garfinkel, H. (1967). *Studies in Ethnomethodology*. Englewood Cliffs, NJ: Prentice-Hall.

Goodwin, C. (1995). Seeing in Depth, *Social Studies of Science*. **25**: 2, 237-274.

Harper, R., Hughes, J. and Shapiro, D. (1989). 'Harmonious Working and CSCW: Computer Technology and Air Traffic Control', in *Proc. of ECSCW'89,* 73-86.

Heath, C. C. and Luff, P. (1992a). Collaboration and Control: Crisis Management and Multimedia Technology in London Underground Line Control Rooms, *CSCW Journal*. **1**: (1-2), 69-94.

Heath, C.C. and Luff, P. (1992b). Media Space and Communicative Asymmetries: Observations of Video-Mediated Interaction, *HCI Journal*. **7**:315-46.

Heath, C. C., Luff, P. and Sellen, A. (1995). 'Reconsidering the Virtual Workplace: Flexible Support for Collaborative Activity', in *Proc. of ECSCW'95,* 83-100.

Hindmarsh, J., Fraser, M., Heath, C.C., Benford, S. and Greenhalgh, C. (1998). 'Fragmented Interaction: Establishing mutual orientation in virtual environments', in *CSCW'98*, 217-26.

Hutchins, E. L. (1995). *Cognition in the Wild*. Cambridge MA: MIT Press.

Kuzuoka, H., Kosuge, T. and Tanaka, M. (1994). 'GestureCam: A Video Communication System for Sympathetic Remote Collaboration', in *Proc. of CSCW'94*, 35-44.

Kuzuoka, H., Oyama, S., Yamazaki, K. and Suzuki, K. (2000). 'GestureMan: A Robot that Embodies a Remote Instructor's Actions', in *Proc. of CSCW 2000*

Latour, B. (1992). Where Are the Missing Masses? The sociology of a few mundane artifacts, in *Shaping Technology/Building Society*, Bijker and Law (eds.), 225-258. MIT Press.

Robertson, T. (1997). 'Cooperative Work and Lived Cognition: A Taxonomy of Embodied Actions', in *Proc. of ECSCW '97*, 205-220.

Suchman, L. (1996). Constituting Shared Workspaces, in *Cognition and Communication at Work*, Engeström, Y. and Middleton, D. (eds.), 35-60. Cambridge University Press.

Tatar, D. G., Foster, G. and Bobrow, D.G. (1991). Designing for conversation: Lessons from Cognoter, *IJMMS*. **34**: (2), 185-209.

Yamazaki, K., et al. (1999). 'GestureLaser and GestureLaser Car: Development of an embodied space to support remote instruction', in *Proc. of ECSCW'99*, 239-258.

W. Prinz, M. Jarke, Y. Rogers, K. Schmidt, and V. Wulf (eds.), *Proceedings of the Seventh European Conference on Computer-Supported Cooperative Work, 16-20 September 2001, Bonn, Germany*, pp. 139-158.

Spaces of Practice

Monika Büscher[1], Preben Mogensen[2] and Dan Shapiro[1]

1: Lancaster University; 2: Århus University

{d.shapiro, m.buscher}@lancaster.ac.uk; pmogensen@daimi.au.dk

Abstract. This paper compares the properties of physical and digital workspaces in the context of a prototype of a collaborative virtual environment that has been developed with reference to work in design professions and concentrates on the organisation of work materials. Spatial properties are analysed in terms of the sociality of workspace use. Digital spaces can be engineered to mimic or to transcend various constraints and affordances of physical workspaces, and they can be given parallel, folded and tunnelled properties. We examine the consequences these have for the readiness-to-hand, intelligibility, and accountability of the resulting workspaces. We address means of interacting with these extended environments. Using case study scenarios, we demonstrate how ethnographic analysis and participatory design have informed the architecture, features and development of the system.

Introduction

In previous papers (Büscher et al. 1999, 2000a, 2000b) we have described the MANUFAKTUR, a still-evolving prototype of a collaborative virtual environment that permits the manipulation of diverse working materials in a three-dimensional digital space. The MANUFAKTUR was inspired in part by ethnographic observation of design professionals – architects and landscape architects – and has been realised in part through involving them in participatory design. They use a great variety of materials: plans, sketches, diagrams, photographs, scale models, samples of materials, catalogues, and more. We found that manipulating the presence and absence of these materials, bringing them into dynamic spatial relations, and referring between them, happen constantly and are not just a context or prerequisite for design professionals in doing their work; rather, they are an integral part of accomplishing the work itself.

Figure 1 (disregarding, for the moment, the descriptive labels) shows an example of a simple MANUFAKTUR space. It contains references and views onto a set of objects. Double clicking any of the document objects will launch it in its respective application – which might be MS Word, Excel, AutoCAD, Photoshop, etc. – and any changes made to it will be updated in the MANUFAKTUR in near real time. The objects can be sized, and can be moved and rotated in three dimensions, giving a full 6 degrees of freedom. The viewer/viewpoint can also move freely in the space. A distinctive feature of the MANUFAKTUR as a virtual environment is that its emphasis is on representing the *materials* with which people are working, and the actions they are taking with them, and far less on the visual representation, e.g. through avatars, of the collaborating *persons* (cf Dourish et al., 1999, for a different recent approach to providing rich interaction with documents). The intention of the MANUFAKTUR is not at all to displace the physical work environment with a digital one. Rather, the system is based in the observation that design professionals (in common with many other kinds of workers) now find that they already have to spend many hours per day working with the digital forms of their materials, and have only the poorest of digital environments to support them in doing so. The aim is to maximise their choices in how to 'flow' their work between their physical and digital environments, and in how to bridge between them.[1]

Physical and digital spaces

The particular purpose of this paper is to consider some of the properties that the MANUFAKTUR has (and which equivalent virtual environments would have) as a digital space in collaborative use, in comparison to the properties of physical spaces in collaborative use. At first sight it seems obvious that such virtual environments should seek to imitate or emulate three-dimensional physical space, for at least three reasons. First, since our starting point was observing the power for work practice of the arrangement of materials in physical space. Second, to take best advantage of users' highly developed skills and competences in manipulating physical materials and creating dynamic order with them. And third, since one of the ambitions of the design is to make it possible to bridge more smoothly between working with materials in their physical and digital forms, the more congruent the environments are, the easier one might expect that bridging to be.

---

[1] The system is in the process of being redesigned and rebuilt from scratch so that the same code can run on multiple operating systems, and can function across the range from small handheld devices, through traditional desktops/notebooks, to wallsize and stereographic interfaces. The name for this new system is TOPOS™.

The constraints of physical space

It is obvious that a digital environment could only have limited success in emulating its physical counterpart, since the capacity fully to reproduce just the visible dimension of the latter is still quite primitive, before going on to consider other senses; and since emulation encompasses not only the realisation-projection of the environment, but also the means of interacting with it. However, it soon becomes apparent that straightforward reproduction is not even the most appropriate ambition for a digital environment. This is in part because the physical environment has constraints that it may not be helpful to reproduce, and in part because the digital environment may be given different and helpful capacities that the physical environment cannot match. As Smith (1987) observed, there is a tension between the literalism of an interface – those of its features that are true to its metaphor – and its magic – those capabilities that deliberately violate the metaphor to provide enhanced functionality. How such literalism and magic might be applied, however, is a matter that is specific to each system and its context. In our case, the call for a 'sliding relationship' between realism, imaginative transposition of known spatial properties, and the exploration of entirely new possibilities (Benedikt 1992) is not one that can be answered through abstract reflection alone (see also Benford et al 1997). Appropriate features for the design of the MANUFAKTUR need also to be discovered from practice, achieved in our case through our ethnographic studies and our collaboration with professionals.

For example, the three-dimensional arrangement and manipulation of a heterogeneous array of working materials is an integral feature of work in architectural design (Buscher et al 1999). In a physical work environment this is strongly constrained by gravity, in ways that may not always be helpful. Documents etc. can only be placed on horizontal surfaces, or pinned to surfaces in other planes. Related items can be gathered together, but only in very limited numbers. In larger numbers they can be collected in a stack, which does make use of depth but is harder to handle and usually means that only the top item is visible. By contrast, in Figure 1 materials in the MANUFAKTUR are arranged in three dimensions unconstrained by gravity and related materials can 'float' in proximity to each other. It has become customary to refer to 3D spaces represented on a flat screen as "2.5D", but in this quite different sense, physical materials spaces are also only "2.5D" while their digital counterparts, even on a flat screen, are in 3D.

Another constraint in a physical work environment is that of a person's convenient reach. In conjunction with the constraints of gravity, only a small amount of material can fall conveniently to hand, with progressively more effort required to manipulate, and eventually even to see, materials further away. One consequence is to reduce the meaningfulness that can be given to the proximity and distance of materials, as embodying gradations of being more central and less central, more urgent and less urgent. Within the limits afforded by reach, these gradations are highly compressed. As can be seen from Figure 1, in an electronic space they can be far more extended, while the materials remain accessible – one acquires 'very long arms'.

Other constraints of arrangements of materials in a physical work environment concern both their ephemeral and their persistent character (Büscher et al., 2000b). Spatial arrangements of materials are ephemeral in that they are easily created and easily changed or destroyed. This is an advantage in following the flow of work through constantly shifting tasks and purposes. But it is also a disadvantage, in that valuable arrangements are easily disrupted by accident or buried under a continuous flurry of objects on the move. Yet spatial arrangements of materials are also persistent in that things 'stay where they are put'. This is an advantage in that meaningful arrangements have some stability, but also a disadvantage in that they easily outlive their purpose, requiring deliberate activities to clear them up, and they easily become sedimented among other meaningful arrangements in a limited space. The result of this combination of ephemerality and persistence can easily be just a clutter in which materials are neither in a meaningful arrangement nor 'in their proper place'.

The sociality of space

These considerations make it clear that we cannot rely simply on trying to emulate a physical workspace in an electronic space. We need other bases for considering what features of physical and electronic spaces are valuable, for whom, and under what circumstances. The 'work' that dynamic arrangements of work materials are doing can, analytically, be distinguished in terms of three aspects: having materials ready-to-hand; the intelligibility and organisation of materials; and the accountable and communicative nature of material arrangements in a working environment. In real activities, work practices will normally play over these aspects in a seamless and tacit fashion, but they can have different implications for design, support and use. We will now explore these aspects further with some scenarios of use drawn from our fieldwork studies.

A firm of landscape architects has been awarded a contract for the development of a major river corridor in the south of England. The *River Corridor* project brings together 16 sites with very different characteristics and requirements. Although all sites need individual schemes, they also come together as a whole and need an overall strategy. Work on the 16 sites will be scheduled in several phases. Initially, three sites need urgent attention. Site 1 is situated next to an Olympic canoeing course. It should respond to this feature in the landscape, but develop into a more informal and naturalistic wildlife reserve. Site 3 concerns the approach roads to one of the main cities situated on the river. The character of the approach should be enhanced. Site 6 houses a derelict industrial complex and is to be converted into a new business park development. Views of old industrial landmarks should be integrated where possible.

At a start-up meeting with the client, the landscape architects have discussed and elaborated the initial brief. They have received Ordnance Survey maps and plans, and some contour plans, from the client. In addition, several of the landscape architects have been on extended site visits and have taken around a hundred photographs.

Minimal digital spaces

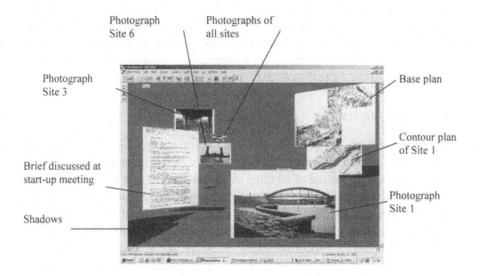

Figure 1. A minimal digital space.

NB: Colour versions of all figures are available at:
http://www.comp.lancs.ac.uk/sociology/spaces/

Figure 1 shows how Chris[2], one of the landscape architects, has brought together some of the work materials in the MANUFAKTUR, in a first attempt to develop some ideas for the individual sites 1, 3 and 6, as well as an overall strategy. He refers to the brief as it was discussed at the start-up meeting, and tries to relate the individual sites to the whole scheme through reference to the overall base plan in his workspace. From a whole array of photographs from different sites he selects

---

2   The scenario presented in this paper has been constructed with reference to the ethnographic fieldwork, but mainly relies upon work undertaken by the landscape architects with the MANUFAKTUR. The project, for example, has been anonymised, but it is 'real', as are the workspaces shown. They were created and discussed in the course of an extended workshop in the landscape architects' studio.

three that capture the specific character of the three sites that are to be developed first. A particular challenge arises from the intricate topography of the Olympic canoeing course, which should inform the design of the adjacent wildlife reserve on site 1, and he examines the details of this on a contour plan provided by the client.

This workspace has quite a simple structure. The space is unbounded, continuous and uniform, with linear perspective. It has no gravity, and objects in it have no momentum or friction: they float freely in space and stay where they are put. Stylistically, it is an abstract space that consists just of the work materials themselves, without decoration or other features. The exceptions are one or more light sources, without which objects would be invisible, and, in this case, an implied 'ground' on which the objects cast shadows. This feature can be switched off but, in a 2.5-D rendering, shadows help to distinguish, for example, a large object that is far away from a small object that is close to. It can be seen as in various ways a 'simplest form' of three-dimensional digital space, although it is already both less and more than a 'copy' of physical workspaces.

Being 'ready-to-hand'

This workspace can, however, already service at some level all three of the aspects we identified above as the 'work' that dynamic arrangements of work materials are doing. The use of all three dimensions means that although there are at least ten items in the space, some of them well forward and prominent, the space does not appear cluttered. Materials are 'ready-to-hand' in that they can easily be identified and handled, and can easily be opened in their native application for further work if necessary. They are available for use and exhibit their relevance to the task through their respective position in a 3-D space. Being ready-to-hand also often means the ability to consider materials in conjunction – a contour plan in relation to a photograph, for example – and that too is easily afforded in the space. All of the objects have a double life, sometimes as materials that are worked upon and at other times functioning as 'equipment' for the task at hand: providing reminders, helping to retain the 'bigger picture', etc. In order for equipment to contribute in the work – that is, to function as equipment – it must withdraw itself ('zurückzuziehen', as Heidegger puts it (1988)). When we use equipment in purposeful and involved engagement, what we are concerned about is not the equipment in itself, but the work to be done. When the equipment can be subordinated to an 'in order to ...', a purpose, then the equipment itself is ready-to-hand (Mogensen, 1994). When, in order to work on materials, we are forced to pay attention to the equipment, then the work breaks down (Winograd & Flores, 1986).

In the MANUFAKTUR workspace, this corresponds to a landscape architect, for example, working on a drawing and having lots of other materials there functioning as equipment for sticking to the overall concept, for reminding about unresolved issues, for remembering site details, etc. The point is that the materials are *there*, providing assistance, without the need to find them, open them, remember them, etc. thus breaking the current flow of work. Materials that she is not working on specifically are still there, offering both a visual reminder and easy availability if she shifts focus from one document to another (e.g. by pushing the first one back and the other forward).

Intelligibility and organisation

The second aspect of the 'work' done by dynamic arrangements is to do with the intelligibility and organisation of materials. Materials can be 'intelligible' in many different ways, but a central component of intelligibility for work practice is to do with being able to perceive the relevance of an item or a collection of items for the particular tasks at hand. It is also to do with the 'intertextuality' of materials and the ways in which their meaningfulness as an assembly can be mutually informing and greater than the sum of their parts. A contour plan and a photograph, for example, may be juxtaposed not only so that they are ready-to-hand and conveniently accessible, but also because each is more intelligible for the tasks at hand – for designing a view, for example – when read in relation to the other. That is often why materials are extracted from their 'proper places' – a particular shelf or a particular computer folder – and arranged in a workspace. The 'proper place' for an item will usually be a rational, but nevertheless often arbitrary, categorisation, such as a collection of all contour plans. That will rarely be the collection of items most relevant for carrying through a particular task.

Hence 'working' spatial arrangements constitute an essential ongoing and ad hoc production of order and working organisation, and dynamic configurations of context. As the example from Figure 1 shows, the MANUFAKTUR is especially powerful in supporting intelligibility in this sense. MANUFAKTUR workspaces are continuously saved, so a particular configuration can always be returned to if work is interrupted. Objects in a MANUFAKTUR workspace are references to the underlying materials, not those materials themselves, so that workspaces can be composed for particular purposes, altered at will, and deleted, without affecting at all the underlying organisation, e.g. in a directory structure, of those materials. In these ways MANUFAKTUR workspaces can avoid some of the difficulties discussed above surrounding both the permanent and the ephemeral character of arrangements of materials in physical space.

Accountability and communication

The third aspect of the 'work' done by dynamic arrangements of work materials concerns accountability and communication and is closely related to the above. The visible order (or disorder) of work materials in the landscape architects' studio is the result of the manipulation of materials under the umbrella of a particular 'in-order-to'. While this purpose makes for, and requires, the readiness-to-hand of working materials, it also guides the creation of contextual arrangements that make the relevance of, and relationships between, a diversity of materials intelligible. At the same time, the spatial sediments of such relevancies and relationships are themselves intelligible. They are an ongoing, contingent and accountable achievement. The notion of accountability has only recently and implicitly been extended to the material world (Heath and Hindmarsh, 2000). It is an ethnomethodological term (see, for example, Garfinkel, 1967; Lynch, 1993) that denotes the fact that human activities are orderly, intersubjectively intelligible and observable.

This includes activities that involve materials in rather interesting ways. 'Orderliness' does not at all refer to a 'tidy' workspace. Instead, it implies that when working with materials people orient towards a particular objective, activity, and/or aesthetics. This orientation – although clearly tinged by personal preferences and styles – nevertheless sediments into meaningful arrangements of work materials (afforded and limited by the constraints imposed by physical space and materials). A tidily categorised workspace is a possibility, but a tangled mess of paper, models, and tools is equally expressive and inextricably tied to the respective orientation that informed its production. Both versions are orderly and intersubjectively intelligible in the sense that members of the community of practice will be able to make sense of the material arrangements that emerge – simultaneously and retrospectively. Their accountability lies in the fact that members will assume that, in principle, any contextual arrangement is the outcome of a meaningful action, even if that is throwing everything on the floor in irate frustration at not being able to find a particular item. However, such difficult forms of meaningful and accountable spatial order lie at one end of a continuum.

If it is to go smoothly, work practice often needs to be visible (or audible, etc.) and comprehensible to others. The connections that are made through this are often serendipitous – for example, one landscape architect may glimpse another working on an area of a plan, and be reminded that she was recently on site and saw that there had been an un-notified change that her colleague needs to know about (Büscher et al., 2001). Sometimes the connections fit into a more direct division of labour, as, for example, when colleagues work side-by-side on a planting plan and a corresponding specification of species. They may share some of their working materials while also involving information that is irrelevant to the other, yet still visible to them and indicative of the kinds of considerations that are in progress. Sometimes colleagues go so far as to stage deliberate 'performances' to ensure that appropriate communication and accountability are achieved, as shown by Heath & Luff (1992) in their examples from the London Underground.

Colleagues may also leave a particular spatial arrangement of materials as an asynchronous resource for others, to enable them to answer a potential client's request while they are away, for example. Considering the work described in conjunction with Figure 1, if Chris were carrying this out in a physical workspace, it would be accountably available in all these ways. A MANUFAKTUR workspace retains very powerfully the intelligibility of activities for others, by contrast with conventional ways of using digital materials. If it is realised on a computer monitor that could have the consequence of privatising this work, but that could be overcome simply by projecting the workspace onto a wall screen (more sophisticated methods of achieving accountability and communication will be considered later).

Spaces with extended properties

Starting out from the 'minimal form' of three-dimensional digital space described in relation to Figure 1, we can consider progressively more complex attributes and features, looked at in terms of how they build support for the readiness-to-hand, intelligibility and accountability of arrangements of materials.

Augmented and stylised spaces

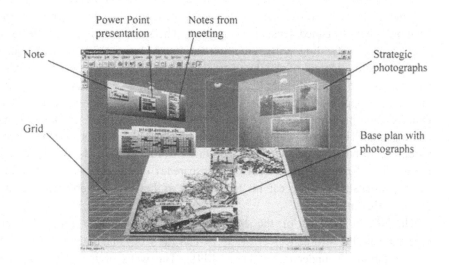

Figure 2. Extended and stylised spaces.

Figure 2 shows how Joanne, one of Chris's colleagues, takes a different approach to the same situation. She lays out the overall base plan and places the same photographs related to sites 1, 3 and 6 on the plan, close to the actual position they were taken in. Her main focus is to develop some ideas for an overall strategy, and a set of strategic photographs from previous projects and magazines serve as an inspiration. She does not want them to intermingle with the materials actually related to the *River Corridor* and so she places them in a glass box that constrains their movement to that box. Similar reasons underpin the placement of her own notes from the start-up meeting, a PowerPoint presentation on industrial regeneration, and a note reminding her to ring an artist working on a different project with her. These three documents are attached to a billboard that confines their movement to the plane of the board (they require an extra 'effort' to pull them off). She also adds an Excel spreadsheet with an outline of the project schedule into her workspace.

This scenario illustrates some of the ways in which the MANUFAKTUR can 'play' with spatial properties to add functionality. The glass box, which can be any size, makes it possible to create a bounded space rather than an unbounded one. The billboard permits the reintroduction of 'gravity', save that now it is capable of acting in any plane. A spatial property that has little parallel in physical space is the ability to give any object a default position, to which it can be returned via a right mouse click on the object. An object can have its own behaviours (if it is a video, for example) or can be given a behaviour, such as animation. It could be made possible to 'flick' an object across the workspace, effectively reintroducing momentum and friction to objects.

This scenario also shows ways in which the space can be made less abstract and more stylised through adding features. Switching on the floor grid, for example, gives an added sense of perspective. The space could be made to look like a 'room' by adding walls, or other 'furniture'. Joanne has chosen a much more interesting variant of this by using one of the work materials – the overall base plan – as a 'static' feature of the workspace itself, on which she places other materials in appropriate positions. The plan has been made non-selectable (and therefore non-moveable) in order to facilitate its function as an 'anchor' for the photographs. This could equally be done, for example, with a 3-D model or wireline of a building or a landscape, so that it would become its own space for the placing of relevant materials. The transparency of objects can be set at any value, so that such features can be 'toned down' if they become too obtrusive and obscure other materials.

The design features of the MANUFAKTUR discussed here are meant to communicate the affordances of the space and the work materials in a way that can be intuitively understood (Gaver, 1991). The walls of the glass box, for example, are easily, and, after initial exploration, visually experienced as boundaries. The way in which the photographs contained within in it are ready-to-hand is made visible. The readiness-to-hand of the plan within the MANUFAKTUR allows it to withdraw as 'equipment', that is, as a background onto which other materials can be placed. These placings add intelligibility to the individual photographs – they refer to 'real' locations. Once this order has been evoked, the combination of map and photographs becomes highly intelligible (and desirable as a shared resource) and accountable (a picture positioned wrongly would be noticed). In constructing her workspace in these ways, Joanne has not only produced a particular intelligibility through these arrangements of materials, but she has also produced a graded distinction in their readiness-to-hand which is tailored to their, and her, purposes. Equally, this is an arrangement with enhanced accountability, in that a colleague glancing at Joanne's workspace will find her orientation to the task 'made flesh' in her division and organisation of materials: the order she has produced 'shouts' at them from the screen.

'Quantum' spaces

So far we have considered spaces that are continuous and unitary. In the digital environment, however, we can have spaces that extend or breach these constraints in various ways. In physical space, there can only be one instance of the same object (which is not a copy), and an object can only be in one place at a given point in time. In the MANUFAKTUR we can create 'quantum' spaces or parallel universes, in which the same material can simultaneously be in different places and different contexts, and encountering different 'experiences'. Since these are multiple references and views onto the same object, they do not give rise to copies and inconsistent versions (though for opening them, their behaviour is dependent on the file locking and sharing implementations of their native applications).

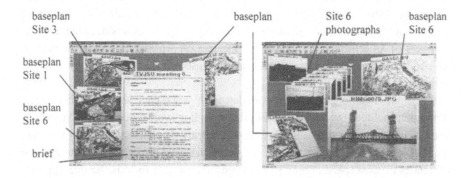

Figure 3. 'Quantum' workspaces: Chris (left) and Dave (right).

Figure 3, developing the same scenario, shows a pair of workspaces with partly overlapping materials. The workspace on the left is being used by Chris to develop the overall strategy for the development of the three urgent sites. It contains the brief, the overall baseplan, and the baseplans for sites 3, 1 and 6. The workspace on the right is being used by Dave, who is working on the detail of site

6. It also contains the overall baseplan, so that he can retain the context, and the baseplan for site 6; hence these two objects are simultaneously present in both workspaces. Dave has a range of other relevant material, including a set of photographs which he has got the system to cascade in date-time order, because that also corresponds to the route he took to explore the site. If Dave moves baseplan 6 in his workspace it will not move in Chris's workspace; but if Dave makes a visible change to baseplan 6, this will also be visible to Chris, and helps him to maintain a 'watching brief' on progress. Of course, individuals can themselves also have multiple workspaces that use the same materials in different ways – Chris, for example, might have an 'administration' workspace and a 'strategy' workspace, both of which contain the overall baseplan. Here, then, we see a particular spatial mechanism – the capacity of an object to inhabit parallel spaces – used explicitly as a mechanism for accountability: changes made to an object in one workspace can be visible in another. We will see this tactic extended much further later on.

'Wormhole' and recursive spaces

Up to now we have only considered individual objects placed in individual workspaces. Evidently, however, it will often be useful to deal with collections of objects together. Initially, we provided for the collection of objects into groups, and for groups to enter into hierarchical relationships. Our approach now is somewhat different. The only spatial entity that we use is the *workspace*, which comprises, in essence, the set of three-dimensional spatial relationships that obtain between a workspace object and a set of documents/materials objects that are its members. A workspace can contain an arbitrary number of objects in arbitrary spatial locations and, as we have seen, objects may simultaneously be members of an arbitrary number of workspaces. A workspace can be opened or closed – when it is closed its contents are collapsed so that only a proxy object is visible (see Figure 4).

Workspaces can contain other workspaces. A workspace shows all the objects of an open included workspace within the including workspace. Workspaces may contain other workspaces at any place, in arbitrary directions and to an arbitrary depth of levels. This is without any constraint via their proxy objects, but circular references to workspace contents are caught: the system forbids the opening of a proxy that would result in a circular reference (Büscher et al., 2000b). Workspaces are in principle unbounded (except for specialised workspaces such as boxes and billboards) and do not monopolise space within their extent, and so can interpenetrate. Hence a workspace does not open in a 'window' or a demarcated space in another workspace; its objects can be mingled freely with the objects and workspaces that are already there. This is, therefore, another instance of how digital spaces can usefully extend or breach the constraints that apply to physical workspaces. Here, space is no longer unitary, but 'lumps' can be torn out and inserted in other places, the space can be 'folded', and 'wormholes' can be opened from one space onto others.

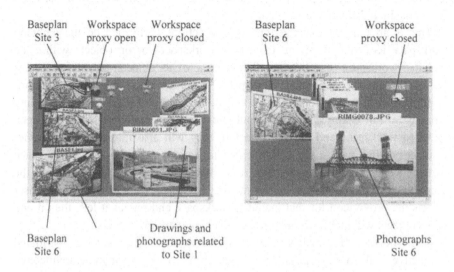

Figure 4. Folded and tunnelled spaces: Chris (left) and Dave (right).

Figure 4 again shows a pair of workspaces. In Chris's workspace on the left, he has created a new workspace, "Sites", which contains the baseplans for the three urgent sites, 1, 3 and 6. He has given it a colour, deep blue, which shows on the workspace icon and on the borders of the objects that are its members. He has placed the overall baseplan and the brief in an "Administration" workspace which is closed, showing only its proxy icon, and pushed to the background. He also has present some Site 1 materials that he is working on. In Dave's workspace on the right, he has created a workspace for his detailed work on Site 6, which he is now working in, showing yellow borders on its materials. He will need, from time to time, to relate his work to what is happening on the other urgent sites, so he has also imported Chris's "Sites" workspace, but it is currently closed.

The potential complexities of these extended and 'breached' spaces call for extended means both for making them intelligible and for interacting with them effectively. We have already seen a simple example of this in the identifying colour that can be given to a workspace and to the borders of its objects. Users can act on a workspace and all its contents as a collectivity in other ways, for example, by moving or rotating it, by giving it a default location, and by returning it and all its contents to their default position from a single right-click selection. A key way in which these issues are addressed in the MANUFAKTUR is through the

152

distinction between a workspace object, represented by the lower half of a workspace icon, and a workspace proxy object, represented by the upper half of a workspace icon. If a workspace is inserted in an including workspace, then one can think of the workspace object as representing the included workspace itself, and one can think of the proxy object as the 'hook' in the including workspace on which the included workspace 'hangs'.

This is an important distinction because actions performed on the included workspace icon (e.g. re-sizing the whole workspace) or on objects within the included workspace (e.g. bringing forward one of its objects) are performed for all of the instances of that workspace wherever else they occur. Actions performed on the proxy object, by contrast, are only performed in the including workspace. For example, if a user multiple-selects all of the objects in an open included workspace and moves them left, they will also move left in all other instances of that workspace. This means that actions carried out in a workspace owned by someone else remain accountable in a way that mirrors the accountability of actions carried out in shared physical workspaces. But if a user selects the proxy icon for that included workspace and moves it left, then it and all its objects will move left only in the including workspace.

The MANUFAKTUR makes sharing of workspaces and real-time distributed interactive collaboration possible through its network distribution architecture (Büscher et al. 2000a). Geometry and textures of 3-D objects are stored in one or more shared relational database servers. Collaborating MANUFAKTUR clients interact via a collaboration server that is used to distribute messages about object updates among session participants.

Shared awareness

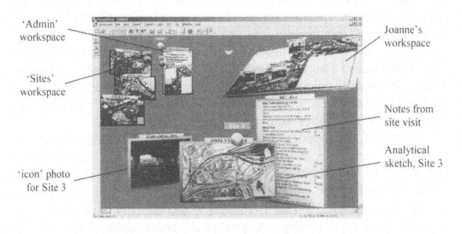

Figure 5. Networked spaces.

Figures 5 and 6 take up some of the issues concerning the complexities of extended and breached spaces, means for making them intelligible, and means for interacting with them effectively, through pursuing our scenario with some slightly more complex workspaces. John and Peter, both junior landscape architects, share responsibility for site 3. In Figure 5, John collects a workspace from Chris, which itself contains two open workspaces: the "Sites" workspace with the baseplans for the three urgent sites (deep blue borders), and the "Admin" workspace with the overall baseplan and the brief. He also collects one workspace from within Joanne's workspace (cf Figure 2) which contains the overall baseplan of the whole river corridor (again), but which Joanne has used as a setting on which to place characteristic photographs. His own working materials include the 'icon' photograph for site 3 – a picture of a motorway bridge that obstructs views from an adjacent public footpath, which is also marked by a red arrow on the analytical sketch on the base plan of site 3 – and some notes from a recent site visit.

Peter's workspace proxy closed, but 'oscillating' to show that there is activity in this workspace

Joanne's workspace

Open workspace with a sketch and inspirational photographs for Site 3

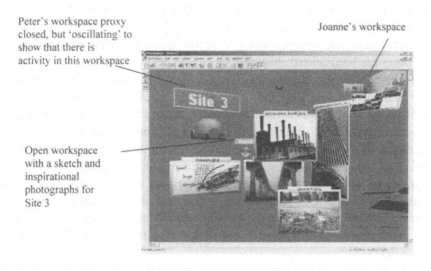

Figure 6. Communicating spaces.

In Figure 6, Peter takes a different approach, but relates it to the overall strategy by including the whole of Joanne's workspace (cf Figure 2) in his own workspace, set well in the background. Like John, Peter is concerned with the experience of travelling through site 3. But unlike John, who concentrates on pedestrian access in the surrounding area, Peter noticed the speed at which most vehicles move along the approach roads to the main city on the river. Pictures of landmark features that are at their best when perceived at speed begin to populate his workspace. Peter and John need to coordinate their work on site 3 so Peter has included the whole of John's "Site 3" workspace in his own. However, Peter would find it too distracting to have it open. The workspace is closed, but nevertheless communicates – as explained below – when John, who is also working on other projects, has a flurry of activity on site 3.

We are currently experimenting with such awareness mechanisms, to the extent that we have found it necessary to supplement the collaboration server with an 'awareness server' to cover these functions. When workspaces are open, awareness is, among other means, provided through the visibility of the work that people are doing on objects within them. When workspaces are closed and only the proxy is visible, some awareness is provided by the awareness server through the proxy. In the current implementation, when objects within a closed workspace are manipulated, the proxy is animated and 'oscillates' a bit around its own centre: the more activity the more oscillation. This is a quite subtle and unobtrusive way of indicating activity here and now, but it does not help to signify whether there has been activity since the user last paid attention to the proxy, e.g. during a coffee break. At the moment, this is afforded through a simple colour scheme for the titles of the workspaces (displayed above the proxy). The normal way of displaying the title is yellow on a blue background. If activity occurs within a closed workspace, the colour of the title becomes orange, until the workspace is opened again. A red title indicates that the workspace under the proxy has been deleted altogether.

If these awareness mechanisms are successful they could easily be extended. For example, the way that the proxy moves (instead of just oscillating) may indicate the sort of activity, and the colour scheme may be elaborated, e.g. by providing an almost continuous colour-change from yellow to deep orange according to the amount of activity that has taken place. These are methods of trying to get objects to display affordances in digital spaces that have no equivalents in physical workspaces. In this respect they are attempting to take over in some regards the mechanisms of accountability that apply when people occupy physical workspaces. Another way of thinking of an affordance in these circumstances, perhaps, is as an accountability practice for actants (Latour, 1996; Law, 1992).

The ongoing manipulation of working materials within the MANUFAKTUR allows people to be, effectively, in several places at once. Or, to put it in other words, it creates a window or 'wormhole' onto activities elsewhere. This may be within the space of the studio, where Peter and John, for example concentrate on work on their own screens. Whereas work with physical materials makes general allowance for peripheral participation, computer screens generally do not. A wormhole onto someone else's workspace may alleviate this privatisation of work on the screen. But a wormhole can be cut to engage with the work of a colleague located at home, on site, or at a client's office. Not unlike the way in which the MANUFAKTUR extends a person's reach (giving them 'long arms'), it also augments their vision. Remote people, places, and materials become ready-to-hand, and accountable parts of an expanded ecological intelligibility. Of course, these possibilities raise serious issues of surveillance, security, and control. At present, we rely in part upon the existing mechanisms for file permissions, and in part upon the emergence of new kinds of conventions among relatively small groups of design professionals who already share their work environments. Moreover, 'real' mutual intelligibility in physical spaces relies on the reciprocity of perspective of co-present actors. This is not easily transposed into any collaborative environment.

Parallel representations

We have shown how the MANUFAKTUR can create extended and 'breached' non-uniform digital spaces with 'quantum', folded and 'wormhole' properties, which offer powerful functionality. In some respects these strange spaces are surprisingly intelligible for users and are easily navigated by them. In other respects, however, they can be confusing. For example, one might easily lose track of who else is also using a 'popular' workspace. It will usually be preferable to try to cope with such issues with awareness mechanisms that are experienced as 'inside' the shared MANUFAKTUR environment. Sometimes, however, it may be helpful to provide parallel mechanisms for overview and navigation.

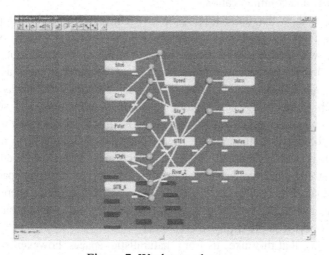

Figure 7. Workspace browser.

Figure 7 reflects the structure of the shared work environment we have outlined above. It shows the three-dimensional workspace browser provided by the MANUFAKTUR (itself, in fact, a specialised workspace), which provides an overview of workspaces and relations between workspaces. It shows that a workspace can have multiple children (e.g. Joanne's River_2 workspace has 'Notes' and 'Ideas' as sub-workspaces), and can also have multiple parents (e.g. Site_3 is part of Peter's workspace and of John's workspace). This nonhierarchical structure is the backbone of our 'tunnels', 'wormholes' and 'quantum' spaces. Workspaces can be opened from any point in the workspace browser. There is an equivalent object browser for objects within a workspace, providing a different kind of comprehensive listing, and making it possible to find, retrieve or go to objects that are 'lost in space'.

Conclusions and future developments

We started from the 'naïve' premise that the more digital workspaces resemble physical workspaces, the more users will be able to 'inhabit' them with ease. On examination we found, of course, that our capacity to mimic physical workspaces is still inadequate; but also that physical workspaces have constraints that digital workspaces can helpfully breach. This leads to the problem of deciding what kinds of digital workspaces to try to 'engineer'. This is not a problem that can be addressed purely in the abstract, and we described how our work with design professionals has underpinned the development. We claim that it is crucial to approach the problem in terms of the sociality of workspace use, here considered under the three aspects of readiness-to-hand, intelligibility and organisation, and accountability and communication.

We tried to show that these aspects can be usefully addressed in different ways and for different purposes: sometimes with a 'minimal' form of digital workspace, which users need never move beyond if they do not wish to; sometimes by reintroducing emulated physical properties such as gravity, stickiness, momentum and friction; sometimes through new behaviours for objects such as returning to a default position, or animation; and sometimes through extended properties that can be given to digital spaces, such as parallel universes, folding and tunnelling. These, and especially the last, mean that simultaneously and in productive ways, objects can occupy different spaces, spaces can occupy different spaces, and people can occupy different spaces. They also mean that users may experience the system as 'beyond being there' (Hollan & Stornetta, 1992), i.e. that the additional functionality may tempt them to use it even when working in proximity to each other.

The distance that this takes us from 'naturalistic' spaces, however, means that appropriate ways of inhabiting them need also, in part, to be 'engineered'. These, too, have emerged through participatory design around social use. They can be divided, approximately, into, (1) metaphorical extensions of familiar uses of space; (2) affordances as metaphors designed for and through new appearances and behaviours of objects (behaviours that indicate 'activity', for example); (3) parallel representations such as workspace browser nets; and (4) menu or shortcut selectable commands. One of the aims of the ongoing development is to find useful ways of 'migrating' functions upwards through this list, making the space itself more intuitively 'ready-to-hand' (cf Shipman & Marshall, 1999). The power that design professionals gain from the disposition of materials in three-dimensional space means that this can usefully be retained as the foundational metaphor for the digital workspace, rather than, for example, seeking to decompose it into myriad 'spatial functionalities' each serviced with a specific tool. But the metaphor must also be critically decomposed to explore the points at which it breaks down and can helpfully be reconstituted or extended.

Our future work around these themes will continue to be anchored in the real work practices of design professionals. It will focus on building better bridges between digital and physical work environments, with three key aspects. Augmenting the design *environment* is about new means – including large scale and stereographic projection and new interaction devices – for designers to inhabit and interact with mixed physical and digital workspaces, collaborating in both co-located and distributed modes. Augmenting *objects* is about making bi-directional connections between physical objects and their digital counterparts, their contexts of use, and their users. Spatial computing *in the field* is about making digital and mixed environments highly portable, so that they can take advantage of 'knowing' their position when users wish to tailor these parts of their work environment according to exactly where they are, whom they are with, and the capacities of the devices that are available to them.

Acknowledgments

Funding for this research has been provided by EU FP4 Open LTR project DESARTE (31870), and by the Danish Research Council's Center for Multimedia (project 9600869). We are very grateful to our colleagues and partners in the DESARTE project for many contributions to the ideas in this paper. Funding for our current and future work is provided by the EU FP5 IST FET 'Disappearing Computer' Programme project WorkSPACE (IST-2000-25290).

References

Benedikt, M. (1992): *Cyberspace*, Cambridge, MA: MIT Press.

Benford, S., et al. (1997). 'Informing the Design of Collaborative Environments', in *Proc. GROUP'97 (Phoenix, Arizona, Nov.16-19)*, ACM Press, New York, pp. 71-79.

Büscher, M., Christensen, M., Grønbæk, K., Krogh, P., Mogensen, P., Shapiro, D and Ørbæk, P. (2000a): 'Collaborative Augmented Reality Environments: Integrating VR, Working Materials, and Distributed Work Spaces', in *Proc. Conf. on Collaborative Virtual Environments (CVE 2000), San Francisco, 9-12 September*, ACM Press, New York.

Büscher, M., Christensen, M., Mogensen, P., Ørbæk, P. and Shapiro, D. (2000b): 'Creativity, Complexity and Precision: Information Visualisation for (Landscape) Architecture', in *Proc. Conf. on Information Visualisation (InfoVis 2000), Salt Lake City*, IEEE Press.

Büscher, M., Gill, S., Mogensen, P. and Shapiro, D. (2001): 'Landscapes of Practice', *Computer-Supported Cooperative Work: The Journal of Collaborative Computing*, Vol. 10, No 1, pp. 1-28.

Büscher, M., Mogensen, P., Shapiro, D. and Wagner, I. (1999): 'The Manufaktur: Supporting Work Practice in (Landscape) Architecture', in *Proc. Sixth European Conference on Computer Supported Cooperative Work (ECSCW'99), Copenhagen*, Kluwer Academic Press, Dordrecht, NL.

Dourish, P., Edwards, K., LaMarca, A. and Salisbury. M. (1999): 'Presto: An Experimental Architecture for Fluid Interactive Document Spaces', *ACM Transactions on Computer-Human Interaction*, Vo. 6 No 2, pp. 133-161.

Garfinkel, H. (1967): *Studies in Ethnomethodology*, Polity Press, Cambridge.

Gaver, W. (1991): 'Technology Affordances', in *Proc. Conf. on Human Factors and Computing Systems (CHI 91), New Orleans, 27 April-2 May*, ACM Press, New York, pp. 79- 84.

Heath, C.C. and Hindmarsh, J. (2000): 'Configuring action in objects: From mutual space to media space', *Selected Papers I*, Kings College, London: Work, Interaction and Technology Research Group.

Heath, C.C. and Luff, P. (1992): 'Collaboration and control: crisis management and multimedia technology in London Underground Line Control Rooms', *Computer-Supported Cooperative Work: The Journal of Collaborative Computing*, Vol. 1, pp. 69-94.

Heidegger, M. (1988): *Being and Time*, Basil Blackwell, Oxford.

Hollan, J. and Stornetta, S. (1992): 'Beyond Being There', in *Proc. Conf. on Human Factors and Computing Systems (CHI 92), Monterey, 3-7 May*, ACM Press, New York, pp. 119-125.

Latour, B. (1996): 'On Interobjectivity', *Mind, Culture and Activity*, Vol. 3, No 4, pp. 228-245.

Law, J. (1992): 'Notes on the Theory of Actor-Network: ordering, strategy, and heterogeneity', *Systems Practice*, Vol. 5, No 4, pp. 379-393.

Lynch, M. (1993): *Scientific practice and ordinary action*, CUP, Cambridge, UK.

Mogensen, P. (1994): *Challenging Practice: an Approach to Cooperative Analysis*, Ph.D thesis, Aarhus University, Daimi PB-465.

Shipman, F. and Marshall, C. (1999): 'Formality Considered Harmful: Experiences, emerging themes, and directions on the use of formal representations in interactive systems', *Computer-Supported Cooperative Work: The Journal of Collaborative Computing*, Vol. 8, No 4, pp. 333-352.

Smith, R.B. (1987): 'Experiences with the alternate reality kit: an example of the tension between literalism and magic', in *Proc. Conf. on Human Factors and Computing Systems (CHI 87), Toronto, April 5-9*. ACM Press, New York.

Winograd, T. and Flores, F. (1986): *Understanding Computers and Cognition: A New Foundation for Design*, Ablex Publishing, Norwood, NJ.

W. Prinz, M. Jarke, Y. Rogers, K. Schmidt, and V. Wulf (eds.), *Proceedings of the Seventh European Conference on Computer-Supported Cooperative Work, 16-20 September 2001, Bonn, Germany*, pp. 159-178.
© 2001 Kluwer Academic Publishers. Printed in the Netherlands.

Collaboratively Improvising Magic:
An Approach to Managing Participation in an On-Line Drama

Adam Drozd[1], John Bowers[2], Steve Benford[1],
Chris Greenhalgh[1], Mike Fraser[1]
The Mixed Reality Laboratory, The University of Nottingham, UK
Royal Institute of Technology, Stockholm, Sweden
asd@cs.nott.ac.uk, bowers@nada.kth.se, sdb@cs.nott.ac.uk, cmg@cs.nott.ac.uk, mcf@cs.nott.ac.uk

Abstract. We describe how a behind-the-scenes production crew managed participation in an on-line improvised dramatic performance in a shared virtual world that was broadcast to viewers. We introduce the approach of collaboratively improvising magic, where participants indirectly request interactions with objects through extended incantations, rather than manipulating them directly. Invisible stage-hands follow these participants around the world, monitoring their activities and granting requests when appropriate. We describe how this was realised in *Avatar Farm*, a two hour long improvised drama that involved four members of the public, seven actors and an extensive production crew. We discuss the provision of technical support within the MASSIVE-3 system to realise our approach. Empirical analysis of interaction in *Avatar Farm* illustrates some key issues. We see how participants weave accounts of technical problems into the narrative; how actors vary the pacing of the narrative to co-ordinate the timing of a local scene in relation to parallel scenes that are happening elsewhere; amongst other matters. We conclude with some general lessons from our approach for CSCW.

Introduction

In *Computers as Theatre*, Brenda Laurel proposed an approach to interaction where computers are considered as a form of theatre rather than as tools, and where the focus of design is on engaging users with content rather than with technology (Laurel, 1992). She suggested that various behind-the-scenes activities are required to maintain engagement and to orchestrate users' experiences.

Nearly ten years later, CSCW technologies such as collaborative virtual environments (CVEs) are being used increasingly for on-line games, performances, role-playing and other leisure and entertainment applications (Dodsworth, 1997). These applications take the idea of computers as theatre quite literally and so have to deal head-on with the challenge of managing participation from behind-the-scenes. What activities are required to ensure the smooth running of an event, and how can participation be guided and shaped, especially in time-critical situations such as performances or TV shows?

One approach, directly derived from traditional theatre and television, is to employ a production crew to monitor events and to intervene where necessary. An example can be seen in *Out of this World*, an experimental inhabited television show in which members of the public and professional actors staged a gameshow in a CVE that was broadcast to a viewing audience (Benford et al., 1999). A member of the production crew used dedicated management software to monitor the show and to move participants to key positions at particular times so as to ensure that the show followed a tightly defined schedule. In contrast, in a recent on-line performance called *Desert Rain*, the production-crew and performers employed more subtle techniques to gently steer individual participants and embed advice and instructions within the performance without fracturing their engagement (Koleva et al., 2001).

This paper describes the experience of managing participation within a recent experimental inhabited television show called *Avatar Farm* in which four players and seven actors improvised a two hour long drama spanning four virtual worlds. The non-linear, branching narrative structure of *Avatar Farm* posed significant challenges for managing participation. We focus on how the players, actors and a behind-the-scenes production crew collaborated to improvise complex interactions with objects, wrapped up in the metaphor of magic. In essence, the players and actors would use objects to invoke magical effects within the world and the production crew, including a team of invisible stage-hands, would try to respond appropriately. Our paper motivates this approach and describes the organisation of the production crew and the design of new management software to support them. We follow this with an account of how *Avatar Farm* was practically managed including an examination of how magic was collaboratively improvised in one scene presented in detail. We close by highlighting issues pertinent to the management of similar events and to CSCW at large.

An Introduction to *Avatar Farm*

While *Out of this World* had demonstrated the potential of dedicated software to support the management of a relatively fast-pace on-line event, it had also been roundly criticised for a lack of empathy for and detail in its characters and adopting a clichéd format from conventional television. Our goal for *Avatar Farm* was therefore to engage members of the public in a more richly dramatic experience and also to explore the potential of CVEs to support new narrative forms. Our overall approach involved three steps:

1. We began by establishing a small on-line virtual community called *Ages of Avatar* alongside Sky Television's [.tv] channel using Microsoft's VWorlds dial-up CVE platform (Craven et al., 2000). This provided us with a pool of established characters and worlds from which to draw inspriation and material, as well as a group of committed players who were familiar with one another and who shared a common history.

2. We recreated new versions of the virtual worlds, selected avatars and objects from the *Ages of Avatar* within the MASSIVE-3 CVE platform running on a dedicated Local Area Network at Nottingham. This enabled us to take advantage of MASSIVE's real-time audio capabilities, desktop and immersive interfaces, and also new facilities for managing events in virtual worlds and post-producing 3D recordings of these events.

3. We selected four key members of the *Ages of Avatar* community to be players in *Avatar Farm*. These persons were notable for their liveliness and commitment in participation in the on-line community. They joined us in a purpose built inhabited television studio in Nottingham for two days in June 2000 where they collaborated with seven professional actors, a story writer and a production crew, to improvise a drama loosely based around their familiar characters and worlds. We chose actors who were experienced in engaging members of the public in more conventional role play situations and improvised theatre.

The result of these activities was *Avatar Farm*, a two-hour long improvised drama structured as four 25 to 40 minute long 'chapters', involving 15 virtual characters, played by 11 people that was both web-cast live and also recorded. *Avatar Farm* was a fable involving gods, tricksters and innocents abroad. The four players from the *Ages of Avatar* were reawakened in the more or less familiar virtual worlds to find them repossessed by the feuding gods Virbius, Egeria and Attis and their various sidekicks. The players were initially enslaved and used as pawns in the gods' struggles. However, by observing closely they came to learn the history of the feud as well as the secrets of magic within the worlds, and so gained the power to free themselves, resolve the feud and restore harmony to the worlds.

In chapter one, the four players were reawakened and were then immediatelly separated and taken to different worlds to meet the gods for the first time. Chapter two involved the players learning how to gain special powers such as flying, changing appearance and becoming invisible. They also learned how to trigger "time-rifts" – ghostlike playbacks of scenes from the past (part of a backstory that had been recorded by the actors on previous days). In chapter three, the players' loyalties to one another were tested as part of a series of cruel games to the point where they rebelled. Further time-rifts revealed more of the history of the feud. Finally, in chapter four the players, rose up to overthrow the villains of the piece.

From the point of view of this paper, a key characteristic of this drama was its complex and non-linear, branching narrative structure. The core of the story was based upon the four players' experiences. For much of the time they were separated and involved in parallel scenes, often taking place in different worlds. As each followed their own thread through the story, their paths would cross at various points and occasionally they would all meet for a pivotal scene before splitting up again. Even when not directly involved with the four players, the actor-controlled characters remained active, carrying out their normal background activities. Replaying pre-recorded scenes within the live worlds gave the story a relatively complex temporal structure. Finally, the use of props and other objects in the worlds to achieve various special effects was central to the story and involved the participants in relatively complex sequences of utterances and gestures as we shall see.

Managing Participation in *Avatar Farm*

Managing participation in *Avatar Farm* proved to be challenging for several reasons.

- The non-linear and distributed nature of the drama required the crew to monitor and manage concurrent scenes.
- There was greater scope for improvisation and automony by the players than there was with the tightly-scripted gameshow format of *Out of this World*.
- A subtle approach was required so as not to break the player's engagement with events and to ensure that their actions appeared to be a natural part of the story at all times (in contrast to *Out of this World* where relatively obstrusive interventions such as suddenly moving all players to a new location seemed to be broadly acceptable within the context of a television gameshow).

Given these challenges, we chose an approach to managing *Avatar Farm* that combined three key elements.

1. We adopted the approach of 'improvising magic'. Rather than directly manipulating objects to achieve an effect, participants would have to indirectly request the effect by gathering key objects, moving, gesturing and speaking aloud. Invisible stage-hands would observe these incantations and would invoke the desired effect on the player's behalf. These helpers could also grant the players new special capabilities. This collaboration between the participants and stage-hands was then wrapped up in the metaphor of magic.

2. We distributed the responsibilities for management among a behind-the-scenes crew and provided them with various physical and on-line facilities for monitoring *Avatar Farm* and for communicating with one another.

3. We extended MASSIVE-3 with new interfaces to allow crew members to intervene in events, directly manipulating objects and players as well as granting and revoking the capablities for the players to do this themselves.

The following sections focus on each of these three elements in detail.

Granting Capabilities and Improvising Magic

At the start of *Avatar Farm*, the players were able to perform only a few basic actions with their avatars. These were: moving around on the ground plane; talking so that they could be heard by other nearby avatars; picking up an object, waving it about and putting it down; carrying an object while moving; and replaying one of ten pre-recorded gestures. At times, the story required the ability to limit even these basic actions; for example, particular players might occasionally be frozen to the spot or disallowed from picking up certain objects.

Central to the story was the way in which different players subsequently gained additional capabilities or learned how to invoke various magical effects. These included: flying up to a fixed height; becoming invisible; changing appearance between a number of pre-determined avatars; moving through the portals that linked the four worlds together; snooping on other players' distant conversations; becoming immune to the powers of particular gods; and triggering a time-rift (the replay of a pre-recorded scene within a live world). In terms of the story, these capabilities and magical effects might be granted by other characters, especially the gods, or might arise from the correct use of particular objects. Examples of the latter include:

- feeding a purple tuft to the world serpent by depositing it on a feeding hole and then making the correct incantation could trigger a time-rift;
- licking a camouflage lizard could confer the ability to change apearance;
- eating a blue mushroom would render one temporarily impervious to the powers of the god Virbius.

One approach to supporting these capabilities and effects would have been to program them directly as part of the *Avatar Farm* application software as if it were an interactive computer game. A player directly manipulating an object (e.g., selecting it) would, through this, invoke its effect. However, we were concerned make the structure of *Avatar Farm* as open as possible to improvisation and a pre-programmed approach seemed did not seem flexible enough in this context.

A key element of improvisation in the theatre and in other arts is the possibility of taking advantage of interesting, yet unforeseen, interactions between participants. To allow flexibility for this, we wanted to be able to choose at any moment whether it would be appropriate to grant an effect and if so, exactly how and when it should be realised. In this way, the timing of an effect could be controlled to fit in with ongoing interaction between participants. Indeed, whether an effect is granted at all could also become a dramatic element. These are outcomes which would be impossible or excessively complex to program in advance. Some effects would also require coordinating multiple players. For example, a time-rift would be a major moment in the story and it would make sense to gather several players together to witness it. However, this would involve finding these players (who might be engaged in activities elsewhere) and persuding them to move to the location of the time-rift. It would be difficult to predict how long this might take. Finally, we were well aware of the possibility that the coordination of the narrative might break down – especially for such a multi-threaded, branching structure as *Avatar Farm*. We needed an approach which would enable us to repair and recover from breakdowns. Pre-programming object-behaviours might have hindered this if, for example, a set of behaviours were to execute autonomously and erroneously.

In the light of considerations, we adopted an alternative strategy – improvising object-interactions. In this case a number of crew members, 'stage-hands', were also present but invisible within the worlds. These had the ability to manipulate objects and avatars and to directly trigger special effects such as replaying pre-recoded scenes; moving or constraining players and objects; making players and objects appear, disappear and change apearance; and granting and revoking permissions to pick up particular objects and move through portals. The invisible stage-hands followed the players around, monitoring their activities and triggering effects in response. Improvising a single logical action from the point of view of the players would often involve the stage-hand in a quite complex sequence of more atomic actions. For example, actions such as eating a mushroom or feeding a tuft had to be composed out of more basic actions such as moving objects and making them invisible. Particularly complex sequences involving more than one player would require several stage-hands to coordinate their behind-the-scenes manipulations.

The players' interactions with objects were therefore indirect and collaborative; they had to request that something happen and a stage-hand then had to respond. However, this collaboration was somewhat unconventional as the stage-hand was invisible and the player was not meant to know that they were present.

Another key characteristic of this approach is that interaction was slowed down. It could take from a few seconds to several minutes for one or more stage-hands to spot that an action was being requested, to decide whether to respond and to make the response happen. We therefore decided to dress up the process of improvising interactions in various extended incantations. We would require the players to act out elaborate rituals involving gathering objects and placing them in key locations and making extended sequences of movements, gestures and utterances in order to invoke an effect. Even where the players gained new abilities such as flying at will, these would be granted in a magical way – as a gift bestowed from the gods or as a result of an extended incantation. We anticipated that this approach would result in two key benefits.

1. The result and timing of any request could be left open – everyone knows that magic is dangerous, unpredictable in its timing and liable to go wrong if the magician makes only the slightest mistake. We hoped that the mataphor of magic would enable the players to accept and work around delays and failures.

2. Extended sequences of actions would be more visible, predictable, dramatic and therefore interesting to watch. Helpers would have sufficient time to spot that a request was being made, to marshall the necessary resources and to plan their response. The camera crew creating the broadcast from the virtual world would similarly be able to predict in advance when and where interesting action was likely to happen. In particular, it would be clear a long time in advance that an interaction was building and that the crew would be required to act in the future. Finally, viewers would hopefully find the interaction easier to follow and more interesting to watch.

The following sections describe the organisation of people and technology that supported this approach of collaboratively improvising magic within *Avatar Farm*.

Organisation of the Production Crew

There were two categories of people involved in *Avatar Farm*. The cast (four players and seven actors) and a behind-the-scenes production crew as follows:

Story director – assumed overall responsibility for directing events within the world. This involved monitoring the progress of the event as a whole, deciding on the course of the plot, and instructing actors and crew members accordingly.

Director's assistant – supported the story director and assumed particular reponsibility for coaching the actors.

Software manager – assumed overall charge of MASSIVE-3.

Stage-hands – the four invisible helpers who were charged with the task of improvising interactions as decribed above. In general, each was assigned to follow a different player, although the story director might ocasionally assign them other specific duties. One was also responsible for cueing and replaying the pre-recorded time-shifts.

World-manager – a further invisible helper specifically responsible for granting and revoking access controls on portals, thereby controlling which characters could move into which worlds at which times. They were also responsible for access control on the ability to pick up some objects.

Actor helpers – two crew members who physically supported the two actors who were using immersive VR interfaces, for example, helping to put on and take off the equipment and also holding their microphones.

Player helpers – two crew members to support the players.

Virtual camera operators – were responsible for capturing different views of the action in the virtual worlds using purpose built virtual camera interfaces, each of which could track four different camera views at a time.

Camera director – responsible for selecting which camera view would be web-cast live at any moment in time.

Web-cast team – a team of two people who maintained and monitored the web-cast software and content.

Floor manager – responsible for coordinating activities and communication within the physical inhabited TV studio.

These people were located in a shared studio space as shown in Figure 1. Several freatures of this arrangement are relevant to this paper. First, the only partitions in the space were black curtains. As a result, the players could not see the behind-the-scenes production areas when the world was live, but there was some potential for audio overspill, which also meant that the production crew had to be careful not to talk loudly or make other noises. Second, the space was designed to encourage mutual awareness among key members of the crew. In particular, the story director, their assistant, world manager, helper responsible for temporal links and camera crew were arranged facing across a shared table so that they could peripherally monitor each other's affairs. A large projected view of the actual broadcast was also visible to the camera crew and many of the other crew-members.

(a)

(b)

(c)

Figure 1: views from the studio:
(a) the story director (foreground) with the row of actors and two helpers and curtain separating the players beyond (background)
(b) looking over a players shoulder (foreground) with the curtain open towards the actors (midground) with the remaining crew in the background
(c) the central table with helper and world manager (foreground), story director, assistant and camera crew (background)

There were also opportunities for physical communication within this set-up and in particular, the floor manager and various actor and player helpers could move freely around the space in order to monitor events and pass messages.

In addition to the physical design of the studio space, the MASSIVE-3 software was also configured to allow different roles to oversee events and to communicate. The story director and assistant were invisibly present within the worlds and they and the stage-hands, world-manger, camera operators, camera director and software manager could monitor the conversation between the actors and the players in the part of the world were they were currently located. A separate audio talk-back system allowed the story director to speak directly to any individual stage-hand, actor or the world manager in order to pass out instructions.

In other words, there were many opportunities, both in terms of on-line communication and the design of the physical studio space for the various crew members, especialy the story director, helper and actors to monitor events within the world and to communicate with one another in order to support the process of improvising magic within *Avatar Farm*.

The Stage-Hand and World-Manager Interfaces

We now focus on the design of the stage-hand and world-manager interfaces in more detail as these were central to the process of improvising magic. The stage-hand interface consisted of two windows, one containing controls for manipulating entities (objects or avatars) as shown in Figure 2 and a second offering a view of the world.

A stage-hand would select an entity to be managed from the list in the lower part of the interface. Upon selection their view of the world would be moved to centre on this entity. The stage-hand could zoom and rotate this viewpoint while focused on this entity using the camera controls at the bottom right of the control panel. The virtual camera would lock onto and track the entity as it moved. Once selected, the entity could be managed.

The constraint control manoeuvred the entity around the world with the speed of movement being goverened by a slider on the control panel. Depending on the type of entity selected, different properties could then be altered using the controls at the top-right. If the entity was an object, the stage-hand could select whether it was visible or not. For an avatar they could:
- set whether it was visible or invisible;
- select its appearance from a among a pre-defined selection of geometries;
- alter the scale factor of its geometry (making it grow and shrink);
- grant or revoke its ability to fly, control its own visibility and appearance.

The world manager interface was similarly split into two parts. The world manger could select a world to view and could position their viewpoint either relative to the origin of the world or to a specific entity (by selecting one from the given

168

list). To change the access control on either a portal or an object, they would select the portal or object from a list, select an avatar from a second list, and then set whether this avatar had access.

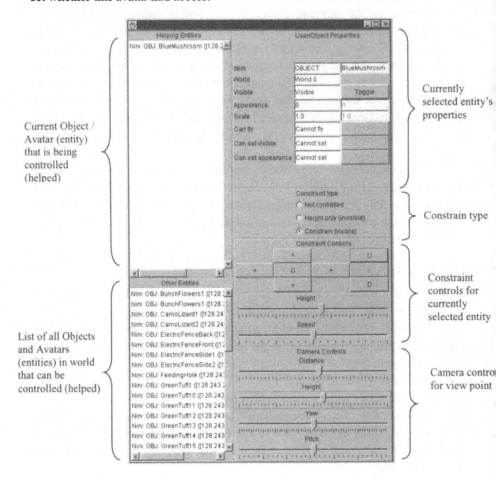

Figure 2: the stage-hand interface

In Practice: The Management of Magic

To appraise our approach to the management of participation in *Avatar Farm*, we now explore a specific example of the process of improvising magic at work. Our example is taken from chapter 4, the final chapter of *Avatar Farm*. It takes place within the child-like world called Kindergarten and involves three main characters: the player Maple, Squeaky Clean (sidekick of the arch-villain Attis and a scheming trickster) and Botchov (authoritarian butler to the chief-god

Virbius). We focus on an extended section of narrative that lasts for approximately fifteen minutes in which Squeaky persuades Maple to play a trick on Botchov, causing him to be eaten by the world-serpent. We have chosen this because it is one of the more complex sequences in the drama in terms of interactions with objects and hence behind-the-scenes-activity.

Using 3D Record and Replay to Analyse *Avatar Farm*

The following analysis of our chosen sequence has exploited a novel 3D record and replay mechanism that we have implemented within MASSIVE-3. This logs and timestamps every action within a locale (a region of a virtual world) (Greenhalgh et al., 2000), including every movement, object interaction, and speech of every avatar within that locale. A recorded log file can then be linked back into a live locale at a later time using a "temporal link" so that when it is replayed the recorded action appears to be recreated within the live world and mixed with the live action. Live participants can then fly around the recording, viewing it from any angle, listening to the audio or following any character.

To support our analysis, we have edited the 3D recordings of *Avatar Farm* so that the invisible stage-hands are now made visible in the virtual world so that we can see their actions alongside those of the players and actors. We could repeatedly view and hear the process of improvising magic in the virtual world from any angle. We also have access to a parallel video recording of the production crew in the physical studio space during this sequence. The images of the virtual world that are included in this paper were generated by replaying the 3D recordings, positioning a live-virtual camera within them and then using a screen-capture tool. They therefore show snapshots of the action as it happened.

How Maple and Squeaky Clean Tricked Botchov

The story director originally planned our chosen scenes to unfold as follows. The player Maple, aided by Squeaky, would feed a purple-tuft to the world-serpent and perform a specific incantation in order to trigger a time-rift. This would show them both a scene from the past in which Botchov was playing with his long lost sister Octavia and discussing various family secrets, especially "the secret of the green teapot". Squeaky would then teach Maple how to change appearance by picking up and licking a camouflage lizard and performing a second incantation. Maple would then take on the guise of Octavia in order to trick Botchov. Maple, disguised as Octavia, would encounter Botchov. He would use the secret of the green teapot (that surely only Octavia could know) in order to convince Botchov that he is indeed Octavia. He would tell Botchov that he has to stand on the feeding hole if he wants to join Octavia in the land where she now dwells. He would then be eaten by the world serpent, but not before Maple and Squeaky have first revealed how he has been duped!

In fact, as the following description shows, enacting this sequence of events is not straightforward due to various unforeseen circumstances involving other threads of the narrative that are taking place elsewhere as well as various local technical and interactional difficulties. However, Maple, Squeaky and Botchov eventually do manage to successfully improvise a version of the trick on Botchov, supported by the stage-hands. The table below summarises some of the key moments in this sequence of events along with our commentary as to what is happening behind-the-scenes. Figure 3 shows various moments from this scene. Maple appears as a red humanoid figure with brown hair. Squeaky has a green body, no legs and long ears and horns. Botchov is wearing a butler's uniform. Octavia (Maple in disguise) appears as a girl with pigtails. Finally, the stage-hands appear as cameras pointing at the character that they are currently controlling (though, remember, stage-hands are rendered from the 3D recording here, they were not originally seen by participants). White rings around a character's head indicate the current volume of their speech.

Event	Commentary
Squeaky Clean briefs Maple about the trick - see Figure 3 (a).	
Maple, guided by Squeaky Clean, begins the incantation to cause a time-rift.	Initially we can see one stage-hand on Maple, but they are soon joined by a second.
	Squeaky Clean's dialogue at this point makes various explicit references to how Maple should use their computer to trigger the gestures that are required by the incantation (e.g., "press key 9").
Squeaky Clean places the tuft on the feeding hole. Maple finishes the incantation. However, no time-rift occurs.	Squeaky Clean and Maple do not know that a 3D replay cannot be triggered at this point because another one is already taking place in the world Nirvana as part of a parallel thread of the story. The *Avatar Farm* set-up does not include the resources required to replay more than one recording at a time.
Squeaky Clean: "Try the incantation once more." Squeaky Clean continues guiding Maple through the second incantation.	A third stage-hand has now become concerned with the progress of events and has attached themselves to Maple. All three can be seen in Figure 3(b). It should be noted that, in the performance itself, the stage-hands are invisible to one another as well as to Maple and Squeaky Clean.
Maple: "Has it worked?" (at the end of the second incantation)	The second incanation hasn't worked either as the parallel time-rift in Nirvana is still playing out.
Squeaky Clean: "No … there is a time distortion already in place which is breaking up the equilibrium of the world"	Squeaky Clean has now heard (probably from the story director over the talk-back system) that there is a problem triggering the replay and is providing an account of this in terms of the narrative.
Squeaky Clean now suggests that Maple use the camouflage lizard in order to turn into Octavia. He explains the necessary actions and incantations.	Squeaky is pressing on anyway. Again, his dialogue contains more references to pressing particular keys on the keyboard.
Maple grasps the camouflage lizard	At this point one of the stage-hands leaves the scene

Maple completes the relevant incantation.
Squeaky Clean: "... and you've changed into ..."

Squeaky Clean: "... Desmond! ...try again!"

Squeaky Clean: "... No ... Tock-Tock!! ..."

Squeaky Clean: "... No ... Octavia!!!. You are an incredibly powerful avatar to have gone through so many changes"
Maple: "Wow" (laughs).

Squeaky Clean now instructs Maple about using the secret of the green teapot to convince Botchov that he is indeed Octavia.

Botchov arrives. Squeaky Clean now makes himself invisible.
Maple: "I am the spirit of Octavia ..."

Squeaky Clean: (evil cackle)

Maple continues to act out the trick on Botchov. He reveals the secret of the green teapot and lures Botchov onto the feeding-hole.

Squeaky Clean explains to Maple that he needs to reveal himself as Maple

Maple: "I am Maple not Octavia"

Squeaky Clean makes himself visible (Figure 3 (f))
Botchov acts surprised.
Maple: "Bye Bye"
Squeaky Clean: "Well done Maple"
Maple: "I think I got everything in there"
Squeaky Clean now engages Maple in conversation for a couple of minutes, recapping recent events. He then asks him whether he has ever seen the maze in this world.

(see Figure 3 (c)), shortly followed by another, leaving just one stage-hand on Maple. They change him into Desmond, the wrong character (he is supposed to become Octavia).

The stage-hand now changes Maple into Tock-Tock (still the wrong character). The exclamation "try again", of course, can be heard by Maple and the stage-hand and understood as an instruction to both.

The stage-hand now changes Maple into Otavia, correctly (Figure 3 (d)).

Squeaky Clean is once again accounting for technical problems in terms that make sense to the narrative at this point

A second stage-hand attaches to Maple, followed by a third.

He needs to do this through dialogue as the replay that would have given this vital information was never seen. He also reminds Maple to talk in a high pitched voice. One of the stage-hands leaves so there are now two in attendance.

Note: As an actor, Squeaky does not need a stage-hand to do this for him.

Forgetting his instructions, Maple begins in a low voice but then switches to a higher register.

Squeaky Clean is using a stage-whisper here. Botchov and Maple will be able to hear this.

One stage-hand now moves over to be on Botchov while the other remains on Maple.

The other stage-hand now moves from Maple to Botchov (being unaware that a stage-hand is already there). There is now no stage-hand on Maple. The stage-hands move Botchov downwards so that he is halfway into the hole (Figure 3 (e)).

Squeaky Clean again uses a stage whisper. However, Maple's microphone connection has temporarily failed and it takes several such whispers before it resumes and Maple is heard to respond. Botchov acts as if he doesn't hear, but Squeaky's whispers help him to understand that there is a technical problem with Maple.

This is the cue to change appearance. One stage-hand now moves back onto Maple. He switches Maple's appearance back to being his normal self.

The stage-hand on Botchov drags him entirely down through the hole and out of sight.

Squeaky is delaying Maple at this point. The main action will soon move to the world Trade and Power. However, the portals between worlds are all closed right now because a time-shift is happening

172

Squeaky Clean: "Soon we will be going to Trade and Power"

elsewhere (a known bug in MASSIVE triggered by using a portal during a time-shift)

Squeaky Clean has received instructions from the story-director over talkback that he now needs to ge Maple to the world Trade and Power where the cast is being assembled for the final climatic scene.

(a) Squeaky Clean (left) briefs Maple (right)

(b) Maple incants with 3 stage-hands present

(c) Maple grasps the camouflage lizard

(d) Maple is changed into Octavia

(e) Botchov is lowered into the hole

(f) Squeaky Clean reveals himself

Figure 3: snapshots from the trick on Botchov

The above sequence of events shows how the cast and stage-hands struggle to overcome various unforeseen circumstances to more or less successfully improvise a version of the planned scene. Maple certainly manages to pull off a complicated trick on Botchov, albeit with extensive support from Squeaky Clean.

However, this sequence of events also sheds light onto the ways in which improvisation occurs and the relationship between the work that is taking place "on stage" and the work that is taking place "behind-the-scenes".

Making Drama out of a Crisis

Previous studies of CVEs and other CSCW technologies have observed how participants often account and compensate for technical difficulties through their talk (Bowers et al., 1996; Hindmarsh et al., 1998). In our example however, Squeaky Clean not only provides such accounts but carefully embeds them into the context of the drama. When a stage-hand struggles to find the correct new appearance for Maple we hear that this is because he is: "an incredibly powerful avatar to have gone through so many changes". Earlier, when it was not possible to replay a 3D flashback we heard that "there is a time distortion already in place which is breaking up the equilibrium of the world". Indeed, it is often possible for an actor or player to formulate their contribution in such a way that it can be heard (by another actor or player) and overheard (by a stage-hand or other production crew member) simultaneously (e.g. Squeaky Clean's instruction to "try again" above). We suggest that the approach of improvising magic provides skilled actors with plenty of room for manoeuvre when it comes to improvising such accounts and we are sceptical whether this would be so easy if interaction were more mechanical and immediate.

Indeed, we have examples of the (non-professional) players also engaging in such creative accounting for events. In a scene a few minutes after our description ends, we see Maple improvising an account for another delay in a purple tuft triggering a time-rift. Squeaky Clean observes: "The purple tufts sometimes take a long time to work" to which Maple retorts "I should imagine so especially after he [the serpent] has had a long meal". Such accounts, even or perhaps especially when ironic, allow the participants to maintain their engagement with the story while providing improvised content which an actor could further develop, all the while covering a delay while the production crew troubleshoots a problem.

Coordinating Help

We have noted in our extended example that, at various times, up to three stage-hands can be seen in the vicinity ready to help out with events. This testifies to the ability and willingness of the stage-hands to monitor unfolding events, check up on them and be ready to help. However, in the example given, we see several moments where two or more stage-hands have attached themselves to a character, even though only one is necessary to bring about a necessary effect. This suggests that there were occasional coordination problems between the stage-hands. This is confirmed by noting that, at the crucial moment in the trick on Botchov, we see the two helpers on Maple both detach and move over to Botchov, when what was required was one to change Maple back to his normal appearance as the other lowered Botchov into the hole.

This and other examples indicate that an awareness of the talk between participants and having visual access to the graphical worlds they inhabit are not enough to cue one in how to effectively deliver help as a stage-hand. One also needs to have an awareness of what other stage-hands are doing as well as be sensitive to instructions given by the story director. During the example above, there was occasional use of talkback to facilitate this. We also have examples of people physically leaving their workstations to go over and talk to stage-hands or check behind the curtain separating the players from the production crew, and so forth. In other words, our technical arrangements did not compensate for the occasional need for activity in the physical world to coordinate help. Indeed, when their responsibilities in the virtual world eased off, a number of members of the crew were willing to spontaneously serve as 'runners' if the need arose.

Delaying and Hurrying Tactics

As noted previously, the branching, non-linear structure of *Avatar Farm* posed a number of challenges to its producers. In particular, a scene that is taking place in one location might be affected by parallel scenes that are happening elsewhere. This might be for technical reasons such as in our example when the time-rift cannot be triggered and the portals between worlds cannot be used because another time-rift is already happening. It might be for dramatic reasons, such as when a major scene takes place that requires the players to gather together. For whatever reason in a non-linear narrative that involves groups of people in different scenes, local plans will often have to accommodate events elsewhere.

The approach of improvising magic provides some flexibility for managing the timing of local scenes. It is easy to prevent participants from triggering effects that would be dangerous or inappropriate and actors can employ various tactics to delay players or hurry them along. We see Squeaky Clean employ such tactics towards the end of our chosen sequence where he first reiterates the events which occurred, thereby delaying Maple from engaging in any subsequent activity while also making it clear to anyone who might be overhearing that the essential elements of the scene are completed. Squeaky Clean then changes pace, hurrying Maple along, after instructions have been received from the story director. Throughout, Squeaky Clean and Maple remain 'in character', improvising narratively appropriate talk as they go.

Technological Interaction within Improvised Talk

Our approach has been one of organising a narrative so that the improvised enactment of it contains adequate cues for behind-the-scenes personnel to realise that certain actions of technical significance need to be performed. For the most part this works implicitly in that talk about a purple tuft or a blue mushroom will be heard while this cues associated technical changes to be actioned. That is, typically, it is not necessary to directly refer to technical arrangements to get technical consequences. Exceptions to this worked rather inelegantly. In the above example, on several occasions we hear Squeaky referring to specific key presses. Players are required to use the keyboard to trigger up to ten different pre-canned gestures in particular sequences as part of making incantations. Such references stand out awkwardly against the general flow of the dialogue. Rather than refer to particular gestures by name (e.g. 'bow'), Squeaky explicitly instructs Maple in the key presses the player should use. There are several reasons for this. Although the association of keys to gestures was fixed throughout *Avatar Farm*, both actors and players had trouble fluently remembering it. To ensure correct performance, actors kept extensive notes close to hand and took to mentioning keys by their names rather than risk a misunderstanding. Hence, inelegant mentions of "key9" and so forth intrude the dialogue. In this and other ways, it seems that the complexity of the gesturing hindered the process of improvising. While extended rituals may be useful in slowing down the pace of interaction both for viewers and behind-the-scenes crew, they need to be designed carefully.

Now You See Me, Now You Don't

A key feature of *Avatar Farm* is the way in which various participants and crew members were made invisible and/or inaudible. Invisibility featured in the story itself, for example, when Squeaky Clean made himself invisible during the trick on Botchov. It was also used to separate front-stage from back-stage; the stage-hands were present within the worlds but were both invisible and inaudible. However, these manipulations of visibility raised some interesting issues.

The stage-hands were invisible to the actors, players and viewers front-stage, but also to one another and to the story director and other crew members back-stage. Even though they had been assigned to follow different players before the event, they appeared to find it difficult to coordinate their actions. We have already seen how it was problematic for the stage-hands to coordinate amongst themselves in giving help. Naturally the fact that they were invisible to each other in the virtual environment did not help in this.

The relationship between audibility and visibility also requires deeper consideration. Squeaky Clean's various stage whispers provide a good example. He cannot be seen, but his whispers can be heard by anyone nearby including Maple and Botchov. Botchov benefits from hearing them (even though the story says that he can't) as presumably they help him determine his own reaction to events. Maple can also hear them. Does he believe that Botchov cannot (it can be difficult to judge who can hear whom in a virtual world) or is he going along with the convention of the stage whisper? If these matters are ambiguous for us as analysts, then it is likely they were unclear to at least some of the participants too.

Conclusion

We have described an approach to managing participation in an inhabited television show called *Avatar Farm*, an example of an on-line interactive drama with a branching, non-linear narrative structure. Rather than directly manipulate virtual objects, participants are required to indirectly request interactions that may then be granted by invisible stage-hands who follow them around the world as part of a larger behind-the-scenes production crew. These requests are then dressed up in the metaphor of invoking magic. We met with partial success in following this approach in *Avatar Farm*. On the one hand, players, actors and crew-members did manage to collaboratively improvise some quite complex scenes involving a variety of magical objects. However, this process was not without its difficulties, especially with regard to the behind-the-scenes coordination of the invisible helpers. Our experience suggests several useful refinements to this approach.

First, the use of invisibility to separate front-stage from back-stage needs careful handling. It may be that a more flexible mechanism for supporting variable views within CVEs would be more appropriate. The technique showing different participants different layers of information in a CVE (Smith and Mariani, 1997) might help alleviate these problems. Indeed, MASSIVE-3 includes a mechanism called aspects that can be used to define subjective layers of information. Future events might more gracefully handle the separation between front-stage and back-stage through aspects rather than through global invisibility. The players and actors would appear in a front-stage aspect that would be seen by everybody. The crew would be in a back-stage aspect that would not be seen by the viewers and players (but would be by the actors). Ideally, participants would be able to dyanmically move between aspects so as to pass from front to back stage and vice versa in order to make dramatic entrances into the action (cf. similar remarks about the visibility of cameras in *Out of this World*, Bowers, in press). An analogous treatment of the distribution of audio is also pointed to so that dramatic conventions like stage-whispers can be supported.

Second, while the approach of using a stage-hand to realise object-behaviours was worked with here fairly exclusively, more mixed approaches might be appropriate in future explorations. For example, one can imagine a narrative world in which some object-behaviours could be programmed in advance and directly triggered by participants, alongside others which require mediation from a stage-hand. Perhaps simple object-behaviours or those which are relatively inconsequential in terms of unfolding the narrative could be given advance programmatic support, while more complex behaviours or those which trigger significant shifts of drama need to be collaboratively worked through. Similarly, some behaviours and capabilities need to be granted in a precisely timed fashion to mesh with surrounding dialogue sensibly (imagine an actor saying to a player "… now you can fly…") while other behaviours (e.g. a serpent which autonomously slithers around the scene) could be initiated without such specific timing.

Third (and giving a further example of the relations between narrative structure and interaction), it must be observed that some interaction sequences were hard for our (non-professional) players to pick up. It was not always easy for them to follow what was required of them – especially when an extended sequence of actions had to be performed to accomplish some goal. Several of the actors who were trained in improvisation complained that the players sometimes "blocked offers" (i.e. refused to take up a suggestion that might carry the improvisation forward). This commonly occurred not because the players were naïve in improvisation but because they were still trying to get up to speed with the last thing that was demanded of them or were in the process of practicing some action sequence which was soon to be required. This argument is another example of the close ties which should exist between reflections on narrative form, improvisation, technical provision and interaction formats: narrative space needs to be reserved for trying out new powers or in-line rehearsal.

All this said, we suggest that the approach of improvising object-interactions can provide a useful alternative to programming object-interactions in advance. It might be especially appropriate when the narrative or technology are likely to be unpredictable. With the former, actors and producers need to respond as freely as possible to participants' actions. In the latter, failures and unforeseen constraints in the technology need to be woven into the framework of the story. In *Avatar Farm*, as a research project, we needed to accommodate both.

We believe that our approach opens out a number of new directions for research. First, we suggest that future applications of CVEs may be based more on improvised performance and less on pre-programmed gameplay and that our approach of recognising and supporting behind-the-scenes roles is a viable solution to the production problems of such applications. Where necessary cover-stories can be often be elegantly included in a narrative to explain technical performance and other constraints and anomalies to participants: dreams, sci-fi physics, ghosts and other supernatural phenomena all suggest themselves!

Second, as a general topic of interest within human-computer interaction (HCI) research, we suggest our application area presents boundary conditions on 'direct manipulation' (DM) interfaces. The DM approach emphasises interaction routines with immediate feedback, physical manipulation of interface objects and reversibility of operations (Hutchins et al., 1985). For very good practical reasons to do with the nature of improvised drama and supporting its production, we might occasionally prefer routines which are protracted with delayed or withheld feedback, involving social exchange not just physical manipulation, and with, if the narrative so demands it, irreversible consequences! It is perhaps time to overhaul classical HCI design-lore in the face of the manifold requirements of cooperative systems.

Finally, it is worth noting that our general design emphasis is one of giving people technical resources which they can use as part of their coordination activities, rather than mandate coordination in a heavyweight way. The unfolding of a narrative and the provision of associated technical capabilities are socially mediated matters in our approach. The narrative is not automatically maintained (e.g. through the use of some narrative 'parser' which checks progress against a script), nor are object-behaviours pre-programmed. Our whole design philosophy has been to embed technologies in social practice. We have maintained this theme right from the establishment of an on-line community from which 'players' were drawn, through to designing technologies, interfaces and interaction methods which are intended to cohere with experimental narrative forms and improvised dialogue. While we cannot promise magic from socio-technical design strategies, we hope we have shown a reasoned approach to the support of novel forms of participation in on-line virtual worlds.

Acknowledgments

We gratefully acknowledge the support of the EPSRC and the European Community i^3 programme for this research. Many thanks are also due to all of those at Illuminations Television and British Telecom who worked with us to stage *Avatar Farm* and especially to the players, actors, behind-the-scenes crew and in particular Alex Butterworth who wrote and directed the show.

References

Benford, S. D., Greenhalgh, C. M., Craven, M. P., Walker, G., Regan, T., Wyver, J. and Bowers, J., Broadcasting On-line Social Interaction as Inhabited Television, Proc ECSCW'99, Copenhagen, Denmark, 12-16 September, 1999, Kluwer, pp 179-198.

Bowers, J., Pycock, J. and O'Brien, J., Talk and Embodiment in Collaborative Virtual Environments, Proc. ACM CHI'96, ACM Press, 1996.

Bowers, J. Crossing the line: A field study in inhabited television. In press in Behavior and Information Technology, expected 2001.

Craven, M., Benford, S., Greenhalgh, C, Wyver, J., Brazier, C. J., Oldroyd, A. & Regan, T., *Ages of Avatar*: Community Building for Inhabited Television, ACM CVE'2000, San Francisco, September 2000.

Dodsworth Jr., C., Digital Illusions: entertaining the future with high technology, Addison Wesley, 1997.

Hindmarsh, J., Fraser, M., Heath, C., Benford, S. and Greenhalgh, C., Fragmented interaction: establishing mutual orientation in virtual environments, Proc. ACM Conference on Computer Supported Cooperative Work (CSCW'98), 14-18 November, 1998, Seattle, WA, AC, New York, pp 217-226.

Hutchins, E., Hollan, J. and Norman, D. Direct manipulation interfaces. In Norman, D. and Draper, S. User centered system design, Lawrence Erlbaum, 1985.

Koleva, Taylor, Benford, Fraser, Greenhalgh, Schnadelbach, vom Lehn, Row-Farr, Adams, Orchestrating a Mixed Reality Performance, to appear in Proc. CHI'2001, Seattle, USA, April 2001, ACM Press

Laurel, B., *Computers as Theatre*. Addison-Wesley 1992.

Smith, G. and Mariani, J., Using subjective views to enhance 3D applications, Proceedings of the ACM symposium on Virtual reality software and technology, 1997, Pages 139 - 146

W. Prinz, M. Jarke, Y. Rogers, K. Schmidt, and V. Wulf (eds.), *Proceedings of the Seventh European Conference on Computer-Supported Cooperative Work, 16-20 September 2001, Bonn, Germany*, pp. 179-198.
© 2001 Kluwer Academic Publishers. Printed in the Netherlands.

Music Sharing as a Computer Supported Collaborative Application

Barry Brown[1], Abigail J. Sellen[2], Erik Geelhoed[2]

[1]Department of Computer Science, University of Glasgow, Glasgow, U.K.
[2]Hewlett-Packard Research Labs, Filton Road, Stoke Gifford, Bristol, U.K.
barry@dcs.gla.ac.uk, {abisel,eg}@hpl.hp.com

Abstract: New computer applications, such as the infamous "Napster" system enable the sharing of music over the Internet, with limited communication around this sharing activity. This paper discusses the use and opportunities for these music sharing technologies using interviews with users of both conventional and new music sharing technologies. The data show that music sharing is a practice that is richly linked with other social activities. New music is often discovered through friends, by listening to music together, or in the form of compilation tapes. In these environments, sharing music is a natural activity. With music sharing over the Internet, however, much of this social context is removed. This suggests opportunities to turn music sharing into a more collaborative and community-related activity. These opportunities are explored with the "Music Buddy", a system for browsing others' music collections without infringing the copyright of artists.

Introduction

One of the most controversial computer applications of late has been the "Napster" file sharing system. Napster has made front-page news worldwide, with the legal drama around the service causing much comment and attention (see for example (Hellmore, 2000, Richtel, 2000)). Napster is a program that allows a user to copy MP3 music files over the Internet from other machines running the Napster program. When a user runs Napster, their music files are automatically shared onto the Internet creating a community of users from which music can be downloaded. At the time of writing, the Napster web site from which the program can be downloaded has become one of the most popular web sites worldwide, and the Napster system itself has more than 6.7 million active users (Konrad, 2000).

While sharing music over the Internet was possible before Napster, it involved setting up a server on which music could be stored and downloaded. Since sharing music over the Internet is an activity that is at best of dubious legality, finding individuals who would be willing to do this was difficult and such servers were easily shut down. Napster, however, uses a peer-to-peer sharing model in that any machine running this application can act as a file server without needing to have a permanent connection to the Internet. This extends the number of possible servers to just about any machine that can be connected to the Internet. By enabling the sharing of music between its users, Napster has attracted the attention – and lawsuits – of the music industry. Currently, Napster is still involved in numerous lawsuits, but has settled with a number of the labels and is attempting a transition to a pay-for-use service.

Napster computerises an activity that has been commonplace for many years – the sharing and piracy of music between individuals. In this paper, we would like to investigate what lessons there are for CSCW from investigating music sharing with both conventional and new media. The data we have collected for this paper come from in-depth interviews with users of both conventional music media and early adopters of the new MP3 technologies. This lets us unpack some of the contrasts between sharing with physical tangible media (such as tapes or CDs) and sharing with MP3 files over the Internet.

We start the paper by exploring the relevance of music sharing to the field of CSCW and briefly review the existing literature on this topic. We then move on to discussing the study itself which was based around thirty-six interviews with music enthusiasts. The paper then looks specifically at how conventional music media were shared, and in particular the social activities which took place around sharing music. We then discuss sharing music online, and in particular the differences in *tangibility* between MP3 and physical music media. In the implications section, the paper then draws out the relevance of these findings and discusses two new concepts we are developing using the results from the empirical study to explore new opportunities for digital music media.

Relevance of music sharing to CSCW

While music sharing is a novel activity in terms of CSCW, its importance is underlined in both its massive popularity and the opportunities it presents for exploring socialisation. Online music sharing through Napster has been very successful. Along with the media attention and controversy, the system itself has gathered a huge user base in a very short time. Indeed, Napster is something of a large-scale live experiment in online file sharing. By investigating the success of Napster, we can learn lessons for more conventional CSCW applications. In turn, by understanding the social processes which are involved in conventional music sharing, we can gain understandings of both how new music technologies might evolve and how better to design products and services which support music activities.

Music sharing is also an activity that allows us to explore issues surrounding friendship and community. Many existing Internet and CSCW technologies are used for communication between friends. Perhaps the most researched are instant messaging systems (Bradner, *et al.*, 1999, Nardi and Whittaker, 2000), but other systems such as IRC and photo sharing sites (e.g., Shutterfly http://www.shutterfly.com/) also support friendship. However supporting the activities associated with friendship has not, until recently, been a topic in its own right in CSCW, although it has attracted research more broadly in the CMC field (Kollock and Smith, 1996, Preece, 2000). Its relevance to CSCW was highlighted by Robert Putnam's keynote to CSCW 2000 where he asked researchers to look to design technologies that *bring people together*. That is, to design technologies which enable people to enrich existing friendships and make new friends and social contacts both in leisure and work activities. In this paper, we explore music as one potential platform for this.

As a medium, music is also of interest as an example of computerisation. In earlier research we have looked at the differences between paper and electronic documents (Sellen and Harper, 1997). This work emphasised the different affordances of both physical and digital documents. While electronic documents are easily manipulable, they lack many of the affordances of paper documents, in that they are harder in some ways to share, control and use. Music is an interesting new genre to explore in this way. Only recently have computer-based tools to store, share and manipulate music become readily available to users. Furthermore, by contrast to paper documents, music recordings require some kind of technology in order for users to access them. Thus it is possible that the advantages of physical *tangibility* may not apply as they do in the case of documents. However, as we will discuss later, we discovered that this was not the case, and that with music, the tangibility of physical music recordings is still a very important issue.

Music technology is also an area which is itself attracting increased interest. For example, Bowers and Hellstrom (Bowers and Hellstrom, 2000) have discussed the creation of music using innovative music technologies for improvising music in live performance. There has also been work on interfaces to pre-recorded music (Pauws and Bouwhuis, 2000). However, research in this area has yet to address the opportunities that the new distribution and compression technologies offer.

Lastly, while music sharing is an activity that is not normally thought of as "work", household and social activities have increasingly been recognised to be of relevance and importance to CSCW in that both the methods and findings in these areas have relevance to the core issues surrounding collaboration and work. As an example of this, McCarthy and Anagnost's 1998 CSCW paper describes the *music-fx* system (McCarthy and Anagnost, 1998). This system was designed to support group music choices in a fitness centre. The system automatically chose music channels to play based on the music preferences of who was in the fitness centre at that time. While this system was obviously not designed directly for the workplace, (it supported *workouts* rather than *work*), it has had relevance for other research in CSCW. There is also an increasing body of work that applies the techniques of CSCW to the design of non-work technologies (Hughes, *et al.*, 2000, O'Brien and Rodden, 1997).

Legality

A more contentious issue surrounding this area is the legality of music sharing. Value judgements about music sharing are inherent in the terminology that one uses to talk about the activity – does one speak of music piracy, or music sharing? Very different values are evoked by both of these terms. One evokes the values of theft and abuse, the other of community and reciprocity. For example, showing careful use of language, the UK anti-piracy organisation calls itself the "federation against copyright theft" (FACT), evoking a direct analogy between theft and piracy. However, as has been discussed in the legal literature on piracy there is no simple analogy between theft and piracy (Couser, 1999). For example, theft as an activity denies someone else the use of an artefact, whereas in music piracy, almost the opposite happens - the use of some media is extended to whomever pirates a copy of it. This is not to downplay the damage that can be done to recording artists if they are not properly compensated for their efforts. This provision – that artists are compensated sufficiently to record new material – is at the heart of American copyright law. It is for this reason that within the U.S. the sharing of music between friends for personal use is legal (Plumleigh, 1990). While an in-depth discussion of these issues is outside the scope of this paper, it is an important consideration that any technology we build helps, rather than hinders, the reward of artists.

Music Sharing in the Literature

One of the first recorded instances of music piracy was the copying of Allegri's *Miserere* by Mozart in 1769:

> "Young Mozart attended a performance of the celebrated *Miserere* of Allegri which could be heard only in Rome during Holy Week performed by the papal choir. By papal decree it was forbidden to sing the work elsewhere, and its only existing copy was guarded slavishly by the papal choir. Mozart, however, had heard the work only once when, returning home, he reproduced it in its entirety upon paper. This mind-boggling task soon became the subject for awed whispers in Rome; it was not long before the Pope himself heard of this amazing achievement. The Pope summoned Mozart, but instead of punishing the young genius with excommunication, he showered praise upon him and gave him handsome gifts." (Galan, 2000)

Despite young Mozart's efforts (or perhaps even because of them) copyright entered international law with the signing of the Berne convention in 1886. Copying music and the associated problems of piracy have remained ever since. Chesterman and Lipman (Chestermann and Lipman, 1988) describe three types of pirated music. *Counterfeits* are copies of music sold for profit in shops or markets and often passed off as original copies, *bootlegs* are unauthorised release of artists work, such as recordings from live performances, and *home-taping* is the copying of music by individuals for use in their car or to be given to friends. It is home-taping which we will have most interest in here, since it is the category of piracy which is most relevant when discussing new technologies such as Napster.

Controversy has raged around "home taping" since the event of the compact cassette tape in the sixties. While the record industry has claimed at various times that home taping is "killing music", tape manufacturers have claimed that home taping increases sales, as individuals come to hear music they would not normally purchase (ibid, 141). For example, the British music industry's representative body conducted a study that claimed that 55% of the population used tapes to copy music, whereas the tape manufacturers claimed 22%. For the music industry, however, the key question was what proportion of copied music would otherwise have been bought. Their own surveys suggested 51% of copied music would have been otherwise been bought, whereas the tape industry argued that copying actually increased sales as individuals copied music to "try before they buy". This debate has generally remained unresolved, with the arguments moving onto legal measures (Plumleigh, 1990).

These issues have been cast into sharp relief with the advent of technologies such as Napster. Along with Napster there is a bewildering array of new technologies which attempt to provide similar functionality. Gnutella, for example, allows files to be shared without any form of centralised server. While few of these technologies have yet to reach the notoriety of Napster, peer-to-peer file sharing is a rich developing topic for both software developers and researchers (Oram, 2000).

Turning to understanding the usage of these new file sharing technologies, the literature on conventional piracy is of only limited use. There are no descriptions of the details of copying practice, of why media is copied, for what purposes, from whom, and as part of what other activities[1]. These issues come to the fore if we are to understand (and perhaps better exploit or control) music sharing applications. The main focus of piracy research has been the economics of the situation, where it has been argued that piracy – in certain contexts – can be of net benefit to a market (Bakos, et al., 1999). However, there is little empirical data in the literature from the actual sites in which piracy occurs. In one recent study of online file sharing Adar and Huberman (2000) have argued that there is a "tragedy of the digital commons" using a study of usage of the Gnutella system. While widely reported, this research has been criticised for over-generalising from the specifics of one system (Shirky, 2000 and see also Turner, 1993 for a discussion of solutions to the 'tragedy'). Moreover, the tragedy of the commons scenario is itself one which has been open to considerable debate (for example, McCay and Acheson, 1990), not least because it fails to consider how communities might self-organise. This suggests that there may be opportunities for investigating the activities surrounding music sharing in more depth.

Methodology

The data for this paper were collected as part of a more general study looking at the consumption of music media. The aim of this study was to uncover the details of music consumption and to draw implications for the design of new music technologies. A particular focus was on how the affordances of different kinds of

---

[1] There has been some work on software piracy but this work has tended to treat software piracy somewhat blankly as a form of immoral deviancy rather than investigate it in-depth (Gopal and Sanders, 2000).

music media and technology (e.g. tapes vs. CDs vs. digital music files) influenced these activities. The study looked at the whole "lifecycle" of how consumers use music, from how people first find out about it, to how they obtain it, listen to it, share it, organise it and collect it. A major finding from this was the importance of *sharing music* in both conventional and new media formats. In other work we have discussed the results from this study more generally (Brown, *et al.*, 2001); in this paper we will focus specifically on music sharing and the implications that this has for technology design.

Group	No	Criteria	Av.	% Male
Teenage conventional	12	> 11 music purchases a year and age <20. No use of MP3 files.	16	42%
Adult conventional	12	> 11 music purchases a year and >=age 20. No use of MP3 files.	30	42%
MP3 early adopters	12	> 11 music purchases a year. listen to MP3 files > 5 times a week	27	71%
Total	36		24	56%

Table 1: Choice of participants

Choice of participants

We felt that in a study such as this it was as important to study conventional music media use as much as use of the new music technologies. Accordingly, we chose thirty-six music consumers from three different groups: teenaged users of conventional music media (e.g., CDs, vinyl, and tapes), adult users of conventional music media, and a group of new music media users (MP3 users). The rationale for focusing on music enthusiasts came from an analysis of market data collected in the U.K. by Mintel (Mintel, 1998). Mintel's survey asked consumers how many music products (singles or albums) they had bought for themselves in the last year. These data show that while only 16% of the population make eleven or more music purchases a year, this relatively small group accounts for 65% of the total number of music purchases made in the market. It seemed to us, then, that understanding this influential part of the population would be a good first step to understanding music use. We therefore screened for participants who fell into this category. We were also interested in understanding teenagers' behaviour, since teenagers are particularly heavy purchases of music (Mintel, 1998), and are a key market for the music industry. The selection criteria we used for the three different groups are summarised in Table 1.

Procedure

As the aim of our original data collection was to uncover the details of music behaviour across a broad spectrum, we used semi-structured interviews to ensure that the important issues we wanted to discuss were covered. The questions we asked were designed to probe a range of activities from first awareness of music through to collecting and archiving behaviour. As much as possible we also tried to unpack specific examples of participants' activities around music. So, for example, we asked participants to describe the last three times they had copied or purchased music. Here the focus was not just on their interaction with the music but also on the context within which the activities took place (such as where they were, who they were with, and what other activities they were engaged in). We also asked a more extensive set of questions for the MP3 group. In addition, rating scale questions were interleaved with the open-ended questions to complement the qualitative data. In total, participants were interviewed for between 1 to 1½ hours. All of the interviews were audio-taped and transcribed. The rating scales were subjected to simple descriptive analysis (means, histograms etc), as well as analysis of variance (ANOVA) for group differences.

Results and Discussion

To our surprise, in terms of the quantitative data collected through the rating scales, we found very few differences amongst the three user groups. With the obvious exception of the activities MP3 users carried out using MP3 files, there were no major differences between the conventional adult group and the MP3 users. For example, there was no significant difference in the amount of materials copied by both conventional and MP3 users. With regard to the teenagers, apart from the fact that they on average owned less of all types of media, the only difference we found between them and the adult groups had to do with Internet and email use. This was high for the MP3 group and overall quite high for the both adult and teenaged enthusiasts, but the teenagers indicated significantly less use, probably due to more limited Internet access. Further, in terms of what we unearthed in the interviews, many of the same issues arose in all three groups. More interesting were the common themes that arose, with little evidence of any systematic differences for the different groups.

For this reason, we will focus on the interview data from this study rather than the rating scale data. Further, rather than discussing each group specifically, we will discuss the findings from the interviews in two different sections. In the first section we will discuss the sharing of conventional media. In particular these results show how music sharing is linked with friendship, collecting and identity. Then we will move on to discuss music sharing over the Internet, focusing on some of the issues which result from the lack of tangibility of digital files. These findings are drawn together in the implications section where we discuss two concepts developed directly from these results.

Music sharing with conventional media

While market surveys report that 15% of the UK population copy music using conventional, non-Internet means (Mintel, 1998), all of our interviewees (both MP3 using and not) had copied some original recordings with conventional formats:

"Oh, [I copy] at least once a week. This week I've probably made about six or seven but at least once a week I'd say"

"It's about 50-50 whether I copy it or buy it. It really depends on how available it is to be copied."

The mean amount of copied material in our enthusiasts' collections was 28%. This suggests that copying was an important part of our enthusiasts' music consumption behaviour. Perhaps unsurprisingly, the major motivation for copying music was to avoid buying the music. The primary advantage of copying is that one saves money and can experiment with music that one might not have otherwise bought:

> "That is one of the advantages of (home) taping, quite often you're not sure whether you'll like it enough to get it on CD but by taping you can listen to things and find out about a lot of different types of music and find out what your taste is."

However, this is not to say that those who copied did not buy music. We found no significant correlation (negative or otherwise) between the amount of copied material people owned and the amount they bought. Suggesting that copying did not inhibit his buying, one enthusiast who copied music heavily commented:

> "Whatever I've been doing I've always spent as much as I can of my money on music without going bankrupt."

While this could be a feature of our sample (we chose individuals who frequently purchased music), Mintel has also reported that only 2% of their sample of the UK population copy music regularly but did not buy music regularly (ibid).

Music and friendship

The major source for material to copy came from friends. Indeed, copying music was an activity very much embedded in existing social networks. For the teenagers we interviewed, a common social activity would be to visit friends' homes and play video games or relax together. In these settings, music would nearly always be played, providing both a way of moderating the mood of the group, as well as a forum for finding out about new music. The older music consumers we spoke to also discussed music being played in groups, as a way of producing amicable social situations when friends or family visited their house. In these setting it is natural to ask for a copy of music from a friend, since it is easily available at the point where the music is listened to.

These settings are important for spreading the all important "word of mouth" about new music. Friends would play to each other new music that they had purchased or discovered. These social music listening environments promoted the exchange of information and taste about new music. Not only did friends get to listen to each other's music collections, but friends filtered music for each other, deciding what they thought others would like to listen to. This involved a form of mutual understanding; friends would get to know each other's taste in music and so design their recommendations, and in turn their opinion of each others recommendations:

> "I really value (my boyfriend's) opinion as he usually gets it spot on for me"

> "I think its because you get to know a person's musical profile, for want of a better word, you can trust certain people's recommendations"

In this way, our enthusiasts and their friends acted as a form of collaborative filtering mechanism in how they found out about music and passed on recommendations (and copies). Friends also often searched through each other's collections, looking for music that they might borrow or perhaps copy. Thus friends' collections were used as sources of new media to experiment with and explore. Another important social method by which music tastes were shared was through the swapping of compilation tapes (see also (Willis, 1990) on this topic). This sharing of music, although time consuming and cumbersome with most current technology, was particularly valued by our interviewees:

"All the cassettes and CDs that I treasure are the ones which are compilations. And it tends to be the way I get into a new music area. I recently have been getting into dance stuff because of John who taped his DJ collection for me and is gradually getting me into harder and harder stuff."

Overall, these social methods of finding out about music were very important for how our participants found out about music. In asking them to rank 14 different ways they could find out about music, "Someone I know played it to me on their Hi-Fi" was the highest ranked. This notwithstanding, a number of enthusiasts also underlined the frustrations they had with finding out about new music:

Int: Do you ever have troubles finding out about music?

A: Yes I do a hell of a lot actually, I always hear it off my mates they always seem to find out about it but I seem to miss it all the time.

These frustrations highlight the potential for new technologies that help individuals to discover and expand on their music tastes. This is a point we will return to later when we discuss implications.

Identity and collecting

As has been remarked before in the literature (Frith and Goodwin, 1990), music choice is tied up with the formation of identity and membership of different groups. Often youth sub-cultures identify themselves using music as a way of forming and establishing their identity. Examples of this include "mods and rockers" (Cohen, 1972), "skinheads" (Clarke, 1975) and more recently "ravers" (Redhead, et al., 1997). To our interviewees, this connection between identity, sub-culture and music was also apparent, if in a less extreme way. The participants often would have friends who shared a taste in music. This gave them opportunities to socialise together around music, by going to nightclubs or live music together. Particularly for the teenagers we interviewed, a shared taste in music was an important bond for groups of friends. However, the older enthusiasts we spoke to also talked about having groups of friends with whom they frequently discussed new music, often swapping popular recordings and recommendations. Some enthusiasts even went as far as saying that if someone liked the same music they liked, this created an instant bond which would make friendship far more likely:

"There's an instant connection, like if I meet someone who listens to the early Verve stuff then I think there's something really important going on inside them [...] I think it brings me a lot closer to people if you can share the exhilaration that music can bring you."

This is perhaps not surprising: music taste, as with other tastes, can be seen as part of an individual's identity. Others who have similar tastes may have other aspects of their identity in common. Later in the implications section we will discuss how this connection between identity and music can be exploited to enhance socialising online.

This connection between identity and music also followed through into collecting music. In many ways a music collection acts as a tangible presentation of one's taste in music. Music collections were something that the enthusiasts took pride in:

> "Your library expresses who you are. If everyone had access to the same stuff [...] it's not the same."

In particular, a collection of *original* recordings (as opposed to copies) was very much valued. Over and over again in the different interviews the enthusiasts returned to their perception that originals were better than owning a copy. While this was often described in terms of the superiority of a purchased original – having the sleeve notes, having a CD over a cassette tape, better quality recording – there was also a strong perception that a copy was less legitimate than an original:

> "It's nice to have something permanently and properly, a bit of a feeling that (home) taping is quite scab [...] I don't think it's a moral thing, it's a more sort of genuine thing that you actually like it and gone out and bought it. I'm mildly embarrassed about taped things"

> "If it is a band I really like I'll buy it for collectors use."

> "I buy something if I think I'm going to listen to it lots, I mean its easy to buy something like the Beatles White album because it's going to last a long time. Although I listen to it far more on the [copied] tape version than I ever do on the CD – that's kind of the irony of it all"

One possible reason for this could be the connection between collecting and identity. In some ways, a music collection is a physical manifestation of an individual's taste in music. Thus if music taste is part of identity, then so is a music collection. A frequent comment from our participants was that if they found they really valued some music they would then go out and purchase an original to replace the copy. This suggests that having a collection of originals that reflects your taste in music is an important reason for buying rather than copying. Having a collection of originals of good music indicate good taste in the owner of a collection. As Belk puts it:

> "[A] benefit of collecting is in enlarging the collector's sense of self. [..] the choice and assembly of objects to form a collection is ostensibly a self-expressive creative act that tells us something about the collector. [..] The surest way to undermine a collector is to observe that the collectible or collection 'is not you'" (Belk, 1995, p89)

To some of our enthusiasts, having an impressive collection of originals was a way of standing out from others. In this sense displaying the music collection became important, since the collection says things about us that it would be socially unacceptable to express aloud:

> "I believe I've got optimal music tastes and I think my record collection reflects that, other people should respect it! (laughs)"

As will be discussed later, these findings have implications for the design of new music technologies, in that digital music fails to properly support this collecting behaviour.

Music sharing over the Internet

We now move onto music sharing activity over the Internet, as conducted by our MP3 users. Many of the MP3 files which our enthusiasts had on their computers were recordings that they also owned in conventional formats. A CD can be placed into a computer and the music "ripped" onto the computer's hard drive in MP3 format. However, one of the key advantages of MP3 files is that, because they are computerised, they can be copied over both local networks and the Internet. Our MP3 enthusiasts exhibited the same kinds of motivations behind copying as the conventional enthusiasts, but took advantage of MP3 files by either downloading from the "Napster" file sharing system or by exchanging them with friends.

In some cases, copying MP3 files followed a similar pattern as conventional copying. In these cases, files would be shared between friends over local networks, such as at work or on a college campus. For example, many of the university students we talked to had personal computers connected to the university network meaning that music could easily be shared between friends' machines:

"You can [download songs] off the network. I discovered Stereolab, and I liked one of their songs and one of my mates said oh so and so got it on his computer so I went and had a look at that and he's got both albums on MP3 so I downloaded them off and listened to them."

Napster

However, the main method of music copying which the MP3 users discussed was the use of Napster. A Napster user obtains music files by searching the machines of users also connected to the Napster system, and downloads music files directly from them. Accordingly, unlike conventional music copying, this form of copying goes on generally between individuals who do not know each other and will probably never meet. This difference in technology also means that the number of tracks available far exceeds what could be copied from friends. At the current time, there are over three million tracks available for downloading. While many of these are duplicate files, this does give an idea of the amount of music available.

As might be expected, this change in the amount of music available changes the copying which is done compared to conventional music sharing. The enthusiasts talked about using Napster to experiment with new types of music that they would not have necessarily bought. This music was downloaded from strangers, without a social context, yet from a far wider range of music than available from friends. In doing so they complied somewhat eclectic collections of tracks from Napster, instead of downloading whole albums:

"I think there was a Quincy Jones song, the theme from "Minder" – don't know what came over me that night – and it would have probably been… Jolene by Dolly Parton. I wouldn't dream of going and buying them."

"I sort of do it in batches, just old classics that I have in my collection and I want to copy or just records I never got round to buying and I don't want to go back and buy an old album because I just wanted the one track off it"

So rather than downloading music to directly replace buying, this downloading was more a way of exploring music that the enthusiasts would not normally have bought. Certainly, for the enthusiasts we interviewed they claimed that using Napster had encouraged them to experiment with new music and did not make them any more reluctant to buy CDs. In fact, some said that this had increased their music purchasing (a finding also confirmed by other questionnaire studies of MP3 users (Jupiter, 2000)):

"I wouldn't say its cut down on my music purchases at all, in fact to a certain extent it would make me go out and buy it in a way if I hear something by an artist on MP3 if I like it that much I'll go and buy it."

"It's influenced which ones I buy but if I like it 9 times out of 10 I will buy it. I don't think it has replaced buying the physical thing."

This behaviour may have in part been caused by the time that it takes to download music from Napster (it takes about three hours to download an average album using a conventional modem). However, our enthusiasts with broadband connections showed similar behaviour - the physical media still had a crucial role in their music use. This finding led us to investigate what advantages physical media had which were causing our enthusiasts to purchase music that was potentially available for free over Napster.

Tangibility

Digital files have very different properties from physical music media. Files on a computer do not have a persistent physical presence which can be arranged to create an aesthetically pleasing display. Browsing through these on-line collections is also very different from browsing through physical collections with their accompanying artwork and sleevenotes. In addition, because they are not physically embodied, they are not as linked with social interactions. For example, digital files are not as desirable as gifts. Currently they cannot be as easily purchased as physical media. Moreover, digital files also have a number of serious practical problems with durability. File formats change frequently, and playback devices change:

"I wouldn't be so keen on that [...] if everything is not physical then you've got worries [...] it will be harder to lend to friends who haven't got the technology to access your collection and also not having sleeve notes and things like that"

"No, there's no point. I like choosing – I like going through my records and then spotting one, if it was digital I'd have to [...] scroll down and it would be words"

These limitations seem to impact on the *collectability* of digital files. Our participants saw a collection of digital files as inferior to a collection of tangible physical media. When we asked our participants about collecting digital files rather than physical music objects they were consistently negative, even those who used MP3 files extensively. Digital music files were untrustworthy, of lower quality, and unreliable:

"I think I'd always like to have something there – the solid thing. The option of being able to do that [collect the music digitally] would have to be a lot cheaper than having a CD, I don't know whether I'd actually trust it."

This suggests that physical objects are more suitable for collecting and that current digital files do not support all the subtle activities involved in collecting. Of course, this is not to say that collecting digital music files does not have its own attractions (as discussed above). As mentioned in the introduction, this finding is similar to our findings on the use of paper documents (Sellen and Harper, 1997), and suggests some barriers to digital music superseding physical formats. For these reasons, we would argue that MP3 should not be seen as replacing physical media but rather as a *complementary* format, at least in the short to medium term. Later in the implications section we will discuss how by connecting virtual and physical media this might be exploited technologically.

Music browsing

New digital media do have some advantages over conventional media in that they can be used in new ways. For example, one user described how new technology allowed him to bring together a whole collection of songs to be chosen and played at will:

> "I copied all my Aerosmith ones [into MP3 format] so I could listen to them all on the computer – I could listen to them randomly – I could listen to any of the CDs. There's about 150 [songs]. Mainly for the random capability."

The new properties of digital media also enable new forms of collaboration around music. For example, one user (who we shall call Julie) developed a way of browsing the Napster system for new music. Julie would search Napster for particular songs from her favourite artists, and be presented with a list of users from whom these tracks could be downloaded. Julie would then use this information to browse through these individuals' music collections. She assumed that since these users liked (or rather, had) a particular piece of music that she liked, there was a good chance that they would also have new music that she would like. In this way, users can navigate around the Napster network, finding users who have similar tastes in music and going on to search the music that they like. This is a form of music browsing, exploiting the fact that music tastes are often clustered in similar ways. Julie went further with this Napster browsing, turning it into a collaborative application. She would discover music through this browsing, sending the usernames of particularly interesting users on to two of her friends who were also keen Napster users, who would then "co-browse" these individuals. Common songs downloaded then became topics for conversation, both online and through the buddy chat systems that they used.

This use of Napster appears to combine some of the aspects of the collaborative filtering normally done through friends with the ability to browse strangers' music collections. This usage suggests opportunities for expanding the socialising around music, and music sharing; points we will return to in the next section.

Implications for Technology Design

In the above two sections, we have highlighted some of the details of sharing music in both conventional and MP3 form. Music sharing with conventional media is deeply embedded in social activities, connected with both friendship and identity. For these activities, the physical nature of conventional media is highly important in how it affords certain uses, particularly the collection of music. For computer-based media, we have discussed the use of Napster: how it differs from conventional copying, and how it can be used as a tool for browsing and exploring new music. We now turn to some of the implications of this work for the design of technology. We will discuss general implications of this work for CSCW, and then move on to discuss two specific concepts which we are building based on these findings – the "Music Book" and the "Music Buddy".

One important finding from this study concerns the tangibility of physical music media. It appears that even though music requires intervening technology in order to make use of different physical forms of media, those physical objects are still of value in and of themselves. Activities such as collecting, sharing, ownership and purchase seem to be deeply embedded in the physical artefact. This suggests that digital music will not inevitably supersede physical formats. Indeed, we would argue that it is in the mixing of physical and digital formats that many opportunities lie.

A second finding of relevance to the design of CSCW systems concerns the ability to easily share electronic media over the Internet. While the web has enabled the sharing of documents more easily than before, even the web presents some barriers to sharing files in that one must establish and maintain a web site. Even well designed lightweight systems such as BSCW suffer from a similar set-up cost (Bentley, et al., 1997). Napster demonstrates an even simpler model: simply run a program and your files are shared over the Internet. This suggests that the peer-to-peer file sharing model may offer opportunities for the lightweight sharing of work documents over the Internet, in particular for *ad hoc* groups where the lifetime of the group may not justify the setting up a CSCW shared space. Napster's peer-to-peer nature means that there is no need for a centralised server, and in turn no need for the administration of that server, reducing complexity and cost.

As we mentioned in the introduction, Napster is of immense popularity. A major part of this popularity is the ability to browse through media, sampling different types of music. This suggests entertainment media as a powerful "hook" for Internet communities more generally. The results above show that while conventional music sharing occurs with friends in social environments, with online sharing much of this sociality is stripped away. Certainly, sharing music online with current technology is an activity that is very 'lean' and involves little communication[2]. These findings imply that online music applications could better support communication with friends around their music collections. Further, as discussed above, music taste is also part of an individual's identity. This means that those with similar tastes in music may have other aspects of their identity in common. If we meet someone who shares a particularly eclectic music taste then there is at least the potential of a bond of friendship. At the very least, there is a common conversation topic. This suggests that online music applications could exploit this to support community and the generation of new friendship around music.

Within CSCW this connection between identity and ownership has been discussed in work on collaborative filtering systems, specifically systems which support filtering for individuals with particular expertise, such as "Who Knows" and "Expertise Recommender" (Mcdonald and Ackerman, 2000, Streeter and Lochbaum, 1988). However, looking at the example of music emphasises a connection between

---

[2] While Napster does provide limited opportunities for socialising around sharing music (chat rooms, a messaging system), these are limited aspects of Napster which is mainly designed for sharing music.

identity and *collecting* behaviour which has been previously neglected. This suggests that for some collections there is a special connection between the owner and the collection – since the collection has been selected in part to represent that person. In this case it is music, however other examples are collections of movies, art, books or academic papers. These collections could prove to be especially valuable for identifying individuals.

Experimenting with tangibility: The "Music Book"

Using the results from this study, we have developed two new concepts. The first concept is called the Music Book and combines some of the advantages of physical music media identified above with the flexible nature of digital media. The concept takes the form of small CD sized books. Each book represents one album, yet, rather than storing the music itself, the book is designed to connect with an online copy of the music. Music books contain a small RF tag that acts as a unique identifier. The book itself contains information and articles on the artist and album, much like an extended version of the sleevenotes that currently come with an album. When the book is waved in front of a suitable player, the RF tag is read and the music connected with the book is downloaded from the Internet and played. In this way, the Music Book can be used just as a conventional record or CD would have been, giving a tangible and substantial representation of the music.

However since the music is stored centrally, what is played can be of near unlimited duration and can be accessed from any device connected to the Internet. This means that any Internet connected player – either portable or home-based – can access the music without having to be physically close to the Music Book. This combines the advantages of the physical and virtual. Music Books can be collected and displayed just as conventional CDs are. This supports the all important sense of ownership and collection which was discussed above. Searching for a piece of music can be done by physically looking through the collection of Music Books, rather than having to choose a album on a computer interface. Music Books can also be lent or borrowed. Music Books therefore combine the advantages of both the physical and the digital music distribution worlds. With this system, users can choose to buy music digitally online. If the music is bought online, the music (or the rights to access the music) can be downloaded to their player. This gives them the ability to instantly listen to the music on their digital player as soon as it is purchased. Soon after this, the corresponding Music Book is sent to them using the conventional post. The music tag on the book links to the digital music content. The individual therefore has instant gratification in that they can listen to the music digitally as soon as they buy it, but they also have the corresponding advantages of the physical artefact. Music can also be sold through existing retail outlets, even though all the actual music is distributed electronically.

Experimenting with music and friendship: The "Music Buddy"

A second invention we are investigating looks specifically at the differences in music sharing online and in conventional media, in particular the amount of *socialising* that takes place around music sharing. As we discussed above, music is an application that is particularly suited to linking with creating friendship or community bonds, since in the physical world it is strongly linked with social activities. A similar observation comes from the collaborative filtering of friends' music tastes for each other. This suggests that the music collections of friends, and those with similar music tastes, would be a useful resource for discovering new music. With conventional music media, the enthusiasts we interviewed would look through friends' music collections to discover new music and experiment with music that they would want to listen to. Therefore there may be value in browsing through other's on-line music collections as a way of exploring music.

These observations led us to develop an application called "the Music Buddy" to help support discovering new music, and making friends through music. In designing the Music Buddy, our aim was to design an application that would combine some of the advantages of physical music sharing with those of Internet music sharing. We also wanted to support the browsing of music collections, yet in a legal way. We were conscious of the various legal and moral implications of sharing music in an on-line application. This in mind, we wanted to design a system which would support rather than undermine the purchasing of music. The system we have designed and are prototyping is shown in Figure 1.

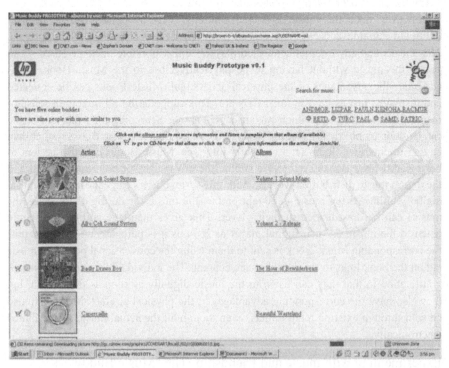

Figure 1: The Music Buddy

The system starts by uploading a list of a user's music collection onto a centralised server. This is done by an application running on the user's machine which collects a list of MP3 files using MP3 format ID3 tags which list album, artist and song. This list is then sent to the centralised server which records which users have which songs. The server then supports the browsing of this and others' music collections using a normal Internet browser. To start, the system displays lists of songs by user. By clicking on a song, album or artist, a list of other users who also have that music is then listed. In turn, these related collections can be browsed. Importantly, this design does not enable copying music or infringing copyright. Instead, it only provides the names of individual tracks which are held on the server. The system then offers links to on-line music retailers to listen to legal samples of the music. In this way, users can explore new albums with the convenience of having an immediate link to a retailer if they should wish to purchase new music.

This "music browsing" functionality is an attempt to address some of the frustrations our interviewees expressed with finding out about new music. Different music collections act as a form of collaborative filter, in that one can browse through different music tastes in a structured way. Existing collaborative filtering systems (such as the Firefly and RINGO systems) work by a user specifying a set number of items which they like (Shardanand and Maes, 1995). With the Music Buddy, however, a user's music taste is automatically uploaded in the form of a list of the MP3 files they already have on their machine. This provides a more reliable and less troublesome way of getting at different users' tastes in music. Once a user's music taste is in the system, the system can then use techniques for matching the user with other users to suggest music that they might like.

While this functionality supports the browsing and discovery of new music, we also want to explore how this system could support friendship and socialisation, exploiting many of the algorithms which have already been developed in the collaborative filtering community (Ungar and Foster, 1988). We are exploring how the system could join small groups of users together with similar music tastes. Our aim is to make this as lightweight as possible so as to encourage new social interactions. We are also exploring how this messaging functionality could connect with existing instant chat and email systems. While the Music Buddy is currently in prototype form, we hope to make the system available over the Internet so as to collect as wide a range of data on music tastes as possible. In this way the Music Buddy is a platform for experimenting with individuals' music tastes. The data in the Music Buddy will be used for the development of agents to predict music tastes based on existing data, and systems for collaborative rating and ranking of music.

Conclusion

In this paper we discussed a study of music sharing in both physical and Internet forms, drawing implications from this for CSCW, as well as describing two concepts which we are building to support the lessons from this study. Using empirical data collected with interviews with 36 music enthusiasts we explored consumers' music sharing practice. While the group that we studied in this paper – music enthusiasts - is relatively small, it is worth emphasising again that this type of consumer makes the majority of music purchases. This group is also likely to be the one most likely to use new music technologies, such as those discussed throughout this paper.

This discussion took two parts. First, the paper discussed conventional music sharing practice. This was a practice very much tied up with existing social processes, such as socialising with friends. In particular, friends were important for finding out about new music through recommendations and searching through friends' collections. In this way, friends act as a form of collaborative filtering for new music. Moving on to the use of Napster and other new digital music sharing technologies, we commented on the differences between copying music physically and over the Internet. Unlike conventional copying, Napster involves copying music from a vast collection, from people that the user does not know and is not likely to meet.

An important finding from this discussion was the importance of physical original recordings. In particular, collecting original recordings was linked to our enthusiasts' identities; a good collection formed (in part) one's music taste, and contributed to a sense of identity. Taking this implication on board, we designed the "Music Book" as an attempt to combine the advantages of physical and on-line music media. In turn, the implications regarding the advantages of sharing music were used to develop a second concept, the "Music Buddy", which allows users to share the list of the music they have stored on their PC.

To conclude, the research discussed in this paper has investigated the controversial activity of sharing music in both digital and physical forms. Our work suggests that rather than placing barriers to copying and sharing practices, the music production and distribution industry might seek to exploit these practices for their own benefit, recognising that the sharing of digital material might actually facilitate buying in the long run. New music technologies which support sharing and the community around music could turn out to have large value for individuals, as well as encouraging new friendships and new opportunities for social interaction.

Acknowledgments

The authors would like to thank Jon Hindmarsh and Kenton O'Hara for helpful comments on this paper, along with the study participants for their time and patience.

Bibliography

Adar, E. and B. A. Huberman (2000): "Free Riding on Gnutella", First Monday, vol. 5, No. 10, URL: http://www.firstmonday.dk/ issues/issue5_10/adar/index.html

Bakos, Y., E. Brynjolfsson and D. Lichtman (1999): "Shared information goods", Journal of Law and Economics, vol. XLII, no. April, pp. 117-155.

Belk, R. (1995): "Collecting in a consumer society", Routledge.

Bentley, R., T. Horstmann and J. Trevor (1997): "The world wide web as enabling technology for ECSCW: The case of BSCW", Computer-Supported Cooperative Work, vol. 7, no. 21

Bowers, J. and S. O. Hellstrom (2000): "Simple interfaces to complex sound in improvised music", in Proceedings of CHI' 2000 extended abstracts. The Hague, The Netherlands: ACM Press.

Bradner, E., W. A. Kellogg and T. Erickson (1999): "The adoption and use of babble: A field study of chat in the workplace", in Proceedings of ECSCW '99. Copenhagen, Denmark: Kluwer Academic Press.

Brown, B., E. Geelhoed and A. J. Sellen (2001): "The use of conventional and new music media: Implications for future technologies", Proceedings of Interact 2001. Tokyo, Japan.

Chestermann, J. and A. Lipman (1988): "The electronic pirates: Diy crimes of the century", London, Routledge.

Clarke, J. (1975): "The skinheads and the magical recovery of community", in S. Hall and T. Jefferson (Eds.) Resistance through rituals: Youth subcultures in post-war britain. London: Hutchinson.

Cohen, S. (1972): "Folk devils and moral panics: The creation of mods and rockers", London, MacGibbon and Kee Ltd.

Couser, J. (1999): "Software piracy and the Doris Day syndrome: Some legal, ethical and social implications of contemporary conceptions of property", International journal of law and information technology, vol. 7, pp. 1-30.

Frith, S. and A. Goodwin (1990): "From subcultural to cultural studies", in S. Frith and A. Goodwin (Eds.) On record: Pantheon Books.

Galan, R. (2000): "Wolfgang Amadeus Mozart". Composers' Network. Available on the internet: http://www.composers.net/ database/m/MozartWA.html

Gopal, R. D. and G. L. Sanders (2000): "Global software piracy: You can't get blood out of a turnip", Communications of the ACM, vol. 43, no. 9, pp. 82-89.

Hellmore, E. (2000): "Music industry is caught napping", The Guardian. London. March 16. Available on the internet: http://www.guardianunlimited.co.uk/ Archive/Article/0,4273,3974240,00.html

Hughes, J., J. O'Brien, T. Rodden, M. Roucefield and S. Viller (2000): "Patterns of home life: Informing design for domestic environments", Personal Technologies, vol. 4, pp. 25-38.

Jupiter (2000): "Jupiter finds napster users are 45 percent more likely to increase music spending". New York, Jupiter communications. July 20, 2000. Available on the internet: http://www.jup.com/company/pressrelease.jsp?doc=pr000721

Oram, A. (2000): "Peer to peer: Harnessing disruptive potential", O'Reilly & Associates.

Kollock, P. and M. Smith (1996): "Managing the virtual commons: Cooperation and conflict in computer communities", in S. Herring (Ed.) CMC: Linguistic, social and cross-cultural perspectives. Amsterdam: John Benjamins.

Konrad, R. (2000): "Napster among fastest-growing net technologies", CNET News. October 5, 2000. Available on the internet: http://news.cnet.com/news/0-1005-200-2938703.html

McCarthy, J. F. and T. D. Anagnost (1998): "Music FX: An arbiter of group preferences for computer supported collaborative workouts", in Proceedings of CSCW '98. Seattle, WA: ACM Press.

McCay, B., J. Acheson (2000): "Question of the Commons: The Culture and Ecology of Communal Resources", University of Arizona Press.

Mcdonald, D. and M. S. Ackerman (2000): "Expertise recommender: A flexible recommendation system", in Proceedings of ECSCW '2000. Philadelphia, PA.: ACM Press.

Mintel (1998): "Mintel report: Records, tapes, cds". London, Mintel. February 1998.

Nardi, B. and S. Whittaker (2000): "Interaction and outeraction: Instant messaging in action", in Proceedings of ECSCW '2000. Philadelphia, PA: ACM Press.

O'Brien, J. and T. Rodden (1997): "Interactive systems in domestic environments", in Proceedings of the ACM conference on designing interactive systems - DIS'97: ACM Press.

Pauws, S. and D. Bouwhuis (2000): "Programming and enjoying music with your eyes closed", in Proceedings of CHI 2000. Amsterdam, Netherlands: ACM Press.

Plumleigh, M. (1990): "Digital audio tape: New fuel stokes the smoldering home taping fire", UCLA Law review, vol. 34, pp. 733-776.

Preece, J. (2000): "Online communities: Designing usability, supporting sociability", New York, Wiley.

Redhead, S., D. Wynne and J. O'Connor (1997): "The club cultures reader: Readings in popular cultural studies", Oxford, Blackwell.

Richtel, M. (2000): "Napster and record industry clash over sales and copyrights", The New York Times. New York. July 4, 2000, Tuesday.

Sellen, A. and R. Harper (1997): "Paper as an analytic resource for the design of new technologies", in Proceedings of CHI '97. Atlanta, GA: ACM Press.

Shardanand, U. and P. Maes (1995): "Social information filtering: Algorithms for automating word of mouth", in Proceedings of CHI'95. ACM Press.

Shirky, C. (2000): "In Praise of Freeloaders", OpenPTP.com article, 1 December 2001, http://www.openp2p.com/pub/a/p2p/2000/12/01/shirky_freeloading.html

Streeter, L. A. and K. E. Lochbaum (1988): "Who knows: A system based on automatic representation of semantic structure", in Proceedings of RIAO '88 conference on user oriented content-based text and image handling. Cambridge, MA.

Turner, R. M. (1993): "The Tragedy of the Commons and Distributed AI Systems", in Proceedings of the 12th International Workshop on Distributed Artificial Intelligence, Hidden Valley, PA.

Ungar, L. and D. Foster (1988): "Clustering methods for collaborative filtering", in Proceedings of the workshop on recommendation systems. Menlo Park, CA.: AAAI Press.

Willis, P. (1990): "Common culture: Symbolic work at play in the everyday cultures of the young", Open University Press.

W. Prinz, M. Jarke, Y. Rogers, K. Schmidt, and V. Wulf (eds.), *Proceedings of the Seventh European Conference on Computer-Supported Cooperative Work, 16-20 September 2001, Bonn, Germany*, pp. 199-218.
© 2001 Kluwer Academic Publishers. Printed in the Netherlands.

PolyLens: A Recommender System for Groups of Users

Mark O'Connor, Dan Cosley, Joseph A. Konstan, and John Riedl
Department of Computer Science and Engineering, University of Minnesota, Minneapolis, MN 55455 USA

{oconnor;cosley;konstan;riedl}@cs.umn.edu

Abstract. We present PolyLens, a new collaborative filtering recommender system designed to recommend items for groups of users, rather than for individuals. A group recommender is more appropriate and useful for domains in which several people participate in a single activity, as is often the case with movies and restaurants. We present an analysis of the primary design issues for group recommenders, including questions about the nature of groups, the rights of group members, social value functions for groups, and interfaces for displaying group recommendations. We then report on our PolyLens prototype and the lessons we learned from usage logs and surveys from a nine-month trial that included 819 users. We found that users not only valued group recommendations, but were willing to yield some privacy to get the benefits of group recommendations. Users valued an extension to the group recommender system that enabled them to invite non-members to participate, via email.

Introduction

Recommender systems (Resnick & Varian, 1997) help users faced with an overwhelming selection of items by identifying particular items that are likely to match each user's tastes or preferences (Schafer et al., 1999). The most sophisticated systems learn each user's tastes and provide personalized recommendations. Though several machine learning and personalization technologies can attempt to learn user preferences, automated collaborative filtering (Resnick et al., 1994; Shardanand & Maes, 1995) has become the preferred real-time technology for personal recommendations, in part because it leverages the experiences of an entire community of users to provide high quality recommendations without detailed models of either content or user tastes.

To date, automated collaborative filtering systems have focused exclusively on recommending items to individuals. In some domains, such as Usenet News (Konstan et al., 1997; Resnick et al., 1994), this limitation is understandable. Few users read articles collectively. In other domains such as books or music (Shardanand & Maes, 1995), it is common both to enjoy the media alone and in groups. (Indeed, the MusicFX system (McCarthy & Anagnost, 1998), which did not attempt to use collaborative filtering, was designed specifically to address the challenge of selecting music for the often-large groups of people using a corporate gym.) Moreover certain items, among them restaurants, board games, and movies (Hill et al., 1995), are more commonly enjoyed in groups. Recommender systems that identify items such as movies for individuals do not address the user's key question, which is not "what movie should *I* see?" but rather "what movie should *we* see?"

This paper explores the design space of collaborative filtering recommenders for groups and presents our experience deploying the PolyLens group recommender to over 800 MovieLens users. The design space includes issues such as: What is the nature of a group? How are groups formed? How are recommendations computed for groups? What interfaces are best for sharing recommendations with groups? What are the privacy issues in showing recommendations to groups?

In our field trial with PolyLens we explored user experiences with one set of design choices. We kept detailed logs to measure how users formed groups, how they used the groups, and how the experience of users who used groups differed from the experience of users who did not use groups. We also surveyed the group users to learn their reactions to group recommendations, including their opinions about the value of the recommendations and the tradeoff in lost privacy.

In the next section, we present related work in recommender systems and in other systems with related group dynamics issues. We then introduce PolyLens and review the design space for group recommenders, looking at group properties and member rights, algorithms for group recommendation, and interfaces for displaying group recommendations. We follow with results of our user trial and survey, and we conclude with a discussion of lessons learned.

Related Work

Though we know of no previously published studies of groups in recommender systems, the work is related to previously published work on collaborative filtering, group formation, roles in collaborative systems, and awareness in collaborative systems.

Collaborative filtering. Many different approaches have been applied to the basic problem of making accurate and efficient recommender systems, ranging from nearest neighbor algorithms to Bayesian analysis. The earliest recommenders used nearest neighbor collaborative filtering algorithms (Resnick et al., 1994; Shardanand & Maes, 1995). Nearest neighbor algorithms are based on computing the distance between users based on their preference history. Predictions of how much a user will like an item are computed by taking the weighted average of the opinions of a set of nearest neighbors for that product. Opinions should be scaled to adjust for differences in ratings tendencies between users (Herlocker et al., 1999).

Model-building methods work by creating a model offline, and then running the model online. The model may take hours or days to build. The goal is for the resulting model to be small, fast, and accurate. Several techniques have been shown to be successful, including: (1) Bayesian networks, which create a model based on a training set with a decision tree at each node and edges representing user information (Breese et al., 1998); (2) dimensionality reduction using eigenvectors (Goldberg et al., 2000) or singular value decomposition (Sarwar et al., 2000), which creates a low-dimensional space within which latent relationships between users or items can be discovered; (3) clustering techniques, which identify groups of users who appear to have similar preferences (Ungar & Foster, 1998); and (4) Horting, a graph-based technique in which nodes are users, and edges between nodes indicate the degree of similarity between two users (Aggarwal et al., 2000).

In this paper we focus on the basic question of whether group recommendations can be useful to users, so we use nearest neighbor algorithms. These algorithms are appropriate for our purpose since they are the most thoroughly studied, and since our users on MovieLens are most familiar with nearest neighbor algorithms.

Group formation. Many studies have examined systems that support group formation. Two interesting ends of the spectrum are Kansas and MusicFX. Kansas is a virtual world in which a user can join a group by moving towards other users (Smith et al., 1998). Kansas groups are similar to chatting in physical spaces in an office environment. MusicFX accidentally enabled group formation by creating a system in which the music in a corporate gym was selected according to the taste of the people working out at a given time (McCarthy & Anagnost, 1998). People began modifying their workout times to arrive at the center with other people, often strangers, who shared their music tastes.

Our work involves intentional groups, like Kansas, and unlike MusicFX. Unlike Kansas, the groups are explicitly selected for an external reason: these people want to see a movie together.

Roles. Roles for participants in collaborative systems have been studied by many researchers. For instance, Kansas includes an object-oriented programming language within which arbitrary roles can be described (Smith et al., 1998; similar to Edwards, 1996). Roles confer rights and responsibilities on the users. Other collaborative systems provide mechanisms to directly control the operations users can perform (Dewan & Shen, 1998).

Experimental work on roles in practice suggests that complicated roles are not necessary in many cases, since social protocols will evolve to manage the interaction tasks. For instance, studies of the Grove and Aspects multi-user editors show that users avoid conflict effectively without system support (Ellis et al., 1991). Further, one study of a large number of Lotus Notes databases shows that even though users say they expect moderators to increase the amount of communication in Notes discussion boards, the moderators actually significantly decrease the amount of communication (Whittaker, 1996). For these reasons, our work uses only very simple roles and permissions, which we address when we discuss design issues.

Awareness. One of the necessary conditions for social protocols to evolve is awareness of other users in the system. For instance, user group drawing tools often show where other users are in the drawing space, and what objects they are currently manipulating (Gutwin & Greenberg, 1998). Experience with group writing tools shows that awareness is important for group dynamics (Mitchell et al., 1995). The Prep collaborative editor treats awareness of other users explicitly, by creating separate columns to record the edits performed by each user (Neuwirth et al., 1994). Our work follows the Prep model of making awareness explicitly visible through separate columns of data about each user.

Designing PolyLens

PolyLens is a group recommender extension to the MovieLens recommender system (<http://movielens.umn.edu/>). MovieLens is a free movie recommender site with over 80,000 users and their ratings of over 3,500 movies (with a total of nearly 5 million ratings). MovieLens users rate movies on a five-star scale.

The MovieLens front page shows users several lists of recommended films, including movies in theaters and movies recently released on video tape or DVD formats. The front page also provides access to special features, experiments, and a query interface. Users may search for movies by title, retrieving a list of matching movies with predicted ratings, or may select categories of movies by date and genre, retrieving lists of recommendations sorted by prediction.

PolyLens was integrated with MovieLens in three places. New links were added to the front page to allow users to create or manage groups; a new field was added to the query interface to allow users to select whether they were looking for group or individual recommendations; and a membership consent interface was added to alert users who were invited to join groups of their pending invitation.

Our goals in designing PolyLens were to:

- gain experience with the design and use of group recommenders;
- create a system that MovieLens users would find valuable;
- simplify the implementation by using our existing infrastructure; and
- keep the trust of MovieLens users by implementing policies and algorithms that respected their privacy and presented accurate recommendations.

We explicitly were not trying to experimentally identify the best design or to compare design alternatives in any systematic way. We knew that several of our goals depended upon having happy users, and therefore focused our efforts on designing a system that would satisfy our users.

Given the novelty of group recommenders, we were forced to start design from scratch. We identified five specific questions about groups and membership, group recommendations, and group interfaces. We reviewed the design alternatives in each area, choosing those that seemed appropriate for our goal of supporting groups of people who were going to see a movie together. In this section, we discuss those five design questions, the alternatives we explored, the choices we made for PolyLens, and different design goals for which alternative designs would be more appropriate.

What is the nature of a group?

Are groups ephemeral or persistent? Public or private?

The persistence of groups is an issue related to both usage patterns and privacy issues. If users want to repeatedly receive recommendations for the same group of people, it saves time and effort to make the group persistent. On the other hand, if groups form and dissociate for a single use, ephemeral approaches better meet the need. This issue interacts with consent (discussed below) as a time-intensive consent process may render ephemeral groups inconvenient, but users may be willing to reduce the amount of consent required if they know the group is only used once, or only in their presence.

A related issue is whether groups are private, known only to group members, or public and accessible to all. Public groups can become community meeting places of sorts (e.g., the *Titanic-haters* group) or even soapboxes where famous critics such as Roger Ebert and Richard Roeper might define a new taste. Private groups serve as clubs where a group of friends or family may share tastes away from the noise and scrutiny of the masses.

In PolyLens, we chose to design the system to support many persistent private groups. Given the nature of movie going, we believed users would often choose to go to the movies with members of the same groups. We also expected that any individual user would be part of only a few groups, but that the system might have many small groups. Private groups minimized both naming problems and concerns about privacy.

Alternative designs would be more appropriate in other cases. A bookseller creating on-line book clubs, for example, might prefer to have a small number of public groups, both to make it easier to find a group and to focus attention on the selected books. Systems to support casual recommendations, such as the workout music playing in a gym might be better designed to support rapid ephemeral group formation (McCarthy & Anagnost, 1998). Similarly, a movie recommender in a kiosk in a video store, rather than on the web, might make use of ephemeral groups by having group members scan their membership cards to receive impromptu group recommendations.

How do groups form and evolve?

All group support systems, from e-mail lists to physical invitations, must address the question of creation and maintenance of the groups. Three important issues are: who creates groups, who can join them, and how are they managed.

The decision on who can create groups frequently determines the nature and quantity of groups. An administrator who creates every group may provide a level of quality control, but may also be a bottleneck that reduces the number of groups created. At the other extreme, some systems allow any user to create groups, encouraging group formation but possibly resulting in a large number of duplicate or otherwise underused groups (particularly when they are public). A middle position limits group creation to people with certain privileges.

A related question is who may join groups. Some systems let users apply to join private groups while others require members to be invited. Systems with large, public groups often allow members to simply join without the group's consent. Other issues include the ability to set qualifications for group membership and the question of whether group membership is restricted to members of a larger community (e.g., members of the recommender system).

Group management ranges from anarchy (where all members have all rights, including the right to disband the group) to dictatorship (where a group's founder or administrator has all rights, and members have none) with a variety of compromises in the middle such as voting systems. Particular rights relevant to administering groups include adding and removing members, viewing the membership list, disbanding the group, and delegating administration privileges.

In PolyLens, we wanted to encourage group formation while keeping administration and membership simple. We decided to allow any MovieLens user to create a group, and limited membership to the people that the group creator invited. All group members could view the membership list and remove themselves from the group, but only the creator of the group could invite new members or remove another member. The creator of the group must already know the person she wants to invite; there is no mechanism for finding other users through PolyLens.

Most of our decisions make less sense for systems with public groups or larger groups. In particular, public group systems need either open joining or an application process to avoid in-band membership requests. For instance, mailing list systems such as majordomo usually have careful rules that separate membership requests from the list traffic. Systems with larger groups also need a way to delegate administrator privileges and may want to have additional levels of administration, such as a system-wide administrator who has the authority to disband a group that violates site policies.

How is privacy handled within a group?

Since the goal of a group recommender system is to recommend items for the group as a whole, membership entails at least some minimal loss of privacy. We look at what control users have over their own membership in groups as well as what control they have over sharing their personal data.

There are three common policies for membership control. One policy, often used in "groups" formed by junk mailers and spammers, neither notifies members nor asks their consent. This gives users no control and awareness of group membership but does make it easy to form groups. A second policy notifies the user that she has been added to a group, providing awareness but no explicit consent. This policy also makes it easy to form groups, but sacrifices user control over private data. The third policy requires consent from an invited group member before that member enters the group and before her data is used by the group. This policy makes it more difficult to create groups but provides the greatest privacy protection to the users.

Once a user joins a group, what control does he retain over his personal data? In recommender communities, data can be divided into two categories: ratings data and recommendation data. Ratings data comprises the opinions the user has entered about items he has experienced. Recommendation data comprises system-derived predictions of how well a user would like a particular item. In the example of movies, a user may have ratings data indicating that he liked *Titanic* very much (giving it five stars) as well as recommendation data indicating that the system thinks he'll dislike *Star Trek VI*.

A recommender system can use personal data without revealing it, or may reveal it to other users. Any user joining a recommender system community, with or without groups, consents to having his ratings used by the system to generate recommendations for others. This consent is fundamental to collaborative filtering recommenders and is the basis for forming the community. Similarly, in order to influence the items recommended to a group, a group member must implicitly allow the system to use his ratings (and possibly recommendations) in the formation of group recommendations, even if they are not explicitly revealed.[1] On the other hand, the ratings and recommendations of individual users need not be revealed to other group members. Particular implementations may make this information available, may hide this information, or may leave control over the information to each individual user.

In PolyLens, our concern for our members' privacy led us to require explicit consent before an invited member could be added to a group. We tried to make the process of consent as easy as possible. If the member is physically with the inviter, she can simply enter her ID and password to provide instant consent. Otherwise, the user is notified of the pending invitation when she next logs in to MovieLens. For people who are already MovieLens users, we also send a notification e-mail if they have consented to receive e-mail from us; for invitations to non-users, we have no choice but to send e-mail. During the consent process, the user is also asked whether she is willing to share her recommendations with the other group members. She can change this decision or leave the group at any time. We do not provide a way to share actual ratings.

How do we form recommendations for groups?

There are two issues to address when forming recommendations for groups. First, there is the general issue of defining a social value function that describes how the tastes and opinions of individuals affect the group's recommendation. Then there is the technical, algorithmic implementation of that social value function to create an efficient recommendation based on the tastes of many users.

The social value functions for group recommendations can vary substantially. Group happiness may be the average happiness of the members, the happiness of the most happy member, or the happiness of the least happy member (i.e., we're all miserable if one of us is unhappy). Other factors can be included. A social value function could weigh the opinion of expert members more highly, or could strive for long-term fairness by giving greater weight to people who "lost out" in previous recommendations.

Once a social value function is selected, an algorithm must be developed to implement it. Single-user collaborative filtering systems commonly use nearest neighbor algorithms that identify a set of community members most like the target user and evaluate items as a similarity-weighted average of the normalized ratings from those users. This algorithm is not directly applicable to group recommendations because each group member has different tastes and therefore different individual ratings profiles. There are two basic approaches for retaining

---

[1] We recognize that groups with few members can attempt to infer individual tastes from group predictions, particularly if members can form groups with and without a target member. This type of inferential attack on privacy is well known (Beck, 1980) and addressing it is beyond the scope of this work.

the essence of nearest neighbor algorithms in a group setting: creating a single neighborhood for the group and merging individual recommendations.

The most direct way to support group recommendations is to create a "pseudo-user" that represents the group's tastes, and to produce recommendations for the pseudo-user. The pseudo-user could be created manually by group members as a reflection of their shared tastes, or it could be created automatically by merging the rating profiles of the group members. Manual creation allows groups to come to explicit consensus on movie ratings (in a way, they can define their own social value functions), but this is time-consuming and hard to keep current. Automatic creation of pseudo-users from group member profiles is more practical, but it raises several issues. In particular, the formula for merging ratings may give unequal weight to the ratings of different users. For instance, using the union of the group's individual ratings leads to recommendations biased toward users with more ratings. A related approach is to avoid merging profiles and instead choose a set of neighbors to best fit the group overall, for some best-fit criteria. By representing the taste of the group before making recommendations, these single neighborhood approaches increase the chance of finding serendipitously valuable recommendations. On the other hand, these algorithms can produce recommendations that satisfy many, but not all, members of a group, which may not match the desired social value function. Furthermore, the group prediction may lie outside the range of any individual predictions, which may be disorienting to users and difficult to explain (Herlocker et al., 2000).

Instead of creating pseudo-users, the recommender system can generate recommendation lists for each group member and merge the lists. Merging strategies have several advantages. They present results that can be directly related to the results that would be seen by individual group members. This means that the results are relatively easy to explain (e.g., "the system believes that three of you would like it a lot, but two of you wouldn't like it at all"). Also, since these approaches compute individual recommendations it is efficient to display them alongside the group recommendation, giving users more information with which to make decisions. On the other hand, group recommendations based on merge strategies are less likely to identify unexpected, serendipitous items.

In PolyLens, we expected most groups to be small—just two or three users—and therefore chose to use a social value function where the group's happiness was the minimum of the individual members' happiness scores. We also decided not to recommend movies that any member of the group had already rated (and therefore seen). We used an algorithm that merged users' recommendation lists, and sorted the merged list according to the principle of least misery.

We know that both our social value function and our recommendation list merge algorithm are unlikely to work well for large groups. It is an open research question to understand the types of social value functions that best satisfy large groups and to implement them algorithmically.

What interfaces support group recommenders?

Two key components to a group recommender interface are the interface for requesting recommendations and the display of returned recommendations. We intentionally omit discussion of graphic design to focus on the data being presented and the queries supported. We explored three models of organizing the available information when displaying recommendations: a group-only interface, a composite interface, and an individual-focused interface.

Group-only interfaces display items with the group recommendation. These interfaces avoid revealing preference information from other group members, but also prevent group members from balancing the interests of others in selecting an item. In Figure 1 we show a modified group-only interface that also displays the predicted value for the group member who is requesting the recommendation.

TITLE	GENRE	GROUP	YOUR
King of Masks, The (Bian Lian) (1996)	Drama	★★★★✔	★★★★✔

Figure 1. A modified group-only interface.

Composite interfaces display a list of recommended movies with both group and individual member predictions. Depending on the privacy policy of the system, particular group members may be omitted from the listing. These interfaces allow group members to balance the system's estimate of group welfare with the predicted happiness of each group member. Figure 2 depicts a simple composite interface for a two-member group.

TITLE	GENRE	REVIEWS	GROUP	YOUR	lam@cs.umn.edu
Frequency (2000)	Drama, Thriller	MOVIE REVIEW	★★★★✔	★★★★✔	★★★★✔

Figure 2. A two-member composite group interface.

Individual-focused interfaces show the items in the context of individual user preferences. They may even entirely omit group recommendations, though such recommendations could be either displayed or used to filter the movies being displayed. In Figure 3 we illustrate a "manual" group recommender that simply brings together individual recommendation list displays.

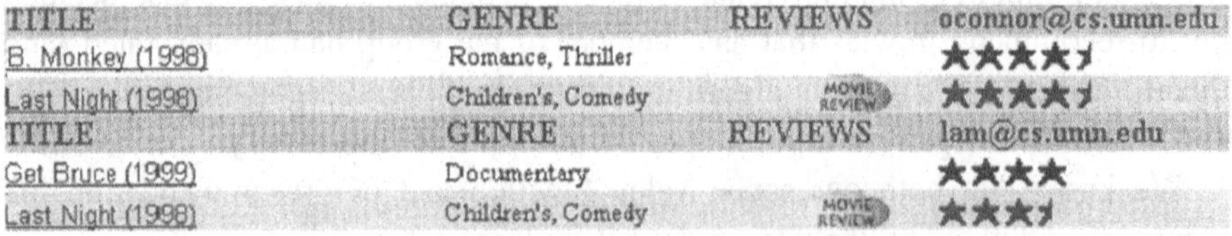

TITLE	GENRE	REVIEWS	oconnor@cs.umn.edu
B. Monkey (1998)	Romance, Thriller		★★★★✔
Last Night (1998)	Children's, Comedy	MOVIE REVIEW	★★★★✔
TITLE	GENRE	REVIEWS	lam@cs.umn.edu
Get Bruce (1999)	Documentary		★★★★
Last Night (1998)	Children's, Comedy	MOVIE REVIEW	★★★✔

Figure 3. A manual group recommender.

We implemented a composite interface for displaying recommendations in order to provide maximum information while minimizing the load on users. Recommendations are sorted in order of decreasing group prediction. The interface for making recommendation requests is the same as the standard MovieLens interface: users can request group recommendations by searching for titles or by specifying restrictions on date and genre. The only difference is that with PolyLens the user may also specify whether to receive group or individual recommendations. We expect that group recommender applications, including PolyLens, may warrant more advanced, custom interfaces, but have deferred study of these until after establishing the value of group recommendations *per se.*

The PolyLens Field Trial

We conducted a nine-month (and still ongoing) field trial of the PolyLens system beginning in May 2000. Figure 4 shows the progress of the field trial.

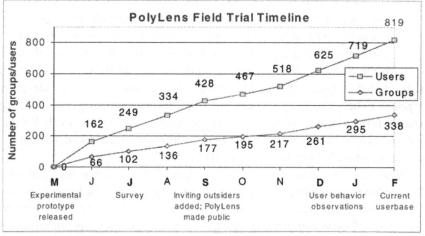

Figure 4. Timeline of the PolyLens Field Trial.

We released PolyLens as an experimental feature of MovieLens in May. This meant that users who consented were allowed to use the feature. In July, we surveyed the experimental users and revised the prototype based on their comments, allowing group creators to invite people who were not yet MovieLens members. We released the revised prototype to the entire MovieLens community in September. After three months, we conducted observations of how the group recommendation features affected user behavior. As of February 2001, PolyLens has 338 groups with 819 members. They have made about 7,000 requests for group recommendations, and have received over 114,000 recommended movies.

Several sources provide the data cited below. Group membership, creators, and names were pulled directly from our database. We logged the user, group, and time when users created groups, joined groups, and made individual or group recommendation requests. In July we conducted a survey of group users. The survey received a total of 143 responses (57% of the experimental users). The survey contained six "agree/disagree" type questions as well as a question soliciting additional comments.

How Groups Were Formed and Used

Most PolyLens groups are small, and they are made of up people who know each other. Table I shows the distribution of group sizes.

Group names followed several common patterns. A pair of proximate personal names (*Jess and Wes*; *Brett&Corrie*) accounts for about 35% of all groups. Families (*The Vails*; *maxwell family*) created another 10%. The rest fall into several categories:

Members	Number of groups
2	257
3	53
4	16
More	12
Total	338

Table I. Group sizes.

- in-jokes (*monkeychickens*; *Ninety-Percenters Know nothing!*);
- salient group characteristics (*College Swimmers*; *MommiesWeBe*); and
- names about being a movie group (*Must See*; *Film, thy name is... film*).

Both the distribution of group sizes and the characteristics of group names suggest that PolyLens groups are composed of people who go to the movies together rather than people drawn by film characteristics (e.g., sci fi groups, Danny Elfman fans). Since movie-going groups tend to be small, PolyLens groups were small as well. This is not surprising, since MovieLens has no mechanism to help users to find other, like-minded users.

What was surprising was that 492 people tried to form groups and failed. Misspelled e-mail addresses, users who ignored invitations, duplicate groups, and flaws in the group interface explain some of these cases. We suspect, however, that many of these one-member "groups" were born when people thought that a movie group would be neat, created the group, and only then realized that they would not be able to recruit MovieLens users that they did not already know.

We wondered whether requiring the consent of members to join groups caused them to form slowly. We measured this consent lag during the prototype period. The median lag was 46 minutes, the mean 4.9 days. The shortest time was 16 seconds, the longest 110 days. Once formed, groups rarely formally disband: only 14 groups (4%) did so.

Groups follow one of three lifecycles. About one-quarter of all groups are used only on the day they form. These are probably either ephemeral groups, meant to be used only once, or else groups that users tried and decided they did not like. Another set of groups appears to be "permanent". One-quarter of the groups created in the first two months of the trial were still in use as of February, seven to nine months later. This may be a high estimate for the entire population of groups, as these groups belong to enthusiastic experimental "early adopters"— but it does imply that groups give long-term value to many users. The rest of the groups are used for a few weeks or months and then lay fallow, with the break-even point around 55 days: half of all groups are used for less than 55 days, half for more. Groups may be abandoned for several reasons: the members decide that group recommendations are not worth the effort; the members stop seeing movies as a group; the members leave MovieLens altogether; the group is dormant; etc.

Most PolyLens users joined (89%) or created (93%) exactly one group; Table II gives a detailed breakdown.

n	Member of n groups	Creator of n groups
1	628	286
2	55	19
3	19	2
More	6	2
Total	708	309

Table II. Number of groups users belong to and create.

There are 708 unique users filling the roles of 819 members, so there is about a 14% overlap between groups. Much of this overlap occurred in situations where a set of users created several overlapping groups.

Across the entire field study, the group's creator was the only member who requested group recommendations for 73 of 338 groups (22%). On the other hand, the group's creator never requested recommendations for 34 groups (10%). Overall, 659 of 819 (80%) of group members requested group recommendations.

Users have made a total of about 7,000 group recommendation requests, or about 10 per user. We do not know the exact number because of a data collection failure; our estimate is based on 11,432 pages of group recommendations viewed and the average number of pages viewed per request (about 1.7).

How Groups Affect the Way Users Use MovieLens

So how do 10 group requests per user stack up against their overall MovieLens usage? And how do new users who came to MovieLens via a group invitation behave differently than others? We made three comparisons to find out how the group recommendation features affected the way users use MovieLens:
- new users invited to join MovieLens through groups vs. other new users;
- new invited users vs. established users who joined groups; and
- established users who joined groups vs. other established users.

The statistics in this section are mostly descriptive; those that are statistically significant are noted. It is hard to establish statistical significance for behavioral differences among MovieLens users because their behavior has high variance. Some rate ten movies while others rate hundreds; some log in once per month, others, once per day.

We studied the 77 "invitees" (users who came to MovieLens because of group invitations) who joined MovieLens between September and January. These users differed from other new users in two ways: friends invited them to join groups, and they had to learn how to use both MovieLens and its group features. Because our server's response time varies (publicity causes usage spikes) and could affect whether new users continue to use the system, we chose a control group of 77 users who joined at about the same times as the invitees. We measured system use for their first 30 days; Table III gives the results.

Use	Invitees	Other new users
Recommendation requests	872	459
Total logins after first visit	103	61
Users who returned after their first visit	36 (47%)	25 (32%)

Table III. New invitees' use of MovieLens vs. that of other new users.

Invitees use the system more actively than other new users, making significantly more recommendation requests ($t(152)=2.01$, $p<0.05$). We believe several factors caused this. First, people who refer invitees may have introduced a selection bias, only inviting users they thought would like MovieLens. Their endorsement of MovieLens also probably carried weight, making invitees more disposed to experiment with the system. Finally, users responding to the survey said that group recommendations add value. Invitees saw a more useful system than did the other new users, and so used it more actively.

We next compared how these invitees used MovieLens to how established users who joined groups used the system. A total of 59 invitees used the system to get recommendations, so we chose a control group of 59 established users who joined groups during the same period and measured requests for group and individual recommendations for 30 days. Table IV shows what happened.

Use	Invitees	Established users
Group recommendation requests	112 (18%)	356 (23%)
Average movies recommended/group request	20	17
Individual recommendation requests	527 (82%)	1193 (77%)
Average movies recommended/individual request	101	46

Table IV. New invitees' use of MovieLens vs. that of established users.

These data show that established MovieLens users made more overall requests than the invitees ($t(116)=2.68$, $p<0.01$). This is sensible, since some invitees never returned to MovieLens, while the non-returners had already been shaken out of the group of established users.

Established users used groups for a greater percentage of recommendation requests than did invitees, although the difference was not statistically significant. We believe that the difference is not statistically significant because user behavior will be different between the short term and the long term. In the short term, invitees had more to do—rate movies, learn how MovieLens works, and explore the group features—while established users could concentrate on using group recommendations. In the long term, we expect that invitees would use the system for more group recommendations than other group users because that is how the system was first presented to them.

Both invitees (t(58)=4.14, p<0.01) and experienced users (t(58)=4.34, p<0.01) view more movies per individual recommendation request than they do per group request. Three factors contribute to this. First, users can rate movies that MovieLens recommends and they have seen, but only when they request individual recommendations. Many users like to rate movies; these users would tend to pursue individual searches. Second, for group recommendations, the system's predicted score falls off quickly because of the "minimum individual score" social value function we use. Some users probably cut off searches once the prediction falls low enough. Finally, users may be able to make decisions based on group recommendations without looking at as many movies as they need to when they make decisions based on individual recommendations.

We wanted to see how joining groups affected MovieLens use among established users. We compared the 59 established users mentioned above who joined groups to another set of 59 established users who only used the system for individual recommendations. We measured system use for 30 days. Users who joined groups made a total of 1,549 recommendation requests. Users who were not group members made a total of 1,666 requests, slightly more than the group joiners, but the difference was not statistically significant.

User Satisfaction

Four of our survey questions focused on how well users liked the group recommendation features. Table V shows their responses.

	Strongly agree	Agree	Disagree	Strongly disagree
I found the process of creating groups easy.	45%	50%	4%	0%
I found it easy to add members to groups.	33%	45%	21%	0%
I found group recommendations more helpful than individual recommendations when deciding on a movie to see.	22%	55%	23%	0%
	Very satisfied	Satisfied	Dissatisfied	Very Dissatisfied
Overall how satisfied are you with MovieLens groups?	41%	54%	5%	0%

Table V. Survey results for user satisfaction questions.

These results suggest that users were pleased with the ability to receive group recommendations, with 95% satisfied or very satisfied with the group recommendation feature, and 77% finding group recommendations more useful than individual ones. Several users emphasized their approval in their comments:

"A delightful and substantive addition to your offering. I love movielens. And now even more."

However, 21% of users found it difficult to add members to groups. Quotes from respondents indicated that the main problem was that in order to add a member to a group, that person had to already be a MovieLens user:

"I'd like very much to be able to invite non-movielens users to a group. Then when they receive the invitation, they can sign up. It's a lot easier than convincing someone to go to the site, sign up, and give me the e-mail address they used for your site."

Outreach

Group creators invited non-MovieLens members to join their groups 391 times. The invitees accepted 95 of these invitations. In 15 cases, one group creator brought in two or more new users (the highest was 12). These invitees add value to the system. As shown above, they are more active than other new users. Recommender systems do better as more people use them, so when users are active the entire community benefits. Group recommenders also provide an opportunity to make explicit the normally anonymous underlying community that allows recommender systems to work.

Privacy

Two survey questions asked users how they felt about seeing others' recommendations and sharing their own. Table VI gives the results.

	Strongly agree	Agree	Disagree	Strongly disagree
I prefer being able to see each group member's personal recommendations.	60%	34%	4%	2%
I prefer having other group members see my personal recommendations.	47%	46%	4%	3%

Table VI. Survey results for privacy-related questions.

Nearly all users preferred to allow other group members to see their personal recommendations (93%) and to see the personal recommendations of other group members (94%). The MovieLens database shows that over 97% (798 of 819) of group members actually do share their recommendations, confirming the survey results. Some users also commented that seeing individual recommendations was essential to making good use of group recommendations.

Mailing group invitations to new users presents a privacy issue. We e-mailed group invitations to MovieLens users only if they had consented to receive e-mail from us. Since we could only contact non-users by e-mail, we designed the invitations to be as personal as possible. We allow group creators to include a personal message, and we send the mail in the name of the group creator if the name appears to be a valid e-mail address. To date, we have received no spam complaints resulting from sending group invitation e-mails.

Lessons Learned

We studied a number of aspects of group recommenders during the field trial, including how groups formed and who used them, how group recommenders affect the use of a recommender system, how satisfied users were with group recommendations, the effect of being able to invite members from outside the recommender system, and how users reacted to the loss of privacy required when joining a group. Here we summarize key lessons learned.

Users like and use group recommenders. PolyLens users expressed a clear desire for group recommendations. Both survey results and observations of user behavior support this claim. We believe that the utility of group recommender systems will generalize to most domains where groups consume entertainment together, such as book clubs, dining out, travel, and concerts. Whether group recommendations are useful in non-entertainment domains is less certain, as there is less shared consumption.

Users trade privacy for utility. The vast majority of PolyLens users were willing to trade privacy for group recommendations. Three factors contributed. First, users had direct control over sharing recommendations. Second, people in PolyLens groups already know each other and probably discuss their reactions to movies. Third, personalized movie recommendations have limited intrinsic value to others. All of these factors are important: if users do not control their data, if they must share their data with strangers, or if the items recommended are of a sensitive nature (e.g., stock picks), people will be less likely to share personal recommendations.

For maximum group use, users must be able to find each other. Most PolyLens groups were very small, and many groups were stillborn. This is partly because of the nature of our userbase, and partly because users were required to know each other outside of MovieLens. We feel that most group recommender systems should have features to help users find each other. These features would help users form groups and would make the community aspect of recommender systems more explicit, although they would raise new privacy issues.

Better social value functions for group predictions are needed. Several users disliked the "minimize misery" policy that PolyLens uses, and one pointed out that our implementation does not take into account differences in rating scales (e.g., Mark's "5" is Dan's "3"). We got away with this simple method for combining recommendations because the groups were small and because users could review the individual recommendations to make a final decision.

Groups are permanent, but also ephemeral. We were right that groups would be permanent, but failed to address situations where only part of the group wanted to go to a movie. Several sets of users created multiple groups, each of which contained a subset of the members, to support temporarily removing group members. One user explicitly asked for such a feature:

"We need to be able to select certain group members and generate suggestions specifically for those members only. For instance, if only three of us are going to the movies, and there are five in the group, we don't want the other two skewing our average."

Group recommenders should support temporary removal of group members.

Groups are valuable to all members, not just the creator. We expected that group creators might have the role of primary decision maker for movie selections for their groups and might therefore be the main users. We found to the contrary that 80% of group members requested group recommendations. This suggests that the group recommendation interface should not require administrative privileges to use. Also, a group administration policy that allows all group users to add members might be effective and might encourage groups to grow.

Using the group mechanism to reach out to new users is effective. New users who came to MovieLens through group invitations used MovieLens more actively than other new users. Group creators no doubt did some filtering of users who were not likely to use the system—but that's a good thing.

Conclusion

We presented the first example of a collaborative filtering recommender system that recommends items to groups of people based on their collective preferences. Surveys and usage studies show that users like group recommendations. Further, even though group recommendations require users to give up some of their privacy, our users indicate that the tradeoff was worthwhile for them. One reason the reduced privacy was less of a problem in this study is that most of the groups were very small, probably comprised of a group of close friends. Future work is needed to understand the tradeoffs for larger or more anonymous groups, as well as to establish appropriate social value functions for such groups.

While the PolyLens system was designed specifically for users of a movie recommendation site, we also reviewed the design space for group recommenders to help others design group recommender applications. The results of our field trial are limited to the particular set of design decisions we made for PolyLens. Further study is needed to understand which designs best serve users of other recommender applications.

Acknowledgements

We would like to thank members of the GroupLens Research Group for their contributions to this research, and particularly Tony Lam for developing the MovieLens experimental framework. We would also like to thank the members of MovieLens.

This work was supported by grants from the National Science Foundation (IIS 96-13960, IIS 97-34442, and IIS 99-78717) and by Net Perceptions, Inc.

References

Aggarwal, C., Wolf, J., Wu, K., & Yu, P.S. (1999): 'Horting hatches an egg: A new graph-theoretic approach to collaborative filtering', in *Proceedings of the Fifth ACM SIGKDD International Conference on Knowledge Discovery and Data Mining*, San Diego, CA, 1999, pp. 201-212.

Beck, L. (1980): 'A security mechanism for statistical databases', *ACM Transactions on Database Systems*, vol. 5, no. 3, 1980, pp. 316-338.

Breese, J.S., Heckerman, D., & Kadie, C. (1998): 'Empirical analysis of predictive algorithms for collaborative filtering', in *Proceedings of the Fourteenth Conference on Uncertainty in Artificial Intelligence,* San Francisco, CA, 1998, pp. 43-52.

Dewan, P., & Shen, H. (1998): 'Flexible Meta Access-Control for Collaborative Applications', in *Proceedings of the ACM 1998 Conference on CSCW,* Seattle, WA, 1998, pp. 247-256.

Edwards, W.K. (1996): 'Policies and roles in collaborative applications', in *Proceedings of the ACM 1996 Conference on CSCW,* Boston, MA, 1996, pp. 11-20.

Ellis, C.A., Gibbs, S.J., & Rein, G. (1991): 'Groupware: Some Issues and Experiences', *Communications of the ACM*, vol. 34, no. 1, January 1991, pp. 39-58.

Goldberg, K., Roeder, T., Gupta, D., & Perkins, C. (2000): 'Eigentaste: A Constant Time Collaborative Filtering Algorithm', UCB ERL Technical Report M00/41, August 2000.

Gutwin, C., & Greenberg, S. (1998): 'Design for individuals, design for groups: tradeoffs between power and workplace awareness', in *Proceedings of the ACM 1998 Conference on CSCW,* Seattle, WA, 1998, pp. 207-216.

Herlocker, J.L., Konstan, J.A., Borchers, A., & Riedl, J. (1999): 'An algorithmic framework for performing collaborative filtering', in *Proceedings of the 22nd Annual International ACM SIGIR Conference on Research and Development in Information Retrieval*, Berkeley, CA, 1999, pp. 230-237.

Herlocker, J.L., Konstan, J.A., & Riedl, J. (2000): 'Explaining Collaborative Filtering Recommendations', in *Proceedings of the ACM 2000 Conference on CSCW,* Philadelphia, PA, 2000, pp. 241-250.

Hill, W., Stead, L., Rosenstein, M., & Furnas, G. (1995): 'Recommending and Evaluating Choices in a Virtual Community of Use', in *Conference Proceedings on Human Factors in Computing Systems*, Denver, CO, 1995, pp. 194-201.

Konstan, J.A., Miller, B.N., Maltz, D., Herlocker, J.L., Gordon, L.R., & Riedl, J. (1997): 'GroupLens: Applying Collaborative Filtering to Usenet News', *Communications of the ACM*, vol. 40, no. 3, March 1997, pp. 77-87.

McCarthy, J., & Anagnost, T. (1998): 'MusicFX: An arbiter of group preferences for computer supported collaborative workouts', in *Proceedings of the ACM 1998 Conference on CSCW*, Seattle, WA, 1998, pp. 363-372.

Mitchell, A., Posner, I., & Baecker, R. (1995): 'Learning to Write Together Using Groupware', in *Conference Proceedings on Human Factors in Computing Systems*, Denver, CO, 1995, pp. 288-295.

Neuwirth, C.M., Kaufer, D.S., & Chandhok, R. (1994): 'Computer Support for Distributed Collaborative Writing: Defining Parameters of Interaction', in *Proceedings of the Conference on CSCW*, Chapel Hill, NC, 1994, pp. 145-152.

Resnick, P., Iacovou, N., Suchak, M., Bergstrom, P., & Riedl, J. (1994): 'GroupLens: An Open Architecture for Collaborative Filtering of Netnews', in *Proceedings of the Conference on CSCW*, Chapel Hill, NC, 1994, pp. 175-186.

Resnick P., & Varian H. (1997): 'Recommender Systems', *Communications of the ACM*, vol. 40, no. 3, March 1997, pp. 56-58.

Sarwar, B.M., Konstan, J.A., Borchers, A., Herlocker, J., Miller, B., & Riedl, J. (1998): 'Using filtering agents to improve prediction quality in the GroupLens research collaborative filtering system', in *Proceedings of the ACM 1998 Conference on CSCW*, Seattle, WA, 1998, pp. 345-354.

Sarwar, B.M., Karypis, G., Konstan, J.A., & Riedl, J. (2000): 'Application of dimensionality reduction in recommender systems—a case study', in *ACM WebKDD 2000 Web Mining for E-Commerce Workshop*, Boston, MA, 2000.

Schafer, J.B., Konstan, J., & Riedl, J. (1999): 'Recommender Systems in E-Commerce', in *Proceedings of the First ACM Conference on Electronic Commerce*, Denver, CO, 1999, pp. 158-166.

Shardanand, U., & Maes, P. (1995): 'Social Information Filtering: Algorithms for Automating "Word of Mouth"', in *Conference Proceedings on Human Factors in Computing Systems*, Denver, CO, 1995, pp. 210-217.

Smith, R.B., Hixon, R., & Horan, B. (1998): 'Supporting Flexible Roles in a Shared Space', in *Proceedings of the ACM 1998 Conference on CSCW*, Seattle, WA, 1998, pp. 197-206.

Ungar, L.H., & Foster, D.P. (1998): 'Clustering Methods for Collaborative Filtering', *in AAAI Workshop on Recommendation Systems*, Menlo Park, CA, 1998.

Whittaker, S. (1996): 'Talking to Strangers: An Evaluation of the Factors Affecting Electronic Collaboration', in *Proceedings of the ACM 1996 Conference on CSCW*, Boston, MA, 1996, pp. 409-418.

W. Prinz, M. Jarke, Y. Rogers, K. Schmidt, and V. Wulf (eds.), *Proceedings of the Seventh European Conference on Computer-Supported Cooperative Work, 16-20 September 2001, Bonn, Germany*, pp. 219-238.
© 2001 Kluwer Academic Publishers. Printed in the Netherlands.

y do tngrs luv 2 txt msg?[1]

Rebecca E. Grinter and Margery A. Eldridge
Xerox PARC, USA and Xerox Research Centre Europe, Cambridge, UK
grinter@parc.xerox.com, eldridge@xrce.xerox.com

Abstract: "Text messaging" — using a mobile phone to send a message — has changed how teenagers use wireless phones to communicate and coordinate. While the media reports rapid growth in text messaging, less is known about why teenagers have adopted it. In this paper, we report findings from a study of teenagers' text messaging practices. Specifically, we show that teenagers use text messages to: arrange and adjust times to talk, coordinate with friends and family, and chat. Moreover, we argue that the reasons teenagers find text messaging quick, cheap, and easy to use, are grounded in their social context. Finally, we show that teenagers encounter three problems when text messaging: understanding evolving language, determining intent from content, and addressing messages.

Introduction

In the UK, many people call friends and family on Christmas Day to wish them seasonal greetings. Typically, this leads to heavier than normal call volumes. Last year something different happened on December 25th: mobile phone networks experienced heavy loads. It was not voice calls that congested mobile networks but rather text messages creating the heavy volume (Verkaik, 2000).

To many this will not come as a surprise, because "text messaging" is a recent communications phenomenon. Text messaging — using a mobile phone to send a message — has changed mobile phone usage. Originally expensive voice-calling devices, mobiles have become mini-terminals for text-based communications, and

---

[1] Why do teenagers love to text message?

now something that was originally designed as "spare" bandwidth has become a popular way to interact with others.

In Europe, teenagers have been among the quickest to adopt text messaging. It is a common sight to see teenagers typing away furiously on their mobiles. One type of service plan, known as "pay-as-you-go," has fueled the growth of mobile ownership among teens. Pay-as-you-go plans have three advantages for teenagers: first, they do not require credit checks; second, they help the teenagers manage their expenses because costs are managed up-front through the purchase of vouchers; and third, those vouchers are available everywhere, making it easy for teenagers to get them. As pay-as-you-go plans made mobile phone ownership possible for teenagers, so these teenagers began using text messages to communicate.

The Rise of Text Messaging among Teenagers

Text messaging uses the Short Message Service (SMS) capacity built into the Groupe Spéciale Mobile (GSM) wireless standard (Newton, 2000). Text messages can be up to 160 characters in length and sent from any mobile to any other wireless phone on the GSM network. It is also possible to send text messages from the Internet to mobile phones.

SMS was deployed with the first GSM networks, and the first text messages were sent in the early 1990s. Initially SMS capacity was used infrequently. The explosion in usage came later, as Rautiainen and Kasesniemi (2000) describe in their own study of mobile practices:

> A significant change took place in the spring of 1998. Suddenly, instead of talking about calling and changing color covers on their mobiles, all the teenagers wanted to give their views on text messaging. In a few months the number (of) text messages sent attained the number of calls made and surpassed it. (Rautiainen & Kasesniemi, 2000).

Groups who track SMS usage rates support Rautiainen and Kasesniemi's observation. For example, the Mobile Data Association (2000) — which tracks SMS usage in the United Kingdom (UK) — reports that UK residents sent 90 million text messages in August 1999. One year later, in August 2000, UK residents sent 560 million text messages; by November 2000, it was 680 million. What makes these numbers more significant is that UK residents do not use SMS as frequently as residents of other countries including the Philippines, Finland and Germany.

In Europe, teenagers were among the earliest and biggest users of text messaging. Reports from Scandinavia show that teenagers have adopted text messaging, despite the potential limitations of the system itself, for example, the poor user interface (Ling, 2000; Rautiainen & Kasesniemi, 2000). Media reports confirm this rise in usage, but offer little systematic examination of why teenagers use text messages. Moreover, other than Ling's (2000) usage analysis, research studies of text messaging are currently in progress, so we only have limited knowledge of why teenagers use text messages.[2]

In addition to being interested in understanding why teenagers have adopted text messaging, we believe that this study can inform some broader CSCW concerns. First, although teenagers do differ from adults because of their circumstances, some of our findings do extrapolate to the work practices of adults. Second, these teenagers will soon enter the workplace themselves and they will bring their already well-developed text messaging practices with them. This study reveals what those practices are and may offer insight for how they fit into future workplaces. Third, we believe that CSCW has taken a broader concept of the notion of what "work" constitutes. Specifically, this study focuses on the coordination teenagers engage in as part of the work of being a teenager. Our findings help deepen our understanding of how they are managing and coordinating their interactions with others.

We begin by describing the teenagers who participated in the study, and the methods we used to study them. We then present data about teenagers' text messaging practices, including how often they sent and received text messages, and their physical location. We then turn to a more detailed analysis of what teenagers use text messages to accomplish. Specifically, we show that they use text messages to: arrange and adjust times to talk, coordinate with friends and family, and chat. We also show that they send text messages because they are quick, cheap, and easy to use. We argue that the teenagers have overcome potential technical limitations of SMS, such as poor input device and limited message length, and even turned them into advantages within their social context. Finally, we show that teenagers encounter three problems when text messaging: understanding evolving language, determining intent from content, and addressing messages.

Participants in the Study

Five girls and five boys participated in the study; seven of the teenagers were recruited through their participation in an earlier study carried out by the second author; the other three were friends of the earlier participants. They were paid for their participation, and consent forms were obtained from each teenager and one parent.

The teenagers were 15 to 16 years of age and attended full-time secondary school in south Cambridgeshire, an area of England that reports higher than the national average affluence. Many high-technology companies have offices and headquarters in the Cambridge area, and, in line with a recent study in the UK, all

---

[2] See http://www.info.uta.fi/winsoc/projekti/mobileco.htm for details. At the time of writing this paper, results had not been fully published.

the teenagers had computers at home with Internet access (BBC, 2000). Three of the boys had their own computers, while the rest shared one with other members of their families. The following information about the teenagers was obtained from a questionnaire that was distributed prior to beginning the study.

The teenagers reported using the Internet regularly: six reported being connected to the Internet less than one hour per day, and four more than one hour per day. Only two of the teenagers (both boys) paid for any part of their Internet use. Three of the teenagers had their own website. All of the teenagers reported regular use of e-mail, giving estimates of sending and receiving from 5-10 e-mail messages per day.[3] In addition to using e-mail, eight used instant messaging and five used chat rooms.

Having a mobile phone was a requirement for participating in the study. Three of the teenagers shared a phone with other members of the family; the others had their own phones. Two of the teenagers, one boy and one girl, had phones with monthly contracts; the rest all had pay-as-you-go phones.

Three of the teenagers, the two on contracts and one using a shared pay-as-you-go phone, paid no part of their mobile phone costs. All others paid for all of their phone costs, although one girl said her parents sometimes bought her phone vouchers. Most of the teenagers reported making less than 5 voice calls per day and receiving less than 5 voice calls per day on their mobile phones. In contrast, most reported sending 5-10 text messages per day and receiving 5-10 text messages per day. Most teenagers reported sending and receiving the bulk of their text messages from mobile phones, but many also sent and received text messages from the Internet using a variety of applications.

Not surprisingly, all teenagers had use of landline telephones from home, with a few having an additional landline dedicated to Internet use. Most teenagers estimated making 5-10 landline phone calls per day, and receiving about the same number. One boy estimated making and receiving more than 20 landline phone calls per day.

In summary, then, the teenagers participating in this study had a number of different technologies available to them to support communication with others. Their options included: Internet-based communication methods including e-mail, instant messaging and chat rooms; making and receiving landline phone calls; making and receiving mobile phone calls; and sending and receiving text messages.

Data Collection

Ideally, we would have liked to directly observe teenagers' text messaging practices. However, we knew that text messages were sent from many locations,

---

[3] We used e-mail to coordinate with the teenagers and found that all but one read and replied regularly.

including from school and late at night from home, making direct observation highly impractical. In addition, in some of our earlier discussions with teenagers, several reported that direct observation would inhibit their normal text messaging behaviour. For these reasons, we were forced to adopt more indirect approaches to capturing data.

In addition to the questionnaire distributed prior to the study, we collected quantitative data in a logging study and qualitative data in discussion groups held later. Each of these data collections methods will be discussed in turn.

The Logging Study

Two log forms were designed, one to record text messages sent, and one to record messages received. The teenagers were given written and verbal instructions before beginning the study. They were asked to enter details of all sent and received messages for seven consecutive days. Figure 1 shows an example of two logged entries from one girl's log form for sent messages. The headings at the top of the figure illustrate the information logged for each message. The log form for received messages was very similar.

ID No.	Date	Time	Sent by phone (P) or Internet (I)	Reply to other rec'd msg? If yes, give ID	Sent to?	Your physical location	Briefly describe content	Why did you send a Text Message instead of phoning, emailing, etc.?	Length (letters or lines of text)	List any abbreviations, shorthands, etc. in message	Did it lead to a phone conversation, meeting, etc? If yes, explain.
S5	22	20:05	P	R7	Nikki	still eating a meal in dining table.	I could not cause her us the pub soon.	Because she could not be in such message from the pub, do'nt complex phone answered.	2 lines	V. = Very	meaning - I met her not say pub, that she intended
S6	23	10:55	P	R8	Lizzie	Sitting up in bed at home.	I said I wasn't going shopping, I had wanted to do etc.	I was in bed so I didn't want her to know that.	4 lines	2day = Today Gr8 = Great :) = Smiley face.	No.

Figure 1. An example of two entries from one teenage girl's log form for sent messages.

The Discussion Groups

Once the teenagers had completed the logging part of the study, we looked through the data to help us formulate questions and topics for further discussion. About three weeks after the logging study, we held two discussion groups of five people each. Based on our previous experience, we felt that one group with ten people would not provide each person with opportunities to contribute to the discussion. Each session lasted about two hours, including time out for a pizza dinner.

We used the discussion groups as opportunities to address weaknesses of relying exclusively on the logs and questionnaires, and to get deeper explanations about patterns of text messaging. During each session, the following topics were discussed: reasons for getting a phone; initial experiences with the phones (most embarassing, most pleasant, most unpleasant); phone customisation; actual recorded versus reported frequencies of text messaging; and reasons for choosing text messaging over other methods of communication. We designed the questions so that the teenagers could discuss their answers with each other. One of us led the discussion, while the other identified opportunities to follow unexpected and interesting conversational topics. Each of the sessions was audio and video taped, and the tapes were then transcribed.

Text Messaging in Practice

We will begin our discussion of text messaging by focusing on the results from the logging study. Specifically, we describe how often the teenagers sent and received text messages; what media they chose for text messaging and why; and where text messaging occurs.

Frequencies of Text Messaging

A total of 236 sent messages and 241 received messages were logged. Not all participants logged for seven days. Table I presents the number of days each participant kept logs, and the average number of text messages sent and received by each participant.

Participant	Number of Days Logged	Mean Number of Messages Sent per Day	Mean Number of Messages Received per Day
G1	8	3.0	3.8
G2	15	2.8	1.9
G3	7	4.0	3.3
G4	7	3.7	4.3
G5	8	3.4	4.0
B1	7	3.0	2.4
B2	8	0.9	1.8
B3	7	4.1	2.3
B4	6	3.3	4.7
B5	7	1.7	3.2
Overall		3.0	3.0

Table I. Number of days logged and mean number of text messages sent and received by each participant (G1-5 are girls; B1-5 are boys).

Although the overall averages for both messages sent and received were 3.0 messages per day, these averages differed slightly for the boys and girls. The girls tended to send and receive more messages than the boys; the average messages sent were 3.3 for girls and 2.5 for boys, and the average messages received were 3.2 for girls and 2.8 for boys. This follows Rautiainen and Kaseniemi's (2000) observations that while boys and girls are equally as likely to own phones, the girls tend to send and receive more text messages. Two girls (G2 and G3) and two boys (B1 and B3) sent more messages than they received.

The logged frequencies of sending and receiving text messages are quite a bit lower than the estimated frequencies reported by the participants in the questionnaire distributed before the study. Most estimated sending from 5-10 messages per day, but no one logged this many. It is quite possible that the teenagers over-estimated their text messaging frequencies, as these types of self-report frequency measures are somewhat unreliable. We had asked for these estimates to get some idea of their use of text messaging relative to their use of other communication methods; hence the absolute numbers were not of such interest.

Nevertheless, we brought this discrepancy up at the discussion groups. One person (B5) said he was short of money that week and couldn't afford to buy another voucher; one other person (B2) who shared his phone said his step-mother was using it for most of the week. Two others (G2 and G4) mentioned that logging the calls made them aware of how much they were spending on text messages; for these girls, the logging method itself may have inhibited them from sending more text messages. Although the teenagers reported being very careful about logging all of their messages, it is possible that actual frequencies were higher than those logged.

Sending Text Messages via the Internet

Sending text messages via the Internet is free, compared to a cost of about GB£0.10 per message sent from a phone.[4] However, fewer messages were sent via the Internet (22%) than via a mobile phone (78%). One girl (G2) sent nearly as many messages via the Internet as from her phone, and two boys (B1 and B5) sent more via the Internet. In the discussion groups, cost was given as the main reason for the heavy use of sending messages via the Internet. However, three boys never used the Internet to send messages; of these, two (B3 and B4) paid none of their phone expenses, and thus saving money may not have been such a motivation for them.

Messages sent via the Internet tended to be longer, on average, than messages sent via a mobile phone (123 characters versus 71 characters), though both were well within the 160-character limit. We have no explanation for this difference, but it could be due to the relative ease of typing using a keyboard and to the reduction in the number of abbreviations used when typing on the keyboard. It could also be that because messages sent via the Internet are necessarily composed when sitting at the computer, the sender is rarely engaged in other simultaneous activities and hence has more time and attention to devote to typing longer messages.

---

[4] Approximately 0.15€.

Where Does Text Messaging Occur?

The participants logged their physical location for each text message they sent. We classified these locations for each of the 185 text messages sent by mobile phone (messages sent via the Internet were not included in this analysis, since we knew that the computers they used were at home). Table II shows the number and percentage of text messages sent from different physical locations.

Location	Number of Sent Messages	Percentage of Total*
At own home	116	63%
Unspecified	40	22%
In own bedroom	52	28%
In kitchen	12	6%
In lounge/study	9	5%
In bathroom	2	1%
On stairs	1	<1%
In transit	23	12%
On bus	8	4%
Waiting for bus	5	3%
In car	6	3%
While walking	3	2%
While bicycling	1	<1%
In town	19	10%
Unspecified	9	5%
In a shop	5	3%
In a pub	4	2%
In a restaurant	1	<1%
At other person's house	12	6%
At school	11	6%
At work	2	1%
Unspecified	2	1%
Total	185	99%

* Percentages do not always total due to rounding errors.

Table II. The number and percentage of text messages sent by mobile phone, classified by the sender's physical location.

More than half of the messages (63%) were sent from home, with most being sent from the teenager's own bedroom. One message (in reply to a received message) was sent from the bath (G5). Some messages were sent while in transit (12%), with one boy (B2) logging a message sent while bicycling. Interestingly, another boy (B4) during a discussion group also admitted to sending a text message while bicycling. Note that although the teenagers reported sending 11 messages while at school, only two explicitly said it was during classes. This is perhaps surprising given the amount of media attention devoted to how text messaging disrupts lessons.

What Do They Use Text Messaging For?

Teenagers use text messages for a variety of reasons. The percentages reported in these sections are percentages of all logged sent messages (236 in total; for some messages, multiple reasons were given). We illustrate the findings from the logs with explanations provided by the teenagers during the discussion sections.

Arranging Times to Chat and Adjusting Arrangements

Teenagers often used text messages to coordinate times and media for communicating. Communicating involves selecting among different technologies, such as e-mail or the phone, and then among specific instances of some media, such as what Internet instant messaging system to use. It is not surprising that they need to coordinate and clarify how, as well as when, they will communicate. Teenagers find text messaging useful for this coordination role.

The teenagers sent 35 messages (15%) arranging a time to phone each other. Specifically, the text messages were coordinating a time to talk on the home landline phone. Teenagers prefer to call a landline phone because the actual call cost is lower. During the discussion groups, the teenagers explained that they pre-arrange these calls because they prefer not to talk with the other family members who might answer the home phone.

The desire to avoid talking with other family members is sufficiently high that the teenagers are even willing to make voice calls to other mobiles — which is expensive — to ask their friends to prepare for a call on the landline, as these two quotes illustrate:

B5: I phone mobiles because then you know that you're going to get them straight away, instead....

G1: yeah.

G2: yeah.

B5: ....instead of having to go through all the family and things. You get straight to the person.

At another point during the discussion:

B5: Even people I know sort of phone my mobile and then say oh, can I phone your house.

G4: That's because it's cheaper

G1: They're phoning to make sure that you're standing by the phone when it rings.

The teenagers sent 13 messages (6%) to coordinate a time and system with which to Instant Message each other. Finally, they sent 10 messages (4%) to arrange times to have face-to-face conversations. Strub (1997), in a study of teenagers at a rock concert, also found that two-way radios were frequently used to arrange subsequent face-to-face meetings.

In addition to making initial plans to communicate, the teenagers also used text messages to revise those arrangements. They sent 11 messages (5%) to say that events — often at home — would conflict with their ability to make the arranged time. They had a number of reasons, some peculiar to being teenagers, which made it sometimes difficult to keep arrangements. One that rarely affects adults is being barred from using communications technologies; we found five instances where text messages were apologies for not using instant messaging or phoning, because they were not allowed on the computer or phone. However, other reasons could affect all users of shared resources. Specifically, we saw two messages rearranging commitments because someone else in their home was using the required resource. Another two messages were sent because the sender suspected the recipient of using the required resource.

Coordinating with Friends

Another activity that the teenagers often used text messaging for was coordinating an outing or activity with friends. They sent 61 messages (26%) arranging activities such as going to the pub, seeing a film, meeting at the cinema, and getting tickets for a club. We noticed that over half of these messages did not focus on making initial plans, but focused on coordinating the arrangements in real-time. In fact, many of the messages sent from town (see Table II) were these kinds of communication.

The logs showed that the teenagers were text messaging their friends to give them updates about the state of the plan. For example, they did not usually send messages asking "want 2 go c a film?"[5]; instead, they used text messages to reaffirm or adjust plans. In the case of seeing a film, we saw text messages saying that people had arrived at the cinema, or were running late.

We think that this is an example of Ling and Yttri's (1999) idea of hypercoordination. Simply put, hypercoordination is the practice of frequently revisiting and revising arrangements with others using a mobile. People make hypercoordination possible because they usually have their mobile wherever they go. This allows people to remain in almost continuous contact and consequently review and revise commitments as circumstances change. Our study suggests that teenagers use text messages to do precisely that.

Chatting and Gossiping

The teenagers also sent many conversational text messages. They sent 48 messages (20%) mainly to gossip or chat. Luckily, they also recorded more details of some of these chatting text messages, giving us some insights into their conversations.

Weekend plans were one topic that they often chatted about (11%). These messages included discussing the upcoming weekend as well as how the previous weekend had been. They also used text messages to talk about what they did that

---

[5] "Want to go see a film?" We will return to abbreviations later.

day (2%). We even saw text messages used to have a more difficult kind of conversation: apologising to friends (2%). Other topics that they discussed included teachers, family rows and the next day's lessons.

During our analysis, we noticed that the teenagers frequently used text messaging to ask questions. For example, they recorded 20 instances (8%) of asking how someone was, which would lead to chatting. They also tended to ask their friends what they were doing (3%), how an event went (2%), what homework was due, and whether people had done their homework (6%). They also used text messages to ask their friends about how a previous evening went (3%), whether auditions (4%) and job interviews (6%) went well, and when someone did not show up at school, others sent text messages to that person to ask them whether they were feeling alright (1%).

Coordinating with Family

The teenagers also used text messages to coordinate with their families. We saw two different kinds of family coordination in the logs: updating and revising arrangements and coordinating with absent family members. The teenagers generated far fewer messages in this category when compared to the messages they sent coordinating with their friends. During the 80 days of logging, they only sent 23 messages (10%) to family members.

We saw a number of messages where the teenagers were hypercoordinating with family members. Teenagers sent their parents messages saying they did not need dinner, wanted to be collected from a friend's house, or that they would be late home. The logs also showed that siblings sent each other text messages. For example, one asked another to come downstairs, unlock the door, and let them in without waking up their parents!

The second use of text messaging with family members was sending messages to those absent from the home. Parents and siblings can be absent for a variety of reasons including divorce, siblings having left home to attend college, and parents working abroad. In these cases, the content was much closer to a conversational contact as opposed to any event-based coordination.

Why Do They Pick Text Messaging?

Teenagers often chose text messaging in surroundings when they could have used other communications media. Once again, we illustrate the findings from the logs with explanations given during the discussion groups.

Text Messaging is Quicker

The teenagers frequently (77 times; 33%) told us that they found text messaging quicker than using other media. Initially this surprised us, since we find typing on the phone keypad difficult ourselves. However, during the discussion groups, the teenagers explained that they found it quicker for two reasons: first, they have grown accustomed to the interface and have adapted it to their needs; and second, it avoided long conversations.

It was clear from watching their demonstrations of text messaging that they knew their phone interface intuitively. Knowing instinctively how many key presses are required to generate a specific character gave them a familiarity with the interface that neither of us has.

Despite that, we wondered whether they used predictive typing technologies to help them type faster. Some mobile phones come with software that predicts and completes the word you want as you type. However, when we asked about predictive typing schemes, we did not find them in widespread use. Moreover, we found some of the teenagers had difficulties with them. As two teenagers explained:

B5: I did have this thing on my phone that, I can't remember what they call it, but it sort of guesses the word you want to type.

G1: Oh, predictive typing.

B5: yeah.

G1: that's annoying.

B5: I deleted it off my SIM card somehow, thank god, because it was so annoying. You type like an 8 and it instantly comes up with hello and it's gets annoying because....

G1: And you can't delete it.

B5: I had the dictionary you could change, because I had like two other phones before, it was just easier, I got used to writing the words.

As they point out, predictive typing can interfere with an expert's knowledge of the interface. Most of the teenagers in this study knew the interface so well that they did not even look at the screen as they typed their messages. Predictive typing, by completing words and often making it difficult to rectify the changes, got in the way of typing rather than supporting it.

Another way that they made input quick was by using abbreviations. As they told us while one of them was demonstrating:

B3: You're typing 'where are you', and it's bound to be quicker than dialling.

G1: If I was to write 'where are you', ok, (she's typing on her phone)...

B5: You use like an 'r' for are, and 'u' for you.

G1: That's it. I've done it.

We counted 146 unique abbreviations used at least once during the course of the logging study. Many of these abbreviations use numbers (e.g., l8r for later) which some predictive typing systems do not support. A language of text messaging, based on abbreviations, has evolved to help make typing faster; however, as we discuss later, it does not come without problems.

The second reason that the teenagers gave us for using text messages was that it avoided long conversations. We expected the teenagers to find the 160 character limit restrictive, but to our surprise it was used as a way to avoid social conventions. As they explained:

> G4: ...say if you just want to say one little thing to someone, otherwise you'd have to ring them up and go through, you know a massive long conversation and it costs a lot more, and text messaging is just ten times easier.

> B5: You can't just sort of phone someone up and go where are you. You've got to say hi, are you alright, nnnh....

> G2: Like if you're phoning someone up you can't avoid that they might want to talk to you about something else, where as when I'm texting someone then it's just what you want to say, and you don't have to commit yourself to a whole other conversation or whatever.

In this discussion, the teenagers revealed two disadvantages of conversations on the phone that they can avoid by sending text messages. First, they can avoid the time, and cost, of all the various conversational protocols required before they can ask a question or get to the reason why they called. The character limit of the messages themselves makes this terse and otherwise rude behaviour completely acceptable. Second, they can avoid the other person going "off topic" and making the conversation even longer than planned. Again, the character limit forces both sender and respondent to stick to the topic. In summary, then, text messaging is quick because the teenagers know the interface and the terseness of the medium speeds up the exchange and focuses it.

Text Messaging is Cheaper

The teenagers often (63 times; 27%) told us that they chose text messaging over other media because it was cheaper. Cheaper meant two things to the teenagers: that the total cost was less than the cost using other media, and that they could control their expenditure. The general cost of calls, and communications generally, came up several times in the discussion groups. It was often associated with the ability to control costs, as the following quotes illustrate:

> B5: Well you know how much it's going to cost before you start.

> G4: You're more in control of it.

> B5: Yeah.

> G4: Otherwise you'd be broke within two minutes.

> B3: Say you're talking to an Orange phone and you're Vodafone, it's about 40p call time whereas text messages only cost 12p.

And in another discussion:

> G1: I went for the pay-as-you-go Vodafone first and just 'cause it was like the idea of topping up and being in control of how much you spend was kinda good.

Managing expenses was particularly important for these teenagers, since their sources of income were restricted to their pocket money and, for a few, payments for after-school and weekend work. Another reason some teenagers mentioned was that in the past they had run up excessive bills with the home phone and their parents had made them pay those costs. They did not want that to happen again.

The teenagers also preferred to text message people who were abroad since that was considerably cheaper than placing a voice call. Both the data in the logs and the discussions revealed that the teenagers sent text messages to several countries. One teenager text messaged her friends in Spain regularly, another sent text messages to her father in Hong Kong, and others used their phones while abroad to send text messages to people at home. Text messages, unlike voice calls, do not change price when used internationally. Some providers do not allow international text messaging in certain plans, but when they do, the messages do not vary in cost from local text messages.

Text Messaging is Easier or More Convenient

The teenagers often (53 times; 22%) said that text messaging was easier or more convenient. If we also include some specific examples of what easier or more convenient meant, such as it being too late or early to call (18 times) and the sender being in a public place (14 times) it became the most common (36%) reason for sending a text message.

We asked the teenagers what they meant by text messaging being easier than dialling and talking. Two reasons are illustrated in the following discussions:

B5: Because if it's like really late you're not going to sort of phone them up, because you could wake up the whole house. So I sort of text message and if they're still awake then I might phone them.

And:

G4: I find I know who I want to talk to on the phone and who I don't. There are some— particularly males— that don't really talk back on the phone.

G1: Yeah, yeah…

G4: …just one syllable answers and it is so frustrating talking to them on the phone, it's so much easier just doing them a text message. Because you're only just talking to yourself. So, it's, that's why I normally text them.

As the first quote above illustrates, one reason that text messaging is more convenient is that it is quieter than calling. Although many mobiles have silent ways of alerting their owners to incoming communications, voice conversations still involve the noise of talking. Text messages give the teenagers a way of communicating silently that does not disturb others.

As the interaction between the two girls (G4 and G1) above illustrates, it takes work to have a conversation. As we mentioned earlier, voice exchanges have lengthy and costly protocols associated with them. While this can take time or be expensive with anyone, it can get more awkward with someone who finds conversation difficult. As another girl commented, continuing the discussion above, the problem does not just apply to boys[6]:

> G2: I know girls as well, I mean at school I talk forever with them and as soon as I phone them up there are just these long silences on the other end of the phone and I realise I've been talking for the past five minutes. And it's really awkward when you know you've got friends like that and you want to contact them but you don't want the long awkward silences, cause that's really awful.

The teenagers find it easier to text message someone who finds phone conversation difficult. The teenagers also used text messages to avoid making conversation with people they did not know well (2%). One occasion where teenagers find it difficult to talk, and may be chatting with someone they do not know well, is when they flirt with each other. Flirting was also observed by Strub (1997) in his study of two-way radio use. Although flirting was not mentioned in the logs, we asked the teenagers about it during the discussion groups:

> Q: Have you ever used text messages to flirt with people?

> (All nod, say yes.)

> G4: It's also very handy, I mean say if you're meeting a bloke or something and you want to give them your number or get theirs, it is so much easier getting a mobile number than a home number and it's a lot less embarrassing if you want to meet up with them again just doing a text message.

A final, pragmatic reason the teenagers gave for text messaging someone was their physical location. Some physical locations require discretion. When they wanted to discuss something that they did not want other people to hear, they sent text messages. Many of the "in transit" messages (see Table II) were of this kind:

> G4: you could be on the bus, you don't really want to talk to them, because you know everyone's listening.

In fact, we noticed that many of the teenagers sent text messages from public places and spaces where telephone conversations would probably be unacceptable.[7] These places included cinemas, school dances, and the supermarket. Text messaging provides anytime, anywhere contact with other people, but in public settings, it is a way to be discrete.

New and Familiar Communications

Finally, we wanted to know whether text messaging made any new kinds of communications possible. The data from our logs suggest that the teenagers use text messages to have conversations about traditional topics. In theory, other media could allow them to have the same kinds of conversations. However, as we have shown in previous sections, text messaging changes how they communicate.

---

[6] Interestingly both comments about the awkwardness of telephone conversations come from girls.

[7] It is interesting to compare this with Palen et al.'s (2000) study of wireless phone adoption in the United States where people with mobiles are getting less sensitive to conversations in public spaces.

For example, the terseness of the media makes it possible to have short, blunt conversations.

Text messaging also makes it possible to communicate from places from which they previously could not. For example, shortly after mobile phones became popular many cinemas started generating and enforcing rules about not using mobiles during the show. Text messaging has made mobile conversations possible again by turning them into more discrete interactions that do not disturb others watching the film.

We found several examples (10; 4%) of one type of message content that seemed novel and was made possible by the discrete nature of text messaging; we call this the goodnight message. The recipients of these messages were either boyfriend or girlfriend, or just a close friend. The goodnight message relies on quiet interactions in two ways. First, the sender can send the message quietly without disturbing his or her own household. Since these messages get sent late at night, this silence is necessary. Second, we noticed that this works because while the teenagers are awake, they keep a close eye on their mobile phones to watch for incoming messages. When they go to bed, they turn off or down the incoming alerts, so that it does not disturb the recipient's house.

Some Problems with Text Messaging

Although we did not begin this study searching for problems, the teenagers described three difficulties with text messaging. What struck us was that some of these problems seemed very familiar, because they were similar to problems that previous studies of e-mail uncovered (e.g., Dunlop & Kling, 1991; Sproull & Kiesler, 1991). In this section, we briefly review three problems.

Evolving Language

Text messaging, like e-mail, has a specialised language associated with it. Unlike e-mail, the language of text messaging is still evolving; consequently, it can be confusing. The teenagers mentioned finding it difficult to understand some of the messages people sent them:

> G4: It's annoying, though, if you get a text message and you don't know what the abbreviations stand for.
>
> G2: It is.
>
> G1: Yeah.

We found several reasons that made the text messaging language difficult to parse. First, the teenagers reported using several different abbreviations for the same words. For example, different messages shortened tomorrow to: "2moro," "2morra," "tomor," and "2morrow." Second, non-obvious long phrases were also shortened such as "dofe" which stands for the Duke of Edinburgh, "gal" meaning get a life, and "bdtd" implying been there done that. Third, some abbreviations already have meanings, such as "lol." On the Internet, "LOL" typically means laugh out loud. However, we also found it in use in text messaging, sometimes meaning lots of love. Imagine confusing the two!

An additional problem for the evolving language of text messaging is that people have different levels of knowledge of the abbreviations in use. As the conversation above continued:

> G4: It is. I think my Nana (Grandmother) gets annoyed as well because obviously she doesn't know any of them and I'm writing them. See you don't actually realise you're doing them, you get into a habit of it.

> G1: You have to sit there thinking l-8-r, or oh, later...

> G4: It depends who you're writing to, you know, how many abbreviations you use.

The language of text messaging has not stabilised sufficiently to make all communications seamless. Indeed, we noted a few (3) instances of text messages being sent in response to previous messages asking people to explain their previous message. Over time, if text messaging shares similar properties to e-mailing, we could expect these abbreviations to stabilise and become more widely-known. Books which explain text messaging abbreviations have begun to appear, which may resolve some confusion as well as guide standardisation (Michael O'Mara Books, 2000, 2001).

Determining Intent from Content

Another difficulty with text messaging concerns the ability to determine the intent from the content. Specifically, the teenagers sometimes found it hard to figure out whether the message was serious or a joke, and consequently did not know how to react. As they explained:

> B5: Well it's difficult to get them into context because you don't know someone's being sarcastic or sort of jokey or really serious and so you might sort of misinterpret what they're trying to say and in your reply you get it completely wrong, and look a fool.

> G1: I've done that two or three times.

It also seems, unsurprisingly, that they are learning to adapt text to be more expressive, as happened with e-mail. I asked them whether they used things like capitals to emphasise words.

> G1, G2: Yeah.

> G1: If you're really good you go to special letters and you can kind of put accents and dots and little squiggles, and it's kind of fun.

It will be interesting to see how and whether teenagers find ways of adapting the media to make the intent behind their content easier for others to understand.

Mis-addressing Messages

The final problem we discussed with the teenagers was the ease of mis-addressing a message, and some of the resulting unintentional social consequences. E-mail addresses have the property of being text, and often people's names, or some part of their name. This makes them easier to remember and distinguish than telephone numbers, which are used as the addresses for text messages.

The United Kingdom has further complicated the problem of remembering numbers: unlike landline numbers, mobile numbers are not geographically locatable. The equivalent of the area code usually signifies the mobile service provider (or increasingly, as people swap service providers but keep their numbers, not even that anymore). This may be helpful in determining whether you are contacting a mobile, and whether it's on another network, but it also makes everyone's number very similar. As the teenagers explained:

G4: And they're all very, very similar so you can easily call the wrong person.

G1: 07780...

However, there are consequences of sending messages to the wrong person:

B4: I uh — someone came around mine and I had a bit of an argument with them as they were leaving, and, uh, they left, and I thought, oh I'll apologise, so I write this text out apologising, um, and sent that to someone that wasn't them, and then, uh I sent it to this girl who — I wanted to say, can I come around now, and I wrote a text message saying can I come around now to the person that just left — that I'd just fallen out with, and he got really, really confused.

The combination of multiple simultaneous communications with people who have extremely similar numbers creates confusion for the sender. Learning to manage communications, in the same way that e-mail programs have evolved to help people save, sort, search and filter their messages, may be necessary for text messaging systems in the future.

Conclusions

This paper has described why text messaging has become popular among teenagers. Our findings show that teenagers use it to coordinate media and times to interact, revise and adjust arrangements, and chat. We found that text messaging mainly happens among peers (71%) and at home (71%).

The teenagers told us that they found text messaging quicker, cheaper, and easier. They find it quicker because they have mastered the interface and optimised their language. The restrictive length of text messages — rather than being a technological disadvantage — allows teenagers to forego conversational conventions and reduces the overall time spent on the interaction. Text messaging is cheaper for them because it reduces the total costs and helps them to predict and manage their expenses. They find text messaging easier and more convenient because it supports quiet interactions and it supports communications with people who have difficulty holding conversations.

We found that text messaging changed the dynamics of how teenagers communicate. For example, it let them coordinate from many more places because it is a discrete and mobile communications medium. However, the content of the majority of messages focused on traditional topics. One kind of message — the goodnight message — used the affordances of text messaging to allow the teenagers to interact in a new way.

While our findings focus on teenage use, they have revealed affordances of text messaging that may well extrapolate to adult use. For example, it seems plausible that adults may also find the terseness and directness of the medium useful for asking questions of colleagues, scheduling meetings and appointments, and coordinating with family members while at work. This may be particularly true for mobile workers (Palen et al., 2000).

Although infrequent, teenagers sent their parents text messages. We did not ask their parents whether this had encouraged them to use text messages more frequently. However, if today's adults do not find text messaging useful, then tomorrow's adults who are already "power users" probably will. We expect them to find job-related uses for text messaging in the office.

In conclusion, when we view work broadly as the "work" of interacting in the social world, our study reveals why teenagers use text messaging. Text messaging gives them opportunities to coordinate from new places. It lets them conduct brief but rich exchanges. It also lets them coordinate opportunistically, finding out in real-time whether people are proximate and then adjusting their commitments on the fly. For teenagers, text messaging fills a gap left by other communications media.

Acknowledgements

We'd like to thank all the teenagers who participated in our study. We would particularly like to thank Kyle Duncan who helped us find people to be involved, and who distributed and collected materials. Finally, thank you to Allison Woodruff for reading and commenting on an earlier draft of the paper.

References

BBC (2000): *UK Internet access rises*. http://news.bbc.co.uk/hi/english/business/newsid_1077000/1077747.stm.

Dunlop, C. and Kling, R. (1991): *Computerization and Controversy: Value Conflicts and Social Choices,* Academic Press, San Diego.

Ling, R. (2000): *Norwegian teens, mobile telephony and text messages*, Report No. 2-2000, Technical Newsletter from Telenor Research and Development, Oslo.

Ling, R. and Yttri, B. (1999): *Nobody sits at home and waits for the telephone to ring: Micro and hyper-coordination through the use of the mobile phone.* Report No. 30/99, Telenor Research and Development, Oslo.

Michael O'Mara Books (2000): *LUVTLK: ltle bk of luv txt.* Michael O'Mara Books Ltd., London.

Michael O'Mara Books (2001): *WAN2TLK: ltle bk of txt msgs.* Michael O'Mara Books Ltd., London.

Mobile Data Association (2000): *SMS statistics.* http://www.mda-mobiledata.org/resource/hot_topics.asp.

Newton, H. (2000): *Newton's Telecom Dictionary* (16th ed.), Telecom Books, New York.

Palen, L., Salzman, M. and Youngs, E. (2000): 'Going Wireless: Behavior and Practice of New Mobile Phone Users', in D. G. Durand (ed.): *Proceedings of the ACM Conference on Computer Supported Cooperative Work (CSCW 2000)*, ACM Press, Philadelphia and New York, pp. 201-210.

Rautiainen, P. and Kasesniemi, E.-L. (2000): 'Mobile communication of children and teenagers: case Finland 1997-2000', in R. Ling and K. Thrane (eds.): *Proceedings of the Workshop on "The social consequences of mobile telephony: the proceedings from a seminar about society, mobile telephony and children"*, Oslo.

Sproull, L. and Kiesler, S. (1991): *Connections: New Ways of Working in the Networked Organization,* MIT Press, Cambridge.

Strub, H. (1997): 'ConcertTalk: a weekend with a portable audio space'. In S. Howard, J. Hammond and G. Lindegaard (eds.): *Human-Computer Interaction: INTERACT'97*, Chapman & Hall, London, pp. 381-388.

Verkaik, R. (2000): *Millions of messages clog mobile networks.* http://www.independent.co.uk/news/UK/This_Britain/2000-12/mobile261200.shtml.

W. Prinz, M. Jarke, Y. Rogers, K. Schmidt, and V. Wulf (eds.), *Proceedings of the Seventh European Conference on Computer-Supported Cooperative Work, 16-20 September 2001, Bonn, Germany*, pp. 239-258.

Coordinating Heterogeneous Work: Information and Representation in Medical Care

Madhu C. Reddy, Paul Dourish, and Wanda Pratt
University of California, Irvine, USA
mreddy@ics.uci.edu, jpd@ics.uci.edu, pratt@ics.uci.edu

Medical care involves intense collaboration amongst a number of practitioners including physicians, nurses, and pharmacists. Their work is concentrated on a single patient, and yet their activities, motivations, and concerns are very different. We explore the use of a shared information system in helping these individuals coordinate their work. In particular, we use the idea of a common information space to explore how the shared information is incorporated into the diverse work practices of an intensive care unit. In addition to physical co-location, we found that providing information in many specialised representations is critical to managing their coordination. Unlike paper records, computer systems offer the ability to decouple information from its representations. This decoupling opens up a rich design space for systems that allow people with different interests, concerns and work practices to work together effectively.

Introduction

The concept of a common information space, or CIS, has become an influential way to think about the use of shared information in collaboration. Originating in the work of Schmidt and Bannon (1992), and further explored by Bannon and Bødker (1997), it was designed to extend then-current notions about the role of technology and shared information.

At the time this was originally proposed, a great deal of technical attention was being paid to the development of "shared workspace" systems (e.g. Lu and

Mantei 1991; Ishii et al. 1992). These systems attempted to extend the workspaces of conventional single-user applications such as word processors and drawing tools, allowing synchronous or asynchronous collaboration across digital networks. Designing effective shared workspace systems presented a range of technical challenges concerning appropriate network protocols, synchronisation, concurrency control mechanisms, and user interface design. Still, over time considerable progress was made, resulting today in the widespread use of systems such as Microsoft NetMeeting that emerge directly out of the "shared workspace" tradition.

However, by introducing the concept of common information space, Schmidt and Bannon sounded a note of caution about the technological conception of shared information. They pointed out that information is not shared unproblematically. It has to be explicitly *placed* in common – extracted from one person's work context, and reformulated in some way that displays its relevance to others (by being related to some common conceptual scheme, for instance). Similarly, when individuals come to examine shared information, they need to recontextualize it, making it relevant for their immediate needs. Further, the same information may be relevant to two people in quite different ways; for instance, a purchase order has different consequences for the person who must process the shipment and the person who must balance the budget. A common information space according to Schmidt and Bannon incorporates not only a repository of information held in common amongst different parties, but also the work practices surrounding that information – how it is used, managed and integrated into the work of those who share it. The practices by which information is placed in common, and then made relevant to individuals' activities, make the information meaningful in the context of their work.

The value of the common information space concept, then, is that it relates shared information to the activities that are conducted over and through the information. While the precise formulation has, lately, been subject to a certain amount of critical scrutiny (see, for example, Bannon 2000; Randall 2000), there is still considerable value in the perspective that it offers on how shared information is incorporated into daily work practices.

In this paper, we report on a field study of the use of a shared information repository in medical work. In particular, we describe the challenges to using a computer-based patient record system as a CIS in an intensive care unit. The paper is structured as follows: in the following section we discuss in greater detail the CIS concept and related work. Next, we present our field study: the research site, staff, and technology as well as examples of daily work activities in the unit. We then discuss the implications of our findings for the construction and use of a CIS, and finally, present some design considerations for CIS systems followed by some concluding remarks.

Background

Schmidt and Bannon (1992) introduced the concept of common information space by contrasting it with technical conceptions of shared information:

> Cooperative work is not facilitated simply by the provisioning of a shared database, but rather requires the active construction by the participants of a common information space where the meanings of the shared objects are debated and resolved, at least locally and temporarily. (Schmidt and Bannon, p.22)

A CIS, then, encompasses not only the information but also the practices by which actors establish its meaning for their collective work. These negotiated understandings of the information are as important as the availability of the information itself:

> The actors must attempt to jointly construct a common information space which goes beyond their individual personal information spaces....The common information space is negotiated and established by the actors involved. (Schmidt and Bannon, p. 28)

This is not to suggest that actors' understandings of the information are identical; they are simply "common" enough to coordinate the work. People understand how the information is relevant for their own work. Therefore, individuals engaged in different activities will have different perspectives on the same information. The work of maintaining the common information space is the work that it takes to balance and accommodate these different perspectives. A "bug" report in software development is a simple example. Software developers and quality assurance personnel have access to the same bug report information. However, *access* to information is not sufficient to coordinate their work. Instead, it is their more or less shared *understanding* of the record's organizational structure that allows developers and quality assurance personnel to coordinate their activities. They know where to find certain information, what it means if the information is not present, and what implications this information carries for their own work.

The distinction between access and practical understanding is at the heart of the CIS concept. Moving from one to the other is not straight-forward. Schmidt and Bannon discuss potential problems actors face in interpreting information when the information's creator, the context of its creation, or politics of its use is unknown to the actors involved. They provide examples of what occurs when this contextualizing information is not present and discuss how common information spaces are created in different work situations.

In many work settings, a CIS involves not only local work practices but also crosses group boundaries. The information artifacts at the heart of the space are the focus of heterogeneous workgroups and have characteristics of "boundary objects" (Star and Griesemer 1989). Boundary objects are information artifacts flexible enough to fit local work practices but also stable enough to convey information across group boundaries, enabling them to act as coordinating mechanisms for interactions between diverse workgroups. For example, Berg and

Bowker (1997) examine the medical record as "an organizational infrastructure...[that] affords the interplay and coordination between divergent worlds." They argue that the patient record is both a representation of the patient as well as a representation of the *work being carried out* on the patient. The record is used by different groups (e.g. physicians, nurses, administrators, etc.) in their own local work context. To each group, the record has a localized meaning, but it also serves to coordinate the different activities of these groups. The patient record functions as a boundary object, spanning the borders of a number of different groups.

Bannon and Bødker (1997) use boundary objects as a lens for viewing common information space. They contend that, as with a boundary object, the dialectical nature of the common information space is an important characteristic:

> It is this tension between the need for openness and malleability of information on the one hand, and on the other, the need for some form of closure, to allow for forms of translation and portability between communities, that we believe characterizes the nature of common information space. (Bannon and Bødker, p. 86)

Resolving the tension between the need for both openness (supporting diverse work practices) and closure (supporting coordination) depends on features of the work and work setting. Bannon and Bødker use a variety of examples to discuss CIS construction in different settings, and suggest that physical co-presence plays an important role in making it easier to construct a common information space:

> In the case of physically shared workspace, due to the common work setting and exposure to the same work environment, actors are able to co-operate with each other, both in the production and reception of utterance and information, without having to resort to extended descriptions or elaborated codes, due to their understanding of the shared context within which they work. (Bannon and Bødker, p. 83)

The physical co-location of the workgroup members provides a number of benefits. First, the work related to the information is highly visible. Participants can see not only what other individuals are doing, but also when and how they are doing it. Second, in a physically shared space, individuals can easily ask other individuals for explanation of something they do not understand – "popping your head over the cubicle wall." Participants can ask their neighbors questions about the work before looking elsewhere for the information. Finally, a shared workspace allows human mediators to play a more effective role in sharing and communicating knowledge about the artifact. Blomberg and colleagues' (1997) study of attorneys in a law firm highlight the role of human mediation of an artifact. Over a period of time, M, a firm attorney, had amassed a large collection of legal documents that he deemed potentially useful or reusable. These documents were available to all, but stored in a filing cabinet in his office. When other attorneys wanted to find a document in the cabinet, M acted as gatekeeper, helping them locate and interpret the needed documents:

> The utility of M's file for other attorneys depends on his knowledge of its contents and organization, derived in turn from his creation, maintenance, and regular use of the file. Other

attorneys rely on M to help determine whether the form file contains documents relevant to the transaction on which they are working, to point them to likely places in the file where relevant documents might be found, and to justify the choice of particular documents. (Blomberg et al., p. 195)

M mediated the other attorneys' search for documents in the filing cabinet. This was successful because he was physically available along with the files.

Although physical co-location provides a number of benefits, how much of a role it actually plays in the creation of a common information space remains unclear. We know that when the work of the participants is similar (e.g. as with the attorneys using M's filing cabinet), the physical co-location of actors helps them to create a usable common information space. This depends, though, on some mutual intelligibility of action, so that when participants observe each other at work with the artifacts, they have some understanding of what work is being carried out. However, what if the work practices are so heterogeneous that the work of different actors is no longer intelligible to others? What role does physical co-location play then? And what other elements can be brought to bear in order to resolve the tensions of openness and closure?

A Common Information Space in Medical Work

We explore these issues by looking in detail at an example of a common information space supporting divergent forms of work. We focus on medical work in an intensive care unit (ICU) supported by a shared patient record system called HealthStat.[1]

Research Site and Methods

The surgical intensive care unit (SICU), where we conducted our fieldwork, is one of nine ICUs of a large urban teaching hospital. The majority of participants in this study worked in the SICU. The research team had access to the SICU staff. In addition, we observed and interviewed the HealthStat technical team members from the hospital's information systems department. The first author observed work in the SICU for approximately three months during summer 2000. He collected data through 30 formal interviews, as well as a number of informal interviews, and observations. The formal interviews were taped and transcribed. The research team had access to the HealthStat application and internal communications, including written policies, procedures, and meeting notes.

Each ICU provides rigorous invasive and non-invasive care-monitoring for patients requiring special attention due to a critical medical condition. Specifically, the SICU is a 20-bed unit that treats the most seriously ill surgical

---

[1]   A pseudonym

patients, including those who have undergone liver transplant, major trauma, or major elective surgery. It is equipped with sophisticated equipment including digital physiological monitors and a fully computerized patient record system. The SICU is an extremely busy unit with 15 out of 20 beds occupied on a daily basis. Patients usually stay in the unit for 5-6 days and are the focus of a team of health-care workers. In most cases, patients are in such critical condition that any minor change in their condition could have rapid and severe implications. Therefore, the specialised equipment and staff in the SICU allows even small changes in a patient's condition to be detected early, thus permitting rapid changes in treatment to prevent problems from developing.

SICU Staff

The SICU staff includes surgical critical care nurses, physical therapists, social workers, respiratory therapists, surgical residents, critical care fellows and faculty. We focus on three SICU work groups: physicians, nurses, and pharmacists because these groups interact with each other and the computerized patient record system on a daily basis. We will now briefly discuss each group.

Physician Staff

The physician staff is organized hierarchically and consists of three rotating surgical residents, two critical care fellows, and four attending physicians. At the bottom of the hierarchy are residents. They are considered physicians-in-training and provide the most hours of patient care in the unit. The fellows are in the middle of the hierarchy. They have completed their residency and are undergoing specialized training in intensive care. Fellows supervise and monitor residents' activities on a day-to-day basis. They resolve a majority of problems that residents cannot handle. If a fellow cannot resolve a problem, an attending physician is notified. The SICU has four attending physicians, each with many years of experience in intensive care. The attending physicians supervise fellows and residents to ensure that they receive proper training as well as maintain a high standard of patient care. The ultimate responsibility for success or failure in the unit lies with the attending physicians.

Nursing Staff

The nursing staff has more than fifty registered nurses certified in critical care, supervised by a SICU nurse manager. Depending on the number of patients, there are 10-12 nurses on each 12-hour shift. The nursing experience in the unit varies; some nurses have more than 20 years of experience but the majority of nurses have been in the unit less than five years. The nursing staff has experienced high turnover due to the stress of ICU work. The nurse's responsibilities range from patient assessment and monitoring to medication administration. Because of the serious condition of the patients in the unit, each nurse is responsible for only 1-2 patients per shift. (In the non-ICUs, the nurse-to-patient ratio is 1:6.) Therefore, SICU nurses can provide more focused care for their patients.

Pharmacist

A pharmacist is assigned to the SICU on a regular basis. She spends 3-4 hours per day in the unit. The medical staff, especially the residents, rely heavily on her knowledge to help them make the appropriate medication decisions. She is also the primary resource for the nurses on any questions concerning drug dosage or usage. The pharmacist participates in the SICU team's rounds each morning and is familiar with the conditions and medications of all the SICU patients.

Diverse Work Practices

The patient is the center of the work activities in the SICU. The primary goal of the SICU staff is to stabilise patients so they can be safely transferred out of the unit. On a daily basis, physicians, nurses, and pharmacists successfully coordinate their patient care activities. However, although patient care is the central focus, the various groups have their own work to do; their motivations, concerns, and activities are quite different (Strauss et al. 1985).

Consider one case that we observed. A nurse noticed that her patient's fingers were turning blue. She knew that blue fingers were an indication of blood vessel constriction and correctly attributed the condition to the medication. The patient was in obvious discomfort. The nurse did not understand why this medication was being administered since it clearly caused so much distress to the patient. She asked the physician if they could stop the medication. However, he insisted that, despite the discomfort that it might cause, the medication was necessary to improve the patient's overall medical condition.

This example highlights the distinct roles and concerns of the physician and nurse. To the physician, the patient's discomfort was not as important as treating the other medical problems. On the other hand, the nurse was primarily concerned with the patient's comfort and well-being. The different emphases of their work continually feature in the life of the unit; with their different concerns, physicians and nurses frequently do not understand the details of each other's work. As one SICU physician stated,

> There is a scope of practice for nurses. There are certain nursing actions,[but] they are not the same as my actions. They are involved with patient care and they make patient care decisions on a routine basis. It is true that they cannot do what I do. They cannot order medications, [but] when I order it they administer it. That is her job. But they make nursing care decisions. I am not minimizing them. It is a different sphere of things. For example, patient comfort measures. I don't prescribe that. I don't tell them when to clean a patient, when to put a pillow here or there, and yet they are important to the patients. Patients remember that. Nurses are the ones

who make those decisions and decide that care. I think that they have a very specific sphere of care, just different from mine.

If physicians view their activities as distinct from nurses' activities, then nurses too view their work as differing from that of other groups (e.g. physician, pharmacist). Berg and Bowker (1997) and Bowker and Star (1999) discuss the creation of the Nursing Interventions Classification, a classification of nursing work that was developed by nurses as a way to describe their activities independently of other groups' work. Nurses created this classification as a means to legitimate their activities and make them visible to physicians and other hospital staff who otherwise neither recognized nor understood their work.

While their work practices may be quite diverse, effective and timely coordination between physicians, nurses, and pharmacists is critical otherwise the patient will suffer. In one example we observed, a nurse failed to notify the physician that the patient's sodium was raising to dangerous levels. If the physician had been notified quickly, he would have been able to give the patient medication to lower the sodium. However, the physician only found out about the sodium levels six hours later, by which time the patient's condition had deteriorated so far that the physician had to intubate the patient to protect her airways. As the example highlights, these groups work under constant time pressure that can effect patient care. They do not have the luxury of waiting an extended period of time for important patient information.

HealthStat: A Common Information Repository

Information technology plays a crucial role in the SICU. A computerized patient record system, HealthStat, mediates much of the work among the physicians, nurses, and pharmacists. The staff has used HealthStat for more than nine years and is well acquainted with its functionality. Originally implemented in the SICU, the system is now in use in eight of the other nine ICUs in the hospital.

Almost all patient information is in the computerized record. Since the patient's bedside monitoring systems are linked to HealthStat, physiological data such as temperature, blood pressure, heart rate, and fluid levels are downloaded automatically into the patient's HealthStat record. However, before the information is permanently entered into the record, the patient's nurse ensures the validity of the data by cross-checking the data in the record with the displays on the bedside monitoring systems. The record also contains medication information, progress notes, and laboratory results.

Most of the data that is not automatically downloaded into HealthStat is entered by nurses. They can spend up to 15 minutes every hour entering data into the system. In a busy ICU, this is a great deal of time but is still shorter than the time that would be spent entering the same information on a paper chart. Physicians, by contrast, do minimal data entry; they largely use HealthStat to monitor the patient's status and to find needed patient information. Finally, pharmacists are interested in ensuring that the patient is receiving the appropriate medication and that all the information related to the patient's medication is correct; the SICU pharmacist spends a couple of hours each day using HealthStat.

The Work of the SICU

We present three examples of activities related to patient care in the SICU. These activities highlight the collaboration required for successful completion of work tasks.

SICU Morning Rounds

SICU morning rounds play an important role in the unit's patient care process. A multi-disciplinary team led by a fellow and consisting of three residents, attending physician, pharmacist, and nurse visits each patient. The goal of morning rounds is to discuss and decide upon a plan of care for that day for each patient. The team uses HealthStat workstations outside patient rooms to find patient information. The team begins by viewing x-rays of all the SICU patients. After examining the x-rays, the team "rounds" on each patient. Each of the three residents are responsible for a certain number of patients in the unit. During rounds, the residents "present" their patients to the team. As a resident outlines the patient's current condition, vitals and other information, the fellow and other team members view the patient's record on the HealthStat workstation. They do this both to verify the resident's information and to gather other pertinent information. As one fellow stated, "It is much easier for me to find the information in the system than to wait for them [residents] to give it to me." After the resident presents, the fellow examines the patient. The team then discusses the patient's condition and decides on the plan of care for the day. After all the decisions are made, a resident writes a progress note in the patient's HealthStat record. The following vignette presents a typical patient round.

> MC, a resident, presents the patient to the team. The patient has recently undergone a male to female gender change operation. She was admitted to the unit because of complications from the administration of high levels of progesterone and estrogen. TK, a fellow, suggests that the hormones be discontinued. However, MC argues that the patient needs them for the gender change. WK, another fellow, looks at HealthStat and asks MC whether the patient is getting both Heparin and TPA (both drugs prevent blood clotting). MC tells WK that the patient is only receiving Heparin. AL, an attending, asks whether estrogen and progesterone have a dose response level. None of the residents know the answer to this question. Later, TK asks the JC, the pharmacist about dose-related complications for estrogen and the relationship between estrogen and progesterone. JC tells TK and WK that the drugs are dose independent of each other. After a discussion, the team decides not to discontinue the progesterone and estrogen.

As the example illustrates, rounding involves a collaborative dialogue among physicians, nurses, pharmacists and the patient record system. Different questions were raised during the interaction: Should the estrogen and progesterone be stopped? What other medications is the patient receiving? Are there dose level concerns between estrogen and progesterone? HealthStat provided some information, but the different team members brought their individual perspectives to understanding the information so the questions could be answered. MC gave the context of the case and explained the need for the high level of estrogen and progesterone. She also answered WK's question about the patient medication. JC answered the question about the drug interaction. HealthStat played a role in answering questions, but only as a component of the entire collaborative process. For instance, WK raised the medication question after looking at the patient's physiological data in HealthStat. Instead of asking the resident, WK could have also looked up the medications in HealthStat. However, she was interested in not only the patient's medication but also the rationale for giving the medication. MC was in the best position to provide that information. The information itself, in HealthStat, does not tell the complete story. During rounds, team members actively collaborate to integrate that information into the context of their work.

Medication Administration

Ordering and administering medication requires collaboration between physicians, nurses, and pharmacists. In routine situations, most surgeons use a standard set of drugs. However, for complex cases, nurses and pharmacists often provide information that help physicians tailor the medication prescription. Since nurses are constantly by the bedside, they can inform physicians about the patient's physical and mental state. This information can help physicians to decide whether a current drug and dosage are appropriate. If physicians need to prescribe a drug for a problem with which they are not familiar, pharmacists can provide a list of appropriate medications.

Nurses must collaborate directly with both physicians and pharmacists. When ordered to give an unfamiliar drug, nurses commonly ask the physician why it is being given, especially when the drug causes discomfort or pain to the patient. Most physicians want the nurse to understand the plan of care and will answer such questions readily. The nurses also ask the pharmacist questions concerning the medication and dosage administration. For certain kinds of drugs, such as pain relievers, it is the nurse who observes the patient's response most directly, and whose opinion is usually given high regard by physicians for subsequent pain medication orders.

HealthStat plays an important role in supporting the collaborative process of medication administration. The central element that HealthStat provides in this

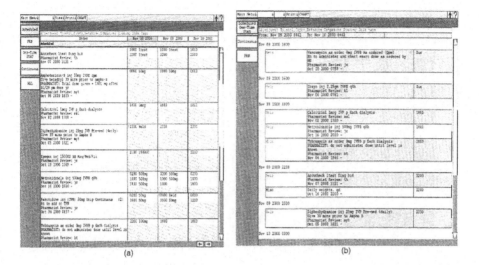

(a)   (b)

Figure 1 Different Representations of Medication Information: (a) Pharmacists use the Medication Administration Record (MAR) to provide them with the more detailed information on each medication. (b) Nurses use the Medication Worklist to keep track of their medication administration work activities.

---

process is the Medication Administration Record, or MAR (Figure 1a). The MAR coordinates both the prescription and administration of medication. When the physician writes a medication order, a nurse or pharmacist enters the order into the MAR, recording the details of the prescribed medication. Although the MAR provides the detailed information necessary for the pharmacists, it provides too much detail for the nurses to allow them to plan their medication administration activities for a shift. Consequently, to administer medications effectively and on-time, nurses use another "view" of the MAR, the Medication Worklist (Figure 1b), which provides a time-ordered list of dosages, and administration times for all drugs due to be administered on the current nursing shift. The nurses use the Worklist to plan their medication administration activities for each of their patients.

Each group uses the system to view a patient's medication information, although in different ways. For example, pharmacists check the appropriateness of the medication based on the patient's condition. If they do not believe that the drug is appropriate, they will offer the physician advice about alternative medications. Physicians may consider the pharmacists' recommendations when making their final medication decision, based on the information that HealthStat provides them concerning the patient's response to previous treatments.

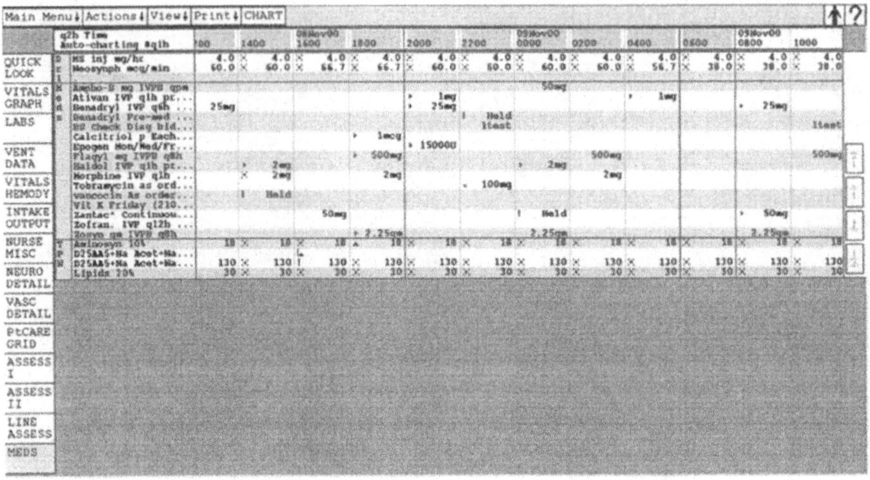

Figure 2 HealthStat Flowsheet's MEDS Section: The ICU staff especially physicians use the MEDS section to quickly check on patient medications.

Configuration Group

HealthStat is implemented in eight ICUs in the hospital. Due to technical constraints, any changes to the various interfaces to the system are replicated to only seven of the eight ICUs (the eighth ICU uses HealthStat on an independent platform). Still, coordinating interface changes for seven ICUs is a difficult process. Although all ICUs have some information in common, much is particular to each ICU and its specialized work. Terms used in one unit may not be used in another. To prevent any misunderstandings between the different ICUs, a committee called the Configuration Group was created. The group consists of nurses from the different ICUs, HealthStat programming team members, and the HealthStat director. Any interface changes must be discussed in the Configuration Group meeting. The group then decides whether changes will be implemented.

An important aspect of these meetings is dealing with changes to the HealthStat Flowsheet (Figure 2). In our observations and interviews, nurses and physicians described the Flowsheet as the most widely used interface of the computerized record. Each of its fourteen subsections contains information about the patient. For example, the MEDS subsection contains brief information about the patient medication. ICU staff use the Flowsheet to get a quick overview of the patient's condition.

Since interface changes made to the Flowsheet for one ICU are propagated to the Flowsheets in the other ICUs, the Configuration Group has to mediate the differing requirements of the various ICUs. For example, both the medical and the surgical cardiac units are interested in the section of the Flowsheet dealing with cardiac data. Because HealthStat was implemented first in the medical unit, the nurses there had the data visually arranged in the Flowsheet to fit their work activities. However, when the nurses in the surgical unit began using the system, they complained about this arrangement, arguing that they could not easily find needed information because the data was not arranged according to *their* work activities.

The responsibility for resolving these problems falls to the Configuration Group. The group plays an important role in minimizing friction between different units concerning changes to the system. The Configuration Group meetings also provide a rare opportunity for practitioners to cross organizational boundaries and discuss their work with others from different organizational groups. As such, the Configuration Group engages in an explicit negotiation of the meaning and role of the information in HealthStat.

HealthStat as a CIS

As we have outlined, HealthStat is a shared repository of information used to coordinate the different aspects of medical care in the SICU. However, looking at HealthStat as a CIS leads us to focus less on the idea of shared information, and concentrate more on the practices by which that information is put to use and is made meaningful for the different sets of people who use it. For example, although much information is automatically logged from systems that monitor the patient's vital signs, that information is not accepted into HealthStat until it has been reviewed and approved by a member of the SICU nursing staff. In other words, the information needs to be explicitly "vetted" according to a set of SICU expectations in order to determine its acceptability. In turn, this vetting allows the SICU staff to maintain a common understanding about the appropriateness and accuracy of the information contained in the system. Thus, the notion of "information" here is not uncontested; rather, HealthStat is a repository for approved and trusted information.

Prospective and Retrospective Use

The patient record in HealthStat incorporates a broad set of concerns and a wide range of information about all aspects of a patient's current treatment regime and medical history. The amount of information that it contains about a given patient is potentially overwhelming. One way that the system's design deals with this problem is by providing a range of interfaces tailored to the needs of either the different practitioners who may deal with the patient or the different activities that make up the patient's care.

For example, physicians interact with the system primarily through the Flowsheet. Since they do not have a great deal of time, the Flowsheet provides them with quick information about the patient's condition. Pharmacists have a different set of goals. They are less concerned with the overall medical treatment of each individual patient and more concerned with ensuring proper medication administration. Their interactions with the system consist largely of checking on patient medications through the MAR. On the other hand, the nursing staff, who are primarily responsible for the moment-by-moment care of the patients, interact with the system through a number of screens, depending on their particular tasks. One of the primary interfaces that they use to coordinate their work is the Medication Worklist.

HealthStat stores information about the administration of medical care. However, the different screens reflect very different aspects of that care. The physicians' primary concern is with diagnosis and monitoring of the effectiveness of a treatment regime. The process of rounding, for example, is about describing how the patient has responded to treatment since the previous round, and on the basis of that, deciding what path should be taken next. So, the physicians' primary use of HealthStat's information is *retrospective*; they want to know what has happened over the last 24-hour period. In contrast, the nurses, who must arrange their activities in such a way as to ensure that each patient receives appropriate attention at relevant points in the shift, look to HealthStat for *prospective* information about the activities which will need to be carried out in order to effect the prescribed regime of care. HealthStat sits at the nexus of these two concerns – retrospective and prospective – both detailing what has gone before and projecting what will come next (See Berg (1999) for a similar argument concerning "reading" and "writing" a computerized patient record).

There are two consequences to this use of HealthStat. The first is the issue of temporal coordination in a CIS. Previous investigations of CIS have pointed out how the activities that surround an information store, and the practices by which information is explicitly transformed in order to "place it in common" are frequently oriented towards the anticipated lifetime of the information. At the most banal level, when information is placed into some form of storage, it is with an expectation that the information may need to be retrieved at a later date. Participants record information in such a way as to anticipate the circumstances under which it might be found again at some time in the future. Discussing the case of the Danish National Labour Inspection Service, Bannon and Bødker (1997) point out that records about encounters with companies may be reused years later, and that inspectors need to be sensitive to the potential future uses of the material they create; while Dourish et al. (1999) discuss how the evolution of a "common" classification scheme presented problems for the long-term storage of engineering documents. In contrast, in the SICU, temporal coordination through the CIS is both much more explicit and much finer-grained. The system not only stores information but also *transforms the information into a hour-by-hour schedule* by which work activities can be coordinated. This mediation between retrospective and prospective information is a key feature of how the different groups within the SICU make use of the CIS.

Our second point concerns the coordination of these multiple representations of information.

Information and Representations

One of the motivating concerns that we have been pursuing through this work is the following problem: if the work practices of the different groups whose work is coordinated through HealthStat are sufficiently diverse that many of the benefits of co-location, as discussed earlier, are effectively lost, then what compensates for this loss? How can coordination be re-established?

The issue of prospective and retrospective uses of information by nurses and physicians offers a clue. Through its multiple screens, HealthStat offers different views of the same information, and these different views are attuned to the needs of the different groups who use them. For the nursing staff, HealthStat transforms information about a treatment regime into a schedule of tasks and activities that will need to be carried out. The information that HealthStat records gives rise to many different representations (Flowsheet, MAR, Medication Worklist), according to how the information is used by the different groups.

This decoupling that HealthStat allows between the information and its representations is unusual amongst the CIS scenarios explored in the research literature. In the case of a CIS that is based on physical records, there is, clearly, only a single representation or physical form for each information artifact. However, even in cases where the information is recorded electronically, a single representation is still the norm (e.g. Trigg et al. 1999). HealthStat, however, expresses the same information through different representations. As we have seen, these representations are crucially integrated into the different working styles and practices of the groups who collectively carry out the work of the SICU. However, this need for *different representations* is balanced by the need for *shared information*. It is not enough that the representations be different, as would be afforded by translation-based approaches (Simone et al. 1999), but that these be different representations of *identical* underlying information, since it is through the sharing of this information that coordination is achieved.

The tension between the need for diverse representations (matching diverse work needs) and common information (for stable coordination) is reflected in the need to coordinate over the forms of the representations themselves. The staff needs to coordinate their activities through more than simply the information; they need to be able to discuss, to exchange, and to compare representations. The work of the Configuration Group reflects this concern. The seven ICUs have varied work practices requiring not only disparate information but also different arrangements of the same information. This diversity is a common feature of a

CIS, but one interesting element here is that the diverse needs of the units are explicitly negotiated through the Configuration Group. Here, the issue is not different representations of the same information, but compatibility between the representations used in different places. Since, the ICUs all use the same system, there has to be clear understanding of the representations' meaning to each unit. Unlike most CIS negotiations which are informal in nature and carried out during the course of the actual work, the Configuration Group allows nurses from the ICUs to meet and exchange information about their different work practices. The Configuration Group meeting is an opportunity for the group members to find out in *explicit* detail how the same information might be differently used in the various ICUs. By exchanging information about each unit's local work practices, Configuration Group members have a better understanding of how making changes to representations can effect each unit.

Discussions in the Configuration Group meetings help overcome the problem that each group has understanding the other's work. This problem is manifest in the SICU itself. While previous investigations described in Bannon and Bødker (1997) have suggested that physical proximity is a key feature in allowing different groups to coordinate their work in and around a common information space, our field data suggests that this is true only in the cases where the work of the different groups is sufficiently integrated (or, at least, mutually comprehensible) that the information can have some general relevance. In these circumstances, then, the ability to see how the work of others is being carried out with and through the information allows participants to coordinate their actions. In cases where the work is more disparate, though, physical proximity is of less immediate value. Even though they work in the same environment, the different groups in the SICU do not feel that their work is understood by the others. The role of a single information representation as a site of work coordination breaks down. However, electronic information systems allow us to present multiple, coordinated representations of information. When the system can present the same information in ways that are differently attuned to the information needs of different groups, participants see other's work transformed in ways that make sense from their own perspective.

Design Considerations for CIS Systems

Our exploration of the use of HealthStat in the SICU has highlighted a number of interesting issues concerning the role of information in coordinating work. In particular, we have seen that work coordination through HealthStat depends on the separation it offers between the information and its representation (how that information is configured for particular uses). Although the observational material presented in the paper has been very specific, our findings suggest a number of broader implications.

First, the work of the SICU suggests that we should reconsider the role of physical proximity and accessibility in coordinating cooperative work. As we have already noted, previous studies have observed that physical proximity is critically important in a range of collaborative settings, affording participants visual and auditory access to each other's activities and facilitating easy communication. Clearly, this is true, but it rests on a more fundamental assumption that the activity going on in the physical space is intelligible to those who witness it. For example, Heath and Luff's (1992) classic analysis shows how the London Underground control room operators achieve a remarkably smooth and intricate coordination between their activities through a combination of, first, continually monitoring the actions of others in the room, and, second, explicitly organising their actions so as to disclose what is happening to others nearby. However, this depends not only on their proximity, but on their ability to interpret what is going on around them, through their familiarity with the work of the control room and the practices by which their colleagues organise that work. It is precisely this in-depth familiarity with the detail, motives and consequences of each other's work that is absent in the case of the SICU. The physicians and the nursing staff have only a limited and superficial understanding of each other's work – certainly not enough to achieve the delicate choreography that Heath and Luff observe. So, the observation that physical proximity and accessibility support the coordination of group work glosses over an important detail. More accurately, physical proximity and accessibility afford the mutual interpretation of working activities to those who share a sufficiently detailed understanding of those activities in the first place. In cases such as the SICU, where this understanding is not present, physical proximity is not, by itself, sufficient.

Second, the case of the SICU shows us that although participants interact with the information through different representations, coordinating their activities depends on these representations reflecting the same underlying information. Because it is the same underlying information, the different representations are always sychronised; any changes in the underlying information will be immediately reflected in all the different representations. The alternative would be to maintain two different systems in parallel – perhaps an information store that describes medication information, and a separate schedule that outlines nursing tasks, such as that observed by Bardram (1997). However, the possibility for inconsistency and the difficulty of moving information back and forth would compromise the SICU's ability to coordinate activities around the patient; it is important that the underlying information be shared. The role of shared information in promoting coordination has been explored extensively in CSCW, particularly in the form of technologies promoting awareness (e.g. Dourish and Bellotti 1992; Gutwin et al. 1996; Mark et al. 1997). The effectiveness of most of these approaches, however, depends on a common representation of the underlying information: a common information structure in the case of Dourish and Bellotti or Mark et al. and a common set of spatial arrangements in the case of Gutwin et al. There has been much less exploration of uses of awareness techniques in a coordinated fashion across multiple distinct representations, although an exploration by Greenberg and his colleagues (1996) provides an interesting example of the opportunities. Cases where the different forms of work are highly diverse, such as in the SICU, may require this sort of approach. In turn, our attention to the ways in which information representations can be designed to naturally convey a sense of the activities in which they are involved. This is not, in itself, a new observation (see Nygren et al. (1992) for an exploration of this issue, also in the medical domain), but the separation between information and representation implied in our study suggests that this meta-information must also be coordinated with multiple representations of the information.

Finally, the separation between information and representation also highlights how the same information is enmeshed in a variety of work processes. It serves multiple purposes and enables multiple individuals to carry out their own work. Traditional software architectures, however, typically provide no direct support for this feature of information work. Often, the information is embedded in a structure (such as a schema or hierarchy) that makes it tractable and manipulable by software systems. However, these information structures make it harder to pick information up and move it from place to place, decontexualising it and recontextualising it according to the situation of need; and similarly, they only reflect a single point of view on the role of the information rather than the many different points of view that we see at work in situations such as the SICU. Our fieldwork, then, provides support for approaches to information architecture that separates the information from the structures that surround and describe it (Dourish et al. 1999; Parsons and Wand 2000). By decoupling information from its structure and supporting diverse representations of the same information, these approaches can facilitate better coordination of heterogeneous work.

Conclusion

Common information spaces exist in diverse work environments. In our study of medical work in an intensive care unit, we focus on the use of a CIS in which the actors are physically co-located. The work of the SICU, like that of many other workplaces, is detailed, demanding, time-critical, and involves interaction among many different groups. At the center of the SICU work is the patient whose health is dependent on the effective coordination among physicians, nurses, and pharmacists. However, in many ways, each group's work practices are opaque to others. Although being physically co-located does help coordinate their activities, the diverse work practices of these groups prevent them from receiving the full benefits of co-location. Under these circumstances, our observations in the SICU point to the important role played by specific information representations in coordinating diverse work activities. For example, the system's ability to present both retrospective and prospective representations of the same information is important for coordinating physician and nursing activities. Unlike paper records, computer systems offer the ability to decouple information from its representations to help smooth coordination. This decoupling opens up a rich design space for systems that allow people with different interests, concerns and work practices to work together effectively.

Acknowledgments

We thank the SICU physicians, nurses, and pharmacists and the HealthStat technical team for allowing us to observe and interview them. We also thank Erin Bradner, Ulrik Christensen, Beki Grinter, and Suzanne Schaefer for their helpful comments on this paper. This work was supported by the University of California's Life Science Informatics grant #L98-05.

References

Bannon, L. (2000). "Understanding Common Information Spaces in CSCW," Paper presented at the Workshop on Cooperative Organisation of Common Information Spaces, Technical University of Denmark, August 2000.

Bannon, L. and Bodker, S. (1997). "Constructing Common Information Space," *Proceedings of the European Conference on Computer-Supported Cooperative Work ECSCW'97.*(Lancaster, UK), Dordrecht: Kluwer, pp. 81-96.

Bardram, J.E. (1997). "Plans as Situated Action: An Activity Theory Approach to Workflow Systems," *Proceedings of the European Conference on Computer-Supported Cooperative Work ECSCW'97.*(Lancaster, UK), Dodrecht: Kluwer, pp. 17-32.

Berg, M. (1999). "Accumulating and Coordinating: Occasions for Information Technologies in Medical Work," *Computer-Supported Cooperative Work* 8: pp. 373-401.

Berg, M. and Bowker, G. (1997). "The Multiple Bodies of the Medical Record: Toward a Sociology of an Artifact," *The Sociological Quarterly* 38: pp. 511-535.

Blomberg, J., Suchman, L. and Trigg, R.H. (1997). "Reflections on a Work-Oriented Design Project" in Bowker, G.C., Starr, S.L., Turner, W. and Gasser, L. (eds.) *Social Science,Technical Systems, and Cooperative Work: Beyond the Great Divide.* Mahwah, New Jersey: Lawrence Erlbaum Associates.

Bowker, G.C. and Star, S.L. (1999). *Sorting things out: classification and its consequences.*Cambridge, Mass.: MIT Press.

Dourish, P. and Bellotti, V. (1992). "Awareness and Coordination in Shared Workspaces," *Proceedings of the ACM Conference on Computer-Supported Cooperative Work CSCW '92.*(Toronto, Canada), New York: ACM Press, pp. 107 - 114.

Dourish, P., Edwards, K., LaMarca, A. and Salisbury, M. (1999). "Presto: An Experimental Architecture for Fluid Information Spaces," *ACM Transactions on Computer-Human Interaction* 6 (2): pp. 133-161.

Greenberg, S., Gutwin, C. and Roseman, M. (1996). "Semantic Telepointers for Groupware," *OzCHI'96.* (Hamilton, NZ), IEEE Press, pp. 54-61.

Gutwin, C., Roseman, M. and Greenberg, S. (1996). "A Usability Study of Awareness Widgets in a Shared Workspace Groupware System," *ACM Computer-Supported Cooperative Work CSCW'96.* (Cambridge, MA), New York: ACM Press, pp. 258-267.

Heath, C. and Luff, P. (1992). "Collaboration and Control: Crisis Management and Multimedia Technology in London Underground Line Control Rooms," *Computer-Supported Cooperative Work* 1 (1-2): pp. 69-118.

Ishii, I., Kobayashi, M. and Grudin, J. (1992). "Integration of Inter-Personal Space and Shared Workspace: Clearboard Design and Experiments," *Proceedings of the ACM Conference on Computer-Supported Cooperative Work CSCW'92.* (Toronto, Canada), New York: ACM Press, pp. 33-42.

Lu, I. and Mantei, M. (1991). "Idea Management in a Shared Drawing Tool.," *Proceedings of the European Conference on Computer-Supported Cooperative Work ECSCW'91.* Dordrecht:Kluwer, pp. 97-112.

Mark, G., Fuchs, L. and Sohlenkamp, M. (1997). "Supporting Groupware Conventions through Contextual Analysis," *Proceedings of the European Conference on Computer-Supported Cooperative Work ECSCW'97.* (Lancaster, UK), Dordrecht: Kluwer, pp. 253-268.

Nygren, E., Lind, M., Johnson, M. and Sandblad, B. (1992). "The Art of the Obvious," *Proceedings of the ACM Conference on Human Factors in Computing Systems CHI '92.* (Monterey, California), New York: ACM Press, pp. 235-239.

Parsons, J. and Wand, Y. (2000). "Emancipating Instances from the Tyranny of Classes in Information Modelling," *ACM Transactions on Database Systems* 25 (2): pp. 228-268.

Randall, D. (2000). "What's 'Common' about Common Information Spaces?," Paper presented at the Workshop on Cooperative Organisation of Common Information Spaces, Technical University of Denmark, August 2000.

Schmidt, K. and Bannon, L. (1992). "Taking CSCW Seriously: Supporting Articulation Work," *Computer-Supported Cooperative Work* 1: pp. 7-40.

Simone, C., Mark, G. and Giubbilei, D. (1999). "Interoperability as a Means of Articulation Work," *Work Activities Coordination and Collaboration (WACC'99).* (San Francisco, California), pp. 39-48.

Star, S.L. and Griesemer, J.R. (1989). "Institutional Ecology, Translations and Boundary Objects: Amatuers and Professionals in Berkeley's Museum of Vertebrate Zoology, 1907-1939," *Social Studies of Science* 19: pp. 387-420.

Strauss, A., Fagerhaugh, S., Suczek, B. and Wiener, C. (1985). *Social Organization of Medical Work.* Chicago: University of Chicago.

Trigg, R.H., Blomberg, J. and Suchman, L. (1999). "Moving document collections online: The evolution of a shared repository," *Proceedings of the European Conference on Computer-Supported Cooperative Work ECSCW'99.* (Copenhagen, Denmark), Dordrecht: Kluwer, pp. 331-50.

W. Prinz, M. Jarke, Y. Rogers, K. Schmidt, and V. Wulf (eds.), *Proceedings of the Seventh European Conference on Computer-Supported Cooperative Work, 16-20 September 2001, Bonn, Germany*, pp. 259-278.
© 2001 Kluwer Academic Publishers. Printed in the Netherlands.

Cognitive Properties of a Whiteboard: A Case Study in a Trauma Centre

Yan Xiao, Caterina Lasome, Jacqueline Moss, Colin F. Mackenzie, and Samer Faraj*

University of Maryland, Baltimore and *University of Maryland, College Park
yxiao@umaryland.edu, lasometc@home.com, jmoss001@umaryland.edu, cmack003@umaryland.edu, and *faraj@rhsmith.umd.edu*

Abstract. Distributed cognition as an approach to collaborative work holds that a work unit is cognitive system in which cognitive activities are carried out jointly by workers with the use of tools. This approach has several direct implications to the study of collaborative work. In this paper, we analysed staff interactions with a large display board in a Level I trauma centre operating room unit. Coordination needs are exacerbated by the unpredictability of incoming emergency surgery patients admitted to the trauma centre as well as other contingencies (such as changes in scheduled surgery cases or staffing). The public display board has evolved into a key component for supporting collaborative work. The physical and perceptual properties of the board are exploited by the clinicians to support rapid paced, highly dynamic work. The canvas-like appearances of the display board, combined with magnetic objects attached to the board, afford its users to taylor the board as an effective coordinative tool and to invent new ways of representing information. Based on the concept of display-based cognition, our analysis illustrates the role of public displays in facilitating negotiation of scheduling, joint planning, and augmenting inter-personal communication.

Introduction

The field of computer supported cooperative work has brought into focus the importance of studying work activities in their natural context (Bannon & Schmidt, 1991). Detailed studies of the interaction with the physical environment and collaborative work can lead to insights into how we work together (Suchman, 1987; Hutchins, 1995a). As reported by those researchers who have paid attention to the work environment and to the way in which people exploit and inventively use the physical and perceptual properties of the work environment (e.g. Hutchins, 1995b; Segal, 1994; Berg, 1999; Bardram, 2000), much can be learnt still about collaborative work. An equally compelling reason for studying artefacts in collaborative work is to inform design. Increasingly human collaborative activities are mediated by tools with computing and telecommunication capabilities. With rapid advances in technology, ever more powerful tools are being built to support collaborative work. One useful source of insight into how collaborative tools should be designed comes from observing ways in which non-computerised artefacts are exploited for supporting collaboration. Studies of computer systems (e.g. Bardram, 1997) have shown that these systems failed because of an inadequate understanding of existing work practices. Paper-based forms, for example, perform functions beyond simply conveying information. Ignoring these other functions may have detrimental effects on the usability of computer systems (e.g. Bardram, 1997).

In this article, we present an ethnographic study of a public display board in an operating room (OR) unit in a Level I trauma centre. Coordination needs are exacerbated by the unpredictability of incoming emergency surgery patients admitted to the trauma centre as well as other contingencies (such as changes in scheduled surgery cases or staffing). The board has evolved into a key component for supporting collaborative work.

After describing the study setting and methods, we will present the visual and physical properties of the display board. We will then present the cognitive properties of public displays through the analysis of the observed interactions between the staff and the display board. Discussions will follow the presentation of findings in each of the three areas: display-based cognition, distributed cognition, and articulation work. We will conclude with implications of our study for future research on public display boards and for design of such boards driven by computers.

Large public display boards have previously been studied by researchers (e.g. Bardram, 2000; Garbis and Waern, 1999; Whittaker & Schwarz, 1999). With the advance of technology, more and more such boards will be based on computer displays (Stefik et al, 1987; Mynatt, 2000; Berkowicz et al, 1999). It is also the aim of the current paper to help researchers to better understand existing public display boards in use, so that the development of technology can be guided and driven by our understanding of the role of public displays in supporting collaborative work.

Coordinating schedules in operating rooms

Setting

The six operating room (OR) unit is part of a busy, urban trauma centre with over 6,000 admissions per year. Trauma patients are brought directly from incident scenes and are first evaluated in the trauma resuscitation unit (TRU). Emergency surgery may be performed in the OR unit for those patients who need immediate life-saving surgery within a few hours of their admission to the TRU. The OR unit is separated by a door from the TRU. When surgery is over, the patient is transferred to the post-anaesthesia care unit (PACU), which is also nearby on the same floor (Fig.1).

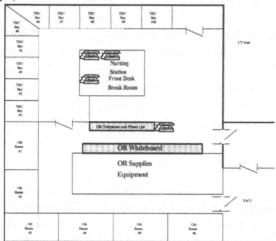

Fig. 1. Layout of the Trauma Resuscitation and Operating Room Units

The majority of the OR surgeries are, however, non-emergency in nature. Non-emergency patients, either previously admitted to the TRU or referred through doctor's offices and clinics, are scheduled for surgery the day before. The OR unit is open around the clock. The number of operating rooms open fluctuates over the course of the day. Generally, more operating rooms are open during the day and weekdays than other times; most of surgery cases occur between the hours of 7:30am and 3:00pm.

OR staff members work a combination of eight and twelve hour shifts. Staff members on an eight-hour shifts are usually relieved for lunch earlier and subsequently complete their shift earlier (3:00pm) than those working twelve-hour shifts (7:00pm).

A list of surgical cases is scheduled ("posted") the day before and distributed to the OR unit by a print-out. The list of cases posted is almost never the list of cases performed the next day. As with many other highly complex and dynamic work environments, uncertainty arises from various sources when changes are frequently introduced. In the study setting, change is constant and unpredictable. Examples of changes affecting the planned surgery schedule include cancelled surgeries, unexpected additional surgeries (which result from both newly admitted cases as well as deterioration of previous patient cases necessitating re-visits to the operating room), multi-patient trauma situations in which demand exceeds resource supply, and any external variables impacting OR operational status (unavailable or malfunctioning equipment, lack of supplies, and changes in staffing patterns).

The charge nurse's primary duty is, to paraphrase one of the charge nurses we observed, "to make the ORs work." The charge nurse takes requests for surgery and translates them into a schedule of specific times and sequences in each of the individual operating rooms (one of six). If a case is not scheduled as the first case, its starting time cannot be scheduled. The order of the case is then scheduled "to follow" another case. The charge nurse does not have clinical duties ordinarily, although all three charge nurses we observed had extensive clinical experience as OR nurses. Charge nurses work in a corridor connecting the TRU and the OR unit, although they are scrubbed and attired to work in the ORs. For the sake of description, we will use "the charge nurse" as a representative of all three charge nurses observed.

Methods

As part of a larger study of coordination through the trauma care process, access was gained to conduct an ethnographic study of the OR scheduling board used by staff. Data were gathered by direct observation, interviewing, and photographing. Due to the sensitive nature of the work observed, most of the data were in the form of notes and photographs but not transcriptions of audio-taped verbal communications.

Most of the intensive coordination activities for the OR unit occur early in the morning. Researcher observations started 6:30am when the day shift charge nurse began shift for the ORs. All three charge nurses were observed. Over a six month period, three researchers (two were registered nurses) observed in the OR board area on eight days. Short interviews were conducted with nurses, physicians, anaesthesia providers in front of the OR board for explanation on its use.

Notes were taken about the people who came to the board and their interactions with the board as well as with other people at the board. When opportunities allowed, the research team conducted brief interviews about board users' purposes and views on the board. Still images were taken.

Visual and physical properties of the OR board

Layout and size

The OR board measures 365x122cm (12 feet by 4 feet) and holds magnetic materials which themselves can serve as surfaces for writing. The board is partitioned into three major areas (Fig. 2a). The left-most area is for displaying which patients are scheduled for surgery in which operating rooms. The second section of the OR board is used to hold those surgical cases that are not planned ("add-ons") and are not assigned a start time nor a sequence for surgery. The far right section of the board is used to hold magnetic nametags for all OR staff (Fig. 2b) as well as a variety of indicator magnets. Across the top of the board are various other messages to announce important items. Additional messages may be posted in paper format held in place by magnets or annotated via erasable marker directly on the board.

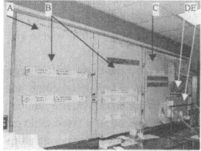
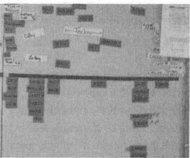

Fig. 2a. Overview of the OR board. (A: General staff information/announcements; B: magnetic case strips for all six ORs in the unit; C: Holding place for case strips, especially unscheduled add-on cases; D: Magnetic staff name tags for off-duty staff; E: Magnetic staff name tags for on-duty staff).

Fig. 2b. A close-up view of the right side of the OR board. The top portion holds name tags of all nursing and supporting staff assigned to the unit. The name tags of those who were currently on duty for the day were arranged on the bottom according to their assigned shift.

Location

The OR board is located at the intersection of the OR unit and TRU (Fig. 1). The area is accessible to ORs, TRU, and ancillary personnel such as housekeeping, supply, patient transport, and administrative staff. Further, the area is supported by other communication and collaboration tools such as telephones and bulletin boards annotating surgical and anaesthesia staff, pager numbers, and announcements.

Schedule representation

Magnetic strips are used to indicate surgery cases (one strip per patient). Three types of strips are used: a white strip indicates a scheduled surgical case (Fig. 3a);

a blue strip indicates an "add-on" case (those that are not scheduled the day before and are not emergency status); and a white strip with red tape at both ends (Fig 3b) indicates an emergency case (also not placed on the surgical schedule the day prior). With all cases (scheduled, add-on, and emergency), the strip contains essential information about the surgical case. The information is hand-written onto the strip based on written and verbal surgery requests. From left to right, the following information items are usually written: expected surgery start time if the case is the first in a particular OR, current patient location (before the surgery) within the facility, patient name, name of planned surgical procedure, responsible surgeon, specialised equipment/supplies, and expected duration of the procedure (see Figure 3a).

Fig. 3a. Left. Surgical case strip (in white) for scheduled operative procedure. The patient and surgeon names were blurred to protect privacy. On the strip are (left to right): case starting time, location of the patient in facility before surgery, patient name, name of the surgical procedure(s), surgeon's name, special instrument requirements, and estimated length of the case.

Fig. 3b. Right. Case strip for emergency surgery (in white). The ends of the strip are marked with red tape.

For scheduled cases, the strips are usually prepared by the night shift charge nurse. For the add-on cases, the strips are prepared as requests come in. Scheduled, add-on, and emergency cases are placed on the board under a number corresponding to a specific OR or in the holding area. Instead of a fixed table on the display board in which each OR has a cell, the number tags indicating individual ORs are magnets themselves and can be moved; therefore, display space for an OR can be changed by merely moving the OR number tag.

Indicator magnets include a green smiley face (Fig. 4), which when placed next to a patient name alerts the staff that the patient requires isolation precautions (due to a communicable disease) and may require additional staffing.

A small piece of paper is sometimes placed under a magnetic strip (Fig. 5). This paper ("Patient Call Slip") is prepared by the charge nurse to include the date, time, patient's name, current location within the facility, assigned operating room, whether or not the current unit has been contacted, isolation status, and any transfer considerations and equipment that will be necessary while moving the patient to the operating room (e.g. oxygen, monitors, medication pumps, patient weight, and need for escort by anaesthesia services). Patient call slips are used by OR technicians who transport patients from their wards to the operating rooms. This messaging device ensures the correct patient is collected and transported to the appropriate OR.

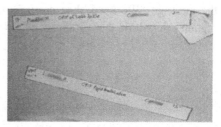

Fig. 4. A green dot (the top case strip) indicating the patient was on special isolation precautions for a communicable disease. There are three strips for three cases here, representing the order in which the cases are to be carried out within one OR. The middle strip is in blue, indicating an unscheduled case. Note the paper slip placed under the bottom strip.

Fig. 5. Patient Call Slip placed behind the top surgical case strip. The paper slip contains information for technicians to transport the patient from the ward to the operating room. A slanted case strip (bottom) indicating that the patient is still in the room but that the surgical case is almost complete and staff can begin to prepare for the next patient.

Staffing representation

Magnetic name tags for all staff members are located in the farthest right section of the board. The name tags are placed to the right of the operating room number (Fig. 6) to represent the staffing assignments. At least two staff members are assigned to each room: one circulating nurse and one OR technician. More staff may be assigned based on the acuity of the patient and the complexity of the procedure.

Those staff members working eight-hour shifts have an indicator magnet with either a star and sunglasses or a cat face next their name (Fig. 7).

Fig. 6. Nursing staff assignment "displayed" on the right side of the case strip using name tags. On the left is the case strip, to which the nurses are assigned.

Fig. 7. Above: A name tag with an indicator magnet showing a "sunglasses" or "cat face" logo identifies that the nurse is working an eight-hour shift. Left: The name tag next to it on the right (RITA) indicates the person who is scheduled to relieve the person on the left (RAMON) for the meal break.

Messages and notices

Notes can be easily written in empty spaces to alert all staff to critical issues. Two examples of such notes are depicted in Fig. 8. In the first example, the message "Please remember to turn off the argon tanks" is placed in a location on the board that is not used for representing daily schedules. In the second example, the message "We need shoe covers" occupies the area of the board that is in regular use (within the workspace of ORs #2 and #3).

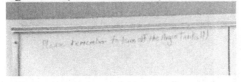

Fig. 8. Sign on top of the board serves as a reminder to staff: "Please remember to turn off the argon tanks." The photo on the right demonstrates one use of the board for passing messages to the charge nurse.

Physical and perceptual interaction with and through the OR board

When observing the activities in front of the OR board, we were amazed by the utility of the OR board. Its immense size easily accommodates 10 or more individuals standing in close proximity either discussing or modifying the board. Its canvas-like appearance invites new uses for its surface. The magnetic strips and name tags are like pieces on a chessboard to be moved about to assess the impact of scheduling possibilities. Below we will examine how the board functions as a critical component of a cognitive system.

Display-based cognition

One of the tasks confronting the charge nurse is to balance demands for and availability of resources, both of which are constantly changing. On the demand side, the number and complexity of the requested surgery cases, their urgency, and the preferences of surgical and nursing personnel must be considered. On the supply side, the availability of staff, the conditions of the operating rooms, and the status of the patient and necessary equipment are also taken into account. The end result is the allocation of an operating room for a case in a given time or order. Arriving at any schedule seems to be difficult, let alone a schedule that approaches maximising the efficiency while at the same time satisfying individual preferences.

With the assistance of the OR board, the difficulty of scheduling appears greatly reduced. Below we will examine some of the ways in which the OR board is used.

- Placing name tags of OR staff according to the staffing pattern for the day (Fig 1b). With one glance, one can tell how many OR staff members there are today and at which shift (8-hour or 12-hour).
- Marking the arrival status of same day surgery patients (Fig 9). Same day surgery patients arrive early to the waiting area and await their surgical case to be performed on that day. Occasionally, there have been problems in that same day surgery patients arrive late for their cases or do not come at all. The charge nurse was observed to confirm the status of same day surgery patients and put a dot near their case strips. In this way, the charge nurse can keep track of when patients arrive for same day surgery on the OR board.

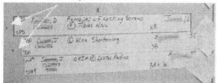

Fig. 9. A list of same day surgery cases. Note the dots to the left of the case strips. The dots were made after the charge nurse confirmed that the patients had already registered in the facility and were ready for surgery.

- Trying out schedules by re-arranging case strips. The add-on cases are always in blue strips and are usually placed in the holding area on the board. They prompt the charge nurse to finish the scheduling task of assigning add-on cases an operating room and a starting time and sequence (i.e. which case the add-on case follows). Since the information for each case is written on a movable magnetic strip, rearranging the sequence and room assignment can be easily accomplished by moving the case strip around the OR board.
- Status tracking. When a surgical case is near completion, we observed that the charge nurse placed the corresponding case strip at a slanted angle on the OR board to indicate that a case was nearing completion (Fig. 5).

Discussions

In the last two decades, many have (re-)discovered the limitations of studying cognitive processes in artificially impoverished settings. Larkin (1989) commented that "problem solving is often done in the context of an external display. Often there are the physical objects that are part of a problem situation. Alternatively the solver may construct equations and diagrams as an aid to solving the problem" (p.319). By having external representation, humans can solve problems leveraging perceptual capabilities. Larkin (1989) noted several features of such "display-based" problem solving: (1) the process is easy, (2) it is largely error-free, (3) it is no degraded by interruption, (4) the steps are performed in a variety of orders, and (5) the process is easily modified.

Payne (1991) discovered the importance of display in users' cognitive activities. Through experiments on how users interacted with word processors, Payne found that human action relies upon patterns in the external environment in the computer display and is to an important degree "display-based".

Zhang and Norman (1994) reported a series of experiments on the role of external representation in problem-solving. The term "distributed cognition" was used to describe the nature of problem solving when information processing is distributed in the environment (external representation) and in the problem solver's mind (internal representation). Zhang and Norman (1994) summarised how external representation helps problem solving: (1) external representations can provide memory aids and (2) external representations can provide directly perceivable information (such as constraints and options).

These and other studies on individual cognition with the support of the external environment point out the importance of examining in detail how artefacts are used, particularly in work settings. One important role of the OR board is to support the cognitive activities of its users. Much of the critical capabilities of the joint human-board cognitive system is accomplished by *externally* representing task status and by physically manipulating objects on the display. The board becomes part of the joint human-board cognitive system:

- It "remembers" cases to be scheduled, the status of the cases, and results of scheduling
- it "displays" constraints and options to the user
- it "simulates" possible scheduling solutions

With constant interruptions to the charge nurse, the OR board enhances the reliability of the joint human-board cognitive system (Larkin, 1989).

Distributed cognition and display-based joint cognition

By some staff members' account, the OR board is the nerve centre for the OR unit. The board area is accessible to a multitude of people who work in the trauma centre. The wide corridor at the intersection of the TRU and OR (Fig. 1) serves as a major gathering point for all providers (e.g. surgeons, nurses, technicians, anaesthesia staff, housekeeping staff, unit clerks, supply staff). Communications of all purposes occur in front of the OR board by all providers.

Although the charge nurse is considered the "owner" of the OR board and is the primarily author of the board, the board is viewed by a number of people. We describe here several types of interaction with the board by people working in the trauma centre and the types of inter-personal interaction with the assistance of the board.

Negotiation of scheduling solutions

On those occasions when complex and dynamic situations require multidisciplinary input, the OR board serves as an excellent site for negotiations. The following are two excerpts from an interview in front of the board between one of the authors (YX) and an attending surgeon (AS), just before the nominal operating room start time:

> YX: So, is this the first time you've come to see the board?
>
> AS: Yeah. You see, usually when I have this kind of the day I try to see if I can stagger the room a little bit because the cases are not that long. If a case is prepared in another room, the patient is put to sleep and prepped, I can go over and start the case in that room.
>
> ...
>
> YX: During the day do you come to the board as well?
>
> AS: If I am trying to do a case quicker I will. I have got to have a look to see how busy it is. If I can move quicker I will....I use [the board] to see if I can push, like "Why can't I follow that case" or "move to there." Like that case [the scheduled case on the right side, with no room assignment yet. It was assumed that the case would go to the OR which has not started yet], I don't see any follow up case. So I might be able to move one of my cases to follow that case.

Surgeons put in requests for time slots in operating rooms. In order to accomplish their goals, it may be to their advantage to understand what the overall schedule is. In this segment, one can see the surgeon (AS) used the board to negotiate with the charge nurse ("Why can't I follow that case") based on an appreciation of what the charge nurse had to consider.

The board facilitates the joint planning and decision-making by allowing workers to reason from the common status representation. It also eases the communication through indication of gaze directions and pointing. Here are several segments from observation notes:

> 06:30 Orthopaedic attending negotiating with OR charge for room and case assignments due to special requirements of the type of rooms. The surgeon looked for cases that may bump his case.
>
> 07:41 Plastic fellow: checking board for availability if he wants to add-on a case.
>
> 07:45 Orthopaedic attending: rearranging cases on board because same day admit patient did not show up. Magnetic strip rearranged. Cases moved to other rooms.
>
> 08:45 Orthopaedic attending: checking board related to which cases have started, who is doing what and expectations. Advises OR charge while pointing to board that one case will take much longer that what is posted.

> 0740 OR charge & Orthopaedic attending: While viewing board Ortho attending asks, "can I get a different scrub tech for my case, one with experience?" OR charge replies, "she will do just fine."

At 06:30am, the orthopaedic attending surgeon wanted to make sure that the room type was suitable for the surgery he was to perform. When asked, he expressed that he also wanted to assess the possibility of the cases preceding his case dragging on longer than scheduled. At 07:41, a plastic reconstruction surgeon ("plastic fellow") came to see if he could add a unscheduled case. By coming to the board, he could assess, jointly with the charge nurse, the likelihood of adding on his case. At 07:45, just after the nominal starting time for the operating rooms, the schedule was already dramatically changed. Note that the surgeon involved came to the OR board to assess the impact of the changes with the charge nurse. At 08:45, the orthopaedic attending updated the charge nurse. On a different day, at 07:40, the orthopaedic surgeon was negotiating with the charge nurse over the OR staff assignment.

Joint planning

The charge nurse is given the responsibility to make decisions related to scheduling. However, our observation found that the charge nurse approached this responsibility with the intention of incorporating individual preferences as much as possible. This is best reflected by the following observation note segment:

> 06:45 OR Staff Nurses and Scrubs: Arriving at board for report from OR charge nurse. OR charge nurse pointing to board while providing staff report. Accepting requests from staff for specific room assignments. Staff placing their names next to room numbers indicating their requests for specific cases while placing indicators for 8 hour shifts next to their names. OR charge nurse points to board while announcing anticipated changes in cases that have not occurred yet. OR charge nurse asks for volunteers for especially difficult cases while pointing to board.

In this segment, the board provided a shared problem space: operating rooms to be staffed, with cases scheduled for each of the rooms. Everyone involved could see which rooms had and had not been assigned, and what were the cases scheduled for a given operating room. According to one of the charge nurses, the board injects a sense of fairness among the staff since everyone gets to see what is available and who selects what.

The following segment shows a different kind of joint planning:

> 07:00 Charge Anaesthesiologist and OR charge viewing the board and deciding how to rearrange rooms for an additional opening.

In this segment, due to the large case load, the charge nurse was exploring the possibility of opening an additional operating room. In order to do this, the charge nurse would need the cooperation from the anaesthesia care providers, who might not have enough resources to support an additional room. The charge nurse and the charge anaesthesiologist jointly viewed the board to evaluate options.

"Intra-system" display

In some sense, the board is a display interfacing various information processors of a joint cognitive system. Many people were observed to come to the board frequently to update themselves. Here are note segments from observation on two separate days:

> 07:10 Radiology technician: "I'm looking at the board to see which rooms I will be needed in through out the day and to see what times I should be there."

> 06:31 Charge anaesthesiologist viewing OR schedules for caseload and acuity of patients; attempting to match ability of anaesthesia care providers with appropriate patient/case. Checking for add-on cases and obtaining overall view of the day's work ahead.
>
> 06:40 OR attendants checking OR schedules to anticipate when they will be needed to collect patients from the floor or same day admits.
>
> 06:57 Resident first meets Charge Anaesthesiologist who explains board so that the resident may anticipate intubation training opportunities.
>
> 07:05 Orthopaedic technician checking board to anticipate any equipment required for specific orthopaedic surgery cases.
>
> 07:06 An anaesthesiologist came by. When asked why came here, he answered "taking the pulse of the ORs".
>
> 07:30 PACU charge: checking board against printed schedule making notes. Estimating type of day the PACU will have by number and acuity of patients.
>
> 07:31 Plastic attending: checking board for when he can anticipate his scheduled case will start.

At 07:10, the radiology technician, who might be needed during surgical cases, came to see the schedule.

On a different day at 06:31, the person who was responsible for coordinating anaesthesia care providers (Charge anaesthesiologist) came to the OR board to get an update. Like a number of other people in similar position, he received a print-out of the day's scheduled cases the day before. As on most days, the print-out he received was already out-dated at such an early time of the day. At 06:40, 50 minutes before the nominal starting time for operating rooms, the technicians (OR attendants) came to plan their own activities. At 06:57, the information on the board was used to anticipate training opportunities. At 07:30, the person who coordinated activities in the "downstream" of the operating rooms, the post-anaesthesia care unit (PACU) came to update her schedule.

This segment demonstrated the central role of the board as a conduit for passing information among collaborative workers. Each worker by him- or herself is agent who plans for his or her own activities. Viewed as a single cognitive system with multiple agents and external environment, how do the agents choreograph and weave individuals' activities into streams of coherent joint activities? The board seems to hold part of the answer to this question.

Augmenting inter-personal communication

Scheduling operating room activities requires the management of multiple conflicts. Conveying situations at hand clearly would likely reduce misunderstanding and facilitate the management of conflicts.

> 08:00 Ortho attending: "which room am I in" while looking at board. OR charge explaining while pointing to board that his room was bumped for an emergency.

In this segment, an emergency case had pushed a scheduled case. As described earlier, emergency cases are on strips with red tapes on the ends and are conspicuous to the viewer. The orthopaedic surgeon was quick to appreciate the circumstances under which "his" case was bumped.

Discussions

People always work in a meaningful physical environment which one can adapt, change and share. Realization of this nature of work has profound implications on the study of cognition and team performance. The approach of distributed cognition (Hutchins, 1995a) has taken this nature of work as the most fundamental premise in studying people at work. In a study of work in aircraft cockpit, Huchins (1995b) demonstrated that the physical environment of a cockpit became part of a cognitive system which "remembers" speed. He also noted the active role of pilots in creating a more informative environment by, for example, placing sticky notes in the instrument panel. Hutchins (1995b) advocates that "system-level cognitive view directs our attention beyond the cognitive properties of individuals to the properties of external representations and to the interactions between internal and external representations. Technological devices introduced into the cockpit invariably affect the flow of information in the cockpit."

Several previous studies have examined the use of public displays like the OR board. In evaluating a computerised patient scheduling system, Bardram (1997) found that users maintained a planning board to re-represent the information in the computer system. The board allows the user to put in post-it notes for additional and detailed information. The board also allowed movement of physical objects (Lego bricks) to represent rescheduling results. Furthermore, Bardram noted the perceptual characteristics: the planning board show schedules to all people and has visual cues of overall workload and visual overview of all case status. In comparison, Bardram noted that computerised system "failed to support ... important aspects of providing highly visible, malleable, and sharable representation of the scheduled treatments."

Bellotti & Rogers (1997) found that news organisations used wall displays for representing personnel/work status and for discussing designs. The shared display of assignment provides a way for teams to visualise current team activities and resource availability. Suchman (1988) examined the role of visual representation in the face-to-face settings. A central theme was that the representation media formed a referential base for interaction. Mynatt et al (2000) investigated how large display boards are used and how objects on display boards are grouped. In a study on operations in emergency resource centres (Garbis & Waern, 1999), public displays (e.g. a flip chart) were noted to perform central roles in indicating status information and facilitating discussions. In a train control room (Garbis, 1999), the wall display of train track status not only supports individual controllers' information needs but also enables the controllers to refer and discuss.

Artefacts and articulation work

Managing interdependency has been noted as the core of coordination (Malone & Crowston, 1990). Given the fact that potentially the activities of everyone in the OR unit are dependent on those of someone else, the effort needed to coordinate could be overwhelming. The OR board alleviates much of the burden of coordination.

The patient call slip (Fig 4) is a good example for reducing the effort in articulating several people's activities. When an operating room is ready for the patient, the charge nurse notifies the appropriate unit that they will be coming for the patient, then assigns an OR technician to pick up the patient. The OR technician removes the patient call slip and leaves to fetch the patient. When the patient call slip is no longer under the patient's case strip, this sends a signal to all staff that the patient has been retrieved for surgery and is either en-route to the OR or is currently in surgery.

As another example, the OR board served as a messaging board (Fig 8). There was an immediate need for a certain supply. One of the OR nurses wrote the message on the board in an area where surgery schedules are usually placed. Without prompting, the first OR technician that saw the message located the appropriate supply, restocked the area, and then erased the message from the OR board.

The following segment is a third example:

0710 OR charge delaying two rooms' start time by placing blue magnetic strips diagonally across white magnetic strips. Rooms delayed due to patient unavailability.

In this segment, the charge nurse wanted to signal to all who might pass the OR board the delays. She placed a conspicuous sign on the board (Fig. 10). In this way the charge nurse did not have to update individually with the essential message yet still achieved purpose of communication.

Fig 10. The charge nurse placed two slating strips over scheduled cases in two operating rooms. The cases in these two rooms were delayed.

As a fourth example, we observed that the charge nurse sometimes slanted the case strip to alert staff that an operating room would soon be vacant and supporting personnel could plan to clean and equip the room.

Discussions

With the support of the OR board, accurate and timely communication is not dependent upon face to face communication nor in real-time. When looking at the OR board, all personnel have an instant understanding of the current state of the OR environment without talking to or interrupting each other.

The first of the five major strategies for coordination described by Bardram (1997) is minimising articulation among collaborators. Bardram noted that artefacts were used to accomplish this strategy. Two examples were given by Bardram: paper-based order forms and in/out trays for holding incoming order forms and outgoing answers. Bardram also described the practice in a hospital that copies were made to share information about patient schedules. By having access to the overall patient schedules, workers could coordinate with minimal effort in articulation.

The use of artefacts, which may be paper notes or otherwise low-technology systems, may have a profound impact on coordination processes. Boguslaw and Porter (1962) give an example about the use of a "spindle wheel" in the short-order restaurant industry. Waitresses could place their written order checks on the wheel. The wheel

"first of all acts as a memory for the cook; he does not have to remember orders, the wheel does it for him. The wheel also acts as a buffer drum. The input rate and output rate need no longer be one-to-one. Ten waitresses may come to the wheel almost simultaneously, but the cook takes the order one by one. The wheel also acts as a double queuing device. Waitresses no longer need to stand in line to put in their orders; the wheel stands in line for them. Moreover, the wheel does not get the order mixed up, but keeps them in proper queue sequence. Finally, the wheel also serves as a display of all the information in the system at a given time. The cooks, by having random access to the information, are enabled to organize their work around larger work units, such as the simultaneous preparation of three or four similar orders. The fact that the order is recorded on a check, equally available to waitress and cook to check back upon when an error has been made, permits feedback and the consequent elimination of habitual errors" (Boguslaw & Porter, 1962, P. 393).

Two important aspects of the above example are that (1) the artefact, spindle wheel, facilitates the communication across the temporal barrier, and (2) it helps to reduce the memory burden.

Berg (Berg, 1999) argues for the approach of treating computerised information technologies with those "low-tech": paper forms, lists, and whiteboards. The rationale is that one needs to focus on what IT does as opposed to what IT consists of. Treating IT as writing and reading artefacts, according to Berg, is one way of understanding IT. Just as Berg has found out in his observational studies of record keeping in intensive care units, the forms (electronic or otherwise) constrain what doctors or nurses do. The forms also change as care progresses as entries are added, thus producing cues of what has been done to the patient and what needs to be done in the future. The paper form co-constructs activities (i.e. documents the progress of activities so far and provides guide of future activities).

Mackay (1999) described a study on the use of paper flight strips used by air traffic controllers. Through observational studies, the controllers were found to exploit the use of paper strips. For example, controllers were found to arrange paper strips to represent the aircraft's spatial positions in the sky. Another study by Berndtsson (1999) on paper strips in air traffic control describes the use of camera through closed circuit TV combined with paper strips in air traffic control. Such a system has the advantage of traditional paper-strip based system while also providing remote users visual access to strips in nearby airspace.

Conclusions and Implications

Public displays are common coordinative tools used in many settings. The users of the OR board in our study made use of the flexibility of the board to satisfy the need of distributed cognition: storing status and scheduling information, communicating tasks and updates, visualising workload and staffing patterns, and referencing during face-to-face discussions. We were particularly intrigued by the clever use of magnetic strips and tags so that the representation of task activities and work schedules could be easily changed to match the frequent changes in the work environment.

In designing intelligent public displays, much of the previous attempts seem to focus on individual operations of objects on display. In the board we studied, the manipulation of the display objects can be accomplished jointly. In addition, the magnetic strips and tags "afford" direct manipulation by moving and placing both demand and supply elements. Our study also suggests that computerised public displays should consider the possibility of inventive use of coordinative artefacts. In complex organisations, changes over time such as the nature of workload and staffing, make it important to consider the possibility of adaptation, or "design

276

enhancement", by the users. It would be difficult to anticipate all possible uses of such boards.

As another implication, the sheer physical sizes of public displays, like the one studied, change the nature of interaction. For example, we observed little access conflicts in front of the board, even when six or more people were observed accessing the board.

. Our research calls for future studies to pay close attention to details in how artefacts are used in support collaborative work. The tailorability issue has recently been discussed (e.g. Teege, 2000). The needs of users change in response to not only their preferences but also changes in task requirements. As the current study indicates, users are very inventive in exploiting tools for coordination. Providing ways for users to improvise is an important function for public displays. Finally, we would like to caution that the current study is limited in that only one board was studied. The types of interactions observed need to be tested in future studies of other public displays

Acknowledgement

This research is supported by a grant from National Science Foundation (IIS-9900406). The views expressed here are those of the authors and do not reflect the official policy or position of the authors' employers, nor the funding agencies. The authors wish to acknowledge the contributions of Dale Downy who collected much of the data, Seokhwa Yun, Richard Dutton, Laurie demers, Charlene Zecha, and Jake Seagull. We would also like to thank many nurses, surgeons, and anesthesiologists in University of Maryland Shock Trauma Center for their generous support and sharing of their ideas and criticisms.

References

Bannon, L. and K. Schmidt, Eds. (1991). CSCW: Four characters in search of a context. *Studies in Computer Supported Cooperative Work*. Amsterdam, North Holland/Elsevier Science Publishers.

Bardram, J. E. (1997). "I love the system - I just don't use it!". *Proc. ACM GROUP97 International Conference on Supporting Group Work*, 251-260

Bardram, J.E. (1998): "Designing for the Dynamics of Cooperative Work Activities", Poltrock & Grudin (eds): *Proceedings of the Conference on Computer-Supported Cooperative Work, CSCW'98*, ACM, pp. 89-98.

Bardram, J. E. (2000). "Temporal coordination: On time and coordination of collaborative activities at a surgical department." *Computer Supported Cooperative Work. 9*: 157-187.

Bellotti, V. and Y. Rogers (1997). "From Web press to Web pressure: multimedia representations and multimedia publishing." *Proc. ACM CHI'96 Human Factors in Computing Systems* 279-286.

Berg, M. (1999). "Accumulating and coordinating: Occasions for information technologies in medical work." *Computer Supported Cooperative Work 8*: 373-401.

Berkowicz, D. A., G. O. Barnett and Chueh, H.C., (1999). eWhiteBoard: A real time clinical scheduler. *Proceedings of American Medical Informatics Association (AMIA) 1999 Annual Symposium, Washington, DC.*

Berndtsson, J. and M. Normakk (1999). The coordinative functions of flight strips: air traffic control work revisited. *ACM GROUP99*, 101-110

Boguslaw, R. and E. H. Porter (1962). Team functions and training. In, R. M. Gagne (Ed) *Psychological Principles in System Development.* New York: Holt, Rinehart & Winston: 387-416.

Garbis, C. (1999), Communication and Coordination Through Public and Private Representations in Control Rooms, in *Extended Abstracts of the Conference for Human Factors in Computing Systems - CHI'2000, 1-6 April, The Hague, The Netherlands*, 67-68..

Garbis, C. and Y. Waern (1999). "Team coordination and communication in a rescue command staff: The role of public representations." *La Travail Humain*: 273-291.

Hutchins, E. (1995a). *Cognition in the Wild.* Cambridge, MA, MIT Press.

Hutchins, E. (1995b). "How a cockpit remembers its speeds." *Cognitive Science 19*: 265-288.

Larkin, J. H. (1989). Display-based problem solving. In K. Kotovsky (Ed.) *Complex Information Processing: The impact of Herbert A. Simon.* Hillsday, NJ: Erlbaum: 319-341.

Mackay, W. E. (1999). "Is paper safer? The role of paper flight strips in air traffic control." *ACM Transactions on Computer-Human Interaction 6*(4): 311-340.

Malone, T. W. and K. Crownston (1994). "The interdisciplinary study of coordination." *ACM Computing Surveys 26*(1): 87-119.

Mynatt, E. D., T. Igarashi, et al. (2000). "Designing an Augmented Writing Surface." *IEEE Computer Graphics and Applications 20*(4): 55-61.

Payne, S. J. (1991). "Display-based action at the user interface." *International Journal of Man-Machine Studies 35*: 275-289.

Rogers, Y. (1992). "Coordinating computer-mediated work." *Computer Supported Cooperative Work (CSCW) 1*: 295-315.

Schmidt, K. D. and C. Simone (1996). "Coordination mechanisms: Towards a conceptual foundation of CSCW systems design." *Computer Supported Cooperative Work 5*: 155-200.

Segal, L. D. (1994). "Actions Speak Louder Than Words: How Pilots Use Nonverbal Information for Crew Communications." *Proceedings of the Human Factors and Ergonomics Society 38th Annual Meeting*: 21-25.

Stefik, M., D. G. Bobrow, et al. (1987). "WYSIWIS revised: Early experience with multiuser interfaces." *ACM Transactions on Office Information Systems* 5(2): 147-167.

Suchman, L. A. (1987). *Plans and Situated Actions*. Cambridge, Cambridge University Press.

Suchman, L. A. (1988). "Representing practice in cognitive science." *Human Studies 11*: 305-325.

Teege, G. (2000). "Users as composers: Parts and features as a basis for tailorability in CSCW systems." *Computer Supported Cooperative Work 9*: 101-122.

Whittaker, S. and H. Schwarz (1999). "Meetings of the Board: The impact of scheduling medium on long term group coordination in software development." *Computer Supported Cooperative Work 8*: 175-205.

Zhang, J. and D. A. Norman (1994). "Representations in distributed cognitive tasks." *Cognitive Science 18*(1): 87-122.

W. Prinz, M. Jarke, Y. Rogers, K. Schmidt, and V. Wulf (eds.), *Proceedings of the Seventh European Conference on Computer-Supported Cooperative Work, 16-20 September 2001, Bonn, Germany*, pp. 279-298.

On Finding Things Out:
Situating Organisational Knowledge in CSCW

Kristina Groth[1] and John Bowers[2]
[1]Interaction and Presentation Laboratory, [2]Centre for User-Oriented IT-Design,
Royal Institute of Technology (KTH), Stockholm, Sweden
kicki@nada.kth.se, bowers@nada.kth.se

Abstract. We present a field study of an organisation which designs and constructs precision mechatronic devices, which typically integrate electronics, mechanical assemblies, computer hardware and software. We study how organisation members seek out answers to questions and solutions to problems as they arise in their work. We examine how project documentation is used, how chance encounters are capitalised upon, how advice is sought, the role of meetings, training and competence-enhancing activities, and the use of the organisation's information systems. We develop an account of 'finding things out' as an orderly and practically situated organisational affair, and compare this with recent studies in CSCW of 'expertise location'. The paper closes with an examination of potential technology development programs to support people in finding things out in organisations while suggesting the re-specification of research on 'organisational memory', 'knowledge management' and allied notions in CSCW.

Introduction

For a number of years, researchers and practitioners in a variety of communities have become engaged with questions of organisational knowledge. There are many strands to this interest. Some researchers regard the knowledge and skills of an organisation's members to be one of the prime resources of an organisation, yet one which is very hard to account for and manage. It is commonly pointed out that organisations lose valued assets as employees move on and some researchers have looked to technical means for externalising and recording members' knowledge (e.g. Conklin and Begeman, 1988). Others are concerned to theorise the 'cognitive' aspects of social groups and organisations and put human collective phenomena on a similar theoretical footing to cognitive science's studies of individual mental phenomena (Hutchins, 1995). Relatedly, yet others write about 'organisational memory' and the management challenges there are once one takes the notion seriously (Walsh and Ungson, 1991).

In CSCW, these topics have been addressed for some time, attracting a range of contributions, including critical analyses (Bannon and Kuutti, 1996) and proposals for supportive technologies (e.g. McDonald and Ackerman, 2000). Most recently a research theme has emerged in CSCW which is concerned to study empirically knowledge and expertise within organisations and documenting the methods used by members to find things out.

McDonald and Ackerman's paper (1998) at CSCW'98 is a clear example of the 'turn to the empirical' in studies of organisational knowledge in CSCW. An extensive ethnographic and interview-based study was conducted at an organisation the authors call MSC which builds and supports turnkey medical and dental practice management systems. The authors were particularly concerned to document how members find relevant 'experts' in their organisation to solve problems as they arise. The study's analysis focuses on expertise identification and expertise selection. 'Identification' refers to how members go about discovering what information or special skills others have, while 'selection' concerns choosing among people with the required expertise (p.317). McDonald and Ackerman refer to seeking help as consisting of identification and selection phases (with identification generally preceding selection), though they recognise that in many actual cases participants 'iterate' (p.317) between these behaviours. Interestingly, McDonald and Ackerman identify a phenomenon they name 'escalation', "... the way in which people repair failures in identification and selection" (p.322). If one attempt at seeking help has failed "people ... may go to less desirable sources (e.g., to people with less expertise or to ill-maintained documents), sources with a higher psychological cost (e.g., to objectionable people), or cross departmental or even organisational boundaries". The impression one gets from McDonald and Ackerman is that there is a preferred ordering in help seeking at MSC: keep it local, avoid interrupting a very busy person, use reliable sources but, in the case of 'failure', be prepared to search further afield, risk a tiresome interruption, and use compromised sources.

We have spent a little time describing McDonald and Ackerman's research as our study is an attempt to build cumulatively upon their work by presenting a new case in a different industrial sector (mechatronics). We do this to help extend the CSCW community's understanding of the observable methods that organisation members deploy to find things out. As we hope to show through the presentation of ethnographic detail, we have observed methods other than those documented by McDonald and Ackerman and, when we observe similar methods, they seem to be deployed in ways which suggest another conceptualisation than that given in terms of expertise identification, selection and escalation.

We have conducted our study as part of a longstanding program of research at KTH into organisational knowledge and specifying technologies for its support (see, e.g., Tollmar et al., 1996). A key theme of this work has been to reject the aim of externalising and recording members' knowledge by technical means. Rather, we have been concerned to explore technologies which facilitate social contacts between individuals in such a way as to promote the exchange of knowledge. In this work, technologies mediate social relations rather than act as a shared storage device for 'organisational knowledge' or 'memory'. In addition to empirically elaborating the corpus of studies of expertise-seeking in organisations, then, we wish to proactively inform CSCW technology development. After a presentation of our empirical research, and a critical discussion of it in relation to other work in CSCW concerned with organisational knowledge, we will close with a consideration of the technical implications of our arguments. We pay particular attention as to whether CSCW need concern itself specifically with 'organisational memory/knowledge systems' as if these had a character distinct from other systems for supporting cooperative work.

The Study

The Company

The organisation studied, which we shall anonymise as 'CompC', is a consultancy company which is part of a larger Swedish corporation with similar companies spread all over the country. CompC describes itself, on its public Web pages, as active in the fields of precision mechanics, electronics, computer science, and the combination of these. At the beginning of our study there were about 100 employees within CompC. Critical organisational changes occurred at CompC during our work. First, CompC bought a smaller mechanical engineering company with 20 people, and as a result CompC was itself considerably re-organised. The new organisational form comprised of a total of ten sections (previously there were just eight) spread over three divisions. The software division had four sections, the hardware one, and the mechanical engineering division had four. An administration section completed the new organisational design. Second, CompC was split into two companies, one consisting of the mechanical division and one consisting of the software and hardware divisions.

CompC has many major Swedish industry companies as customers with whom it engages on a project basis. Usually a project lasts for about half a year, and involves about five to ten consultants. Some projects are carried out within CompC's own premises, while in other cases the consultants are located at the customer's office. Consultants working in projects within CompC's premises are physically co-located by project in a common work space, although they are administratively organised by sections. To find new projects and customers is a major role of the section managers. When a section manager, usually together with a project manager and a technical 'expert', have reached an agreement with the customer, the management group (the section managers and the CEO) at CompC chose a project team. As we shall see, it is at moments of team formation that 'knowing who knows' plays a key role.

Research Methods

Our study is based on nearly a year's contact with CompC. The first author has spent much of this time at the organisation's premises engaged in ethnographic observation. She has sat in on a variety of meetings, as well as shadowed personnel in the conduct of their work. A corpus of materials has been collected which includes field notes, copies of the organisation's documents and brochures, drawings and other specifications which are important to the work and so forth. In addition, several managers, as well as consultants who do not have a management role, have been interviewed in an open-ended style, the discussions being tape-recorded and transcribed. Broadly, our orientation to field research follows the program of 'ethnomethodological ethnography' as exemplified in CSCW by Hughes et al. (1992) amongst several others. Our emphasis is on the description of the observable features of the work in terms which organisation members themselves would recognise. Having set this general scene, let us pick out some features of the work of CompC of analytic interest in the current context.

The Practical Use of Documentation

All projects within CompC are thoroughly documented. It is a strict policy that members regard to be well respected and carefully considered during all project work. In this section, we examine some features of how the organisation's archive of documents was routinely used.

What is Documented and What is Not?

Studies of documentation at least since Garfinkel (1967) have pointed out the selectivity of records. There is not a reasonable sense in which one can attempt to document 'everything'. Indeed, it is not always clear what 'everything' or 'enough' might mean, or at least not clear independently of consideration of purposes. The labour of documentation, and deliberating over what to document and what not, is a central task within a project at CompC. All persons in a project are involved, from time to time, in the documentation task. An archive for a project is likely to contain such heterogeneous elements as product specifications, including co-signed contractural forms of specification documents, order forms, fax papers, lists of suppliers, list of parts needed if something new is constructed, programming code listings and, in electronic form, copies of email written, etc.

Although much in the projects gets documented there are things that are left out. One example concerns an incident where a change in technical equipment affected the precision of the machine built. One of the project members said to us:

> The machine did not work as it should. A supplier came and rebuilt the machine. They were only to upgrade the electronics but it became clear that they actually did much more than that and thereby decreased the precision in one aspect. Then the question is when did this rebuilding take place and who did it. I talked to several colleagues who all gave me the same picture that it was the client's idea to rebuild the electronics. This had been done but there was no protocol on this and it was not written down. Instead I had to go on what I was told.

The change made was never documented, principally because it was made by another supplier under direct instruction from the client, and is not relevant for the documentation of the actions which CompC specifically engaged in and which they uniquely might be held accountable for. However, the problem (of the decreased precision) was solved by talking to other project members and, from that, conclusions were drawn about what had happened. It is worth noting that this example does not entail that more details should be documented than currently are. This did not occur as an upshot to our informant. He did not characterise the records as 'incomplete' or wanting. Other supplier's actions cannot become part of CompC's documentation on pain of doubling the task!

On-Line Overviews and Searching

Each project has its own on-line document overview, a spreadsheet with all documents listed. The document overview is searchable, but only in a limited way by words used in the title or in the document text. There are no advanced search functions available, only those offered by the standard office application which is used. While it is not possible to search in more than one document overview at a time, the absence of such a simple facility did not seem to trouble members. It appeared that people usually knew in which document overview, i.e., project, to look. Consider the following example.

> Mike (a project manager): There was a cable that broke in a test. I needed the guy that made the investigation. I had no idea in which document he had written about it. He was working away so I could not reach him. I tried to search on 'cable' and I got all documents that had the word cable included in the text and by using a method of elimination I found what I needed.

By searching on a specific word in the document overview Mike could, by knowing who had written the document and which area it belonged to, find the right document and begin to address the problem of the broken cable. The simple search facilities work in conjunction with Mike's memory of the document and the person who would have written it. The document archive does not stand as a substitute for his organisational and project knowledge. On the contrary, the archive is used with the knowledge he has to effect the search.

It appears then that the simplified search procedure is satisfactory, as long as you have an idea of what you are looking for. Hence, organisational knowledge about the projects of CompC is often necessary for a successful search. While such knowledge could be commonly attributed to established members (like

Mike), the archive was hard to use for novitiates. However, this was not thought to be an extremely critical organisational problem at CompC as coming to know past projects through speaking to people about them would be precisely the main means for finding out about the organisation's work. Browsing the archive, then, was not seen as an actual or potential substitute for learning on the job from co-workers. For the most part, then, the tolerance of restricted search facilities goes hand-in-hand with a particular image of who would and would not need to access the documents and the circumstances under which this would occur.

Troubleshooting Documents and Situated Searching

To be sure, sometimes documentation is not clear enough without help from a key individual. Mike, a project manager, had been absent for a while. When he came back to the office he could not understand a hardware drawing one of the project members had done in his absence, but he was not available in the office. Mike started to look at the documentation, but did not understand it. He, therefore, contacted a section manger to see if he could explain what had been done. Here, we have an example of an organisation member moving from one resource to another in pursuing a solution. If the most ready-to-hand resource is unavailable, others will be turned to, whatever can get the job done in the available time.

The importance of project documentation was rather obvious when observing Mike. He could not find one of the binders that was usually kept in his bookshelf. He asked around and went looking for it in other rooms, but still could not find it. He needed a CAD drawing made by one of the mechanical engineers in the project in order to make an important decision. However, all the mechanists were away this day and could not be reached, even after persistent trying. Mike also could not find the electronic version of the CAD drawing. After a while he asked Susan, a project member sitting across the corridor, for help to find it. Mike had also called one of the companies manufacturing the construction to fax a drawing, but he still wanted to find the binder. After a while Susan happened across it in the room of a person who had recently started on the project. At the outset of his searches, Mike had not thought about this person as being part of the project and had, accordingly, looked elsewhere and pursued other means of exploration.

This example gives an impression of some quite typical themes in our ethnographic observation. First, the identity of people which are turned to in order to address a problem is a radically situated matter. Mike looks for the CAD drawing as a single item because he can't find the binder which normally contains it. He calls another company to see if they can fax the drawing because he cannot find either an electronic or printed form of it. Largely by happenstance, he finds the drawing in the room of a new team member. While there may be, all other things being equal, 'rules-of-thumb' or 'heuristics' (see McDonald and

Ackerman, 1998)[1], which Mike might wish to follow, other things rarely are equal and ad hoc-ing a search in the face of the specific situation Mike finds himself in is the order of the day. While cases like this bring the situated character of searches for information to the fore, situatedness in applying one's 'rules-of-thumb' is not an exceptional matter. As Garfinkel (1967) remarks, "rules do not apply themselves", they need to be artfully worked with in the face of everyday contingency, the occasional failures of documents being one such contingency.

While searching out people to talk to is a natural practice if documents are inadequate to the task, members often found themselves in the situation that key personnel simply were not contactable. This was a noticeable feature in an organisation involved in much on-site work. Often, then, there is no alternative but to artfully persist with documentation. In the example below a member of a project, Cindy, identified a mismatch in the documentation.

> I was to find out what kind of components we had bought for this large 'Q-project'. So I put together a list of all suppliers that had bought parts and I found there was one supplier that didn't have an address. In fact, there did not exist any such company. I tried to talk to Sam about it but couldn't because he was out of the office at the time. So I sat down and searched among the orders one by one. I did not find the company name which proved that we had not made any registered order from that company of these parts. Then you start getting suspicious that the supplier's list was written wrong. So I searched on a specific drawing and a component and found that it was two other suppliers that had manufactured these parts. I was then able to correct the suppliers list and work out which components we actually had purchased.

This further underlines our remarks about the artfulness of organisational information searching and problem solving. While there is an ordering to Cindy's conduct (notice anomaly, try to contact individual, do item-by-item search, test correctness of list, put things to rights), its exact course is clearly an outcome of the contingencies of the situation (e.g. Sam being unavailable) and Cindy's ingenuity, as it is of any heuristics as to who/what to use as a resource first.

Finding Things Out as a Practical Matter

We have been developing an argument that sees organisational knowledge as a practically situated affair. The rules-of-thumb one observes in people's conduct, or which participants themselves claim to be there, have to be understood in terms of the contingencies of the situations people find themselves in.

Let us give a further vivid example. A member of a project, Bill, first tried to solve a problem by asking the first author of this paper who was the only other person in the room at the time. Unfortunately, she did not have an answer to Bill's question and Bill instead turned to a reference book. Bill needed to use 'structs' in the C++ programming language in an advanced way and he did not know how to

---

[1] McDonald and Ackerman give particular attention to three heuristics: (i) keep it local, (ii) take into account the workloads of people approached and (iii) take into account the known or likely 'performance' of experts consulted. It is the status of these with respect to members' real-time searching activity that we ultimately wish to examine.

do that. He still could not find what he was looking for and, therefore, walked out to the open space area where other project members were working. Bill saw a person standing talking to two other persons sitting at their desks, and said, "you are good at structs". They both walked into his room and solved the problem. Again we see an ordering from the ready-to-hand (Kristina!) to the less accessible (the person outside the office who was good at 'structs'). But, we also see a radical situatedness and contingency in who is asked: the researcher who happens to be there and the 'struct-man' who happens to be passing by (and noticeable through the open-plan office ecology, cf., e.g. Anderson and Sharrock, 1993).

The different considerations that members take account of in finding things out are many and varied. Members' methods for organisational knowing comprise a large and flexible repertoire to sustain their everyday enquiries. Our studies of CompC indicate that this repertoire is differently organised from the practices of others who have been studied (e.g. McDonald and Ackerman, 1998) or from what several theories of social conduct would have us believe. Let us say more.

A Culture of Helping Others Beyond Reciprocity

Many traditional social psychological theories of 'helping behaviour' point to the dilemmas involved in seeking and accepting help, on the one hand, and offering and giving it on the other (for reviews, see various contributions to Hewstone et al., 1988). To seek help is, on these views, a face-threatening act which manifests incompetence. To offer help can be seen to reinforce that view of the person seeking help: let me help you, you look like you need it! Help can be refused, withdrawn or not even sought on these grounds. Other theories would point to a 'market of favours' surrounding help organised around principles of reciprocity and equity: one should not, on these views, offer or receive help beyond some form of 'reciprocal balance' with others (again see Hewstone et al.). While these accounts point to recognisable phenomena (of course people do refuse help on the grounds that it is patronising or whatever), it seems inadvisable to erect any wide-ranging theory of helping-behaviour on these grounds. At CompC, we saw no evidence of people being reticent in asking for help on face-saving grounds. When they were reticent it was for practical, work-related reasons. Equally we saw no market of favours. People were delighted to help there and then, if they had the time and the ability. The demands of getting the job collectively done were more important than any insistence on or hope for return[2].

Steve needed to test a hardware construction. The person working with

---

2   The social psychological literature on helping and reciprocity often takes as its point of departure extraordinary events: e.g. bystanders not intervening to help an injured person. Various theoretical notions are developed for these cases which are then read back into everyday interaction, no matter how implausibly. A full critique of this tendency would take us way beyond the remit of the current paper. We find it necessary to mention this literature, though, as we feel that it lies behind some of the interpretation of interaction between organisation members one encounters in the CSCW literature and could occur to reader seeped in this theoretical background at this juncture in our paper.

hardware in the project was away from the office and directed Steve to a person he thought could help. However, this person was no longer working with testing hardware, but, as Steve had no one else to turn to, she contributed anyway.

Another example: Steve had presented an internal course within CompC. One of the participants came and asked for advice about a problem, but Steve was extremely. Even so, he did not want to re-direct the query because the question was about a course topic he had specific responsibility for. Instead, Steve arranged to discuss the question at a later time. Of course, Steve could have sent the course-participant off to someone else. But, here and on this occasion, Steve's specific relationship to the course defeated this possibility.

Non-Local Help Freely Given

McDonald and Ackerman notice that members at MSC often seem to follow a heuristic of 'keep it local'. However, we (as they must have done) have observed numerous examples of non-local help being sought and freely given. One of the project managers, Mike, received a phone call from a person working at another corporation company. As it happened, the person calling was actually trying to reach another manager, who was not available. Mike himself could not solve the person's problem, but he took the time to distribute a memo about it to people he thought could help. Again we see an organisation member 'geared up' to help. The fact that the enquirer is from outside the company is not a countervailing consideration. Indeed, much effort was expended on this outsider, even though it would have been in one sense 'easier' to have asked the caller to try again when the manager he sought was available or to get the manager to call back.

What is more, we have several examples of personnel directly contacting customers for the answer to a query. If the matter were important, something that the customer might also know about, and if relations with the customer were cordial, there would be no necessary barrier to even these forms of non-local help.

Knowing the Suppliers

It is important for CompC to maintain good relations with suppliers of components. CompC projects typically involve some kind of physical device, e.g. medical equipment, for which components are sourced from different specialist suppliers. CompC's suppliers are selected not just because they offer competitive prices or reliable delivery. Suppliers are also preferred who can serve as reliable information sources that can be trusted to discuss problems with, e.g., when it is unclear what components to use in a construction. In this respect, suppliers are another source of non-local help. This help can go way beyond narrow understandings of customer-supplier relationships. Let us give an example:

> Cindy: I was looking for a certain type of sensor the other day and called around without success. Then I realised after a while that this was the wrong track, I should have another kind of sensor. One supplier was very helpful and we reasoned about it and found another way to

solve the problem: to use [another kind of] sensor. Yes I say but where can I find that kind then. One moment he says, then he starts looking [and says] yes this and this supplier you could call and here is another one. Then I think, but hey you are looking somewhere, do you have some kind of table or something. [The supplier says] no I sit here and look in an advertisement catalogue with many suppliers sorted by branch, it is very good. [I say] couldn't you fax me that page. [The supplier says] yes sure and then I got that page with twenty suppliers that I could start calling.

Managers

Project and section managers were, by most persons interviewed, considered to be a main source of organisationally-relevant knowledge – especially section managers. To be there for questions asked by the section members was something one of the section managers saw as a basic role of a section manager. Managers tended to be the longer serving personnel within the organisation and, through this, had encountered and worked on more projects and were likely to be useful resources not just for their own knowledge but for their ability to 'know who knows'. McDonald and Ackerman (1998) note the existence of personnel who serve as 'expertise concierges'. These are people with considerable knowledge about who knows what: they do not necessarily know the solution to a problem themselves but they know who might. At CompC, managers (especially section managers) often served this role. For many of the people we asked, it was their greater experience, rather than the management role per se or any status that might go with it, which was the justification for consulting managers in times of trouble. In practice, though, whether a manager is consulted or not hinges on all the kinds of situated detail that we have been at pains to emphasise: the manager's availability, how quickly a solution is needed, whether a KTH ethnographer happens to be in the office right now and knows the answer, and so forth.

Not surprisingly, then, we observed people consulting managers, not because of the manager's credentials, but because the manager happened to be available. The example above where Mike turned to the hardware section manager for clarification of a technical drawing, rather than the consultant who authored the drawing and happened to be out of the office, is an instance of this. Once again, we see the sheer availability of persons at the moment to be a major mitigating factor in knowing how to find something out.

Indeed, another feature of section managers, which made them commonly approached over work-issues, was their knowledge of the availability and commitments of others. Through routine reporting, section and project managers were likely to know what the consultants working for them were doing. A consultant working on a project who was taking a course would be highly likely to inform his section and project manager of this commitment. These people in turn would be able to manage how queries directed to the consultant would be dealt with. In short, to paraphrase McDonald and Ackerman, managers often acted as 'availability concierges' with special knowledge of the commitments of others. In an organisation where workers may oftentimes be out of the office or committed on a variety of intercalated activities, knowing the availability of others is at least as important as knowing what others know.

To be sure, at CompC, the long-serving project and section managers tend to be the ones who 'know who knows' too. Commonly a project manager will be able to recall most of the persons active on recent projects. Indeed, we have seen this kind of remembering in practical action in supporting people's use of the document archive. Through working with people, especially if project teams rotate personnel over the years as is typically the case at CompC, the managers become acquainted with people's skills and competencies as a natural byproduct of project work. This is not to say, of course, that managers are never unable to give a recommendation as to who to ask for help.

In interview, Mike described a case where he neither had an answer to a question, nor did he know who else to ask.

> Mike: We had this new guy in the project. We talked about different novel technical solutions that he should investigate. He asked who should I talk to for further information. In this case I had no idea. I gave him the name of a section manager but that was actually a shot in the dark because usually he has a lot of answers to everything but not this time. By chance we had a meeting one morning where we had brought in a guy who had worked in this project before with the software. We sat down and talked about different things and then we happened to come in on this subject and then he said yes but talk to A. He is an expert on those things.

Once every week, all the section managers and the CEO met to review each ongoing project and discuss immediately upcoming ones. Important matters emerging in projects could be raised at this meeting. In this way, the meeting served as a means for participants to become aware of the status of projects that they were not personally involved with. A common topic at such meetings was the allocation of personnel to projects. An existing project might be deficient in a needed competence. A new project might need to have its mix of personnel assembled. A typical format for proceeding with the meeting would be to review the availability of consultants both at the time and over the months to follow, as well as picking out individuals with a needed skill, experience or interest. This review can be quite detailed, enabling all present to pick up on the availability of others and their skills as a natural byproduct of finding out about current projects, planning future ones and keeping the CEO informed. While managers may come to act as 'expertise concierges' (or 'availability concierges'), this should be seen as an entirely natural feature of their work and how it is organised.

Local Questions

We have noted a number of times how personnel at CompC can go beyond the immediately local context in order to find things out. Seeking help with a problem is noticeably opportunistic and a situated matter. Personnel do not experience it as 'face-threatening' or find themselves entering into a 'market of favours' to seek help beyond their own project team, if there are good practical work-related reasons for so doing.

However, this is not to deny that many of the questions asked among the consultants are dealt with locally. Naturally, if these questions are project specific and other project team members are at hand, then it will often be possible to 'keep it local'. This can be so, even if an answer is not immediately forthcoming. Indeed, questions can remain unanswered because the person identified as the one to address the issue is not available and no one else is regarded as having the specific knowledge needed.

For example, Bill, a member of the E project, was discussing whether to make some variables static or not with Barb, another project member. It depended on how the database should be accessed and they both agreed that they needed to discuss this with either the project manager or another project member with specific technical skills in C++, but both of these individuals were away for the rest of the week. In the absence of colleagues with the necessary combination of specific project and technical skills, Bill and Barb had to wait – to ask elsewhere, in this case, would not have been helpful or appropriate.

Let us give a second example of the occasional necessity of local knowledge about a specific project. A supplier to CompC had not fulfilled all of the requirements of a job they were to deliver and yet had raised an invoice at the agreed price. Under such circumstances, CompC would typically withhold full payment or request a credit with the supplier. It fell to Tim, a section manager, to decide exactly how this should be handled. The manager for the project itself, though, was away on a course. Tim did not feel that he knew the background to the problem well enough to make a decision there and then. As with Bill, Barb and their variable declaration problem, it was necessary to wait until uniquely relevant personnel became available again to discuss the matter.

Thus, keeping questions local within the project is often a matter of convenience and necessity. Questions can, simply, be impossible for persons outside the project to answer. In other words, whether a problem needs to be dealt with locally or can be raised elsewhere are practical matters, depending in great part on specific features of the problem and the project-context it arises in.

Existing Information Systems

Several different information systems exist at CompC, each relevant to supporting a different aspect of their work. We have already mentioned the on-line document archive of project-related material. Other systems are available by means of the company's intranet, containing web pages divided into a list of links to, for example, important internal documents, common information for employees, address information to other companies within the corporation, internal web pages of the corporation, and so forth.

On each section's web page there is a list of the section member's names, technical skills, the project they currently work on, where the project is located and how long it will last. On the pages of most of the sections of the software division there are also links to meeting protocols from section meetings and to the competence groups (about which, see below).

Although much information is available on the intranet (over 100 pages), we have observed that its pages are relatively rarely used in day-to-day working activity. Project-specific documents – drawings, programming code, diagrams, specifications, correspondence, et cetera – are the most likely things to be found on a consultant's screen, not corporate web pages.

However, one should not get the impression that the intranet is entirely useless. Indeed, we observed a number of specific uses of it. These include: finding out individuals' telephone numbers, their usual physical location and mailing address, employment-related details such as how to apply for vacation time, local train service information, and other such mundane matters. One section manager had the habit of posting occasional articles on the intranet which a number of people found interesting. In addition, people new to the company were also often directed to the intranet as a way of finding out the basics. Similarly, people who had been working at a customer's site for a long time might use the intranet to alert them of changes to expect on return – for example, new personnel in their section. All these uses are rather more mundane and varied than one would perhaps expect from an information system functioning as an 'organisational memory' or as a 'knowledge management system'. At CompC, you are more likely to use the intranet to check on the time of the last train home than to find out who can tell you about structs in C++!

An impression should be developing about CompC's usage of their information systems. Different systems have different organisationally-specific purposes in their use. The on-line project document system is predominantly used for archival purposes. The intranet is used for a host of everyday purposes which, though seemingly mundane, are nevertheless important to the work (missing the last train home could be a serious matter!). However, none of these systems substitute more routine methods such as talking to others.

Learning on the Job

We have examined the various ways in which people at CompC search out others who can help with problems they encounter in their work. We have looked at some aspects of how project documentation is consulted. We have seen how seeking out expertise or asking for help is a situated affair, contingent upon the availability of others amongst other considerations. Such occasioned instances of raising problems, asking questions or seeking help take place against a background of what we can call 'learning on the job'. That is, CompC workers are continually listening in, finding things out, picking up details relevant to their own and other's projects as well as to CompC's work in general and the kind of business it does. In a sense, learning often takes place as a 'side-effect' of having a problem that needs help from others. Being helped with a solution is often at one and the same time to learn about a technique, principle or useful component which can be used again in similar circumstances in the future. Even when individuals do not have a particular problem that is concerning them, they are often attuned to opportunities to learn and enhance their skills as part of everyday work on projects. In short, much learning takes place as a natural feature of ordinary participation in project work.

In addition to the hurly-burly of everyday activities, there are occasions for learning which are more staged or planned as such. Let us discuss some of these.

Training

CompC provides an introductory course for new, less experienced recruits to the organisation. This is three to five weeks in duration. The course tends to focus on project organisation and management issues, and general matters about CompC, rather than specialised technical topics. Training courses related to more specialised topics are provided or arranged when the need becomes apparent. For example, a course dedicated to BlueTooth was purchased from external consultants with ten people from CompC in attendance.

The E-project at CompC is a long-term activity of several years' duration with a reliable customer whose business is well known within CompC. This project involves only software. Unlike other CompC projects, it is not necessary to get software to interoperate with electronic or mechanical components. The work involves maintaining and updating existing software while also addressing new specifications. This balance of the old and the new in the work, its relative homogeneity (software only) and the fact that it takes place with a well established customer makes the E-project well suited for new, less experienced employees to be assigned to. Indeed, this is routine practice. During management meetings, when personnel are assigned to projects, the E-project is, in many respects, the default assignment for new recruits.

Competence Groups

In 1996, CompC inaugurated 'competence groups' as a means for giving shape to the development of people's knowledge and skills. These enable personnel, who might otherwise be working on different projects, to help each other and to attend or arrange courses or share literature. Members of a competence group might even work together to build a small application or part of a development platform if that was considered to be the most effective way of enhancing their abilities. Additionally, people without a current project might devote their time to building up the resources of a competence group.

Competence groups have formed around topics such as 'internet', 'database techniques', 'user interfaces' and so forth. Typically, a competence group would have between three and eight members with individuals being constrained to be members of only one group at any one time. Groups pass in and out of existence. A group might break up if collectively the members have learned as much about the topic as they wish at the moment or if membership dwindles to one or two persons or if new topics come to be seen as more urgent or relevant. Commonly, new topics and groups emerge as a result of proposals consultants make to the section manager or following from a manager's suggestion. There is no formal procedure governing the formation of groups but CompC does insist that each consultant is a member of one. Equally, there is not a formal allocation of resources to competence groups (e.g. they do not have a 'budget'). However, the existence of a group under a particular topic gives a warrant to group members to ask section managers for support on topic-relevant activities. For example, a consultant is relatively more likely to be released to attend a BlueTooth course if mobile computing has been the topic of their competence group.

Discussion

We have presented in detail some of the methods used by personnel at a consultancy company specialising in mechatronics to find things out. This has included examinations of how documents are used, how people are sought out and consulted, how opportunistic encounters are exploited, how workers learn on the job, how specific support for training and competence development is offered, and how their workplace enables encounters between individuals to take place through which expertise might be disseminated. Our emphasis throughout has been to attend to the real-time, social interactional features of 'knowing' and 'coming to know' as these become visible as everyday organisational affairs. We would like to draw out some features of our research so as to connect with questions of expertise and organisational knowledge as these topics have been discussed in the CSCW literature. We will also suggest some emphases for technology development which we believe arise from our work.

Situatedness and Accomplishing Orderliness

An overwhelming feature of our observations has been the situatedness of members' deployment of methods to find things out (as also strongly emphasised by Ackerman and Halverson, 1998). What a worker at CompC will do is very variable with respect to the character of the problem and the nature of the situation she finds herself in as attempts to seek solutions unfold. Mike assembled a variety of methods to find the missing CAD drawing (see above). These included looking around the office, trying to contact the mechanical engineers, searching for the electronic version and telling others of his plight. Cindy noticed an anomaly with a components listing, tried to contact someone, did an item-by-item check. And so forth. In both of these cases, as in others we have observed, there is a clear ordering to members' conduct as they try to find things out but exactly how their searches unfold, and exactly which method they will turn to next, is strongly contextually tied at each moment.

A clearly noticeable feature of work at CompC is how the availability of personnel impacts upon what can be done. Workers can be at the customer's site, away on courses or attending to other matters which take them away from the office. At any moment who will and who will not be present at their workstation or in their project room is a highly contingent matter. While many features contribute to the situatedness and contingency involved in person's attempts to get answer to questions or to solve problem, it is perhaps the sheer availability of people which most notably influences the course of members' activities.

The fact that people are often not available when desired is, of course, a common non-exceptional feature of contemporary working life. Indeed, many of CompC's 'arrangements' can be thought of as ways to compensate for this or help negotiate it. Managers are folk who are likely to know the commitments of others. Our awkward coinage of 'availability concierge' parallels McDonald and Ackerman's notion of 'expertise concierge' in underlining this utterly mundane feature of managers' knowledge at CompC. The weekly meetings with the CEO allow the exchange of knowledge about persons' availability, as do routine project reporting relationships. The office ecology further enables co-workers to check on each other's presence and freedom to help. It is hardly a grand empirical finding to point out that the availability of people is a major mitigating factor in how people at CompC seek help and advice on work issues. But it does point us in a particular design direction – a matter we return to.

While people within the same project are commonly consulted first when problems arise, this is more for mundane reasons such that co-project members are more likely to share concerns about the issue in question as well as knowledge of the context in which to solve it than others might. It is rarely at CompC to do with any "higher psychological cost" or critical organisational obstruction in looking for help further afield. Indeed, we have many examples of non-local help being freely given, even when this means consulting customers and suppliers. If the supplier in question is trusted and long-serving, they may indeed be the very best source of information. It all depends upon the specific nature of the parties involved, the problem and the situation people find themselves in.

The varied practices surrounding the use of documentation further illustrate our emphasis on the situatedness and contingency in people's efforts at findings things out. We have argued that document archives do not stand in lieu of skilled know-how and organisational knowledge. They are not a repository or an externalization of what people know such that they could substitute the embodied knowledge people do have. On the contrary, as evidenced by CompC's tolerance of unsophisticated search facilities, it is organisational knowledge and skill which enable effective and appropriate use of the archives in the first place. Naturally, one can imagine CompC using more advanced document systems and we do not wish to be heard as arguing that they shouldn't. Rather, our point is to understand the purposes behind project documentation and consultation. The level and kind of detail in a project's archive relates, not to some ideal of a 'perfect' record, but oftentimes to what the organisation might be held accountable for in the future. Supporting the traceability of design decisions is more important than developing an organisational 'knowledge system' whether it is one which supposedly externalises worker-skill or supports 'knowledge brokerage' or whatever. To use organisational records for this purpose would be quite a shift in what they are seen as relevant for and, hence, what they currently consist of.

Under such circumstances, it is entirely typical to work with document archives alongside consulting original authors or other project members when required. However, our observations would not be consistent with any simplification of the activities surrounding document usage. We cannot claim that CompC personnel noticeably follow a heuristic such as 'ask the people first, only then look to project documentation' (or its opposite). If the relevant document is already there, open on your desk, to be sure it might be looked at first. If a document cannot be found, then a relevant person might be approached...if they are available, not on a course, not tied up with urgent business...and so forth. There are many, variable problems which occasion consulting documents and many, varied courses of action in which members partake in consequence.

A summary impression should be developing from our work by now. Our study has emphasised following organisational members in real-time as they address problems in their work and described how they locally and situatedly order their searchings for information and persons for help. In each example we have presented, members are seen to go about such searches in an orderly way. They first do one thing, then do another. If one method fails, another will be explored. And so forth. However, this orderliness arises through locally organised activity. It is not provided for through the mere execution of a rule of conduct. Orderliness in searching out information is a practical accomplishment.

This makes us sceptical of theoretical schemas which might simplify the complexity of observed behaviour. On the basis of their study at MSC, McDonald and Ackerman argue that finding things out in an organisation is often a matter of expertise 'identification' and person 'selection' phases, and that people quite commonly reiterate between them, if necessary 'escalating' their searches to more organisational distant or undesirable sources. While we have observed moments which fit this schema of how searching out expertise is ordered, we have described many which do not. For us, 'escalation' has no special status as description of the orderliness in members' conduct. The subtle rationality of organisational conduct cannot be captured in any simple schema or small set of heuristics. Any heuristic one might identify from our study like 'keep it local' would have no special status above 'go non-local if you have a special trusted source'. Keeping it local and other phenomena are, when observed, a practical *outcome* of members' orderly responses to the situation, they are not the result of a *prior* heuristic appropriately applied. Or, to put the point another way, there is a difference between observable phenomena and the organisational rationale for them. We argue, for example, that problems tend to be kept local *because* co-project members are likely to share contexts of project-relevant knowledge and *because* persons and information in the local environment are more likely to be ready-to-hand. If either of those situational conditions turn out false, then naturally members' activities will be differently ordered.

Designing 'Organisational Knowledge Systems'

These points become important when one considers implications for systems design. McDonald and Ackerman (2000) present ER (for Expertise Recommender) which applies technologies from 'recommendation systems' to problems of expertise location in organisations. This is clearly innovative work in the area of organisational knowledge systems and represents a substantial development activity as both a generic platform and a specific application instance for supporting MSC are worked through. However, in many respects, the platform reifies the model of expertise location we have argued does not compellingly fit our data. ER has separate architectural components for expertise identification and selection, and the process of escalation is specifically supported at a system architectural, and not merely application, level. We have noted above how important the availability of persons and an awareness of others' commitments are in shaping the orderliness of members' efforts to find things out. Architectural components corresponding to this feature (e.g. ones which inform on the patterns of people's availability) are not given focal design effort in ER. ER clearly represents a particular design trajectory for organisational knowledge systems and one which may well work in some organisational settings. However, our study suggests to us an alternative design orientation and set of development priorities.

As a first step it is important to note that expertise and information location problems at CompC, though irksome, are not regarded as major organisational concerns. CompC's mission is not jeopardised because its workers can't get the information they need. In other words, there's no convincing organisational mandate for the extensive redesign of information systems there. The practices we have described, for the most part, work well. If this were not the case, and this was manifest to members and researchers equally, then we would feel more entitled to suggest a radical intervention. The 'lack of fit' of the assumptions embodied in a technical system with observable social practice would not then be an argument against considering a system as changing practice would be the whole point. As it is, as researchers, we can learn from CompC.

In their existing use of IT, CompC are happy to work with a family of loosely connected purpose-specific systems. While the non-integration of systems is an occasional problem, it is (again) not mission-critical. There is no strong organisational reason to devote considerable resources to integrating systems. Theirs is not a business sector which would clearly profit from web-delivery of services and products so there are not, in that respect, strong arguments to integrate around internet/intranet technologies. Equally, their document database has predominantly and specifically an archival function so developing that into a core resource to support additional activities might also be effort ill-spent. It must be noted that the ER system, when applied to real records from MSC, involved McDonald and Ackerman in extensive pre-processing of data to get it into a form that their algorithms could work with. Such a degree of preparatory work and algorithm fine-tuning would be very hard to justify at CompC, even if we could find an analogous records database (and the document archive is not it).

In a sense, it is the entire panoply of office ecology, unexpected encounters, scheduled meetings, training and competence groups which – together with a varied family of information systems – constitute CompC's 'organisational knowledge system' (cf. Anderson and Sharrock, 1993). And an adequately effective one it is too. Improvements need to be seen against that background and here we have a number of modest suggestions.

Recall that an awareness of others' activities and availability is a key issue in shaping how expertise and information are sought. Supporting activity awareness is a longstanding topic in CSCW and has lead to a number of technical developments (e.g. Sandor et al., 1997). This existing line of research can be given a new inflection given our studies of expertise and information seeking in CompC. That is, giving persons a rich understanding of the activities of their co-workers and how their engagement and disengagement with matters of varying urgency and importance is patterned over time might be a valuable resource for facilitating expertise and information seeking. While we (as others have done) started out investigating 'expertise location' and related topics under the rubrics of 'organisational memory' and 'organisational knowledge systems', our empirical work takes us to other topics (how to enhance members' awareness of activity and personal availability).

In this regard the research exemplified by @work (Tollmar et al, 1996) seems to us to be a promising lightweight approach to consider in contexts like CompC. @work enables users to set availability information viewed by others in a variety of simple ways. The essential design emphasis of @work is to capture awareness information from existing sources and allow easy access to awareness setting mechanisms which do not require special hardware or complex applications to be used. This lightweight approach of increasing other person's awareness of one's availability informs the design work we are now embarking on. We want to explore how to support people in knowing about others' availability and activities using technology such as mobile phones, swipe cards, sensors etc, that build upon systems and routines already in place in people's work.

Our fundamental concerns are shared with many researchers in CSCW studying 'organisational knowledge'. We wish to study how people search out information and expertise and we wish to consider technical support for this. However, our study suggests that not all organisations would benefit from systems directly dedicated to the support of such matters especially if those systems would require extensive technical work or organisational redesign in turn. In our case, we feel that considering lightweight approaches which add value to existing systems would be a better strategy. As such we have indicated how research in a different subfield in CSCW – one more concerned with 'awareness systems' than 'organisational knowledge or memory' – might be most appropriately built upon, at least for applications in organisations like the one we have studied. This conclusion we hope is generally instructive. If one's concern is for supporting some feature of cooperative work, X, one does not necessarily have to build an X-system. In our case, the situated features of organisational knowledge have led us to re-situate systems which might support it.

Acknowledgements

We wish to thank CompC for their participation in this study. Kerstin Severinson Eklundh provided valuable comments on a draft of this paper. Liam Bannon pointed out to us the importance of an empirical study of members' methods for finding things out. We hope we satisfy his expectations. A (not so) anonymous reviewer has led us to temper some of our critical examination of earlier work in the field. Thank you, whoever you may be.

References

Ackerman, M. & Halverson, C. (1998): 'Considering an Organization's Memory', *Proceedings of CSCW'98*, ACM Press, New York.

Anderson, R. & Sharrock, W. (1993): 'Can Organisations Afford Knowledge?', *Computer Supported Cooperative Work*, 1 (3), 143–161.

Bannon, L. & Kuutti, K. (1996): 'Shifting Perspectives on Organisational Memory: From Storage to Active Remembering', *Proceedings of HICSS-29*, IEEE Computer Society Press.

Conklin, J. & Begeman, M. (1988): 'gIBIS: A Tool for Exploratory Policy Discussion', *Proceedings of CSCW'88*, ACM Press, New York.

Garfinkel, H. (1967): *Studies in Ethnomethodology*, Prentice Hall, Englewood Cliffs, NJ.

Hughes, J., Randall, D. & Shapiro, D. (1992): 'Faltering from ethnography to design', *Proceedings of CSCW'92*, ACM Press, New York.

Hutchins, E. (1995): *Cognition in the Wild*, MIT Press, Cambridge MA.

McDonald D. W. & Ackerman, M. S. (1998): 'Just Talk to Me: A Field Study of Expertise Location', *Proceedings of CSCW'98*, ACM Press, New York.

McDonald, D. W. & Ackerman, M. S. (2000): 'Expertise Recommender: A Flexible Recommendation System and Architecture', *Proceedings of CSCW'00*, ACM Press.

Sandor, O., Bogdan, C. & Bowers, J. 'AETHER: An Awareness Engine for CSCW', *Proceedings of ECSCW'97*, Kluwer, Dordrecht.

Tollmar, K., Sandor, O. & Schömer, A. (1996): 'Supporting Social Awareness @ Work, Design and Experience', *Proceedings of CSCW'96*, ACM Press, New York.

Walsh, J. & Ungson, G. (1991): 'Organizational Memory', *Acad. of Manag. Rev.*, 16 (1), 57-91.

W. Prinz, M. Jarke, Y. Rogers, K. Schmidt, and V. Wulf (eds.), *Proceedings of the Seventh European Conference on Computer-Supported Cooperative Work, 16-20 September 2001, Bonn, Germany*, pp. 299-318.
© 2001 Kluwer Academic Publishers. Printed in the Netherlands.

The Effects of Network Delays on Group Work in Real-Time Groupware

Carl Gutwin

Department of Computer Science, University of Saskatchewan

Saskatoon, Saskatchewan, Canada, S7N 5A9

carl.gutwin@usask.ca

Abstract. Network delays are a fact of life when using real-time groupware over a wide area network such as the Internet. This paper looks at how network delays affect closely-coupled group work in real-time distributed groupware. We first determine the types and amounts of delay that can happen on the Internet, and then identify types of collaborative interactions that are affected by delay. We then examine two interaction types more closely: predicting others' movements, and coordinating shared access to artifacts. We carried out experiments to measure the effects of two kinds of delay (latency and jitter). When these interactions are isolated and repeated, we found that even small delays can lead to significant increases in completion time and errors. Although people in real-world tasks are often able to adapt their actions to accommodate network delays, we conclude that designing groupware to minimise the effects of delay can improve usability for closely-coupled collaboration.

Introduction

The goal of real-time distributed groupware is to allow people in different places to work together, as naturally and simply as they do in face-to-face settings (e.g. Stefik et al 1987, Tatar et al 1991). Consequently, much attention has been paid to the design, implementation, and evaluation of multi-user software, and considerable gains have been made in improving groupware usability (e.g. Beaudoin-Lafon and Karsenty 1992, Gaver 1991, Gutwin and Greenberg 1998). However, there is one aspect of groupware that that has not received much consideration from CSCW, but one that can cause usability problems: the underlying network.

Distributed operation introduces communication delays between the computers running a groupware application, and in wide area networks, these delays can be substantial and unpredictable. Most people who have used groupware over the Internet have experienced delays of one kind or another, particularly in the real-time display of other people's movements and actions. For example, many shared workspace systems provide each person with a telepointer; under delay conditions, a person's telepointer may seem to get stuck as it moves across the screen, or may be out of synchrony with accompanying speech. Delays are especially noticeable when people work in a closely-coupled fashion and need continuous and up-to-date feedback about another person's activities (Salvador et al 1996).

The goal of this research is to investigate the effects of network delays on the usability of groupware systems. We are primarily concerned with groupware that involves visual artifacts in a shared workspace, and with tasks that involve close coupling amongst the group.

In this paper, we look at three questions: what kinds of delay happen in groupware systems, what magnitude of delay occurs on a real-world wide area network such as the Internet, and how different types and magnitudes of delay affect groupware usability. The main part of the paper reports on a study of how delay affects specific kinds of closely-coupled interactions. The results of these investigations will assist developers in designing and building groupware that is appropriate for the network environment in which it must operate.

Types of delay: latency and jitter

Groupware applications communicate information by sending messages to one another. For discrete information, such as commands and model updates, the order of the messages is important, but timing of a message is independent of other messages. For continuous real-time information, however, messages must be considered as part of a temporal stream. Telepointer positions and other information about people's movements and activities are examples of this type of data stream. Continuous streams have temporal dependencies, in that the timing and pacing of the stream has an effect on how the stream is interpreted. Streams are therefore sensitive to two kinds of delay that can be caused by network communication: *latency* and *jitter* (e.g. Fluckiger 1995, Kum and Dewan 2000). These are described below and illustrated in Figure 1.

Latency is the lag between the sending and the receiving of a message (see Figure 1b). Since messages cannot be delivered instantly, latency will always exist to some degree. Even in a face-to-face conversation, there is a (usually unnoticeable) communication latency due to the speed of sound. In network communication, substantially larger latencies exist, caused by the transmission time of the network medium, slowdowns due to traffic, the overhead of routing messages, and by the processing time required to unpack and process messages.

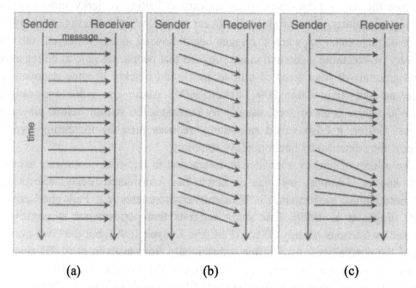

Figure 1. Time-series of messages from a sender to a receiver, with
(a) no latency or jitter, (b) latency but no jitter, (c) jitter but no latency

From the groupware user's perspective, latency means that a data stream (such as another person's telepointer motion) is late compared to when it was produced. The motion of the telepointer will look normal in other respects, however; if the user has no indicator of when the motion started, then the latency will be difficult to detect. Problems begin to occur with latency in two situations. The first happens when two streams (such as voice and telepointer motion) are supposed to be synchronised, but are transmitted with different latencies. The second happens when interaction involves taking turns. Previous research suggests that turn-taking audio interaction such as telephone conversations become difficult to coordinate when latency is greater than about 300ms (e.g. Scholl 2000).

Jitter, in contrast, affects the pacing of the stream rather than its lateness. Jitter is variance in transmission time, and measures whether the amount of time between two messages at the receiving end is the same as the time between them when they were sent (see Figure 1c). For example, if messages are sent at 10ms intervals, but the receiving interval varies from 10ms, then there is jitter in the transmission. Jitter does not exist in face-to-face communication, because all the data in an utterance or a movement travel at exactly the same speed. In networked groupware, however, each message in a stream is encoded as an independent packet; two consecutive messages may be sent to the destination on different routes, or may encounter different overheads and traffic conditions along the way. Furthermore, a message may be lost altogether, and if the transmission protocol enforces in-order delivery, all messages behind the lost message must wait unprocessed while it is resent from the source. These factors imply two means of characterising jitter: size of delay, and percentage of messages that are delayed.

From the user's perspective, jitter appears as halting or jerky movement: a moving telepointer, for example, will appear to stick when a message is delayed, and will then catch up when messages begin flowing again. Research into the delivery of streaming audio and video suggests that people are able to notice even small amounts of jitter (tens of milliseconds), and quickly become annoyed by larger amounts (e.g. Cisco 2000, Scholl 2000). Audio and video applications strive to reduce jitter to zero, usually by buffering the stream before playback begins. Buffering (also called smoothing) reduces jitter by increasing overall latency; the stream starts later but plays smoothly.

The effects of latency and jitter on interaction in real-time groupware are not well known. Limited previous research has considered delay effects on collaborative task performance in 3D virtual environments (e.g. Park and Kenyon 1999, Vaghi et al 1999). One study suggests that performance is negatively affected by latencies of only 200ms (Park and Kenyon 1999), but the "two-person thread the needle" task used differs substantially from tasks in most 2D shared-workspace groupware systems. A qualitative study (Vaghi et al 1999) saw a variety of strategy changes in the presence of latencies from 200ms - 1000ms, and suggests that the task became difficult at about 500ms latency.

The next step for the current investigation is in determining a rough idea of the magnitude of latency and jitter that can be expected for a groupware system working across a real-world network such as the Internet.

Delay magnitude on the Internet

Real-world groupware applications encounter different amounts of latency and jitter, depending upon where and when they use the system. Delays on the internet depend on the power of the client machines, the bandwidth of the network segments, the distance that messages must travel, the number of routers that the message goes through, and the current traffic level (e.g. Acharya and Saltz 1996). This means that it will be impossible to state the exact latency or jitter that developers should design for; nevertheless, we wished to get a general idea of the possible range that could be encountered.

There are ongoing research projects that measure internet performance characteristics such as round-trip latency (Caida 2000, Matrix 2000, NLANR 2000). These projects report mean round-trip times between 100ms and 200ms (ping times) and approximately 5% packet loss between various internet sites (e.g. Matrix 2000). These low results do not entirely reflect reality for groupware applications, however, since they use hosts that are on or near a major backbone, since there is almost no processing of messages required for the tests (which adds to overall delay), and since they do not measure jitter directly.

To get a broader sample of real-world groupware latency and jitter, we recorded and analysed message communication to several sites using an instrumented GroupKit (Roseman and Greenberg 1996) application. Latency was measured by timestamping and sending messages with immediate reply by the other groupware system. Jitter was measured by timestamping arrival times and calculating the difference between inter-send times and inter-arrival times for each consecutive pair of messages. Several different network bandwidths and distances were tested, from local area networks to dialup connections and worldwide Internet links. All trials were carried out during the day (based on the remote host's location). A few examples from these tests are shown in Table I.

Approx. distance	Slowest network link	Max. latency (ms)	Median latency (ms)	Max. delay from jitter (ms)	Median jitter delay (ms)	% delayed by jitter
100 m	10BaseT	99	99	51	31	5
3 km	Dial-up	1040	476	320	303	33
3 km	Cable	4420	492	847	200	34
700 km	Cable	950	500	1245	280	26
3000 km	10BaseT	910	303	343	97	52
12000 km	10BaseT	1000	590	2509	244	41

Table I. Example jitter and latency between skorpio.usask.ca and various hosts. Latency is calculated by dividing round-trip time in half.

In our tests, latency and jitter varied widely, and maximum delays could be several seconds. Average latencies ranged from 100 to 700 milliseconds, and jitter delays ranged from 40 to 1000 milliseconds. These results were used to determine the test conditions for the experiments that are described in the next section. More detail on these delay benchmarks can be found in (Gutwin 2001).

These results give a rough idea of what groupware users can expect in heterogeneous real-world settings. The next issues to be addressed are whether these delay types and magnitudes have a negative effect on the usability of a groupware system, and if so, how and why those effects happen.

Effects of delay on group work

We are interested in several questions about the ways that network delays affect closely-coupled collaborative work, where people have to keep close track of others in order to carry out their own work correctly. Our questions are:

♦ What types of collaborative interactions are affected by delay?

- Does delay reduce task performance and system usability?
- What magnitude of delay is required before usability suffers?
- How do task strategies change in the presence of delays?
- Which kind of delay is worse, latency or jitter?

We considered these questions in two stages. First, we observed groups using a real groupware system (a real-time game) both with and without delays. From these observations, we identified several specific kinds of interactions that seemed to be most affected by delay. Second, two interaction types (predicting another person's movement, and coordinating access to a shared artifact) were examined in greater detail through two lab experiments.

Observations of delay in a real groupware activity

Five pairs of people were observed for approximately one hour each as they played the real-time groupware game GK-Pipedreams (Figure 2). The game is a multi-player version of the arcade game Pipedreams, in which players must place sections of pipe to stay ahead of the water that flows through the pipeline. GK-Pipedreams represents players in the workspace with telepointers, shows all player movements and manipulations as they happen, and gives all players full access to the artifacts in the workspace. People usually play GK-Pipedreams in a mixed-focus fashion: they engage in both independent and shared work, moving back and forth (often rapidly) between loosely- and tightly-coupled interaction.

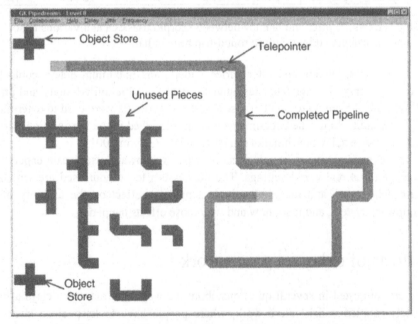

Figure 2. GK-Pipedreams groupware system. Players take pipe sections from the stacks at top left and bottom left, and build a pipeline from an inlet to an outlet.

For this study, GK-Pipedreams was altered to be able to introduce artificial communications delays between the two machines. In particular, the visual representation of the other person's movements could be subjected to controlled latency and jitter. Latency could be set to a fixed time between 0 and 1000 milliseconds. A simple model of jitter was adopted in which a certain percentage of messages would be delayed by a fixed time between 0 and 1000 milliseconds.

Pairs played the game first without any delays, and then with a range of artificial jitter and latency conditions. The players were in the same room (separated by a divider), so they were able to talk normally about their tasks. Two observers watched the on-screen interaction, looking for situations where delays appeared to cause some kind of problem for the group.

In general, people were able to deal with the latency and jitter conditions fairly well. Game performance did not appear to suffer even when large delays were imposed (c.f. Monk et al 1996), and people did not report major difficulties in working together on the task. However, the observers did notice changes in people's behaviour when delays were large. First, several people appeared to ignore the other person's activities entirely when the delay (particularly the jitter) was greater than about 500ms; that is, they reverted to working independently. Second, and perhaps as a result, groups appeared to run into more problems of coordination when delays were large: for example, players would both try to grab the same pipe piece, or would both try to move pieces into the same position. These problems were for the most part repaired quickly and without incident by the players; in discussions after the game, players only sometimes recalled that these problems had occurred at all.

Even though latency and jitter did not cause major problems for the groups, our observations suggested that certain kinds of collaborative interactions were affected by delay, and deserved closer study. These involve the activities of predicting movement and coordinating access.

- ♦ *Predicting another person's movement.* When a person moves around in a shared workspace, others use that movement to predict where the person is going (Gutwin and Greenberg 1998). These predictions are used to anticipate actions, to join someone at their destination, and to plan motion so as to avoid bumping into one another.
- ♦ *Coordinating access to shared artifacts.* Up to date knowledge of another person's activities in a closely-coupled situation is essential for managing access to a shared object or tool. This information is the basis of "social protocols" of concurrency control (Greenberg and Marwood 1994).

We carried out two experiments to test the effects of delay on prediction and coordination interactions in simple repeated tasks. We built two groupware systems with the GroupKit toolkit that implemented the interaction type. The groupware systems were set up such that two participants sat at different workstations and carried out the task by looking only at their own monitor.

Artificial delays were introduced using the same mechanism described earlier.

Experiment 1: Prediction

One type of prediction in a shared workspace is being able to determine where someone else is moving by watching their telepointer. We built a simple groupware system to isolate and test this type of interaction. The following sections describe the task, participants, experimental methods, and results.

The Prediction Task

This task involves two people, one attempting to predict as quickly and accurately as possible where the other person is pointing. One person (the follower) must click on a screen target that has been pointed to by the other person (the leader). Both participants see a set of boxes on their screen (see Figure 3); however, only the leader's screen showed which of these boxes was the target.

Leaders were instructed to move as quickly and accurately as possible to the yellow target as soon as it appeared on their screens. Followers were instructed to move to the box that was indicated by the leader, and click on the box when they arrived. Followers did not see the target highlighted in any way, but they could see the leader's telepointer. Groups were asked not to talk during this task.

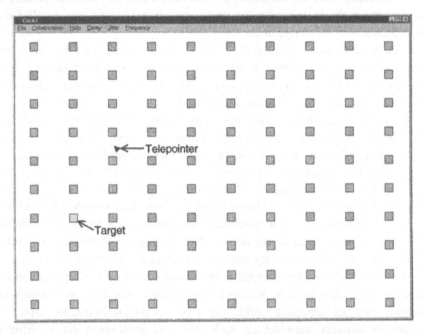

Figure 3. Prediction task system (leader's view). Target is coloured yellow.

Participants

Ten pairs of undergraduate computer science students participated in the study, and were given extra course credit for their involvement. Eight participants were women, and 12 were men; the mean age was 23 years. All participants were regular users of basic networked software (email and web browsers), but they had less experience with real-time groupware. Three participants had used a shared whiteboard system, and six had used internet voice conferencing. Five people were experienced with multi-player networked games. Finally, eight of the ten pairs were familiar with one another (more than three interactions per week).

Study hypotheses and conditions

The primary hypothesis in the prediction experiment was that increasing jitter would result in longer completion times and higher error rates. A secondary goal was to determine the level of jitter at which performance degrades significantly. We considered only jitter in this task because it was clear from pilot testing that simple latency did not have any effect on performance.

The effects of delay were explored by applying several levels of artificial jitter to the display of the leader's telepointer on the follower's screen. The experiment was run on a network that had very low real jitter (mean 10ms, frequency 2%); in the summaries below we consider this as zero jitter. For the non-zero jitter conditions, the groupware system delayed the display of the leader's telepointer by the jitter amount and with a frequency of 10%; however, the system also ensured that at least one jitter event was randomly introduced into the display for each trial. Data was gathered by recording task completion times and errors for several blocks of pointing tasks.

Block	Type	Jitter (ms)	Trials
1	Practice	0	20
2	Practice	1000	5
3-7	Test	0, 200, 400, 600, 1000	12

Table II. Conditions for prediction task; order of blocks 3-7 was randomised.

Pairs completed practice blocks with and without jitter, and then completed test blocks using different delay conditions, as shown in Table II. Test block order was randomised for each group. The first two trials of each block were discarded as additional practice trials, leaving 10 test trials in each condition. Participants were allowed to rest between each block of trials. When the session was complete, the participants changed workstations and repeated the experiment in the other role, resulting in 20 total participants.

308

Results

Completion time and errors were recorded and logged by the groupware system. Results for the five test conditions are shown in Table III and Figures 4 and 5.

Jitter (ms)	N	Completion time per block		Errors per block	
		Mean (ms)	SD	Mean	SD
0	20	20910	5395	0.15	0.3663
200	20	21166	3242	0.15	0.3663
400	20	23349	5813	0.05	0.2236
600	20	25369	6123	0.15	0.3663
1000	20	25060	4773	0.75	1.1642

Table III. Completion times and error rates for prediction task

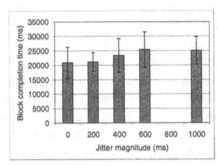
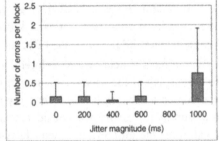

Figure 4. Mean completion times for prediction. One block = 10 trials; error bars represent standard deviation.

Figure 5. Mean errors for prediction. One block = 10 trials; error bars represent standard deviation.

We examined the primary hypothesis by carrying out repeated-measures ANOVA for completion time data and error data. Both analyses showed main effects of jitter magnitude: for completion time, $F(4,76)=4.983$, $p<0.05$; for error rate, $F(4,76)=6.909$, $p<0.05$.

To determine the magnitude at which jitter makes a substantial difference, post hoc one-tailed t-tests were performed comparing jitter conditions with the no delay condition. A Bonferroni correction was used to maintain alpha at 0.05; therefore, only p-values of 0.0125 or less were considered significant. For completion time data, t-tests showed significant differences for jitter of 600 ms and 1000ms ($p<.0125$), but not for jitter of 200ms ($p=0.429$) or 400ms ($p=0.089$). For error data, there were no significant differences between conditions.

In addition to the quantitative data, the experimenter also observed the way that groups carried out the tasks. It was clear that in low-delay conditions, people did use the feedback of the telepointer to carry out the task more quickly. People almost always started moving their mouse before the other person had stopped moving. People would track the other cursor closely, and then click the target as soon as the telepointer stopped moving. When there was larger jitter, however, people adopted different strategies. They would often still track the telepointer, but would pause when it stopped to wait and see if the pointer would begin moving again. In a few cases, people had difficulty finding the telepointer after it had made a large jitter-induced jump. Some participants resorted to a strategy of not starting their move until they were sure that the other person had finished.

Experiment 2: Coordination

The second type of interactive activity we studied was coordinating access to shared resources. A second experiment and a second groupware system were designed to test the effects of delay on coordination.

The Coordination Task

In the coordination task, participants were asked to drag objects from a shared central stack and drop them onto a target region. There were two drop regions, one for each participant, but only one central stack of objects (see Figure 6). In this system, both participants see the same objects on their screens, and carry out the same task actions. Participants were instructed to drag and drop a set number of objects from the stack, but were explicitly cautioned to minimise errors—that is, the number of times they grabbed an object that the other person had already taken. Groups were allowed to talk to each other during this task.

Participants

The same pairs from the prediction study were used in the coordination study, and were run through the experiment later the same day. This meant that all of the study participants had experienced jitter conditions in both the leader and follower role of the prediction task.

Study Hypotheses and Conditions

The primary hypothesis in the coordination experiment was that increasing jitter and latency would result in longer completion times and higher error rates. Again, the secondary goal was to determine the level at which performance degrades. In this task, several levels of either jitter or latency were applied to the display of both participants' telepointers and object moves as shown on the other person's screen. The system was run on a fast network with a consistent latency of 40 ms; as this is the lowest latency we could achieve, this amount was used in the 'no delay' condition.

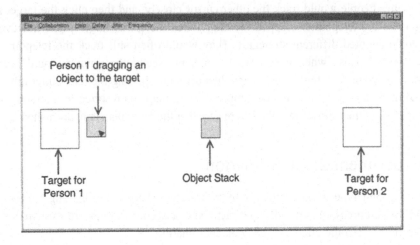

Figure 6. Coordination task system. Rectangles at left and right are the drop regions; filled rectangles are objects to be moved; object stack is at centre.

Groups first completed three practice trials, and then carried out a set of test trials with different delay conditions (see Table IV). In each block of test trials, groups completed 50 object moves, of which the first five were discarded as additional practice trials, leaving 45 test trials per block. Block order was randomised for each group. Data was gathered by recording task completion times and errors for several blocks of trials. Errors were defined as attempts by one person to grab an object with their mouse that another person was already holding. Participants were specifically instructed to try and minimise these "double grabs."

Block	Type	Latency (ms)	Jitter (ms)	Trials
1	Practice	40	0	50
2	Practice	1040	0	10
3	Practice	40	1000	10
4	Practice	440	400	10
5-9	Test	40, 240, 440, 640, 1040	0	50
10-13	Test	40	40, 240, 440, 640, 1040	50

Table IV. Study conditions for prediction task. The order of blocks 5-13 was randomised.

Results - Coordination

Completion time and errors were recorded and logged by the groupware system. Results for the test conditions are shown below in Table V and Figures 7 and 8.

Jitter (ms)	Latency (ms)	N	Completion time (45 trials)		Errors (45 trials)	
			Mean (ms)	SD	Mean	SD
0	40	10	31497	6063	0.9	1.728
200	40	10	32523	11893	1.1	0.994
400	40	10	31133	5463	1.8	1.475
600	40	10	32088	5135	1.4	1.712
1000	40	10	33041	5006	3.1	1.969
0	40	10	31497	6063	0.9	1.72
0	240	10	32940	4980	4.6	2.95
0	440	10	33876	5167	10.8	3.29
0	640	10	33942	5377	14.6	3.4
0	1040	10	31983	5896	16.8	2.89

Table V. Completion time and error rates for all study conditions.

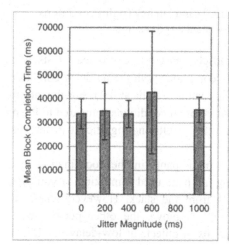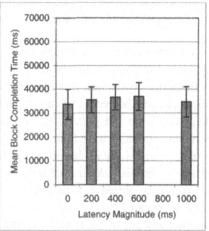

Figure 7. Mean block completion times for jitter (left) and latency (right) conditions. Blocks consist of 45 trials. Error bars show standard deviation.

The a priori hypothesis for the coordination task was that increased jitter and latency would increase completion time and errors. We considered latency conditions and jitter conditions separately, using the no-delay condition in both analyses. Repeated-measures analyses of variance were carried out for both error rates and completion time. For completion time, there were no main effects found for either jitter ($F_{(4,36)}=0.841$, $p=0.509$) or latency ($F_{(4,36)}=1.6$, $p=0.195$). For error rates, significant main effects were found for both jitter ($F_{(4,36)}=6.445$, $p<0.05$) and latency ($F_{(4,36)}=73.11$, $p<0.05$) conditions.

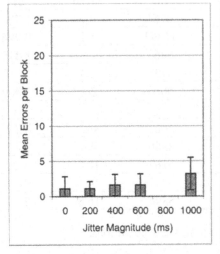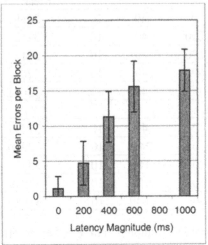

Figure 8. Mean errors per block for jitter (left) and latency (right) conditions. Blocks consist of 45 trials. Error bars show standard deviation.

To explore the error results more closely, post hoc one-tailed t-tests were performed to compare the different delay conditions with the no delay condition. A Bonferroni correction was again used to maintain alpha at 0.05. For the latency results, t-tests showed significant differences for all conditions compared to the no delay condition (all $p<0.0125$). For the jitter results, no significant differences between conditions were found.

Observations were also made of the participants in the coordination task. Strategies in this task all used turn-taking; all pairs used some kind of you-then-me-then-you approach to taking objects from the stack. However, when one person appeared to be taking longer with a move, the other person would occasionally fill in the time by taking an extra object. In low-delay conditions, errors were rare, and usually happened when people were re-starting the turn-taking. With larger delays errors happened regularly, and often occurred when the screen appeared to show that it was safe to take an object from the stack. When people had difficulty coordinating in the high-delay conditions, they would generally slow down and try to establish for certain where the other person was (e.g. by both participants going to their drop regions). They would then restart the turn-taking strategy.

Discussion

Our goals in this research were to find out what kinds of real-world interaction are affected by network delays, to determine the level at which performance starts to suffer, and to determine how task strategies change in the presence of delays. The next sections summarise our findings, interpret the findings in light of our general goals, consider the generalisation of the results, and discuss design approaches that can improve groupware usability in the face of network delay.

Summary of results

An observation of a real groupware system (GKPipedreams) suggested that overall task performance is resilient to the presence of even large delays. However, this resiliency occurred because people were able to alter their work style to be more independent and less collaborative. In addition, certain types of interaction appeared to cause problems even when people ignored the other person's movements. Two of these in particular were predicting others' movements, and coordinating access to shared objects.

In experiments to explore these two interactions in more detail, several of the priori hypotheses were supported by the results. Table VI shows a summary of our quantitative findings. We found significant relationships between jitter magnitude and prediction performance, and between both types of delay and coordination errors. We also found that prediction time is significantly affected with jitter of 600ms or more, and that coordination errors are significantly increased with latency of 240ms or more.

Task	Hypothesis	Sig. Effect	1st sig. level
Prediction	Jitter magnitude increases CT	Yes	600 ms
Prediction	Jitter magnitude increases errors	Yes	None
Coordination	Jitter magnitude increases CT	No	—
Coordination	Jitter magnitude increases errors	Yes	None
Coordination	Latency magnitude increases CT	No	—
Coordination	Latency magnitude increases errors	Yes	240 ms

Table VI. Summary of quantitative results. CT = completion time; Sig = significant.

The two most obvious effects were that of jitter on prediction time, and that of latency on coordination errors. These results can be converted back to real-world terms. With no jitter, predicting another person's pointing action took about two seconds; with jitter of 600ms, prediction took about half a second longer. With no latency, pairs made one coordination error in 50 repeated manipulations of a shared object. When latency was 240ms, they made one error in every 10 manipulations, and when latency was 1000ms, they made one error in every three.

We also found that people's strategies changed in the presence of delays. High jitter in the prediction task resulted in a change from a "start following immediately" strategy to a "wait and see" strategy. Latency in the coordination task seemed to force a "rhythmic turn-taking" strategy, but even this strategy often broke down when latencies were larger. From the experimenter's observations, it seemed clear that delays made the tasks more difficult, and that they reduced satisfaction with overall systems. It was clear that when there were delays in the system, people had to slow down and pay more attention to both their own and others' actions.

Explaining the results

In closely coupled visual tasks, people use the representation of the other person as a kind of visual evidence of the state of the action (e.g. Brennan 1990, Clark 1996). In the real world, people quickly learn to use this information to improve their efficiency. They can become expert at a shared task by learning the task boundaries that are presented by the other person, and gradually pushing towards those limits. This expertise, however, depends upon the information being accurate. In the prediction and coordination tasks, a main reason that delays impaired performance is that delay introduces uncertainty into a situation where certainty is required for expertise. When visual evidence is uncertain, fast perceptual tasks (e.g. simply watching the other person) are changed into time-consuming cognitive tasks (e.g. mentally calculating the other person's location or current activity).

In the prediction task, the most common strategy in the no-delay condition was to follow the other person's cursor as closely as possible, and to choose a target as soon as the telepointer stopped moving. When jitter was introduced, however, it made the telepointer appear as if the leader had stopped moving, forcing the follower to think about whether they had really stopped. In addition, attempts to "think ahead" and predict the leader's location in jitter conditions required the follower to calculate the likely path of the leader's cursor based on its previous speed and trajectory (also noticed in (Vaghi et al 1999)).

In the coordination task, latency made people unsure about what their partner was doing, and made it difficult to determine whether it was safe to grab the next object from the stack. When coordination is based on visual feedback, and the feedback cannot be trusted, coordination becomes more difficult. Perhaps as a result, almost all of the groups fell into rhythmic turn-taking during the delay conditions—an example of a non-visual way to coordinate the task and gain certainty about the other person. As long as people maintained the rhythm, they did not have to depend on untrustworthy visual evidence; unfortunately, the rhythm broke down often when people paused or got out of step, and it was often in restarting where errors occurred.

Jitter was less of a problem in the coordinated-moving task. This may have been because a jittery telepointer was still up-to-date most of the time, and along with the rhythm of turn-taking, may have provided enough information to keep the activity properly coordinated. One situation where jitter did appear to cause a problem, however, was when one person's cursor stuck while they were inside their drop area. This occasionally fooled their partner into thinking that they had paused, and into attempting to grab a second object from the stack. This problem is similar to that of the prediction task, where a telepointer freeze forces the observer to guess whether motion has really stopped.

Generalising the results

The two experiments showed that delays can affect both performance and strategy during closely-coupled activities. However, the experiments were set up to isolate and repeat specific types of interaction, so the question remains of what these results imply for real world group work.

First, the effects of delay on real world task performance will be proportional to the number of delay-sensitive interactions that the task requires. In tasks where predicting movement and coordinating access are common, it is likely that jitter and latency will lead to measurable performance loss. In other tasks these types of interactions will be less frequent (as in GKPipedreams) and so performance losses will not be apparent. Even if overall performance is not affected, however, delays will cause problems that affect system usability: when people have to keep track of others in a groupware system, latency and jitter are simply annoying. Despite the fact that people can concentrate harder and still get the task done, usability suffers.

Second, the strategy change that we observed in the GKPipedreams observation suggests that people tend to work more as individuals when visual information about others' activities cannot be trusted. This strategy protects performance, but means that the benefits of working as a group are largely lost. When groups are fully aware of others in the workspace, they are able to provide assistance, monitor one another, discuss artifacts, and share joint tasks. When people work as individuals, they do not maintain the awareness that provides for these sorts of collaborative benefits. These more subtle effects of delay on real-world distributed work will be the focus of our continued research in this area.

Designing for delay

What can a groupware developer do to design for delay, given that the network is not under their control? The most important things from the designer's perspective are to assess both the coupling requirements of the groupware system and the likely delays in the situation where the application will be installed. If the group task requires close coupling and the network delays are high, the developers may have to rethink their design, since unreliable information about others is often worse than no information at all. Once the requirements are known, there are several approaches that can be used to reduce delays or work around them.

Network techniques. First, different network configuration can be used that have lower delays than the Internet (e.g. dedicated ISDN modems). Second, different message protocols provide different quality-of-service (QoS) parameters than the TCP/IP protocol currently used in most groupware toolkits. For example, the UDP protocol has considerably lower latency and jitter than TCP. It does not provide guaranteed delivery, but for messages such as telepointer position, guarantees are not usually required. Other protocols such as LRMP (lightweight reliable multicast protocol) add some control ability on top of UDP, and may also be useful in groupware.

Smoothing. Buffering incoming messages is one way of reducing jitter at the cost of increasing latency. In situations where tasks are affected more by jitter than by latency, smoothing can be used.

Adaptation. If groupware systems are able to measure the current delay, they could be able to adapt the interface to present the users with interaction techniques that are most appropriate for the current delay conditions. For example, as jitter increases beyond a certain level, the system could offer to switch from the use of telepointers for user awareness to a participant list, which is not affected by jitter.

Explicit indications of delay. People may be better able to adapt their behaviour to delays if they are aware of the presence and magnitude of the delay. Delay can be represented in the interface by devices like delay gauges, or by "ghosting" effects on moving objects (Vaghi et al 1999).

Conclusions

Delay is a fact of Internet life, and is one aspect of a groupware system that is difficult for the developer to control. Since many groupware applications are being built to run across the Internet, we undertook an investigation into the effects of delay, particularly latency and jitter, on group work in real time groupware. Based on observations of a real groupware system, we identified two kinds of interaction in closely-coupled tasks that seemed to be affected by delays, and designed experiments to study them more closely. Significant relationships between delay and task performance were found, and it was clear that task strategies changed to accommodate the delay. Our main direction for future work is in studying the effects of delay on more realistic collaboration. From our observations of GK-Pipedreams, it is evident that there are changes to strategy, interaction, and conversation when information is delayed in a real-world application, but identifying these subtle changes will likely require more sensitive qualitative and process measures.

Acknowledgements

Thanks to Reagan Penner for running an earlier version of the experiments, and to Sean Cocks for conducting the version reported on here.

References

1. Acharya, A., and Saltz, J. (1996) *A Study of Internet Round-Trip Delay.* Report CSTR-37-36, Dept. of Computer Science, University of Maryland, 1996.
2. Beaudouin-Lafon, M., and Karsenty, A. (1992), 'Transparency and Awareness in a Real-Time Groupware System', *Proceedings of the Conference on User Interface and Software Technology*, Monterey, CA, 1992, 171-180.
3. Brennan, S. (1990), *Seeking and Providing Evidence for Mutual Understanding*, Ph.D. thesis, Stanford University, Stanford, CA, 1990.
4. Cisco corporation (2000), *Designing Internetworks for Multimedia*. Currently at: www.cisco.com/ univercd/cc/td/doc/cisintwk/idg4/nd2013.htm.
5. Clark, H. (1996), *Using Language*, Cambridge University Press, Cambridge, 1996.
6. Cooperative Association for Internet Data Analysis (2000). http://www.caida.org
7. Fluckiger, F (1995). *Understanding Networked Multimedia*, Prentice Hall, 1995.
8. Gaver, W. (1991), 'Sound Support for Collaboration', *Proceedings of the 2nd European Conference on Computer Supported Cooperative Work*, 1991, 293-308.
9. Greenberg, S., and Marwood, D. (1994), 'Real Time Groupware as a Distributed System: Concurrency Control and its Effect on the Interface', *Proceedings of the Conference on Computer-Supported Cooperative Work*, 1994, 207-217.
10. Gutwin, C. (2001) *Groupware Latency and Jitter on the Internet.* Technical Report, Department of Computer Science, University of Saskatchewan, 2001.
11. Gutwin, C., and Greenberg, S. (1998) 'Effects of Awareness Support on Groupware Usability'. *Proceedings of ACM CHI'98*, Los Angeles, ACM Press, 1998.
12. Hall, R., Mathur, A., Jahanian, F., Prakash, A., Rassmussen, C. (1998) 'Corona: A Communication Service for Scalable, Reliable Group Collaboration Systems'. *Proceedings of CSCW'98*, pp. 140-149, 1998.
13. Kum, H., and Dewan, P. (2000), 'Supporting Real-Time Collaboration Over Wide Area Networks', *Video Proceedings of ACM CSCW 2000*.

14. Matrix Information and Directory Services, Inc. (2000). *The Internet Weather Report.* http://www.mids.org/weather/

15. Monk, A., McCarthy, J., Watts, L., and Daly-Jones, O. (1996), 'Measures of Process', in P. Thomas (ed): *CSCW Requirements and Evaluation*, Springer-Verlag, London, 1996, 125-139.

16. National Laboratory for Applied Network Research (2000). www.nlanr.net

17. Park, K. and Kenyon, R. (1999), 'Effects of Network Characteristics on Human Performance in the Collaborative Virtual Environment'. *Proceedings of IEEE Virtual Reality '99*, March 14-17, 1999.

18. Roseman, M., and Greenberg, S. (1996), Building Real-Time Groupware with GroupKit, a Groupware Toolkit, *ACM Transactions on CHI*, 3(1), 66-106, 1996.

19. Salvador, T., Scholtz, J., and Larson, J. (1996), The Denver Model for Groupware Design, *SIGCHI Bulletin*, 28(1), 52-58, 1996.

20. Scholl, F. (2000), *Planning for Multimedia*. White paper, Monarch Information Networks. Currently available at: http://www.monarch-info.com/pmm.html.

21. Segal, L. (1995), 'Designing Team Workstations: The Choreography of Teamwork', in P. Hancock, J. Flach, J. Caird and K. Vicente (eds): Local Applications of the Ecological Approach to Human-Machine Systems, 392-415, Lawrence Erlbaum, Hillsdale, NJ, 1995.

22. Stefik, M., Foster, G., Bobrow, D., Kahn, K., Lanning, S., and Suchman, L. (1987), 'Beyond the Chalkboard: Computer Support for Collaboration and Problem Solving in Meetings', *Communications of the ACM*, 30(1), 32-47, 1987.

23. Tanenbaum, A. (1996), *Computer networks*, Prentice-Hall, Englewood N.J., 1996.

24. Tang, J. (1991), 'Findings from Observational Studies of Collaborative Work', *International Journal of Man-Machine Studies*, 34(2), 143-160, 1991.

25. Tatar, D., Foster, G., and Bobrow, D. (1991), 'Design for Conversation: Lessons from Cognoter', *International Journal of Man-Machine Studies*, 34(2), 185-210, 1991.

26. Vaghi, I., Greenhalgh, C., and Benford, S. (1999), 'Coping with Inconsistency due to Network Delays in Collaborative Virtual Environments'. *Proceedings of the ACM Workshop on Virtual Reality and Software Technology*, 1999, 42-49.

W. Prinz, M. Jarke, Y. Rogers, K. Schmidt, and V. Wulf (eds.), *Proceedings of the Seventh European Conference on Computer-Supported Cooperative Work, 16-20 September 2001, Bonn, Germany*, pp. 319-338.

Community Support and Identity Management

Michael Koch, Wolfgang Wörndl

Technische Universität München, Germany

{kochm,woerndl}@in.tum.de

Abstract. Computer based community support systems can provide powerful support in direct exchange of information and in finding people for information exchange. Such applications usually make use of information about the user (user profile information) for personalization and for supporting contact management. As in real life, a user will interact with different communities (community support applications) hosted by different providers. With the current approach users have to provide and update information about their identity and interests for each community independently. That results in cold-start problems with new community support applications and in inconvenience for the user. In this paper we discuss user-centric identity management for community support applications and concentrate on a platform for using user profiles in more than one application. We also propose mechanisms to address privacy issues in this framework.

1. Introduction

Community support and virtual communities gain more and more attention in various areas from marketing to knowledge management. In this context community support includes a large variety of functions supporting groups of people with some kind of commonality and an ongoing rhythm of interaction (Mynatt et al., 1997). Identity plays a key role in virtual communities. In communication, which is the primary activity in communities, knowing the identity of those with whom you communicate is essential for understanding and evaluating an interaction (Donath, 1998). In addition to this, a community support application could offer special personalized services.

The Webster English Dictionary describes the word *identity* as: "*1) the condition or fact of being the same or exactly alike (sameness, oneness); 2a) the condition or fact of being a specific person or thing (individuality); b) the condition of being the same as a person or thing described or claimed*" (Webster, 1988).

For community support applications the aspect of identity as proving to be a specific person is not as important as the aspect of identity as all information that describes a specific person in the real world. Hence, we regard identity more in the context of user profile, a set of information representing a user or clearly related to a user or role in the digital world. In the rest of the paper we will use the terms user profile and identity synonymous.

Managing which information is available for which application is called *identity management*. Identity management is something we do in normal conversation everyday when we decide on what to tell one another about ourselves. In interactions with others we consider the situational context and the role we are currently acting in as well as the respective relationship with the interaction partners. This results in different sets of information being released to different interaction partners. Sometimes this leads to the situation that a person is known under different names in different contexts, e.g. by using special names, nicknames or pseudonyms suiting the occasion (Köhntopp and Bertold, 2000).

Also or especially in the digital world people are using different (digital) identities. When interacting with different applications from different providers and using different identities it becomes hard to keep track of the information which service stores which information, and to keep the information in the services up to date.

An identity management system would allow people to define different identities, roles, associate personal data to it, and decide whom to give data and when to act anonymously. An identity management system would empower the user to maintain their privacy and control their digital identity. For community support systems a user-centric identity management system would make it easy for the user to use different communities and thereby lower the entry barrier to online communities.

In this paper we tackle the technical aspect of user-centric identity management. After reviewing requirements for identity management systems (Section 2) we will present a general architecture for identity management that is developed in the context of the Cobricks project at Technische Universität München (Section 3). Then we will focus on the privacy issues in this architecture (Section 4). The paper concludes with a brief overview of the implementation status and prototypes (Section 5), some comments on related work (Section 6), and a summary and look-out to future work (Section 7).

2. Identity Management Requirements

2.1. Functionality

One of the main motivations for identity management is to enable different services reuse user profile information. The user of an online service should no longer have to enter a lot of data for registration or wait a long time until the application has learned his preferences and can provide properly personalized services. Therefore, identity management support first has to provide functions for creating, storing and accessing digital identities (user profiles). Here it has to be stressed that in contrast to different kinds of customer relationship management systems, identity management has to clearly treat the user providing information as the owner of the profile and not the services using the information.

Identities are created by a user for himself or by a certification authority for the user, and are accessed by services the user is interacting with or has interacted with (e.g. community applications or e-commerce services). For enabling services to access identity information the user has to provide the service with an identity identifier. This identifier could either be transmitted automatically by the user's browser or be entered by the user upon registration or login.

In addition to reading data from the identity, services should also be able (with permission) to add new information to the identity. This can relieve the user from entering all information himself.

Usages for digital identities are:

- Authentification – the identity provides a way for the service to authenticate the user (e.g. password checking function or public key certificates).
- Providing data for different functionalities like
  - (e-commerce) transactions (e.g. delivery address, payment data),
  - personalization, or
  - configuration/initialisation (e.g. email address for sending push information, buddy lists for configuring awareness and communication functions).

For authentification the identity management support has to provide functions that enable a service to check the identity of a user who is directly interacting with it.

Access to the identity has to be logged to provide the owner of the identity with reports about which service possesses which personal data.

The owner of an identity should have the possibility to determine which interaction partner should see what information. This could be done by creating different digital identities or by defining and negotiating special access rights to one identity. In our opinion both solutions have to be provided by an identity management system since it is not possible to foresee every usage of the information by defining a special sub-identity for it. A connection between the two solutions and a functionality to help users managing several identities can be introduced by providing the possibility to link identities to each other. Such a link could define a data path that determines how updates to one identity are automatically forwarded to another identity.

2.2. Privacy

As already mentioned, the identity management system has to enable the identity owner to specify which services can access and write which data. This is one aspect of privacy. (Information) privacy refers to the claims of individuals that information about themselves should generally not be available to other individuals or organizations, and that, where data is possessed by another party, the individual must be able to exercise a substantial degree of control over that data and its use (Clarke, 1999).

Surveys among Internet users show that they are concerned about their privacy. For example, 87% of the participants in a survey conducted by Ackerman et al. (1999) were somewhat or very concerned about threats to their personal privacy while being online. Respondents were less inclined to provide information when personally identifiable information was requested:

"In a scenario involving a banking Web site, 58% of respondents said that they would provide information about their income, investments, and investment goals in order to receive customized investment advice. However only 35% said they would also supply their name and address so that they could receive an investment guide booklet by mail." (Ackerman et al., 1999, p. 5).

There is an obvious need for mechanisms allowing users to specify and enforce their personal preferences regarding privacy. More precisely, requirements for a privacy infrastructure in our scenario are:

- Flexible access right control system, e.g. through rules and negotiation
- Possibility to monitor access rights and accesses
- Possibility to use a pseudonym instead of real identity
- Purpose binding of data accesses
- Possibility to allow access for temporary use
- Possibility to revoke granted access rights
- Control whether user data can distributed to other services (and users)
- Integration of cryptographic techniques for anonymous data transfers
- Possibility of support from privacy authorities

Online services and businesses could also benefit from a powerful privacy architecture because users with less fear of risking their privacy are likely to make more and better personal information available to services (Köhntopp and Bertold, 2000). Our ideas for a technical solution to ensure privacy in this framework are presented in Section 4.

3. Identity Management Architecture

To introduce a user-centric identity management system one has to tackle the following issues:

1) infrastructure/architecture of the system
2) standards for representing and storing user profile information (for making multiple usage and exchange among applications possible)
3) cryptographic means for storing and authenticating identities and pseudonyms
4) privacy issues (this includes negotiation and the possibility to use more than one identity)

In this section we will mainly discuss architectural issues (Issues 1 and 2). The following section (Section 4) will address the privacy issues.

3.1. Server- versus client-side storage of user profiles

Today, user related information is stored on different servers. For example, amazon.com or bn.com keep track of users' interests to make recommendations based on previous transactions or interest specifications users have made available. However, there are several problems with this server-side approach:

- A user has to log on to different community applications manually and provide his profile information again and again; there is no possibility to distribute new information to different communities (i.e. community applications) in one step.
- Information gained by one community cannot be used by another.
- Privacy considerations: users have little or no control over what personal information is collected.

Alternatively, user profile information can be stored on the user's computer. This could lead to higher trust because personal information is located near the user and because the usage of profile information can be controlled and monitored. The user information can be reused for several communities. Client-side user profile storage is usually implemented by so-called *infomediaries*. Infomediaries are (small) applications on the client computer, which maintain user profiles and offer services such as automatic fill-in of Web forms (Cranor, 1999).

The main problem of client-side storage of user profile information is that it is not portable (Mulligan and Schwartz, 2000). Personal information stored on one computer (e.g. at work) cannot be easily transferred to another one (e.g. at home) Therefore, a promising solution might be a *ID-Repository*. It offers server-based storage of user information for different services under the control of the user. A network of repository servers operated by different companies might be the best approach because it adds scalability and allows the user to choose one or more server operators to store her personal data.

3.2. User Profile Repository Network

Our technical approach is to separate user profile information from services that make use of it and store it in a central place where it can be maintained by the user and be accessed by different services (with permission of the identity owner).

The core component in our architecture is a user profile repository service (ID-Repository) that stores information about an identity and offers the identity owner and authorized services interfaces to access this information (see Figure 1).

The server offers a functionality to store more than one identity and to link identities to each other (defining data propagation paths).

For the repository we have several possibilities placed between the following two extremes:

- one central identity server for storing all identities of all people
- one or even several servers per person storing different identities

We imagine that in the real world there will be identity providers – services that operate servers (see Figure 2). These services might also offer certification services for profile information.

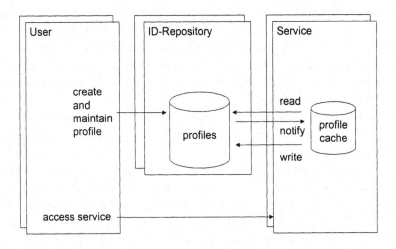

Figure 1. Identity Management Architecture Components.

For accessing the profile information we need a means for name resolution. Here we have to answer the question how a service can find the user profile server? There are two major possibilities for that issue. First we could use a service dependent identity identifier that includes the contact address of the identity repository server. Since it should be possible to move identities between servers this solution is not flexible enough. The only reasonable alternative is to introduce a name service or broker that is presented with the identifier and forwards requests to the correct server or returns the server's name or address.

The services that read the profile information should have a possibility to cache this information for some time. Here we need a means for keeping the cache up to date (and for the user to request deletion of the cached copy). After the negotiation of the basic lease this whole process can be seen as replication of the data with a master copy.

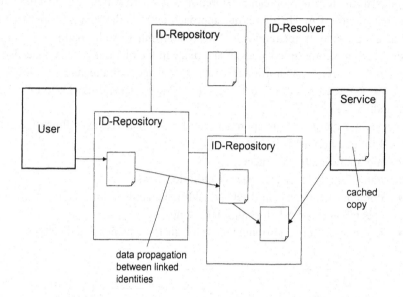

Figure 2. Identity Management Network.

3.3. Profile schema

Now that we outlined the general architecture for storing and accessing profiles, there is the question of how a profile should be structured to be of general use and allow interoperability.

Some information standards have been defined in the past for user profile information. Examples are the vCARD standard (Howes et al., 1998) or the standard included in W3Cs P3P specification (P3P, 2000). These approaches mainly choose hierarchically structured sets of attribute value pairs, i.e. there are attribute names like "personal.address.zip" and values of different data types stored for these attributes. So called ontologies are used to define the attribute and data type names and hierarchy.

When reviewing information needs in community support applications the following types of information can be identified:
- basic and demographic attributes like "name" or "gender"
- information about interests: This can be represented by correlations with predefined clusters or stereotypes (e.g. in iFAY (www.ifay.com)), by ex-

plicit attributes (e.g. "interest.music = 'hip hop'") or by collaborative interest definitions (correlations with other users). The source for all of this can be ratings given by the user to information (implicit by visit or explicit).

- information about relationship networks: colleagues, buddies, ...

Some of this information can be stored in a standard way using attribute value pairs, but not all of it. Therefore, our approach extends the standard approach by new data types mainly for ratings and for relationships. Additionally, there is the possibility to have multiple values in any place in the hierarchy. This is needed to store sets of values for an attribute (e.g. "personal.spokenLanguages = ('de', 'en', 'fr')") or to provide several data sets (e.g. "personal.address(1).street", "personal.address(2).street").

The main features in our approach can be summarized as follows (see also Figure 3 for an overview):

- hierarchical attribute space
- values at any level can be sets (multiple values)
- domain specific standard set and additional application specific attributes
- special types for relationships and ratings
- ontology to define attribute hierarchy, attribute names and data types

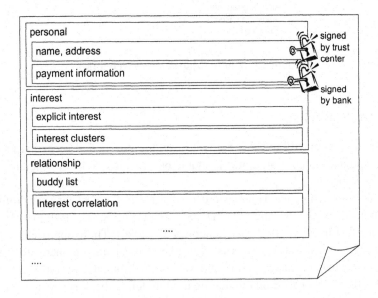

Figure 3. User Profile Structure and Signatures.

Since attributes can be set by different sources they have to store meta information about who has stored them. In addition to knowing who has set some data it might often be necessary to have a prove for this. If attributes are to be used for one application only, the service could store these attributes locally (and only store the other attributes globally in the identity management service) – but there might be needs where attributes should be exchanged among services and still have to be trusted (e.g. attribute that user has bought for more that $1000 at one e-commerce site which entitles him for special discounts in other services). The two solutions to this issue are that the identity management service itself guarantees the source of the data or that the data source digitally signs the data so that any-body can check the origin and the integrity. We have chosen the second possibility. The repository servers offer a possibility to sign any sub-hierarchy or sub-set of attributes in the repository and store the signatures.

4. Privacy

4.1. Overview

The presented ID-Repository network allows reuse of user profile information for different services but does not necessarily improve the privacy situation for the user at first. A powerful access control system to the user profile information is essential in this framework.

Existing access control systems (Sandhu and Samarati, 1994), such as role- or group-based solutions may be suitable within a community where administrators and community members may have different access rights and are all well known. With regard to user profile access, there really are only two groups: the user who should have total control over his profile and services or other users that may access part of the profile. Some communities are more trustworthy to users than others and it is not practicable for users to define different access rights to her profile information for different, not necessarily known, communities. Therefore, a more flexible approach is needed.

Our proposal includes two phases (see Figure 4):

1. Negotiation of access rights using privacy policies and preferences and generation of an access ticket (Section 4.2.)
2. User profile data access with the access ticket (Section 4.3.)

4.2. Negotiation of access rights

The negotiation of access rights is based on the Platform for Preferences Project (P3P) of the World Wide Web Consortium (W3C) (P3P, 2000). P3P is a project to define a standard way for web sites and user agents to communicate about privacy practices. Its goal is to enable the development of tools for making informed decisions about when personal information should be revealed when surfing the WWW.

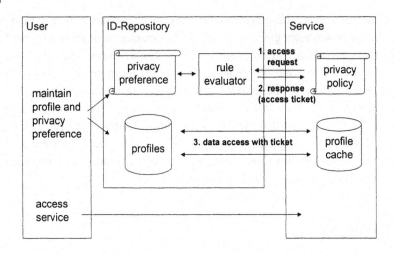

Figure 4. Negotiation of access rights.

Services or communities express their privacy policies and profile access requirements in machine-readable form. The P3P specification defines a vocabulary for describing data practices of a service. For example, a community can make a statement regarding whether information about the interests of a user are explicitly made available to other members of the community. Also, the purpose of data accesses can be modelled.

The user agent, respective ID-Repository, can then check the conformity of the privacy policy of a community with the user's privacy preferences. P3P includes a standard language for encoding the user's privacy preferences called "A P3P Preference Exchange Language (APPEL)" (APPEL, 2000). APPEL rules allow the expression of preferences over anything that can be expressed in the P3P schema. It defines four standard actions: "accept" (privacy policy is compliant to privacy preference), "reject" (privacy policy is not acceptable), "inform" and "warn" (information or warning should be provided to the user).

In our framework, a rule evaluator uses the P3P privacy policy and the APPEL rules in the users' privacy preferences to determine access rights for the requested profile attributes: allowing/disallowing access or requesting user interaction. This access information is stored in an *Access Ticket* (see Section 4.3).

We are currently working on extending P3P and APPEL for our purposes and implementing the rule evaluator which will be the core of our privacy architecture. P3P's data format specifies some commonly used data schemas, such as a person's email and postal addresses. This data format can be extended to match our user profile format described in Section 3.3. In addition, P3P provides a mechanism to extend its syntax and semantics using the "<EXTENSION>" tag.

The meaning of the data within the "<EXTENSION>" element can be defined by the extension itself.

Negotiation was contemplated in earlier draft versions of P3P but omitted in the final recommendation and might be implemented in future versions. In our framework, negotiation is implemented by mandatory and optional parts in privacy policies and preferences and by exchanging different proposals.

Users do not necessarily have to formulate the privacy preferences (or access rules) themselves. Reasonable rule sets could be provided by trusted organizations and a user could choose a suitable set with to option to manually adjust some parameters or rules. A suggestive user interface is also very important in this regard.

4.3. Access Tickets

The actual data accesses do not need negotiation but the access ticket that represents the result of the negotiation. The access ticket manifest the access rights of a certain community application for the user profile information. The ticket must be presented by the community with each data access.

The access ticket can be compared to the XML Tickets proposed in (Fujimura et al., 1999) or XML languages for digital rights management such as XrML (Extensible rights Markup Language, www.xrml.org). It is digitally signed by the ID-Repository on behalf of the user and contains the following information:

- Ticket issuer
- Validity date
- Ticket owner: a ticket is usually valid for one service only but may contain rights to distribute information
- Access modes for user profile attributes which include "Read", "Write", "Delete", "Read Once", "Read & Distribute" and "Read & Subscribe"

A released access ticket may be revoked at any time, e.g. if the user changes his mind about certain rules in his privacy preferences. The access ticket may be passed over from the ticket owner to another service. If the ticket states that some information is distributable (access mode "Read & Distribute"), other services can access this information without further negotiation.

The access control system is independent from caching. If a community has the right to read (or write) data, it may cache data or not do so unless the ticket states something else (e.g. access mode "Read Once"). Caching is allowed until the access ticket expires or is revoked. On the other hand, communities need an access ticket to write or collect user data locally, even if the data is never actually written to the ID-Repository.

Since the ID-Repositories handle the specific access rights of every service, it is possible to notify services when information has changed (access mode "Read & Subscribe"). This might not be the case with a role-based access control system. In addition, functionality in the user interface can be implemented that allow users to check and monitor not only their access rules but also the granted access rights at any time.

4.4. Anonymity

Anonymity is another important issue in any privacy architecture. Users do not want to reveal their true identity to all services. Levels of anonymity/identification include:

- (Real) anonymity (transactions cannot be associated with a user)
- Pseudonymity (transactions can be linked to a pseudonym but not to a particular individual)
- Identification (a user's identity is revealed and authenticated by a certificate)

Anonymizing components in our framework act as intermediaries between user and community components and provide the requested degree of anonymity. The negotiation of the level of identification is part of the negotiation process described in Section 4.2. users can specify rules in their privacy preferences with regard to the favoured level of anonymity, e.g. "do not reveal true identity unless the privacy policy of the service does meet certain criteria".

Anonymity is not always desirable. For example, transmission of credit card information over a secure channel (e.g. Secure Socket Layer, SSL) might necessitate client identification. Also, communities have contrary requirements regarding anonymity of their members, users may have to identify themselves to use certain services.

Several projects try to achieve unobservability and anonymity in open networks, including CROWDS (Reiter and Rubin, 1997) or ONION ROUTING (www.onion-router.net) and anonymizer services such as www.anonymizer.com. These anonymity tools are often based on *mix networks* (Chaum, 1981). A mix network is a collection of routers – the *mixes* – that use layered public-key encryption to conceal the path of a message through the network. Anonymization in the underlying communication network can be integrated in our framework but we will not describe this aspect in more detail in this paper.

4.5. Trust

The storage of user profile information under control of the user and negotiation of access rights based on privacy policies and preferences is a promising technical approach but it cannot solve problems of trust: how to control that the privacy policy is really observed by the service? Organizations such as TRUSTe (http://www.truste.org) or BBB Online (http://www.bbbonline.org) check the compliance of online services with credible privacy policies and provide privacy seals that are part of a P3P privacy policy. The privacy preferences of a user might include the following rule: "grant access rights only if a privacy seal by a trusted organization is presented by the service".

Services might be able to short-circuit the negotiation and access right process and enhance their information of a user without the user's consent, e.g. by tracking web accesses. However, it could be part of the privacy policy that no other information about the user is collected. A violation of the privacy policy can lead to legal consequences (or loss of the privacy seal, at least).

5. Implementation and Prototypes

In the Project IMC/Cobricks[1] we have implemented first parts of the ideas outlined above – the basic repository service is operable and identity caches are finished for different community support applications. The privacy negotiation mechanisms discussed in Section 4 are work in progress and not yet implemented. However, users can already create different identities and link them together, and thereby get different levels of anonymity when giving away access to the data.

In this section we will give a brief overview of the implementation and of the applications which are currently using the identity management system.

5.1. Identity Management Infrastructure

ID-Repository

As described in Section 3, the core component of the identity management system are servers storing user profiles (identities). In our case this are the ID-Repository servers. A server stores user profiles associated with an identity identifier, which is an anonymous global identifier, and offers the possibility to link identities to each other (see Figure 5).

The identity identifier does not include information about where the identity is stored. To resolve this there is a ID-Resolver in the system that acts as a central directory server and knows which ID-Repository is storing which identity. In this context we are currently working on a de-central solution and on other solutions including the usage of existing directory server infrastructures like X.500 and LDAP.

In addition to the profile information (including the meta information about origin of the data and the signatures) the server maintains a log of all access and provides the profile owner with reports from this log. Using the log the profile owner can determine which service currently holds personal information.

---

[1] Cobricks ((Software) bricks for supporting communities) is a project at Technische Universität München aiming at building a infrastructure for communityware (see (Koch and Lacher, 2000)) – The identity management system is a central part of this infrastructure.

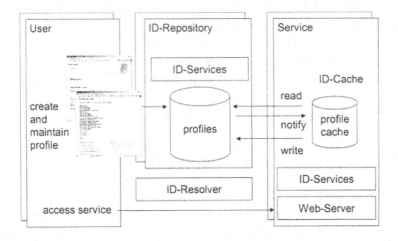

Figure 5. Identity Management Infrastructure.

The server is implemented in Java and offers the following interfaces:
- Corba and RMI interfaces for service-server interaction, for client-server interaction, and for server-server interaction
- ACL (FIPA-ACL interface): we are experimenting to implement the negotiation protocols discussed in Section 4 using the FIPA agent communication language (see (Koch and Lacher, 2000)).
- Web (HTTP/HTML) interface for profile owner

We have created XML based schemas for defining the ontologies. The schemas are used in the web interface for dynamically creating the user interface for entering information, and for entering meta information

ID-Cache

On the community support application side we have built custom made stub solutions all based on a common ID-Cache module for storing data and handling the interaction with the ID-Repository. The module will support the negotiation of access rights and already handles synchronization with the ID-Repository.

We are also starting to make stub modules available for widely used generic community platforms. So we just have finished implementing a user module for the Cassiopeia Community Server (see www.cassiopeia.com).

ID-Services

There are different usages for identity data. We are currently working on a modular approach to this. The so called ID-Services will either be installed in the ID-Repository or on the service side (using the ID-Cache to access data) and perform different services like personalization or generalization on the user data.

5.2. Prototype Applications

The identity management infrastructure is used in several community support applications we are developing and operating in our group. Namely these are our different community portals like the Informationsdrehscheibe Informatik, the knowledge management tool CommunityItemsTool and the recommender application CoMovie (see Figure 6 for the Web user interfaces of the applications).

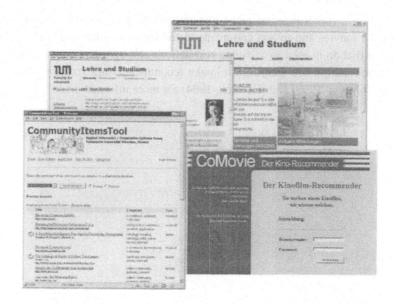

Figure 6. Prototype Community Support Applications.

Informationsdrehscheibe Informatik[2]

This application is a web portal (information source) and online community for the computer science department at Technische Universität München. The application uses a lot of information about the user for personalizing the information displayed – some of which are explicitly about user interests. The user has either the possibility to set the user profile information explicitly or the have them derived from his click stream. Currently, about 1500 registered members of the faculty and students are using this application. Other community portals based on the same technology have been implemented for other departments of for special interest groups at Technische Universität München.

---

[2] Available at http://drehscheibe.in.tum.de/

334

CommunityItemsTool

The CommunityItemsTool is a knowledge management application that helps people to publish and exchange bookmarks and bibliographic references (Koch et al., 2001). Users can assign items to user-specific folders to build personal categorizations and use recommendations based on keyword searches. Personalization features include configurable layout options and notification services.

CoMovie

CoMovie is a classical movie recommender system. It offers users the functionality to rate movies and to add comments to the movies (Koch and Lacher, 2001). The information is used to calculate correlations among users (relationship data), and these relations are then used to make recommendations (collaborative filtering, see (Grasso, 1999) and (Resnick, 1994) for more information).

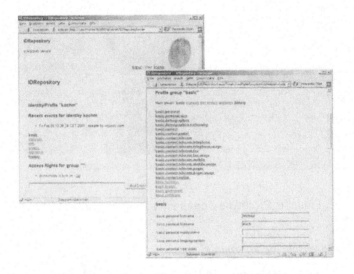

Figure 7. Web User Interface of IDRepository

Usage of Identity Information

The identity framework first offers a single sign-on solution for all these applications. Using the global identifier one can easily register or log in to the services. Both passwords and client side certificates are supported. This single sign-on also includes the reuse of basic configuration information like name and email address (plus mobile phone number for the emerging mobile services in the community support applications). User profiles can be created and maintained in the community support applications or by using the Web user interface of the IDRepository (see Figure 7). First results show that the single sign-on solution and possibility to reuse demographic information such as email and postal addresses has been found very valuable by users.

For the other attributes used by the applications we are currently developing ways how to most generally label the information for making reuse possible. Successful reuse was already possible for relationship data (for collaborative filtering and for buddy lists) and for interest information derived from ratings or explicitly entered by the user. In the latter case however it showed that the current applications are too different in their focus to make large scale reuse possible – there are only some overlapping areas, e.g. leisure activities.

As a result of this finding we are currently setting up new test applications for the identity service. One of them will be a Munich-wide Mobile Lifestyle Community (see www.cosmos-community.org for more information) and another one will be an Entrepreneurship Community that especially focuses on relationship networks (see www.telekooperation.de/tibid/ for more information).

6. Related Work

First we have to mention work dealing with what "identity" is and how the identity is used or determines interaction in online communities. Examples for work in this area are from Donath (1998) on Newsgroups and from Churchill and Bly (1999) on MUDs.

On the technical side one can find different approaches helping users to manage their online identities by collecting identity information like the infomediaries Jotter (www.jotter.com) or Persona (www.persona.com). Most of the infomediaries allow the user to store information in a personal data store and use it in conjunction with automatic form filling features. Some have additional features for automatically sharing information with marketers of products or services they have expressed interest in. The P3P standard described in Section 4.2 is also being integrated in some infomediaries.

Server-side solutions are digitalme from Novell (www.digitalme.com) and Microsoft's passport (www.passport.com). These systems are very similar to what we have in mind for communities, however they concentrate on delivery information (name, address) and payment information only, and not on personalization.

For personalization one can find different services like iFAY (www.ifay.com) or Yodlee (www.yodlee.com) which support clustering users and making the information about the affiliation to clusters available for personalization. However, these services either do not offer sufficient user control or are too concentrated on marketing and personalisation issues so that they cannot be used for configuration or initialisation.

Köhntopp and Bertold (1999) discuss the feasibility of using P3P as a basis for identity management. Their work is more focused on studying legal implications of privacy enabling technologies than technical infrastructures.

For single sign-on there are various solutions based on public-key cryptography and directory services. iPlanet for example is explicitly advertising its directory server and certification authority for this purpose and has extended its servers to accept client side certificates for authentication (see http://docs.iplanet.com/docs/manuals/security/SSO/sso.htm).

Finally, there are services for easily replicating user data. These services currently are used for sharing address information with different peers. Once the information is changed by the owner the business card changes at all places. An interesting approach in this area that can also be extended further is the solution by Onename (www.onename.com) and XNS (www.xns.org).

7. Summary and Future Work

In this paper we have discussed the issue of identity management in community support applications. With every user using more and more applications, and these applications making use of more and more information about the user this issue becomes important both in groupware and communityware.

We presented an identity management infrastructure which separates the identity management from the service applications. This separation is important for making community support applications easier use. In real life people take their identities with them all the time and implicitly give or communicate it to people they interact with. This also has to be possible in online communities to lower the entry barriers and make rich (personalized) services possible.

Our current work is mainly about implementing the privacy negotiations mentioned in Section 4 and about defining interoperable user profile data in different application areas. Here we also look into the application of the identity management service for internet appliances, i.e. tools the user is working with and that have network access. These tools will need more and more information about the user in the future and surely lack proper means for entering this data.

References

Ackerman, M.S.; Cranor, L.F. and Reagle, J. (1999): 'Privacy in E-Commerce: Examining User Scenarios and Privacy Preferences', *Proc. ACM Conference on Electronic Commerce*, Nov. 1999.

APPEL (2000): 'A P3P Preference Exchange Language', W3C Working Draft, 2000.

Chaum, D. (1985): 'Security Without Identification: Transaction Systems to Make Big Brother Obsolete', *Communication of the ACM*, Vol. 28, No. 10, Oct. 1985, pp. 1030 – 1044.

Chaum, D. (1981): 'Untraceable Electronic Mail, Return Addresses, and Digital Pseudonyms', *Communications of the ACM*, Vol. 24, No. 2, Feb. 1981, pp. 84 – 88.

Churchill, E. and Bly, S. (1999): 'Virtual Environments at Work: ongoing use of MUDs in the Workplace', *Proc. Intl. Joint Conf. On Work Activities Coordination and Collaboration*, 1999, pp. 99 – 108.

Clarke, R. (1999): 'Internet Privacy Concern Confirm the Case for Intervention', *Communications of the ACM*, Vol. 42, No. 2, Feb. 1999, pp. 60 – 67.

Cranor, L.F. (1999): 'Agents of Choice: Tools that Facilitate Notice and Choice about Web Site Data Practices', *Proc. 21st Intl. Conf. on Privacy and Personal Data Protection*, Sep. 1999, Hong Kong, China.

Damker, H.; Pordesch, U. and Reichenbach, M. (1999): 'Personal Reachability and Security Management – Negotiation of Multilateral Security', in: Müller, G. and Rannenberg, K. (eds): *Multilateral Security in Communications – Technology, Infrastructure, Economy*; Proc. Multilateral Security in Communications, Jul. 1999, Stuttgart, Addison-Wesley-Longman, pp. 95 – 111.

Donath, J.S. (1998): 'Identity and deception in the virtual community', in: Kollock, P. and Smith, M. (eds.): *Communities in Cyberspace*, London: Routledge, 1998.

Fujimura, K.; Nakajima Y. and Sekine, J. (1999): 'XML Ticket: Generalized Digital Ticket Definition Language', *Proc. W3C Signed XML Workshop*, Apr. 1999.

Grasso, A.; Koch, M. and Rancati, A. (1999): 'Augmenting Recommender Systems by Embedding Interfaces into Practices', *Proc. Intl. Conf. On Supporting Group Work (GROUP'99)*, Phoenix, AZ, Nov. 1999.

Howes, T.; Smith, M. and Dawson, F. (1998): 'MIME Content-Type for Directory Information (vCARD Specification)', *RFC 2425*, Sep. 1998

Koch, M. and Lacher, M.S. (2000): 'Integrating Community Services – A Common Infrastructure Proposal', *Proc. Knowledge-Based Intelligent Engineering Systems and Allied Technologies*, Brighton, UK, Sep. 2000, pp. 56-59.

Koch, M. and Lacher, M.S. (2001): 'The Comovie Movie Recommender – An Interoperable Community Support Application', *Proc. HCI International 2001 – 9th Intl. Conf. on Human-Computer Interaction*, New Orleans, LA, Aug. 2001.

Koch, M.; Lacher, M.S. and Wörndl, W. (2001): 'Das CommunityItemsTool - Interoperable Unterstützung von Interessens-Communities in der Praxis', *Proc. Liechtensteinisches Wirtschaftsinformatiksymposium – Informationsmanagement – Herausforderung und Perspektiven*, May 2001.

Köhntopp, M. and Bertold, O. (2000): 'Identity Management Based on P3P', *Proc. Workshop on Design Issues in Anonymity and Unobservability*, Jul. 2000, Berkeley, CA.

Mulligan, D. and Schwartz, A.: 'Your place or mine? Privacy Concerns and Solutions for Server and Client-side Storage of Personal Information', *Proc. Computers, Freedom and Privacy*, Apr. 2000, Toronto, ON, Canada.

Mynatt, E.D.; Adler, A.; Ito, M. and Oday, V.L. (1997): 'Design for Network Communities', *Proc. ACM SIGCHI Conf. On Human Factors in Computer Systems*, 1997.

Reiter, M.K. and Rubin, A.D. (1997): 'Crowds: Anonymity for Web Transactions', *Technical Report 97-15, DIMACS*, Aug. 1997.

Resnick, P.; Iacovou, N.; Suchak, M.; Bergstrom, P. and Riedl, J. (1994): 'GroupLens: An Open Architecture for Collaborative Filtering of Netnews', *Proc. Intl. Conf. On Computer Supported Cooperative Work*, Chapel Hill, NC, 1994.

P3P (2000): 'The Platform for Privacy Preferences 1.0 (P3P1.0) Specification', W3C Candidate Recommendation, Dec. 2000.

Sandhu, R. and Samarati, P. (1994): 'Access Control: Principles and Practice', *IEEE Communications Magazine*, Vol. 32, No. 9, Sep. 1994, pp. 40 – 48.

Webster (1988): 'Webster's New World Dictionary of American English', Third College Edition, Cleveland : Webster's New World, 1988.

W. Prinz, M. Jarke, Y. Rogers, K. Schmidt, and V. Wulf (eds.), *Proceedings of the Seventh European Conference on Computer-Supported Cooperative Work, 16-20 September 2001, Bonn, Germany*, pp. 339-358.
© 2001 Kluwer Academic Publishers. Printed in the Netherlands.

Reducing Interference in Single Display Groupware through Transparency

Ana Zanella and Saul Greenberg
University of Calgary, Canada
{azanella, saul}@cpsc.ucalgary.ca

Abstract. Single Display Groupware (SDG) supports face-to-face collaborators working over a single shared display, where all people have their own input device. Although SDG is simple in concept, there are surprisingly many problems in how interactions within SDG are managed. One problem is the potential for *interference*, where one person can raise an interface component (such as a menu or dialog box) in a way that hinders what another person is doing i.e., by obscuring another person's working area that happens to be underneath the raised component. We propose *transparent interface components* as one possible solution to interference: while one person can raise and interact with the component, others can see through it and can continue to work underneath it. To test this concept, we first implemented a simple SDG game using both opaque and transparent SDG menus. Through a controlled experiment, we then analysed how interference affects peoples' performance across an opaque and transparent menu condition: a solo condition (where a person played alone) acts as our control. Our results show that the transparent menu did lessen the effect of interference, and that SDG players overwhelmingly preferred it to opaque menus.

Introduction

Single Display Groupware (SDG) is a class of Computer Supported Cooperative Work (CSCW) applications that supports the work of co-located groups (Stewart, Bederson and Druin 1999). The group shares the same display, which can be a large display or a monitor. Each member has his or her own input device, allowing all to interact simultaneously with the system. Figure 1 illustrates this,

Figure 1 – Two people in a Single Display Groupware situation, each with his own input device.

where we see two users, each with their own mouse, interacting simultaneously over a single monitor.

SDG provides its users with many potential benefits. Of course, SDG users can profit from the technological powers offered by the actual SDG application, which may be specialized to fit their task. SDG collaborators also gain the richness of face-to-face interactions for free because they are co-located: they can easily look at each other, see each other's gaze and gestures, have natural conversations, perceive each other's behaviour, and so on (Tang 1991; Whittaker and O'Conaill 1997).

Although these SDG benefits are self-evident, there is a surprising dearth of research in the area. One of the reasons for this deficiency is the difficulty of building SDG applications on personal workstations. These computers typically assume one user per workstation. Its top-level graphical user interface (GUI) provides only one text focus for the single attached keyboard, and one cursor for the single attached mouse. Even when we physically connect multiple keyboards and mice onto a workstation, the operating system just merges the device inputs into a single stream that is then passed onto the GUI. For example, when two users are moving their mice at the same time, the single cursor provided by the standard operating system will respond to both movements. Underlying programming languages and their graphical toolkits also provide poor or non-existent support for developers wishing to program SDG using multiple input devices. Events raised by keyboard or mice actions do not identify which keyboard or which mouse they came from. The standard graphical interface components—buttons, menus, list boxes, tool palettes and so on—are not designed to discriminate and respond to multiple users. This is disastrous for SDG, for by definition SDG users should be able to work simultaneously e.g., by raising and selecting from different menus at the same time. Similarly, SDG user actions must be treated separately e.g., people may be in different drawing modes as a consequent of selecting different colours from a palette, and each person's drawing actions should reflect this mode. The consequence of all this is that SDG designers and implementers often have to start from scratch. Device drivers that recognize multiple input devices must be written; programming languages must be extended to discriminate input from multiple devices; and interface components must be totally redesigned if they are to respond efficiently to multiple users.

Even when the technical problems above are solved, there are other SDG usability issues that must be addressed. One specific interface issue we are investigating, and the focus of this paper, is *interference*: one person can raise an interface component (such as a menu or dialog box) in a way that hinders what another person is doing i.e., by obscuring another person's working area that happens to be underneath the raised component. Interference is a problem because it can distract and impeded SDG users from their tasks.

After first summarizing related work in SDG, we will describe interference in more detail. We will then suggest that transparent interface components may be a possible solution to interference: while one person can raise and interact with the component, others can see through it and can continue to work underneath it. Next, we will describe our implementation of a simple SDG game that we will use to test the efficacy of transparent SDG menus. In the subsequent sections, we will present our controlled experiment and our analysis of how interference affects peoples' performance when playing the SDG game using opaque *vs.* transparent menus: a solo condition (where a person plays alone) acts as our control. We close by describing the broader implications of our results to SDG design.

Related Work

Bier and Freeman (1991) built MMM—one of the first SDG systems—comprising a toy rectangle and text editor. They explored many SDG issues: how input devices are registered in the system; how multiple users are identified and 'attached' to particular devices; how different users can simultaneously manipulate the same data object; how individual mode information is captured and displayed; how multiple selections of data can be done; and so on. While a tour-de-force exposing many SDG issues and suggesting possible solutions, the authors did not, unfortunately, continue this line of research.

Several years later, researchers re-discovered SDG. Most of their efforts concentrated on showing that SDG systems could have a positive impact in educational settings involving children. Inkpen, McGrenere, Booth and Klawe (1997) studied how children share a single mouse *vs.* multiple mice when using a single display containing only one cursor. For the multiple mice situation, two types of turn-taking were tested to mediate access to the single cursor: *giving* (where one passes control to the other) and *taking* (where one takes control from another). In either situation, their results suggest that collaboration increased and that children had more fun when using multiple input devices to control the single cursor. Inkpen et al (1999) then explored the effectiveness of a true SDG setting, in this case testing pairs of children solving a puzzle in three conditions: a paper-based setting, a one-mouse / one-cursor setting, and a two-mice / two cursor SDG situation. Results indicate the advantage of the true SDG situation: most children preferred the two-mice / two-cursor situation since they could play together simultaneously, and they exhibited significantly less off-task behaviour. Another research group based mostly out of the University of New Mexico also explored SDG use by children, in this case through an innovative SDG application called KidPad (Druin, Stewart, Proft, Bederson and Hollan 1997). In particular, Stewart, Bederson and Druin (1999) studied how pairs of children collaborated when creating stories in KidPad. Each pair interacted together in either a one or a two-mice condition for three sessions, and then used the other condition for a last session. As before, children preferred the two-mice situation: they were more engaged in their task and they had more fun. Stewart, Raybourn, Bederson and Druin (1998) summarized several benefits they saw in true SDG: collaboration and communication increases, conflicts are reduced, and children offer and solicit help more often. Research in SDG use by children is continuing. For example, Hourcade, Bederson and Druin (2000) are now exploring how two children using a special-purpose SDG browsing tool can navigate to different parts of a shared library. Benford *et al* (2000) presents an enhanced version KidPad, where some tool functionalities are activated *only* when two children work collaboratively. For example, one child can draw with a basic colour, while two children can create a new colour by combining their colour tools. While we expect all the above findings will generalize to adults, this validation remains to be done.

Another thread of research considers how input devices other than the mouse can be used in SDG settings. Myers, Stiel and Gargiulo (1998) explored personal digital assistance (PDAs) as input devices for SDG in their Pebbles Project. They described several advantages and disadvantages e.g., that PDAs can display output as well as input, that there are screen real estate problems associated with PDAs, and that PDAs can afford much more powerful interaction techniques when compared to a mouse. They created several applications demonstrating the capabilities of a PDA-based SDG system, including a shared editor, a scribble application, and a slide show system. Rekimoto (1998) takes a similar tack, where hand-held computers are used as tool and data entry palettes for inputting the SDG functions. Greenberg, Boyle and LaBerge (1999) considered how personal information created on the PDA could be brought into a face-to-face SDG setting, and how that information could then be manipulated on the PDA, the shared screen, or both. They were mostly concerned with the movement of personal information to a public space and back again, and concluded with a listing of problematic design issues that result from the distinctions made between personal and public information.

Next, researchers in Group Decision Support Systems have a long history of developing special purpose computer-augmented meeting rooms (Stefik et al 1987; Nunamaker et al 1992). The room often has a very large display with its own connected computer. Participants usually have their own computer as well, connected to each other and to the large display through a network. A facilitator often controls the large display, and uses it to collect and show information gathered from each individual. Alternately, each person can switch his or her computer so that it appears on the large display. While related, these meeting rooms are a genre of their own; they are not quite single display groupware.

Finally, many game producers, such as Nintendo and Sony Play Station, have commercial SDG systems in every day use. Unlike standard commercial workstations, these specialized hardware boxes and many of the games often recognize up to four input devices and four players. The standard approach taken in most games is to split the screen, where each player has their own dedicated portion that is a viewport into the virtual world. Unfortunately, there is little in the way of research reporting within this arena.

Interference and Transparency

We now return to our description of *interference* in SDG. We define interference as the act of one person hindering, obstructing, or impeding another's view or actions on a single shared display. Interference can arise when one person raises an interface component (such as a menu or dialog box) over another person's working area. Because interface components are opaque, that other person cannot see beneath it, and is thus precluded from continuing his or her work. Any interface component that appears over the primary working area has potential to cause interference: pull down and popup menus, floating pallets, secondary windows, dialog boxes, and so on. These components may appear as a consequence of several activities: they can be raised directly by one user (e.g., by popping up a menu to make a selection: see Figure 3), or as a side effect of an action (e.g., a confirmation dialog box), or by the system itself (e.g., a system error or warning message appearing in a popup window).

The obvious solution of dedicating a portion of the screen real estate for displaying these components does not really work. First, this will lessen the available working area, which is a serious disadvantage because screen real estate is already very tight in SDG settings. Second, raised components can be quite complex and thus too large to fit e.g., a dialog box or palette with many options. Third, when there is one component type per person (e.g., when it is a component that displays an individual's mode), the number of components could increase with the number of collaborators.

Another solution is to do away with these floating and transient components altogether. For example, Druin et al (1997) proposed the idea of *local tools*, where large simple tools sitting directly on the work surface would replace traditional floating tool palettes. That is, local tools are guaranteed to appear within the space rather than above it. While reasonable for certain applications (Druin applied this approach to interfaces for children), we believe it cannot be generalized to all applications. For example, functionally rich applications may have so many tools and options that it would be unreasonable to map each to a simple tool; they would consume too much screen space.

Yet another solution is to display individual actions on the input device, as possible with PDAs. While promising, the problem here is that an individual's actions are now hidden from view. Thus other participants may no longer be aware of the actions that a person is taking because they cannot see them (Gutwin and Greenberg 1988).

Our own solution maintains the notion of floating and transient interface components while introducing the idea of making them semi-transparent. Transparency makes it not only possible to see the component itself but also what is underneath it. The effect is that when a semi-transparent component appears on top of a person's working area, that person is able to see through it and can continue his or her work. To allow the person to work underneath, each component responds only to its owner's inputs and passes all other inputs to the underlying working area. For example, a semi-transparent menu raised by one person will let only that person select from it; intercepted actions of other people working underneath the menu will be passed on, thus allowing those people to continue their interactions with the underlying working surface.

Our own transparent interface components extend Harrison's previous work on applying semi-transparent interface components to single user applications (Harrison, Ishii, Vicente and Buxton, 1995; Harrison and Vicente 1996). She was mostly interested in how a single person could use these components while still being able to see underneath them. She gave people menus with different degrees of transparency over various background textures, and then explored how well people could differentiate between these foreground and background layers: she found a reasonable compromise using objects that were 70% transparent. At the University of Calgary, researchers also used transparency, but this time as a way for a collaborating group to stay aware of one-another's actions in a distributed groupware setting (Greenberg, Gutwin and Cockburn 1996; Cox, Chugh, Gutwin and Greenberg 1998). They used transparent overviews, where one user would see his or her detailed working area in one layer, with a transparent overview showing the entire workspace layered on the top of it. Their results also indicate that transparency is promising, particularly if used at the 70% level.

Because our SDG transparent components are quite different than these other uses of transparent components, we were uncertain as to whether they would help

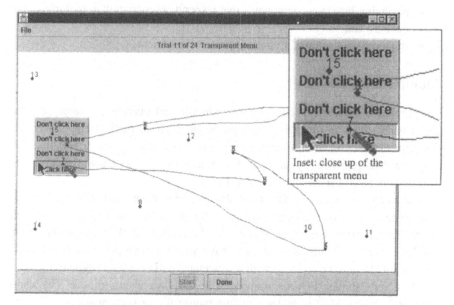

Figure 2 – A snapshot of the SDG connect the dots game. One player has raised a semi-transparent menu over the other player, who is working underneath it. See inset for detail.

or hinder SDG collaboration. To help us judge whether transparent interface components are an effective way to mitigate interference effects, we built and tested an SDG version of a two-person game. In this game, one person would try to complete a task as quickly as possible, while the other person would intentionally try to interfere with the first one by raising a menu in his or her way. The next section will describe this system and its implementation, with subsequent sections detailing the study and our results.

The Game

The SDG game used in the study is based on a "connect the dots" task. One player would try to draw a line connecting a series of numbered dots as quickly as possible, while the other player would try to slow down the first one by raising a menu in his or her way. The menu could be either semi-transparent or opaque.

A screen snapshot of a game session is illustrated in Figure 2. The player connecting the dots (using the pencil cursor) has connected dots 1-6, and has almost reached dot number 7. The other player (the arrow cursor) has raised a transparent menu over the first player.

We had three main implementation challenges when developing this SDG application. Although implementation of SDG is not the focus of this paper, we list these difficulties and how we solved them so that others wishing to replicate this (or similar) study can do so with less effort. These were:

- recognizing and treating multiple input devices,

- designing interface components that respond appropriately to multiple input devices, and
- implementing semi-transparent interface components.

Multiple Input Devices

As previously mentioned, conventional window and operating systems are not particularly adept at managing multiple input devices, particularly if they are mice. In many cases, it is up to the programmer to write device drivers that can interpret data generated by an input device attached to (say) a serial port e.g., as was done in MMM (Bier and Freeman, 1991).

Fortunately for us, Hourcade and Bederson (1999) developed MID—a dynamic link library and Java package running on Windows 98[1]—which implements an architecture that handles multiple Universal Serial Bus (USB) mice. MID extends the Java event mechanisms. In order to have access to multiple mice the standard Java events have to be replaced with the extended MID events. Programming with MID is very similar to programming with the Java events model. The main difference is that MID provides a unique mouse ID for each mouse seen by the system that can be retrieved when a mouse event occurs. In this sense, it is possible to know which mouse triggered the event, and to treat it accordingly. Consequently, our game was written in Java and used MID.

Interface Components that Recognize Multiple Mice

Each player can interact with the connect-the-dots game both simultaneously and independently of the other. Each player (and thus each mouse) is represented by its own cursor: a pencil for the first player who is connecting the dots, and an arrow for the second player who is raising the menu (Figure 2). Each player's actions are interpreted differently: a mouse press and drag by the first player draws a line, while for the second player it raises a menu and positions the cursor over an item.

To do this, we had to redesign and implement the interface components—the menu and the canvas—so they would recognize multiple mice. First, we assigned the drawing functionalities to $mouse_0$ and the menu functionalities to $mouse_1$. Second, we had to make the menu respond only to its owner's input. A player using $mouse_0$ should not be able to select from the menu raised by the other person, and should be able to continue to draw underneath it. Conversely the other player using $mouse_1$ should be able to raise a menu and make a selection from it while not affecting the drawing surface. Yet other shared interface components, such as the pull down menu and the buttons seen on the top and bottom of Figure 2, should respond to both players and consequently both mice.

---

[1] As far as we know, it is not possible to get separate input streams for multiple mice in Windows 2000.

While simple in concept, the problem is that no conventional widget set exists that recognizes multiple mice in this way[2]. This required us to completely re-implement the interface components to take mouse identification into consideration. For example, the SDG popup menu in Figure 2 is our own implementation, using a Java panel containing sub-panels, which in turn contains a label (the menu items). This meant that we had to code all visible effects corresponding to menu interactions, such as the raising of the menu and the highlighting of selected items. The component code also had to make a decision concerning each mouse event it saw. For example, when the menu received an event from $mouse_0$, we had to dispatch it to the drawing surface.

The necessity of redesigning interface components to handle situations such as these is one of the main obstacles to rapid SDG development. Quite simply, existing programming languages do not provide interface components that know how to deal with multiple inputs. This requires them to be redesigned from scratch, adding considerably to the burden of programming SDG systems.

Transparency

The third implementation issue was implementing transparency on the popup menu. Fortunately, Java implements an alpha level for every colour; this can be adjusted to control the transparency level of the drawn object. Because we had already re-implemented the popup menus, it was fairly straightforward to specify the alpha level of its constituent components. For example, our semi-transparent popup menu uses an alpha level of 70 selected from a range from 0-255 to draw the panel and its sub-panels: this makes it slightly more than 70% transparent. However, we leave the text labels opaque for better readability[3].

While reasonable in our case, we recognize that other languages and graphical widget sets may not provide this ability to do alpha-blending. This could lead to significant implementation difficulties and/or performance penalties.

User Study

We ran a controlled user study[4] in order to analyse the efficacy of semi-transparent popup menus when compared to opaque popup menus, using our SDG version of the "connecting the dots game". As we will describe below, we measured the level of interference that both types of menus create when users are

---

[2] SDG Widget development is on-going in several labs: our own at the University of Calgary; at Simon Fraser University (Shoemaker 2000); at the University of Maryland (Hourcade, Bederson, Druin 2000); and previously by Bricker, Baker and Tanimoto (1997).

[3] Harrison et al, (1995, 1996) offers special fonts customized for transparent situations, which we did not use as they were not necessary in our application.

[4] A brief description and preliminary analysis of the study was reported in (Zanella and Greenberg 2001).

doing their tasks as well as their levels of satisfaction. We focused the game towards the worst case of interference, i.e. where one user wanted to interfere with the other. While we do not normally expect SDG users to interfere intentionally with one another, we used this worst-case scenario to increase the number of interferences seen in a short time period, thus making it easier to measure the effect of the menu types.

Null Hypothesis

There is no difference in the *time* for a player to complete a connect-the-dots task or in player's *menu preferences* (as measured by a questionnaire) when playing in a *solo* condition (i.e., by oneself) or in the *opaque* and *semi-transparent* blocking condition (i.e., when an opponent tries to slow down the player by raising a menu of a given type in his or her way).

Subjects

We recruited and ran 30 pairs (60 subjects) in our study. Subjects were solicited from undergraduate and graduate programs at the University of Calgary. Subjects were asked to sign up in pairs, and as a result all but one pair were friends who knew each other. All appeared comfortable playing a competitive game with each other. All subjects were well versed with computers, mice, and popup menus. When asked about familiarity with SDG systems, most answered that they had played multi-user videogames before. Each person was paid CDN$10.

Materials

Our study situation used the SDG game and MID software as described previously running on Windows '98. Hardware included two USB mice, and a standard 1280x1024 19" display, and a modern PC. System performance was not an issue. The physical set up was similar to that seen in Figure 1, except that an observer was also seated behind both participants.

The Task

One subject, who we called *player*, was asked to connect 15 dots in numeric order as fast as possible. The player did this by drawing a line from one numbered dot to its successor using a left mouse button press and drag, and then marking each dot with an 'X' after it was connected by clicking on it with the right mouse button. A pencil distinguishes the player's mouse cursor (see Figures 2 and 3).

The other subject, the *interferer*, was asked to interfere or slow down the player as much as possible by popping up a menu in a location that would obscure the player's view of where to go or what to do. The interferer could raise the menu

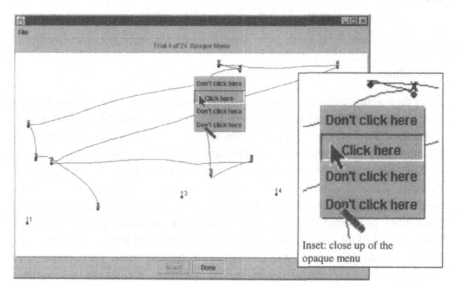

Figure 3 – The opaque menu version of the game. Notice that the player is 'blocked' by the interferer. While she can see her pencil cursor, she cannot see the next dot to connect as it is located on the drawing surface underneath the menu. See inset for detail.

in a given part of the display by right clicking over the desired position. The interferer was also instructed to quickly select the menu item labelled "Click here". This item was randomly positioned in the menu each time the menu was raised, as shown by the differences between Figures 2 and 3. These figures also show that the interferer's cursor is an arrow.

This was a competitive task. The player's goal was to connect all the dots as fast as possible, while the interferer's goal was to slow the player down as much as possible. To keep the game 'fair' for the interferer, we slowed down the player by requiring them to right-click each dot as it was connected. This mitigates those cases where the player is otherwise much faster than the interferer (which we saw in some of our pre-tests). Similarly, we instructed interferers to select the 'Click here' menu option as fast as possible; this guards against them indefinitely blocking the player.

Conditions

There were three different types of trial conditions in the test, where a trial consisted of a single connect-the-dots game.

> *Solo:* the player connected the dots alone, without any interference. This is our control: we expect players will have their best performance in this condition, and we do not expect that they could better this time on average.

> *Semi-transparent menus:* both player and interferer play, and the menus are semi-transparent (see Figure 2).

Opaque menus: both player and interferer play, and the menus are opaque (see Figure 3).

Procedure

After they signed a consent form, we administered a pre-test questionnaire to each pair to collect information about their abilities with computer, mouse, popup menus and SDG systems. Each person in the pair was then randomly assigned to be either the player or the interferer. They kept these roles across all trials.

Each pair played 24 games divided into 8 sets. Each set contains the three different game conditions—solo, semi-transparent, and opaque—presented in randomized order. Each game displayed 15 dots to be connected. As the dots were randomly repositioned for every game, no two games were identical for each pair. All pairs played the same games in the same order but in different conditions.

We considered the first set of three games as training trials, where players and interferers could explore the system and ask questions. We did not include these trials in the analysis.

For the remaining seven sets, we recorded the total time the player took to connect all the dots in a game. We also recorded the number of interferences as the number of times a popup menu was opened on the top of the player's immediate working area. While not part of the study hypothesis, this later data is used to check for situations where gross performance differences exist between the player and the interferer. We also observed the reactions, behaviours, expectations, comments and strategies of participants.

After playing all the games, the participants answered a post-session questionnaire that asked them about their menu preferences and how the menu types affected their tasks.

Results

We watched all the pairs as they played. We wanted to observe their reactions, behaviours, expectations, comments and strategies.

All pairs engaged with the task. They appeared comfortable playing a competitive game. Interferers delighted in blocking the player's view, and both tried to trick each other by developing game strategies. All played in an appropriate manner, i.e. the player connected a dot before going to the next, all the dots were connected before starting a new game, the interferer was selecting the right option from the menu and did not leave the menu opened for a long period of time, etc.

Performance

We analyzed how long the player took to connect the dots across the different trial conditions. As mentioned previously, this gives an indication of the efficacy of each menu type as contrasted to each other and to the solo control. We collapsed the data within each pair into an average time / condition type. To get a sense of this data, we first compared how each pair faired over these conditions. In almost all cases, the average within-subject time relationships when performing these conditions are: solo < transparent < opaque. A single factor ANOVA shows that these differences are statistically significant ($F=16.36$, $p<0.05$). A post-hoc t-test shows statistically significant differences between every condition. Thus the null hypothesis is rejected. Figure 4 illustrates these differences by displaying the average performance time and standard deviation to complete a game for all subjects in each condition.

We performed a few other analyses to look for any hidden effects that could have influenced our results. First, it is entirely possible that people's performance changed over time, perhaps due to learning or fatigue. We analyse each trial type separately, where we calculated the average time for completing a particular game in a particular trial. Results are graphed in Figure 5.

In this graph, we do see a small increase in performance time over the first few games. This is likely a learning effect, where people are getting used to the mechanics of playing i.e., which mouse button to click, how to search for the next number and so on. However, what is immediately obvious by visual inspection is that the average time to complete a particular game is still solo < transparent < opaque. That is, it is unlikely that the statistical differences seen in our analysis are confounded due to some relative performance change in the game over time.

We calculated the average number of interferences per game in each condition, to analyse the relation between interference and performance (Figure 6). While

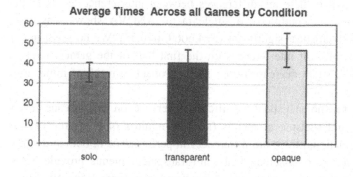

Figure 4 – Average performance time to complete a game for all subjects by each condition. Standard deviation is shown in each bar.

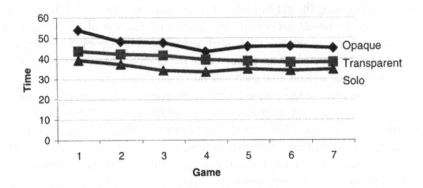

Figure 5 – Average time for players to complete a particular game in a particular trial.

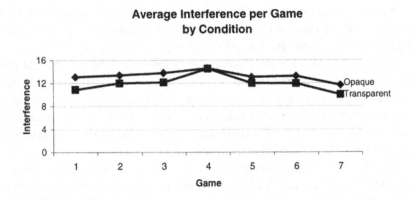

Figure 6 - Average number of interferences per game in a particular trial type.

the graph suggests that there are differences between interference levels in the opaque and transparent conditions, a single factor ANOVA shows that these differences are not statistical significant (F=4.6069, p=0.53). We do see a minor increase in the number of interferences on the first half of the games, likely a learning effect. The slight decrease in the end is probably a result of minor user fatigue.

Although we see no statistical significant difference on interference levels between opaque and transparent menus (i.e., the number of interferences was similar in both situations) there are differences in performance in both situations. These results lead us to conclude that semi-transparent menus provide better performance than opaque menus when interference occurs. However, semi-transparent menus do not eliminate all interference effects, as performance is not quite as fast as in the solo control condition.

Preferences

Through our post-session questionnaire, both the player and the interferer stated their opinions and preferences in terms of how the menus affected their task.

Using a five-point scale, with opaque on one side and transparent on the other, we asked subjects which type of menu they preferred in the SDG situation (i.e., without regard to their player or interferer role). Their responses strongly indicate a preference for transparent menus over opaque ones, as illustrated in Table 1. 34 of the 60 subjects strongly preferred transparent menus, and 9 more had a weak preference. Only 10 of the 60 liked the opaque menus.

Of course, these preferences could depend on whether one was a player (where transparency helped) or an interferer (where it hindered). Using a three-point scale, we then asked subjects how the different menus affected their particular task when acting as player or interferer. In these responses, tabulated in Table 2, almost all players thought that transparent menus made it easier for them to continue their work in spite of interference (28 of the 30 players). On the flip side, almost all interferers thought that transparent menus made it harder for them to interfere with the players (25 of the 30 interferers). While these results are not analyzed statistically, they obviously enforce our rejection of the null hypothesis.

Opaque				*Transparent*
Strong	Weak	Neutral	Weak	Strong
7	3	7	9	34

Table 1: Which type of menu do you prefer (all subjects)?

Players				*Interferers*		
Easier	Same	Harder		Easier	Same	Harder
28	2	0		0	5	25

Table 2: How do transparent menus help your task?

Qualitative Observations

We watched all pairs as they played in all conditions, and interviewed them afterwards. We saw that the pairs quickly engaged with the game, and became very competitive over time.

It was obvious that players greatly preferred the transparent to the opaque menus because it was easier and faster for them to connect the dots. As one player commented:

"After a while I did not even see the transparent menus anymore, it was like I learnt how to ignore them..."

Players become frustrated when they were blocked with an opaque menu. As one player exclaimed to an interferer who was taking their time selecting the item from the opaque menu: "Can you make your selection faster?"

As one would expect, the interferers preferred playing in the opaque over the transparent menu condition because it helped them block the player. This exchange, occurring at the beginning of an opaque menu game, highlights how a one pair's reaction:

Interferer: "I am going to bug you now!"
Player: "I hate these opaque menus!"

One specific pair (a boyfriend who was a computer scientist and girlfriend who was not) was very competitive. As a player, she celebrated every time a dot was connected under the transparent menu. As the interferer, he was noticeably excited when the opaque menus came up, and kept making fun of her when the popup menu blocked her view. In the end of the game, she playfully asked him to give her all the money he had earned; because she had done very well in spite of his merciless teasing, she felt she deserved it.

In informal post-test interviews, one subject said he really liked the semi-transparent menus in SDG, and that he would also want them even in a single user application. He explained:

"Sometimes when you are making a search on [Microsoft] Word the result is positioned near the *find window,* so you have to move the window if you want to see the text related to the search. [Similarly,] the window to format text, to change a colour or font type, usually covers the text you are modifying ... sometimes you open the window and you forget if you selected the right text."

We also observed that most players moved very quickly when playing in the opaque menus situation, for they wanted to minimize the actual times that the interferer raised the menu over their position. Although we told them to connect the dots as fast as they could, the players appeared more relaxed in the solo situation since they knew no interference would happen. We saw a similar relaxed attitude in the semi-transparent situation after players played a few games, probably because they knew they could still continue their job in spite of the interferer's best efforts. While this apparent speed-up in the opaque menus could have confounded our results, we still see that, on average, it took longer for players to complete games with the opaque menus (Figure 4). That is, the differences between conditions still exist *in spite of* the player's best effort to overcome the interferer.

We also saw that most of the pairs developed strategies of play after a few games. At first, interferers moved their cursors by the next point to be connected, and then popped up the menu when the player arrived at that spot. After some time they realized they were sometimes helping the player, as it showed the player where the next point was. To offset this, the interferer moved their cursors around while waiting, or just following the players' cursors before 'pouncing' on them.

Some of the players tried to counteract this by first moving their cursors *away* from the correct dot (in order to 'fake out' the interferer into moving in the wrong direction) before quickly moving their cursor back to it. When this strategy worked, the interferer was unable to respond as quickly as normal. However, the relatively flat performance curve over all games (displayed in Figure 5) suggests that these opposing strategies counterbalanced each other over time, and they likely did not confound our results.

Discussion

Our results suggest that semi-transparent interface components can mitigate interference in Single Display Groupware. This is promising indeed, for it means that the existing genre of popup components (e.g., menus, windows, dialogue boxes, floating palettes) can be adapted to SDG, and that people can use these well-known techniques to interact with SDG systems. The only real difference is that users can see through them, and that they have to understand what component is their own and which belongs to others. From our observations, we saw that people quickly adapted to transparent components, and had no problem manipulating them or working underneath them. While 'standard' interface components would have to be redeveloped in order to work within SDG and to display themselves semi-transparently, the basic interaction technique remains the same. Ideally, transparency in SDG is only a programming issue rather than an interface issue.

However, we recognize that the situation we tested was simple, and that there is a danger of over-generalizing our results to all SDG situations.

First, we used only two users in a very controlled situation, and we are uncertain about what would happen if three or more collaborators were interacting simultaneously. For example, it may be possible for several semi-transparent components to be raised atop of each other.

Second, we tested the worst case of interference, where one user intentionally tried to interfere with the other. Actual interferences in every-day SDG situations are probably far less numerous. If good feedback were provided to collaborators about what others intended to do, social protocols would likely lessen the number of actual interferences. People are, in fact, quite adept at informing others about possible conflicts and at mediating turn-taking when contention is unavoidable. Still there are times that collaborators in SDG cannot avoid interference. For example, one person may popup up a menu or dialog box without realizing that others would be affected. Or the system may have to raise a large error window, but there may be no place to position it that would not cause interference. Even if people do mediate their actions by resorting to turn-taking, we suspect that this sequential rather than simultaneous access to the space will lessen the amount of collaborations and people's feeling of satisfaction (Inkpen, Ho-Ching, Kuederle, Scott and Shoemaker 1999).

Third, we used a 1280x1024 resolution standard monitor as our shared display. Yet the probability of interference may decrease for larger, higher resolution screens (because people have more space to do their work), and increase for smaller ones (because people will likely contend for the same area).

Fourth, the interface component we tested—the menu—is fairly small and usually does not stay long on the screen. Larger and longer-lasting interface components, such as a dialog box, could create more interference problems to users. For example, a 'save as' dialog box is quite large, and it often takes considerable time for a person to find the right folder and type the name of a file. In these cases, transparency could be even more helpful.

Fifth, our game used a foreground and background conducive to transparency. Excepting the drawing marks and the numbered dots, the background was fairly sparse. Thus it was easy to separate visually the text of the menu from the background objects. As Harrison et al (1995, 1996) noticed, backgrounds rich in visual information—pictures, contrasting colours, dense text—may make the visual separation of the layers difficult. Similarly, complex foreground objects may be difficult to separate from the background e.g. the many fields of a complex dialog box. While there are a few design techniques within transparency that help make certain items stand out, these are still in their infancy (Harrison et al 1995, 1996).

In summary, our transparency approach is successful in our test conditions, and we believe they are promising as a way to minimize interference in SDG applications. Users reacted positively to the semi-transparent popup menus, mentioning that the idea could also be applied to other widgets and even non-SDG settings. Still, we recognize that real-world factors can that both increase or decrease the benefits of this technique. To truly understand these factors and their effects, we need to develop serious SDG applications, deploy them into real situations, and study what happens.

Conclusions

There are many issues involved in SDG development. Some are technical, for example, how multiple input devices are seen by the operating system and how programming languages support them. Other problems are related to the design of interface components that are adequate for several users sharing the same screen, such as recognizing multiple users' input and responding accordingly to each input.

In our study we investigated interference as one particular interface problem in SDG. We offered semi-transparent interface components as a way to mitigate interference effects. We then created a 'worst case' of interference, where one person intentionally tries to interfere and slow down another person by blocking him or her with popup menus. As our test results show, our approach of using transparency is appropriate for dealing with interference in our SDG situation. Although our setting was somewhat simplistic, we believe the idea of transparency could be generalized to a certain extent to other SDG applications.

Acknowledgments

Thanks for Ben Bederson and Juan-Pablo Hourcade from the University of Maryland for graciously allowing us to use their MID software. We also thank our research participants for participating in the study, as well as all Grouplab researchers for their input. We are grateful to Microsoft Research, the Alberta Software and Engineering Research Consortium (ASERC), the National Sciences and Engineering Research Council of Canada (NSERC) and Smart Technologies who provided funding, some equipment, and encouragement.

References

Benford, S., Bederson, B., Akesson., K., Bayon, V., Druin, D., Hansson, P., Hourcade, J., Ingram, R., Neale, H., O'Malley, C., Simsarian, K., Stanton, D., Sundblad, Y., and Taxen, G. (2000) 'Designing storytelling technologies to encourage collaboration between young children', *Proc ACM Conf Human Factors in Computing Systems (CHI'00)*, pp. 556-563, ACM Press.

Bier, E. and Freeman, S. (1991) 'MMM: A user interface architecture for shared editors on a single screen', *Proc 4th annual ACM Symposium on User Interface Software and Technology*, pp. 79-86, ACM Press.

Bricker, L., Baker, M., Tanimoto, S. (1997) 'Support for cooperatively controlled objects in multimedia applications', *Extended Abstracts of the ACM Conf Human Factors in Computing Systems* (CHI'97), pp.313-314, ACM Press.

Cox, D., Chugh, J., Gutwin, C. and Greenberg, S. (1998) 'The usability of transparent overview layers', *Summary Proc ACM Conf Human Factors in Computing Systems (CHI'98)*, pp. 301-302, ACM Press.

Druin, A., Stewart, J., Proft, D., Bederson, B. and Hollan, J. (1997) 'KidPad: a design collaboration between children, technologists, and educators', *Proc ACM Conf Human Factors in Computing Systems (CHI'97)*, pp. 463-470, ACM Press.

Greenberg, S., Boyle, M. and LaBerge, J. (1999). 'PDAs and shared public displays: making personal information public, and public information personal', *Personal Technologies*, vol. 3, no.1, March, pp. 54-64.

Greenberg, S., Gutwin, C. and Cockburn, A. (1996) 'Using distortion-oriented displays to support workspace awareness', In A. Sasse, R. Cunningham and R. Winder (eds.): *People and Computers XI*, pp. 299-314, Springer-Verlag.

Gutwin, C. and Greenberg, S. (1998) 'Design for individuals, design for groups: tradeoffs between power and workspace awareness', *Proc ACM Conf Computer Supported Cooperative Work (CSCW'98)*, pp. 207-216, ACM Press.

Harrison, B. and Vicente, K. (1996) 'An experimental evaluation of transparent menu usage', *Proc ACM Conf Human Factors in Computing Systems (CHI'96)*, pp. 391-398, ACM Press.

Harrison, B., Ishii, H., Vicente, K. and Buxton, W. (1995) 'Transparent layered user interfaces: an evaluation of a display design to enhance focused and divided attention', *Proc ACM Conf Human Factors in Computing Systems (CHI'95)*, pp. 317-324, ACM Press.

Hourcade, J. and Bederson, B. (1999). 'Architecture and implementation of a Java package for multiple input devices (MID)', Report HCIL-99-08, Computer Science Dept, University of Maryland, MD USA.

Hourcade, J., Bederson, B. and Druin, A. (2000) 'QueryKids: a collaborative digital library application for children', *Workshop on Shared Environments to Support Face-to-Face Collaboration*, held at ACM CSCW'00.
http://www.edgelab.sfu.ca/CSCW/ shared_environments.html

Inkpen, K., Ho-Ching, W., Kuederle, O., Scott, S and Shoemaker, G. (1999) 'This is fun! We're all best friends and we're playing', *Proc ACM Conf Computer Supported Collaborative Learning (CSCL'99)*, pp. 252-259, ACM Press.

Inkpen, K., McGrenere, J., Booth, K., and Klawe, M. (1997). 'The effect of turn-taking protocols on children's learning in mouse-driven collaborative environments', *Proc Graphics Interface (GI'97)*, pp. 138-145, Morgan Kaufmann Publishers.

Myers, B., Stiel, H. and Gargiulo, R. (1998) 'Collaboration using multiple PDAs connected to a PC', *Proc ACM Conf Computer-Supported Cooperative Work (CSCW'98)*, pp. 285-294, ACM Press.

Nunamaker, J., Dennis, A., Valacich, J., Vogel, D. and George, J. (1991) 'Electronic meeting systems to support group work', *Communications of the ACM*, vol. 34, no. 7, July, pp. 40-61, ACM Press.

Rekimoto, J. (1998) 'A multiple device approach for supporting whiteboard-based interactions', Proc ACM Conf Human Factors Computing Systems (CHI'98), pp. 344-351, ACM Press.

Scott, S., Shoemaker, G. and Inkpen, K. (2000) 'Towards seamless support of natural collaborative interactions', *Proc of Graphics Interface (GI'00)*, pp. 103-110, Morgan Kaufmann Publishers.

Shoemaker, G. (2000) 'Supporting private information on public displays', *Extended Abstracts ACM Conf Human Factors and Computing Systems (CHI'00)*, pp. 349-350, ACM Press.

Stefik, M., Foster, G., Bobrow, D., Kahn, K., Lanning, S. and Suchman, L. (1987) 'Beyond the Chalkboard: computer support for collaboration and problem solving meetings', *Communications of the ACM*, vol. 30, no. 1, pp. 32-47, ACM Press.

Stewart, J., Bederson, B. and Druin, A. (1999) 'Single display groupware: a model for co-present collaboration', *Proc ACM Conf Human Factors in Computing Systems (CHI'99)*, pp. 286-293, ACM Press.

Stewart, J., Raybourn, E., Bederson, B. and Druin, A. (1998) 'When two hands are better than one: enhancing collaboration using single display groupware', *Extended Abstracts of the ACM Conf Human Factors in Computing Systems (CHI'98)*, pp. 287-288, ACM Press.

Tang, J. (1991) 'Findings from observational studies of collaborative work', In S. Greenberg (ed): *Computer support cooperative work and groupware*, pp. 11- 26, Academic Press.

Whittaker, S. and O'Conaill, B. (1997) 'The role of vision in face-to-face and mediated communication', In K. Finn, A. Sellen and S. Wilbur (eds): *Video-Mediated Communications*. LEA Press.

Zanella, A and Greenberg, S (2001) 'Avoiding interference through translucent interface components in single display groupware', *Extended Abstracts of the ACM Conf Human Factors in Computing Systems (CHI'2001)*, pp. 375-376, ACM Press.

W. Prinz, M. Jarke, Y. Rogers, K. Schmidt, and V. Wulf (eds.), *Proceedings of the Seventh European Conference on Computer-Supported Cooperative Work, 16-20 September 2001, Bonn, Germany*, pp. 359-378.

Harnessing Complexity in CSCW

Simon Kaplan, Lesley Seebeck

School of Computer Science and Electrical Engineering, The University of Queensland, Australia

s.kaplan@csee.uq.edu.au; lesley@csee.uq.edu.au

Abstract. We argue that socio-technical systems can be understood as *complex adaptive systems*, that is, systems containing component sub-systems interacting such that they co-evolve. This viewpoint may allow us to understand more clearly the factors that underlie the complexities of socio-technical systems, and allows for a new approach to systems design predicated on unpredictable adaptive processes. System designers, we argue, need to seek to understand the underlying structures, drivers and nature of change within the system and of the system as a whole. This paper presents an outline of the complexity mechanisms that operate within socio-technical systems, and illustrates the concepts and system design implications by way of a case.

Introduction

The challenge of CSCW is the challenge of designing better *socio-technical systems*: systems that involve a mixture of humans and machines such that the components cannot be separated, or are thought to be inappropriate to separate (OUP, 1996). Such systems have proven to be enormously difficult to understand and design (Grudin, 1988, 1994). There are many reasons for this. Understanding and designing for such systems is a wicked problem (Rittel et al., 1973), and the work and activities carried out in such a system are highly contingent and emergent (Seely Brown et al., 2000; Suchman, 1987). However, as Rodden and Blair (1991) pointed out, computer-based systems require some regularities as the basis from which computer systems can be built.

It's therefore useful to look for alternate ways of understanding socio-technical systems in the belief that this will lead to better perspectives from which to provide computer-based support. The particular perspective we adopt here is that socio-technical systems are part of the larger set of systems known as 'complex adaptive systems' (Axelrod et al., 1999). This is an evolutionary perspective, which argues that systems grow by processes of variation, interaction and selection. The problem is complicated by the fact that we are dealing invariably with multiple, interacting systems. Therefore we also need to consider concepts of co-evolution (several systems influencing each other's evolutionary paths) and self-organization (how new systems grow out from old). It is also important to take appropriate account of the role of time in evolution, as the rate of evolution is different for (parts of) different systems, and this, too, can have a profound effect.

From this we distil a systems-oriented view of CSCW systems design. This view extends our prior work on aspect-oriented approaches to systems understanding and design (Fitzpatrick, 1998; Fitzpatrick et al., 1995; Fitzpatrick et al., 1996; Kaplan et al., 1997), and provides a foundation for capturing and reusing useful 'design tricks' (Dennett, 1995) based on the concept of pattern languages (Alexander, 1979; Alexander et al., 1977).

We begin the paper with a case study, and then introduce the notion of complex adaptive systems, ideas of co-evolution and self-organization in complex systems, and discuss the role of time in complex systems evolution. We argue for our perspective on systems design, reflecting on the case study before concluding.

Case

To illustrate the points we will make below, we introduce here a case study: the growth and evolution of the University's IT systems over more than 35 years. The case is based on the personal recollections of staff involved in the changes described, documentation and the personal experience of the authors. One point to note is that while many reports of field study in the CSCW field focus on small details in work practice, systems thinking tends to focus more on big picture issues, thereby complementing other forms of study.

In the 1960s scattered groups of researchers developed, or gained access to, small computing systems for specific research or teaching activities. In the late 1960s the University assisted the engineering department to purchase a large system, on which it was allowed to bill out excess capacity. As this usage grew, the computer group spun out into a separate Computing Centre. Discontent with the service provided by the Centre – including their lack of understanding of other work environments and needs, and subsequent non-responsiveness – led to other units within the university seeking their own technology solutions. Over the subsequent two decades, no fewer than five formal independent IT organizations and systems were established within the university: the original Computing Centre; the library; student administration; finance; and human resources. Consequently, the university had five stand-alone corporate systems, each staffed separately, using three different database technologies and two different operating systems. All these systems could not interoperate. There were also a myriad of systems of varying size, capability and interoperability to be found in academic departments and research programs, and a complex web of social and personal interactions that supported the sharing of information, war stories and warnings among the technical support staffs that grew up in each group.

In the late 1990s resource constraints, the impossibility of any further evolution of the existing corporate systems due to technology constraints, and the need to take account of the Internet, led organizational units to seek a massive shift in information technologies. A 1998 report signalled the deliberate centralization of backbone and corporate support under a revamped Computing Centre, renamed Computing Information Services (CIS), and a higher IT management profile in the university, with key executives appointed responsible for CIS and the Library. The looming Y2K problem was frequently employed as a justification for rapid shifts in technology. Since 1998, corporate email, the student administration system and shortly the human resource system will have been completely rebuilt and migrated to centralized control under CIS.

The individual corporate systems have their own histories. The student administration system is typical. The initial student system was built in-house and evolved over two decades. It was highly restrictive, running on a mainframe, could support only a very limited number of concurrent users, and could not interoperate with other systems. This encouraged the growth of separate faculty, departmental and even course-based records to ensure redundancy and access for non-central staff, in spite of the associated expense. (Exactly the same occurs for finance records within departments.) In the late 1990s, the student system was given a facelift, with a simple web-based interface and shadow database to allow limited access to information by students. All this software was written and maintained by a small technical support staff in the administrative services area.

After the 1998 report recommending centralization, the University decided to move to a COTS-based student record system, called s2000, and hired the same company that had successfully developed and installed this system in another major Australian university. The s2000 system has forced profound changes to the university's business processes and systems. These have included subject and degree restructuring, and significant procedural changes throughout the University. While such change has been difficult, universal access to a single source of student information is now possible, eliminating the need for much duplication, and students can now access their records, and enrol online. Managing the system is beyond the expertise available in the administrative directorate. The adoption of s2000, then, generated greater impetus to the centralization of services under CIS as well as changes to the University's way of doing business, the ramifications of which are not yet understood.

An unexpected side effect of this change has been a shift in the role of CIS. From being the major provider of student computing it has shifted to back-office, server and infrastructure services, and controlling standards. Client (student) access has been devolved to departments (for course-specific needs) or the library (for general web access, email clients, helpdesk, etc.). CIS's remaining direct contact with students is limited to provision of ISP services.

One area has remained largely untouched and unregulated through all these changes: teaching and learning. That's surprising, given that teaching and learning is a core business of any university and that in 1995 and 2000 the University engaged in significant academic restructuring to foster change. To promote online delivery, the University adopted WebCT as a standard, but issues concerning technical and development support, reliability and security remain fraught, so limiting its implementation. This in some ways parallels the late 1980s, where every group in the University built its own network and client/ server strategies. That infrastructure is now managed (or standardized) centrally, but every group is developing its own different way of using web-based services.

Complex Adaptive Systems

The thesis of this paper is based on the insight that socio-technical systems are an example of *complex adaptive systems* (hereafter, simply systems) (Axelrod et al., 1999). Complex systems are difficult to understand, explain and predict because, following Axelrod and Cohen, they 'consist of parts which interact in ways that heavily influence the probabilities of later events' (p. 15). In other words, complexity is a systems property similar to *wickedness* and is closely related to the notion of emergence. 'Complexity' contrasts with 'complicated', which means that although a system has many components, it is simply explained.

Complex adaptive systems comprise populations of *entities*. Entities can be *agents* that act (and interact) to achieve various goals through employment of *strategies* of various kinds, and *artefacts* and *tools* that can be manipulated in various ways as part of these strategies.

These systems are in a continual state of change through processes of *variation, interaction* and *selection* (discussed below). Simply put, variation is the business of changing the population of agents, strategies or artefacts; interaction is to do with the ways that the various elements of a system interact with and influence each other; and selection is to do with how and why some elements of a system survive over time while others are allowed to die out.

Any entity can potentially participate in many systems, for example an agent can be a staff member in an organization, a member of professional societies, etc. Information picked up in one system can be used to foster variation, change selection strategies, passed on through interaction, and so forth, in another. Indeed, it is these interactions across systems that seem to be a key trigger for adaptation in socio-technical systems (Seely Brown et al., 2000).

Variation

There are generally two ways to vary a population, *exploitation* and *exploration*. In exploitation, the variation among systems elements is kept as small as possible, in order to leverage established advantages (for example, a particularly useful tool, or a way of manipulating staff to accomplish a certain outcome, or hiring new agents with particular training). In exploration, new elements are created in order to experiment with alternatives (for example a new strategy, a different tool or agent). Exploitation, then, takes advantages of previously discovered good design tricks, while exploration opens the possibility of uncovering new design tricks that turn out to be effective.

Both these kinds of variations showed up in our case study. For example, at the departmental level if one department successfully implemented a piece of technology, such as a LAN, then another department might well build an almost-identical LAN, thereby exploiting the first group's success. When the University decided to build a new corporate student management system, it chose to bring in entirely new COTS technology. From the viewpoint of the technology base previously at the University, this was quite radical exploration of a new possibility. But the University hired a company that had done this before, to assist implementation, so exploiting a previous success and mitigating its risk.

Obviously, creating new agents or strategies at random is unlikely to be a successful strategy. One popular trick is *recombination*, where parts of existing, entities are combined together (possibly with some 'new' aspects) to create an entity that is likely to be viable yet allows exploration of something new.

The balance between exploration and exploitation in a system can have a profound impact on its ability to survive. Following exploitation-only variation strategies can work in the short term if a system is well adapted to current conditions, but can be disastrous if conditions change. On the other hand exploration can be very expensive so there is a natural tendency to avoid it until it is forced in some way (in our case, by resource constraints, reaching the limits of technology, and the spectre of the Y2K problem).

Interaction

Interactions are literally the ways in which the entities in the system interact with one another. Through interaction activities, and thus eventually adaptation, occur in the system. Examples are the ways in which interactions shape the behaviour of the agents working in Underground Control Rooms (Heath et al., 1992), or among groups of systems administrators (Fitzpatrick et al., 1996). Systems tend to have distinctive interaction patterns that, while not random, also are not regular – they are complex and continually changing.

An interesting question for us is understanding how these patterns of interaction change over time. Whereas ethnographic approaches tend to look to uncover the detail of interaction, we are looking here more at changes over time – the two approaches thus tend to complement one another.

Pressures for change can be external or internal. External pressures modify the system from the outside, such as forced changes to artefacts or policies governing rules of behaviour. Internal changes can be driven by *proximity* – the 'nearness' of entities to each other in some kind of physical, virtual or conceptual space. For example, co-located office workers develop similar cultures and worldviews, as do workers who are distributed but have similar tasks (Seely Brown et al., 2000). Entry to these spaces can be restricted or open, and where restricted the barriers can be physical or virtual, and made semi-permeable by rules, conventions, etc.

Following often drives change in interaction patterns. One important kind of following is 'agent following', where one copies or follows another agent, such as master-apprentice relationships, mentoring, and recommender systems. Another is 'signal following', where one follows a discernable signal, such as teenagers copying what is 'cool' in a subculture, staff moving to companies with higher rates of pay, students choosing a University based on perceptions of a 'quality' education. Both leverage prior effort, especially where it is hard to make a judgment or develop knowledge firsthand.

Temporal aspects of interaction, including activation, sequencing, periodicity and phasing, also are important. Interaction may be triggered externally. Budget cycles, parliamentary sittings, and conferences deadlines may trigger and so to some extent control the activities and interactions in a system. Interaction also may be triggered internally, by everything from receipt of a memo or email, to meetings, conversations and serendipitous hallway interactions.

Barriers of various kinds – cultural, physical or virtual – can limit the flow of information by interaction. In our case, as the Computing Centre focused inward, so barriers at all levels began to grow up. Technical support staff moved into offices protected by swipe cards, so physical access became intimidating and difficult. A culture of not responding to email or requests for help became endemic (more because of pressure of work than deliberate decision). Interaction between the Computing Centre staff and other staff became limited as a result. Communities of IT support practice in departments evolved independently, with only occasional and minimal interaction with the Computing Centre staff. Over time lack of communication damaged the ability of the IT community to deliver the best possible solutions, anticipate and avoid problems, or even agree on common workstation specifications in order to get bulk discount pricing.

Like the entities in a system, interaction patterns need to be able to change if the system is to remain viable and adapt to changing circumstances. Too much internal interaction within organizations or occupational and social groups can lead to exclusive exploitation of known successful approaches, leading to rutted processes and groupthink, with consequences for those groups' ability to adapt.

Selection

Over time the interaction patterns and entities in a system will vary. If the populations in a system are large enough, some entities or patterns will be allowed to try to grow and flourish, while others will die or be suppressed. The process of determining what should be allowed to live or die is termed selection.

Selection is relative to success criteria, which are usually performance measures. For example we might measure efficiency for certain tasks, or the return on certain kinds of investment, or the publication rate of a young academic.

Selection can operate at the agent or strategy level, or a combination. In order to decide the appropriate level, it must be possible to attribute success to agents and/or strategies. For example, if we decide that agents are crucial, then we are likely to reward and/or reproduce the agents. If we decide strategies are important we may decide to reproduce them. Thus in one organization success may be attributed to the individual managers of successful groups, while in another the managers may be seen as interchangeable and expendable, and the 'company culture' attributed with success.

Using our case as an example, once the University decided to purchase a COTS student administration solution, there were three ways to proceed. They could have chosen to purchase the system and get a team that had worked with it before (this is an example of selecting both strategy and agents). They could have chosen to purchase the system and implement it with an in-house team (this is an example of selecting the strategy only). Or they could have chosen a team of excellent IT personnel who had worked on a particular piece of relevant technology before, and had them implement the system with different technology (this is an example of selecting the agents). The University chose the first approach, which is clearly low-risk, exploiting as it does both people and technology that have proven to be successful in the past. But in other circumstances other mixtures of agents and strategy could be more appropriate. For example, our school at the University moved into a new building three years ago and installed a very expensive ATM network. The network proved to be difficult to manage and expand, as well as expensive to run and rather slow, so we chose to replace it by a gigabit Ethernet. This decision was made largely because a gigabit Ethernet had been recently installed in a large research centre with which we have close links, and a junior system administrator had just been hired from that centre. So we had a working technology solution to copy, and links to the appropriate agents to help us out. In this case we selected a strategy, not the agents that had implemented it, and used signal following to make it work for us.

Co-Evolution and Systems Structure

Thus far we have introduced the notion of complex adaptive systems, and argued that they adapt by following evolutionary processes of variation, interaction and selection. Clearly, complex adaptive systems do not live in a vacuum. Any such system is likely to be recursively composed of sub-systems, each of which is likely itself to be complex, and to be itself part of a larger network of systems.

Stuart Kauffman (1995) has been studying the structure of such systems-of-systems, with a view to understanding under what conditions adaptation is more or less likely to occur. To understand his argument, consider the situation of a system that exists entirely in isolation. A certain amount of variation through exploitation and exploration will be possible, but because there are no external factors impacting on the system, it is likely to tend to a 'steady state' in which there will be no discernable benefit in further adaptation.

Of course, systems do not exist in isolation. Any adaptation in one system can create the possibility of adaptation in another. Thus variation in one system will tend to trigger variations in the systems with which it is interdependent. The resulting continuous flow of adaptation called *co-evolution,* and is necessary for the systems to remain fit relative to each other (Van Valen, 1973).

In socio-technical systems the interactions among agents that exist in many systems simultaneously is often a key driver for this. There are many examples of such behaviour ready at hand. In our case study, the decision of the University to centralize IT core services in the CIS group, coupled with general unhappiness at the level of client service provided by that group, created the opportunity for the library to expand into client-side computing services, which in turn led to the growth of a rich family of new online information resources. In many ways this is also an example of signal following, as similar initiatives had been successful elsewhere. The results have been adaptations in the library's budget, staffing and collection profiles. Each of these is triggering adaptations in the various subsystems making up the library. For example, the library now has a large IT group which continually seeks to expand, usually through attempting to provide new services, or take over those previously located elsewhere.

With co-evolution, each subsystem always will seek to achieve the best possible local situation through adaptation, even if this is to the detriment of the larger systems in which it is embedded. While this might seem harsh or unrealistic, it appears to be borne out in practice. For example, we have come across instances of this kind of co-evolution in action, where different parts of an organization locally optimise in ways that are detrimental to other parts.

Thus, in one (unpublished) real-world situation we have studied, the support part of an organization used to hire junior software developers to man the help desk. The advantages of the practice to the system as a whole included a better understanding of customer needs, both internal and external, and so improved product and system support. As these people became more experienced with the systems, they migrated to maintenance and then development groups. This is a fine example of interaction – signal and agent following – working within and across systems, and an example of a selection policy that benefited the company as a whole. Recently, the helpdesk manager chose to stop hiring software developers, because of problems with turnover and training, and instead promote administrative staff to the helpdesk. His rationale was that these people had a limited career path and thus were more likely to stay in place. This has had an impact elsewhere in the company, reducing the quality of programming staff and increasing training costs.

What is happening here is that each subsystem is locally optimising through adaptation, causing the entire organizational system to co-evolve, even if that is not to the overall benefit of the organization as a whole. In this particular case, we see an example of poor selection strategies – the success criterion that the helpdesk manager has chosen is lowest possible staff churn in his group, rather than best intellectual standard over the company as a whole. Ironically, in this case, lowering staff turnover enhanced the manager's performance bonus, an example of poor selection strategies higher up in the organization.

Kauffman further discovered that *size* (by some appropriate measure) is of paramount importance in how well systems can adapt. It turns out that if the systems are too large, they tend to become locked in some form of stasis, while if they are too small the system-of-systems in which they are embedded tends to chaos. Intuitively, this seems reasonable: an organization that manages everything centrally is usually inefficient and unwieldy; an organization that gives everyone too much autonomy is chaotic; but with the right group size and interdependencies, decentralized organizations can operate reasonably well.

The question of what constitutes a good size (or even size measure) for a group is not simple. Kauffman's simple mathematical models don't map directly into socio-technical systems, not least because organizational sub-units (people, users, work-groups) are themselves inherently more complex (Morel et al., 1999) than Kauffman's models. Still, for organizations there are good intuitive 'sizes' for systems: group sizes within successful organizations are a good starting point. The academic restructuring of the University, for example, turned a large number of small and fiercely independent departments into a smaller number of larger schools. Time will tell whether the departments were too small before and thus overly chaotic, or if the centralization will create a system in which schools are too large for their own good and thus tend to stasis.

What about technology? If we consider any fairly complex system the same extremes seem to apply. Large-scale pieces of technology (for example the University's corporate information systems) are notoriously unable to adapt. Many small pieces of technology that can change independently lead to chaos. Between these extremes lie interesting systems sizes.

Thus at our University, initially, the sole computer system was controlled by a central group. This proved to be too clumsy and unresponsive, so departments started to build their own computing systems for teaching and research, then their own LANS. The result was chaotic – the various systems were too small and poorly managed, and the various adaptations that took place, usually as a result of signal or agent following (copying a successful system in a sister department, for example) tended to deepen this chaos. There was little or no reflection on the variation and selection strategies that were in play, and no selection pressure either to reflect or to seek consensus solutions. Now a seemingly successful balance has been struck where certain core infrastructure services (the WAN, standards for interoperability, campus-wide servers and services) are maintained by CIS, and departments can build local subsystems as needed.

Self-organization

But how do sub-systems arise? Kauffman argues they appear spontaneously (in complex adaptive systems, this is a variation choice – one set of systems is varied to create a different set, according to some selection criteria). In general this spontaneity is called *self-organization*: the way in which, under its own dynamics, a system becomes increasingly more organized. Kauffman demonstrates how a large number of interacting elements can display self-organising behaviour given a few simple rules and time, resulting in non-trivial organized configurations.

An example of the development of self-organizing systems is the research groups that form in departments around particular problems. The group may organize further, and develop their own network, which in time may evolve to form a larger entity, just as the 1960s engineers' efforts lead to the genesis of the Computing Centre. A temporary level of stasis may be reached, such as in the corporate IT silos that existed for some 20 years. Or such systems may become extinct as funding dissipates, members leave, or technology changes, and co-evolution can trigger the creation or destruction of systems. For example, MSDOS drove many competing operating systems to extinction. The ubiquity of the PC and its applications drove typing pools – dependant on a lower order of technology – out of existence, with consequences for other workgroups, but created new categories of jobs such as system administrators and webmasters.

The Crucial Role of Time

Time scales are important in complex systems. We consider two ways in which this is so. First, systems have sub-parts that operate on different time scales simultaneously, which has an impact on the kinds of adaptations that are possible. Second, systems achieve moments of 'self-organized criticality' at which sudden radical shifts become possible.

Stewart Brand argues that complex systems can consist of several subsystems each of which tends to adapt at a different pace. He first illustrated this through

Stuff	Fashion	Personal Email/Web Pages
Space	Commerce	Department Policies
Services	Infrastructure	IT Services
Skin	Governance	University Policies
Structure	Culture	Corporate IT
Site	Nature	Teaching Practices

| a. Buildings | b. Society | c. University IT |

Figure 1. Brand Layer Models

what on the surface would seem an unlikely candidate for a evolving system: buildings (Brand, 1994). Buildings, according to Brand, evolve over time, and do so by 'layering' themselves into a number of subsystems, each of which can then evolve reasonably independently, as shown in Figure 1a, with slowest-evolving systems at the bottom and fastest at the top. At the top of the diagram, the 'stuff' layer adapts most quickly as people, furniture, chairs, books constantly move around. The second (space) layer adapts as the space plan for the building (rooms, offices, etc) changes. 'Space' can evolve relatively independently of 'structure' (the structural aspects of the building), although some space modifications will have structural implications (moving a load-bearing wall, for example). Services (plumbing, HVAC) then evolve more slowly than space, and so on down through skin, building structure and building site. All these changes are results of the driving forces of variation, interaction and selection. For example, one company's floor plan, if seen to have advantages, may be copied elsewhere; furniture might be rearranged to accommodate more staff; or IT services may be brought in to improve productivity.

More recently, Brand (1999) has applied a similar layering argument to the continual social adaptation of society, which is represented in Figure 1b. Here Brand similarly argues that different aspects of society evolve at different timescales, with fashion evolving fastest, then commerce more slowly, followed by infrastructure, governance, culture and finally the environment.

Our running example is also amenable to a similar layered structure, shown in Figure 1c. University teaching practices change very slowly, despite pressures to shift to online learning and adopt other 'modern' practices, as they are in many ways a deep embodiment of University culture. It turns out that the University's corporate databases also evolve extremely slowly – a major change is under way at present but the previous successful change was almost 20 years ago. Changes in University policy are often designed to force changes to this culture. Since we're mostly concerned with computer-based systems here, our top three layers show how IT services – for example networking, file servers, email – evolve much more quickly than the big corporate databases or University policies, which in turn are shaped by departmental policies. Material managed by individual students and staff changes most rapidly.

Brand's idea of layers also relates to Kauffman's idea of co-evolution: one layer evolves, with consequences for the adaptability of other layers. Thus, for example, changes to the University's policies trigger adaptation at both the IT services and corporate IT levels, and changes to departmental policies could change both personal email/web pages and underlying IT services.

This idea of time layering is not unique to Brand. Holland, for example, points out that systems patterns become building blocks for persistent patterns at more complex levels (Holland, 1998). Alexander (1977) has built a pattern language for development based on a layering of regions, cities, communities, neighbourhoods, building groups, the house and its surrounds, and the house and rooms themselves, all of which necessarily play out at different speeds. And Simon (1981) has argued that effective management requires breaking an organization into layers, where each layer influences the next, and operates at a different timescale (thus the CEO should be looking at the long-term view, the operating officers at a shorter term view, and lower-level management at immediate issues).

From our point of view, this is all interesting because it helps us to understand how to design systems better. Because layering in time is often not taken into account, new systems can fail because they attempt to push a 'slow' layer too quickly, or because by the time they are built the part of the business for which they are intended has already evolved to some different set of needs.

What, then is the relationship between the Complex Adaptive Systems approach of Axelrod and Cohen, and Brand's system layering approach? We believe that both these approaches tell different parts of the story of complex socio-technical systems, with Axelrod and Cohen focusing more on the mechanisms of change (and less on time), and Brand focusing more on the ways in which we can, or should, take account of time. Clearly both are needed. For example, if we want to vary a system in a hurry, there's no point in focusing on something that will change very slowly. But if we want a lasting effect, chances are we have to account for, and deal with, time in an appropriate fashion.

In slow layers costs associated with variation and selection would appear to be higher than in faster layers, and their consequences appear to be more profound. In corporate systems, reliability and predictability are key selection measures; change is costly, not encouraged and when it must occur must be managed carefully. Thus for example, changing to s2000 was expensive, slow, and is still having ramifications through the entire University, while changing individuals' web pages incurs much less cost and thus change is frequent, ad hoc and can be unpredictable without significant consequence.

Layers are thus shifted by variation and selection, and interaction serves as a key enabler of variation. High interaction costs, such as the cost of international travel (significant for Australians) or breaking cultural norms, can constrain variation by limiting the opportunity for, and increasing the risk of, exploratory or recombination strategies. On the other hand, lowering interaction costs (such as the advent of the internet reducing isolation of Australian universities) can trigger bursts of innovative interaction and thus exploration of new possibilities. Well-travelled interaction patterns are likely to yield efficiency-seeking exploitation strategies, but over time may generate less and less gain: for example, the ways in which the IT innovation in the Computing Centre stagnated as interaction patterns solidified. In assessing the nature and affect of Brand layers, it appears that signals (such as costs, student preferences, incidence of travel, changes in policies, possibilities opened by the Internet) may themselves decay over time. Disruptions in interaction patterns caused by the shearing of layers, as one layer shifts relative to others, potentially offer the opportunity to explore new and unplanned variation strategies, selection criteria, and interaction opportunities.

So Brand's approach is useful because it allows us to see how some parts of a system may evolve more slowly while evolution in other parts can run more quickly. However there are clearly moments where, spontaneously, several different layers all need to change simultaneously.

Why is this? Bak's (1997) work on *self-organised criticality* shows that in complex systems stability is only a passing phase, and that in such systems, change is enacted by unpredictable 'catastrophes' of unpredictable size. Catastrophes need not be bad. From our viewpoint they are merely massive changes in the system, occurring spontaneously. Often good things arise from the result, in the same way that forests are regenerated by massive bushfires.

Self-organized criticality is not in evidence to the eye, but can be seen only over time. The classic example is avalanches of sand piles. Consider making a pile of sand by hand. You will be able to add many grains, which just pile up, but at some moment an avalanche will occur – this is the moment of 'catastrophe'. Another example: the University's corporate IT systems grew fairly successfully over many years, but then passed the point where one change too many was needed. The systems became increasingly unstable, and impossible to adapt further. Bak argues that in such a case the system has self-organised to the point where one further, even negligible, addition or change results in catastrophe. At that point, the functional unit is the system as a whole (Bak, 1997, p60).

When that system is part of a larger network of systems, a catastrophe can trigger the possibility of massive change in its interdependent systems. Thus adding one more staff member could make a space crisis so acute that an entire department needs to shift to a new building; adding one more computer could mean the whole IT network infrastructure needs rebuilding, and so forth.

Clearly, changes at lower layers will be riskier and more costly, and generally take longer, than those at higher layers. Rebuilding the student administration system runs the risk of not being able to enrol students for the year, with consequences for funding and student learning across the University. Failure in department systems affects only the students and staff in that department, with limited consequences for other areas in the University. And if a lecturer's on-line web site were to crash, only he and his students would be immediately affected.

Systems Design

It is our argument that CSCW design, and indeed IT systems design more generally, is complex adaptive systems design. But 'design' as a verb implying conscious, rational decision-making would not apply to the 'design' of complex adaptive systems. Complex adaptive systems are not 'designed' in this sense at all – they evolve. Human insight and decision making comes in through the choices made in variation, interaction and selection. Even when we embark on a conscious, 'rational' restructuring process such as business process reengineering this would be the case. We might take an organization (system) restructure it, forcing the extinction of some of the pieces and encouraging new growth in others. The result will still be a set of interdependent complex adaptive systems, which will immediately continue along some evolutionary path, which may well be different to the one followed before the shake-up.

It follows that the best we can hope to do from the viewpoint of complete systems design is attempt to make informed decisions about which variation, interaction and selection strategies are most likely to be to the benefit of the systems as a whole. Then we can look to implement these through introduction of various kinds of leverage, such as new policies or new technology and tools. Or, turning things around, as we go through the process of software systems design, questions from a systems perspective should be uppermost.

The system designer needs to be aware that though a system in one configuration may seem quiescent and stable, that is not likely always to be the case. Systems self-organise to criticality so that design for a 'normal' state may be nullified when the inevitable catastrophe occurs.

Looking at systems design from a complex adaptive systems viewpoint also makes clearer the ways in which the various disciplines in CSCW might work together more effectively. The 'CSCW design myth' would be that social scientists – particularly ethnographers – develop design insights through study of the world, and that these insights shape the actual systems that are delivered. There is however little evidence to support this view (Plowman et al., 1995). As Schmidt (2000) points out "those workplace studies that have had the strongest influence on CSCW research have been studies which did not aim at arriving at specific design recommendations ... but instead tried to uncover ... the ways in which social order is produced in cooperative work settings, whatever the design implications of the findings may be".

Dennett (1995) draws an interesting distinction between *reverse* and *forward* engineering as design processes. Reverse engineering is the business of understanding the how, what, when, where and why of how things came to be as they are, while forward engineering is the business of designing or modifying to make new things. It is our belief that from the CSCW perspective significant value in field study and other ethnography arises because it is a very effective way of performing reverse engineering on socio-technical systems, in other words uncovering the stories that explain the how and why of socio-technical systems emerge from such study. Such emergence can be aided by using appropriate analysis frameworks such as the Locales Framework, which help to structure the information gained from fieldwork (Fitzpatrick, 1998; Fitzpatrick et al., 1995; Fitzpatrick et al., 1996).

Forward engineering of CSCW systems has proven to be challenging (Grudin, 1988). We believe that an important reason is that CSCW systems designers fail to take account of the fact that they're designing technology for use in complex systems. As a result they omit the potential or need for variation, fail to distinguish between exploitation and exploration and the risks associated with each approach, fail to ask appropriate reflective questions regarding selection and interaction processes, and can overlook temporal layering.

It is our view that a more appropriate 'CSCW design myth' is to view CSCW design as complex systems engineering. In such an approach reverse engineering helps us to understand the variation, selection and interaction trajectories at play in the system. The resulting insights conceptualise forward engineering activities, for example by pointing out ways in which systems adaptation has run fast or slow in the past (signs of layering), interaction patterns that should or should not be supported, selection mechanisms which could appropriately be used to measure success, and the pros and cons of different selection strategies.

One possible basis for performing reverse engineering is to use a grounded theory approach to field data analysis such as Strauss (1993) or the Locales Framework (Fitzpatrick, 1998; Fitzpatrick et al., 1996). The Locales Framework, in particular, provides a structured way of reporting grounded insights based on fieldwork that could easily adapt to the complex systems approach we have employed here. In particular, the framework allows identification of systems elements (agents, artefacts, tools), internal and external interaction patterns, and temporal aspects of systems behaviour. Further discussion of this point is unfortunately beyond the scope of this paper.

Turning to the question of forward engineering, and following Dennett (1995), there are no magic answers to the question of how to design an evolving system – its design is embedded within itself through its evolutionary processes. Rather, by recognizing that as designers we are steering evolution rather than designing tools, we are more likely to account for the factors affecting success.

This opens the question of what means we have of 'steering evolution'. We argued above that purely random variation was unlikely to be a successful adaptation strategy. Instead, using a mixture of exploitation (reusing discovered good design tricks earlier) and exploration (recombination and careful extension from previously-discovered good design tricks), we believe it is possible to make reasonably reliable progress. Self-organized criticality tells us that sooner or later this approach will break down. Once it has, we can pick up the pieces and move forward again – sudden radical moves are almost always a poor idea in evolutionary systems (Dennett, 1995). Once one has experienced a catastrophe a few times, it's then possible to reflect on and design systems adaptation strategies that act to minimize the chances of the catastrophe re-occurring.

Does there exist some methodology or approach that captures this notion of codifying and reusing good design tricks? This is exactly the reason why Alexander developed the notion of 'pattern languages' (Alexander, 1979). Alexander's pattern language are an attempt to create a framework through which design knowledge can be codified, *based on practical experience*, in a way that is concrete enough to allow it to be reused by abstract enough to allow wide latitude in application. A pattern generally specifies a particular problem and context to which it is to be applied, gives an abstract skeleton of the solution(s) to be used in solving the problem in that context, and sketches some practical illustrations of its application. They thus form a kind of practitioners guidebook, which codifies the approaches to take and situations in which they are applicable, but only through application of the skill and local context of the practitioner.

Through the development of appropriate pattern languages, we believe we can we can begin to capture and reuse the 'evolutionary moves' that prove to be useful in complex systems design. As we will see in the following section, the 'rules' of complex adaptive systems articulated by Axelrod and Cohen provide a good foundation from which to build such a language.

The Case Revisited

This section reflects on our case study, drawing out the complex systems at play, and pointing to the kinds of patterns that could be used to describe the good design moves in action. The University system is a complex adaptive system: there are many interdependent actors, each seeking to improve its own performance given its environmental constraints and employing processes of variation, interaction and selection. The result was a highly diverse population of IT systems, although the underlying strategies were often similar. The following bullets capture the essence of those strategies, in the form of highly abbreviated patterns. These examples illustrate capturing design insights in a pattern language.

- *Build a system similar to that used by a group with similar technical needs or budget.* This is both a form of signal following and a form of selection where the performance criterion is that it worked for another group.
- *Build or evolve a system based on recommendations from a trusted colleague.* This is a form of agent following and of selection where the

performance criterion is related to the trust given to the judgements of the colleague in question.

- *Build something different to that used before, or in a sister department, to overcome some deficiency; or deploying a mixture of older, trusted and newer technologies, software and tools.* This pattern encourages a kind of cautious variation.

- *Deploy a new technology that has been demonstrated to be successful elsewhere* (for example email, or connecting to the internet). This is a form of exploration, bolstered by the fact that others have done it successfully overseas – a kind of selection.

- *Deploy a new technology because it is cool and has marketing or differentiation value, even if its use is not yet clear.* This is another form of exploration, based on signal following. Our School has just engaged in application of this pattern – in this case wireless LANs – on the argument that it will help to boost the image of the school as forward-thinking, and create the opportunity for anywhere/anytime network access from student and staff laptops. Here our selection criterion was 'coolness', justified by signal following in the form of evidence of successful use and interaction pattern change in one major research group that had trialled the technology.

Our case shows that, even with the use of these patterns, over time the IT complex system at the University both stalled and tended to catastrophe concurrently. This is particularly true at the corporate level. While each of the many IT systems that were developed was optimised locally to meet the needs of the group hosting it, often using the patterns above, interaction among the various groups became increasingly problematic. We believe that from a systems perspective the combination of being at a slowly evolving time layer, coupled with decreasing interaction and technology not capable of supporting evolution, slowly shifted the systems closer to catastrophe. In parallel, the external environment (the Internet, Y2K, budgetary pressure) was building up momentum for significant change.

In the mid 1990s the moment of self-organized criticality arrived. Further change was impossible without the core corporate systems collapsing. Adaptation to the Internet was impossible, as the various systems were inflexible and inaccessible via the web. The culture of the Computing Centre had become so inwardly focused that it was incapable of support. The University's network could no longer handle traffic demand.

At this point, we can see that system evolution had been bounded artificially by limiting variation and interaction, and so selection choices. But at the time, that didn't seem to matter. Corporate systems evolve slowly, so that interaction and variation seemingly are less important and opportunities for feedback fewer and less apparent than for 'faster' systems. Exploitation was favoured over exploration, and self-organised criticality reached the point of system catastrophe.

Our work leads us to believe that the balance between exploration and exploitation is one that needs to be exercised with care. As connectedness increases, as through a centralised corporate backbone, so does the potential for system-wide catastrophe. Duplication of student records has been eliminated, but in the event of a fire, for example, not only will the University suffer immediate disruption, but core business data will be lost, impeding both rapid recovery and its operations for considerable time. Yet greater connectedness also increases the prospect of adaptive moves through exploratory recombination. For example, a single database containing staff and access data allows a directory server and single log-ins, independent of location, which in turn enable new online services.

Working to maintain good interaction (so providing improved knowledge about possible 'good' moves) is crucial for successful adaptation. Recruitment of a junior systems administrator from an allied research centre provided our school with insights into that centre's systems and strategies, allowing the school to undertake successful evolutionary moves (in this case, the new network). Good interaction also allows us to make some assessment as to the effect of new, emergent groups, systems or activities. Rather than waiting until catastrophe, we need to continually assess system changes and 'look ahead' through variation and interaction strategies to make successful moves. Although the catastrophe of the late 1990s has been successfully negotiated thus far, the ongoing adaptation of the University IT system remains far from certain.

Change also can be amplified or muffled by layering. As we argued above, changes to one layer will tend to ripple through others and these impacts are not well understood. For example, we do not yet fully understand the effect of the academic restructure or the introduction of simple online learning technologies on all these systems. But we do know that the University's teaching culture, and all the other layers mentioned, will continue to shift and change in response.

While on the face of it, the drive to centralization might be seen as inimical to the construction of flexible systems, the University has, by accident or design, centralized the services at the lower levels in Figure 1c, that is, the things that evolve most slowly (and thus are most likely to benefit from centralization and standardization), while creating a solid platform for further development by departments of the parts of the total IT system which they manage and which need to move more quickly (such as file and compute servers, LANS and other specialized services). Time will tell whether the push to centralization goes too far, and if services which would be better left at the department level, to provide needed flexibility and variety, become centralized and frozen.

Conclusion

Recognizing socio-technical systems as complex adaptive systems allows us to gain insights into underlying systems drivers, and, importantly, generate possible new tools and hypotheses. The 'tool-set' we present here builds on a variety of ideas from systems thinking, including Axelrod and Cohen's language of complex adaptive systems, Kauffman and Bak's notions of co-evolution and self-organization, and Brand's work on the ways in which systems shear in time to create a framework from which to gain insights into how complex systems work and change over time. We have suggested that CSCW systems design – and indeed IT systems design more generally – is more apt to failure because computer systems designers are not equipped to take account of these phenomena. Alexander's pattern languages provide a conceptual framework within which ideas and insights gained from studying complex systems can be codified for dissemination and use by the IT systems design community.

Our case, the development of the University IT system over a period of some 35 years, has yielded cogent examples, and allowed us to illustrate insights into the design of socio-technical systems. In the spirit of von Hayek (von Hayek, 1945), we believe that system design is more the nurturing of a garden than the propagation of a seed.

The work of complex systems generally and its application to socio-technical systems is in its youth. Still, we believe complexity theory is a powerful instrument of analysis. There are rich veins of research to be uncovered in this area of application, and more work needed to make it more accessible. Moreover, it is an approach that complements and informs other approaches within CSCW.

Acknowledgments

The authors would like to thank in particular Mr Wilfred Brimblecombe, Mr Alan Coulter and the anonymous staff of the mentioned company for their assistance with the cases.

References

Alexander, C. (1979): *The Timeless Way of Building*, Oxford University Press, New York.

Alexander, C., Ishikawa, S., et al. (1977): *A Pattern Language - Towns, Buildings, Construction*, Oxford University Press, New York.

Axelrod, R. and Cohen, M. D. (1999): *Harnessing Complexity: Organizational Implications of a Scientific Frontier*, Free Press, New York.

Bak, P. (1997): *How Nature Works*, Oxford University Press, Oxford.

Brand, S. (1994): *How Buildings Learn*, Penguin, New York.

Brand, S. (1999): *The Clock of the Long Now*, Phoenix, London.

Dennett, D. (1995): *Darwin's Dangerous Idea*, Touchstone, New York.

Fitzpatrick, G. (1998): *The Locales Framework: Understanding and Designing for Cooperative Work*, Dept. of Computer Science & Electrical Engineering, The University of Queensland, Brisbane.

378

Fitzpatrick, G., Kaplan, S., et al. (1995): *Work, Locales and Distributed Social Worlds*. 1995 European Conference on Computer-Supported Cooperative Work (ECSCW), Stockholm, Sweden, Kluwer.

Fitzpatrick, G., Kaplan, S. M., et al. (1996): *Physical spaces, virtual places and social worlds: A study of work in the virtual*. CSCW'96, Boston, MA.

Fitzpatrick, G., Mansfield, T., et al. (1996): *Locales Framework: Exploring Foundations for Collaboration Support*. Sixth Australian Conference on Human-Computer Interaction (OzCHI '96), Hamilton, NZ, IEEE Press.

Grudin, J. (1988): *Why CSCW Applications Fail: Problems in the Design and Evaluation of Organizational Interfaces*. ACM Proceedings of the Conference on Computer Supported Cooperative Work, Portland, OR., ACM.

Grudin, J. (1994): 'Groupware and Social Dynamics: Eight Challenges for Developers', *Communications of the ACM*, vol. 37, pp. 93-105.

Heath, C. and Luff, P. (1992): 'Collaboration and control; crisis management and multimedia technology in London Underground line control rooms', *Computer Supported Cooperative Work*, vol. 1, no. 1-2, pp. 69-94.

Holland, J. H. (1998): *Emergence: From Chaos to Order*, Oxford University Press, Oxford.

Kaplan, S. and Fitzpatrick, G. (1997): *Designing Support for Remote Intensive-Care Telehealth using the Locales Framework*. ACM Conference on Designing Interactive Systems (DIS), Amsterdam, The Netherlands, ACM Press.

Kauffman, S. (1995): *At Home in the Universe: The Search for Laws of Self-Organization and Complexity*, Oxford University Press, Oxford and New York.

Morel, B. and Ramanujam, R. (1999): 'Through the Looking Glass of Complexity: the Dynamics of Organizations as Adaptive and Evolving Systems', *Organization Science*, vol. 10, no. 3, May-June 1999, pp. 278-293.

OUP (1996): 'Dictionary of Business', Oxford University Press, Oxford.

Plowman, L., Rogers, Y., et al. (1995): *What are Workplace Studies For?* Fourth European Conference on Computer-Supported Cooperative Work, Stockholm, Sweden, Kluwer.

Rittel, H. and Webber, M. (1973): 'Dilemmas in a General Theory of Planning', *Policy Studies*, vol. 4, no. 1, pp. 155-169.

Rodden, T. and Blair, G. (1991): *CSCW and Distributed Systems: The Problem of Control*. Second European Conference on Computer Supported Cooperative Work (ECSCW 91), Amsterdam, Kluwer Academic Publishers.

Schmidt, K. (2000): 'The Critical Role of Workplace Studies in CSCW', *Workplace Studies: Recovering Work Practice and Informing Design*, C. Heath, J. Hindmarsh and P. Luff (eds.), Cambridge University Press, Cambridge.

Seely Brown, J. and Duguid, P. (2000): *The Social Life of Information*, Harvard Business School Press, Boston.

Simon, H. A. (1981): *The Sciences of the Artificial*, MIT Press, Cambridge, MA.

Strauss, A. (1993): *Continual Permutations of Action*, Aldine de Gruyter, New York.

Suchman, L. A. (1987): *Plans and Situated Actions: The Problem of Human Machine Communication*, Cambridge University Press, New York.

Van Valen, L. (1973): 'A New Evolutionary Law', *Evolutionary Theory*, vol. 1, no. 1, pp. 1-30.

von Hayek, F. A. (1945): 'The Use of Knowledge in Society', *The American Economic Review*, vol. 35, no. 4, September 1945, pp. 519-530.

W. Prinz, M. Jarke, Y. Rogers, K. Schmidt, and V. Wulf (eds.), *Proceedings of the Seventh European Conference on Computer-Supported Cooperative Work, 16-20 September 2001, Bonn, Germany*, pp. 379-397.
© 2001 Kluwer Academic Publishers. Printed in the Netherlands.

Decentralizing the Control Room: Mobile Work and Institutional Order

Oskar Juhlin[1] and Alexandra Weilenmann[2] *

The Mobility Studio, Interactive Institute, Sweden[1]

The Mobile Informatics Group, Viktoria Institute, Sweden[2]

Abstract. This paper seeks to inform the ongoing redesign of air traffic management by examining current practices and the adoption of a new system aiming to relieve traffic control from work and reduce radio communication. We report from ethnographic fieldwork among mobile, distributed airport ground personnel. By examining the ways in which they use the 'old' technology, i.e. VHF radio, we identify a set of important aspects of work carried out through radio talk. These are: repairing misunderstandings, discussing the task-at-hand, and negotiating next actions. The new system fails to support this negotiation work, and is hardly ever used by the ground personnel. The distributed workers in the field make their own decisions and negotiate coordination with the tower based on local information. In this respect, current work practice is already decentralized to a certain extent. The problem with the new system, we argue, is the idea to decentralize the organization by providing distributed workers with more information, whereas the current institutional arrangement for coordination is built upon highly formal and hierarchical ideas. When redesigning the system it is necessary to take into account the ways in which radio talk is used to carry out the everyday work among ground personnel.

Introduction

Air traffic is constantly increasing. In the middle of the last century centralized air traffic control was introduced to handle the growing number of planes in a safe manner (La Porte, 1988). Today, as the growth continues, traffic control itself

---

* Authors are listed alphabetically

becomes a problem. In northern Europe, mainly in Sweden, a new concept for air traffic control, called CNS (Communications, Navigation and Surveillance), is being introduced. This is a joint research and implementation collaboration between the Swedish, Danish and German civil aviation administrations as well as Lufthansa, Scandinavian Airlines Systems (SAS) and the European Commission. It is a major effort aiming for a decentralization of the coordination system, by moving some responsibility out of the control tower to the pilots and other vehicle operators. This is addressed by launching a new communication system based on a standard (VDL Mode 4), featuring various new applications to support individual vehicle operators in the system (SCAA,1999). It is in the process of being adopted as a global standard from November 2001.[1] Important keywords in this effort are *collaboration* and *situational awareness*: Air traffic management should "make sure that the best use is made of all available resources and that potential problems are resolved in a collaborative and pro-active manner" (SCAA,1999:5) It introduces ideas of support for group work to a practice that traditionally has aimed for hierarchical and centralized control. Not surprisingly, the approach is therefore considered radical, and is meeting resistance in air traffic management circles.[2]

The purpose of this study is to inform design of coordination technologies by describing the organization of the everyday practices of a certain airport ground personnel category very important for air traffic management, namely those who keep the runways free from snow. The snow clearance personnel we have studied, use two systems two carry out their work: the traditional radio communication system and a new system (the first application for their use based on the design principle described above). The snow clearance vehicles are equipped with SnowCard. It is a "situation display", that provide the sweeping crew with a moving map where they could see dots representing other ground vehicles as well as those airplanes equipped with the new system. This is motivated by work-overload in traffic control, as well as too much talk on the radio system. The radio system is conceived as technically insufficient, and the talk itself can cause mis-understandings and failures in achieving coordination. The SnowCard system addresses these issues by giving the snow maintenance crew and the control tower an awareness system enabling them to see the location of snow clearing vehicles. However, during our fieldwork it became evident that the personnel did not rely on the new system in carrying out their work. Rather, they used the 'old' technology, the radio, to coordinate their work on the runways. Therefore, in this paper, we examine what the snow crew is doing with the radio, in order to be able to draw conclusions about how to design better tools for this activity.

---

[1] Press release, Swedish Civil Aviation Administration, 2000-03-30

[2] Niklas Gustavsson, Swedish Civil Aviation Administration (Luftfartsverket), Norrköping, Interview, October 2000.

In the first part of the paper we present related work, our data collection, as well as explain the tools and manuals that influence snow clearance operations. We then present selected items from the fieldwork, together with our analysis. Finally, we draw conclusions to inform the design of support for this specific type of air traffic management.

Related Work

Two distinct ways of understanding work practice figure in the design of support for traffic control. In the documents from the Civil Aviation Administration, they discuss coordination either between autonomous users, or centralized coordination:

> Concept options will range between a "managed" ATM [Air Traffic Management] environment based on traffic structuring, greater traffic predictability, longer planning horizons and extensive automated support, to a "free flight" environment based on free routings and autonomous aircraft separation (SCAA,1999:6).

The CNS system will provide additional support for traditional forms of centralized management which structure and order the movements of the planes. The new and innovative approach concerns ideas that, in their most radical formulation, allow for free flight where the operators have the freedom to select their path and speed. Then, individual pilots will organize traffic through decentralized collaboration. The traditional perspective in aviation control understands coordination of air traffic as a centralized achievement, where traffic control holds a unique position, monitoring the system. The traffic controller has a number of information sources, e.g. radar and other personnel. Based on this information the controller visualizes the current state of the entire system, and decides on appropriate next action. This decision is based on a list of appropriate actions to take in the given situation. To coordinate the many people in the system, it is necessary that they behave in a predictable way, i.e. follow formal procedures.

The distinction is central in terms of CSCW research, where an important design choice is understood as either automating organizational work, understood as routine work in a predictable environment, or supporting the articulation of contingent and situated organizing activities (Schmidt et al 1996, Gerson and Leigh Star, 1986)

In the new perspective, coordination is achieved as a distributed activity where people and technology in collaboration achieve coordination (Goodwin & Goodwin, 1998 and Hutchins, 1995). Air traffic control holds a less privileged position, as one of many local settings. The controller's understanding of the system is only partial, and decisions about next action must be negotiated with other localities where participants have different understandings. To achieve coordination it is essential that people account for the local circumstances and contingent situations in which they are involved. Thus, people do different things and hold different views on the system. Collaboration and mutual understanding is interactionally negotiated.

In the studies of control rooms of various sorts, it is usually the controllers and their teamwork that are in focus. Hughes et al. (1992) and Sanne (1999) show how the managers make their own work accountable for their colleagues, and how this is seen with peripheral awareness, as a way to e.g. repair mistakes. Hutchins (1993) considered the task of navigating a large vessel as a collaborative and distributed achievement. Watts et al (1996) have considered voice communication support for managers launching a rocket. They argued that a combination of different virtual meeting rooms increased awareness for the benefit of the collaborative work at hand. Further, Mackay et al. (1998) study air traffic controllers who were not located in a control tower, but had radar screens as a visual source of information about the location of the planes.

However, in order to influence the design of a more decentralized traffic control it is necessary to consider coordination as seen from outside of the control room. As pointed out by Bellotti and Bly (1996) with reference to the studies of navigation at sea, the managers in all these settings are themselves 'locally immobilized'. In their own research, Bellotti and Bly point to the importance of 'local mobility' where people walk between office rooms and then often have to leave their computers at the desktop. Consequently, this local mobility penalizes long distance collaboration. However, with the aid of mobile technology it is possible to continuously monitor the activities in the center. A similar approach is taken in the studies of traffic management at the London Underground. Heath and Luff (1992) study the local mobility of the station managers. They also found that the managers had much less awareness of the activities when they left the control room to move around at the underground station.

In this paper we will look at a different form of mobile work. The snow crew is undertaking a job where they are almost constantly on the move. The movement is more than an issue of moving to a different place of work - it is the work itself. The snow crew has this in common with many occupations involved in transportation. The thoroughgoing mobility is visible in the talk, the system that supports the work, as well as in rules surrounding the work. For them, the positioning of their co-workers is under constant negotiation.

Radio talk

This study is concerned with the practices of radio (UHF - ultra high frequency) communication. The use of radio for carrying out work has been studied mainly within the transport sector. In this section, we briefly outline relevant findings from these studies, focusing on features identified as unique for radio talk.

Pritchard and Kalogjera (2000) have examined marine radio communication. They argue that "the conversational structure and format of most messages is simple, routine-like and therefore predictable." (2000:186). They show how the actual maritime VHF communications differ significantly from the highly formal standards.

In another study of marine radio communication, Robert Sanders examined the talk between vessels, commercial as well as recreational. He is interested in the fact that although these radios are intended for safely operating vessels, and with a prescribed language, they are widely used for other purposes, especially by recreational boaters. His focus is on conversational socializing (specifically laughter) observed over the radio. Both studies show how practices have developed for making a highly restricted technology more adjusted to everyday actual use.

The radio technology has some interesting implications for the talk situation. One main difference between face-to-face communication and radio talk is that when talking over the radio it is physically impossible for more than one person at a time to occupy the floor (Sanders, 2000:5).

Another relevant difference, pointed out by Sanders, is the fact that in order to say something on the radio the speaker has to do something more than just vocalize. There is a need to take the microphone and press the button before the talk can be transmitted and heard. This of course has the implication that the person speaking needs to have at least one hand free to operate the microphone. When engaged in physical work, this can sometimes be a constraint, and consequently lead to response delays.

The above-mentioned studies have mainly focused on the talk in itself, rather than looking at it in the context in which it occurs. Luff and Heath (2001) describe a setting (a railway in London) where the practices of radio use are closely linked to the practices of using a computer supported display system. They note how "the displays are utilized to make sense of the ongoing talk and also shape the production of interactions within that setting." (2001:28).

Method and setting

The fieldwork reported in this paper was carried out at Arlanda airport during January-February 2000. Arlanda airport is situated north of Stockholm. With its two runways and intense traffic it is Sweden's largest airport. There is a risk of snow during half of the year. From end of October to middle of April, there are people present twenty-four hours per day to run snow clearance operations. A minor part of their task is to clear the areas around the gates. The major task is to clear the runways and the areas in the vicinity. The aviation administration argues that they currently clean a runway, being forty-five meters in width and 3.3 kilometers long, in eight minutes. Extensive efforts are made to improve the operations.

The snow sweeping operation takes eight collaborating vehicles moving in a falling line (see below). Each vehicle is equipped with means to plough, sweep and blow away the snow. Therefore, they are referred to as the sweeping group.[3] The driver in the first, the lead sweeper, is responsible for radio communication with airport traffic control (the tower). The sweeping group collaborates with a "brake vehicle", a car that measures the friction of the runway before and after snow clearance.

On a total of five snow clearance occasions, we rode with the snow sweepers, sitting in their vehicles while they carried out their work on the runways and the surrounding areas. The vehicles normally had an extra seat next to the driver seat, where the researcher could sit. We normally organized it so that one of us always was in the lead vehicle. Being two people in the field made it possible to get different perspectives on the same situations. Some drivers talked a lot with us and were interested in explaining their work and their use of the systems, whereas others did not take much notice of us. It enabled us to focus more on the work and listening to the radio communication. During all this, we took extensive field notes.

Figure 1. The eight snow vehicles out on the runway, with the lead sweeper in the front and the others in a line behind.

When in the vehicle with the snow sweepers, it was sometimes difficult to hear and comprehend the radio talk. In order to get the details of the ongoing talk, we made recordings. This was carried out during two days of the fieldwork. Due to the nature of the work, we had to wait for it to snow before going out with the snow sweepers. This meant that we spent a lot of time in the recreation room, in the garage, etc. That enabled us to talk to the snow crew and get their opinions of their work situation, as well as getting a sense of the workplace.

The material, the field notes as well as the recordings, were then transcribed. We went through the transcriptions, identifying a set of themes. A few sequences from the transcribed recordings, were then chosen as showing the issues we examine in this paper.

---

[3] We have chosen to use the term 'snow sweepers' and 'sweepers' rather than the more obvious snow plougher or similar, because this is the way that they are referred to at the airport.

The systems

The snow clearance operation is traditionally coordinated through radio communication on the ultra high frequency band (UHF). It is a simplex system, which means that it is only open for one transmitter at a time, but that everybody with radio equipment can listen. Only the strongest signal goes through if several people try to speak at the same time. The speaker has to push a button in order to transmit. It is possible to hear their use of the button since the beginning of a sentence is often clipped off, and the end is often followed by an audible click. This clicking sound is represented by the sign '#' in the transcripts.

In radio talk it is not easy to understand who's talking to whom. To avoid misunderstandings, formal rules define the way the participants speak. Every statement should be initiated by an identification of the speaker. Permission must be granted by the tower before any maneuver. All decisions must also be check-read to make sure that everybody heard it the same way. The manual states:

> When you want to drive onto the maneuver area, you must identify yourself (give your call signal) and tell where you want to go and - when needed - what way. When the tower gives permission to drive on or to remain on the maneuver area, you shall check-read (i.e. repeat) the permission. Even the request to "hold position" or to hold a certain distance from the runways shall be check-read. End the check reading with your own call signal, so that the tower knows that it is the correct vehicle that is acknowledging the permission.[4]

Further, it is strongly requested that radio conversations be "short" and "accurate". This is also expressed more straightforwardly in the manual, in capital letters as follows: "IN OTHER WORDS, NO UNNECESSARY 'CHAT' ON OUR RADIO COMMUNICATION SYSTEM!"

There are a number of radio channels that the personnel could use when they are doing their work. The channels of relevance for the work in the group are mainly channels one and two. Channel one is intended for communication with the tower. When on the runway, the snow crew is demanded to use channel one. This is mainly for security reasons; the tower has to be able to hear all the communication on the ground, and the ground personnel need to be in constant response to orders from the tower. The manual states:

> The Aviation Administration demands ... that radio communication be possible with vehicles are located and working in ... the airports maneuver area. Here there is a demand for constant radio attention (SCAA,1999:14).

As soon as they leave the runways, the snow crew should switch to channel two, so that the tower would not be disturbed by their talk. Channel two is meant for communication within the sweeping group.

---

[4] From the manual *Radio communication on airport* (UHF), page 47. [Translated from Swedish.]

The snow clearance operation has been targeted by the designers behind the CNS concept. In the pursuit of expanding the system concept, a number of aircrafts was first equipped with new equipment. Then some snow clearance vehicles were included in the system and provided with situational displays with a moving map (SnowCard).[5] On a display presenting a map of the airports, a number of the sweeping groups' vehicles are represented by small dots. When the vehicles move around the airport the dots follow on the map. This is made possible by the positioning system in each vehicle and the digital radio communication link. The new data link is considered a "major breakthrough" giving each aircraft and other vehicles the ability to broadcast its position and identity to other vehicles as well as to the central traffic control (SCAA,1999:7). Below is a picture of the inside of one of the snow vehicles (Figure 2).

Figure 2. The inside of one of the snow vehicles. The SnowCard display is in the upper left corner of the picture. The small radio receiver is hanging down from the ceiling of the vehicle, and is visible in the top middle of the picture.

Analysis

In the following we will present our analysis of the fieldwork. First, we will present our observations of the use of the SnowCard system. The remainder of the analysis then deals with the ways in which the snow clearance personnel use the traditional radio system to coordinate their work through talk. The reason for devoting more space to the use of the radio rather than the new system, is simply because the current work practice in the sweeping group relies on radio, and there are several things that the snow sweepers regularly and ordinarily do which do not seem to be possible using the new system. Therefore, in focusing on the current practices we hope to be able to inform the redesign of the new system, something which is discussed later in this paper.

New visual support for situational awareness

The new display system was introduced to increase situational awareness for vehicle operators in conditions of poor visibility due to the snow. Thus, the use of

---

[5] Swedish Civil Aviation Administration, SnowCard Arlanda, leaflet

the system should be observable in the way the drivers looked at the screen in parallel to looking out of the windshield, and in the rear mirrors.

On one occasion during our fieldwork, the sweeping group is sent to clear the runway. They have instructions to vacate the runway by a specific time. The lead sweeper turns and exits the runway. The driver constantly looks at the screen to oversee when all the other vehicles have exited. He then calls the tower telling them: "Tower, the sweeping group has now left the runway". Later he states that the SnowCard system allowed him to report directly to the tower. Before, he had to wait for the last driver to notify him by radio, and only thereafter call the tower. Now he could use the display instead. This lead sweeper consistently used the situational display when turning. He reported it useful for seeing if the group was holding together, and that no one was falling behind. Along with the adoption of the new system, he also frequently looked through the windshield. Interestingly enough, he would look out the windshield first; only after that would he glance at the display.

This lead sweeper had found some use for the new system. However, it was difficult to observe instances of personnel actually looking at the screen. When we addressed the issue, they told us that they did not find it useful. One member of the sweepers, when asked why he did not have his screen turned on, responded: "What does that [the screen] tell me then?" The researcher replied: "It tells you where the others are". The final comment by the driver reflects what many of them seemed to think: "I can tell that by looking out the windshield". Thus, in a sense, there were two competing visuals, the windshield and the SnowCard. The one taking precedence was the view from the windshield.

We conclude that, although the sweeping group found some use for the system, it was not at all important for them in coordinating their activities and doing the work.[6] The SnowCard did not influence the sweeping group's understanding of their situation in any important sense. It follows then that the new system did not have any impact on the coordination of their work. Rather, they continued to coordinate their moves on the runway using the old technology, i.e. the UHF radio. In the following we will therefore concentrate on the radio conversation, and the situational and local awareness provided simply by the view from the windshields of the vehicles.

Making decisions on the ground

During their work on the runways, the sweeping group is in constant contact with the tower to coordinate their movements. The talk between the tower and the sweeping group is regulated by rules (as described above). We will begin by

---

[6] It should be remembered that the situational display is installed only in a small number of vehicles, and that only a small number of the vehicles out on the tracks are sending information on their identity and position. The promises of the system designers should be evaluated when a much larger number of vehicles are displayed. And in this situation it could perhaps achieve more attention from the driver.

looking at how the visual local information is used in the conversation between the tower and the snow crew. In the following example, it becomes evident that the snow sweepers make their *own decisions based on visual information on the ground*, rather than on information from the control tower.

In the first excerpt from the radio conversations, we will see how the lead sweeper and the tower repair a misunderstanding:

Excerpt 1

LEAD SWEEPER: tower to sweeping group #
TOWER: sweeping group #
LEAD SWEEPER: I'm waiting here at Zulu Tango want to go Xray west#
(13.0 sec)
TOWER: sweeping group go Xray out <u>east</u>:: from hh ramp + #
LEAD SWEEPER: sweeping group we would like to go out on zero eight twenty-six later when we have come down towards hh Xray Alpha #
(9 sec)
TOWER: h «sweeping group: » I see so you are going Xray <u>west</u>? #
LEAD SWEEPER: yeah I saw that they took off from there so isn't it best to go from there then? #
TOWER: «<u>absolutely</u> the best» it is the absolutely best thinkable <u>but</u> I thought you said <u>east</u> but go Xray out west (up) to the meeting point #
LEAD SWEEPER: sweeping group ready for meeting point #

In the first section of this fragment, everything seemingly runs according to the manual. The sweeper reports their position - "I'm waiting here at Zulu Tango", and say that they want to continue west. After an unusually long pause the tower repeats, but repeats incorrectly, saying *east* instead of west. The long pause might suggest that the person in the tower was busy doing something else at the moment. The misunderstanding is not revealed until the tower hears the sweeping group's next planned action. The tower then displays uncertainties, shown in the slowly, prolonged address of the sweeping group in the next utterance.

The lead sweeper now states his reasons for wanting to go in that direction. Here is where it becomes evident that the snow sweeper uses visual information as a basis for his decision-making - "Yeah I saw that they started from there so isn't it best to go from there then?" He now shows that he has seen the planes, and from the direction in which the planes are going, has drawn a conclusion about where the sweeping group should go next. The person in the tower agrees with his decision, saying that his planned next action is "absolutely" the best way to go. Here she could have ended her turn, but she continues to explain for the sweeper how the misunderstanding came about. This is all done out of the institutional order of talk. The lead sweeper does not acknowledge her explanation at all in his next utterance, where he simply states that the sweeping group is ready. The repair of the misunderstanding between the tower and the sweeper is done in a conversational mode. They are not using any identification or address. By opting out of the institutional mode, they mark the topic for the conversation as problematic. When the problem has been resolved, they get back into the institutional mode again.

This example nicely shows how the snow sweepers and the tower have different perspectives in the system that the ground air traffic management comprises. There is not one single unit with control; the control is distributed over various people, and the decisions are consequently also distributed, although against the manual considering both legitimate movements and radio use.

In the next excerpt, we will see a very illustrative example of the sweeping group making their own decisions on the ground. In this case, they cross the runway without permission from the tower, something which is highly prohibited:

Excerpt 2

SWEEPER: Tower the sweeping group at Yan::kee (0.5) an we go Zulu south via Zulu Kilo? #
(17.0)
391: Tower three nine one#
TOWER: eh: one (paus) three (paus) nine tower #

[Long section where vehicle 391 speaks with the tower. Meanwhile, the lead sweeper sits ready with his radio in hand, waiting for a response. He looks in both directions, then crosses the runway.]

391: three nine one (0.5) ready to make turns at south Yankee (0.5) at entrance Uniform #
(1.0)
SWEEPER: tower sweeping group (paus) we went Zulu south via the entrance Zulu Kilo (.) Just so you know #
TOWER: the sweeping group driving Zulu south #
SWEEPER: eeping group#

In this excerpt, the driver is asking the tower for permission to cross the runway. The tower does not answer; there is a very long pause suggesting that the tower did not hear. Instead he talks to another vehicle, 391. The driver waits for the tower to give him permission to pass. After a while, still overhearing the tower's conversation with someone else, the sweeper crosses without permission, after having looked in both directions to see that it was clear.

What is interesting in this example is that the sweeper obviously does something that is against the institutional order of work, i.e. crossing without permission from the tower. However, the tower does not comment upon this. Instead, when the sweeper calls the tower to say where they have gone, "just so you know", the tower simply confirms. But the repetition is a repair of the breach against the institutional order of work, in that the tower repeats in the present tense. Instead of repeating "went" he says "driving". Obviously, confirming in the past tense would show that he had recognized that the sweeping group had already taken action; now instead he repairs by saying that they are about to do it. The tower and the lead sweeper thus *collaboratively repair the sweepers' breach of institutional procedure*.

In these two examples, it becomes evident that the mobile workers make decisions based on local, visual information. In the first example, the lead sweeper drew conclusions about where to sweep next from his visual information about where the aircraft were departing. In the second example, the sweeper crossed the runway using the same mundane method as one would use to cross a road: looking in both directions and then crossing. This was done without permission from the tower, thus against the institutional order of work as described in the manual. These examples show how the visual and the local are used in decision-making at the airport.

Inverting institutional order

In the formal plan of how the work at the airport is supposed to be carried out, it is the snow team which is supposed to ask for permission for their actions. In this excerpt we see the opposite; the tower asks the group (here the brake vehicle) for permission for aircraft to enter the area that the snow crew is currently clearing.

Excerpt 3

TOWER: «brake vehicle::» is it okay that we are getting in position e:: directly when you have e: begun clearing on zero eight? #
BRAKE VEHICLE: yeah sure that's okay #
TOWER: thanks #

The tower begins by identifying the recipient (the brake vehicle) in a formal manner. Thereafter, the person in the tower opts out from the institutional to do something rather unusual in the communication between the tower and the sweeping group – he asks for permission for an action. Since asking for permission to do things is not something that the tower should do from the group, there is no institutional way of doing it. The informality of the question and the way it is phrased, leads the brake vehicle to continue in that mode. The rest of the exchange is conversational, in the lack of identification, repetition, as well as in the choice of words. The last part of the exchange is particularly interesting. The tower thanks the sweeping group. It is remarkable that the tower displays thankfulness to the sweeping group for letting the aircraft be on the runway. This can be taken as evidence of the decentralized practice. The control tower does not decide what to do, the mobile workers have a say in the coordination of work as well.

In the next examples something quite similar occurs. In the formal plan of how the work at the airport is supposed to be carried out, it is the snow sweepers who carry out orders and the tower that gives orders. The tower normally does not give any *reasons* for orders; they simply state where the sweepers should go, not why. However, in the following example we can observe how the tower changes plans, and explains her reasons for doing so to the sweeping group.

Before this segment, the tower has displayed uncertainty about the plans by telling the group to wait. Also, there have been problems with the radio, something that the lead sweeper has commented on to the tower.

Excerpt 4

SWEEPER 391: yeah tower we are getting in position then and holding <u>fifty</u> at Yankee Hotel#
(0.3)
TOWER: eh three nine one with suite:: «do you think you can» get in position and begin by Yankee Juliet ((radio problems, unhearable)) later tonight and then we would need it cleared #
SWEEPER 391: yeah we will do that instead then (0.1) three nine one #
TOWER: <u>great</u> (.) hh hold fifty from zero eight on Yankee Juliet (0.1) three nine one #
(2.0)
SWEEPER 391: three nine one we are holding fifty at Yankee Juliet

In the first line in this excerpt, the lead sweeper tells the tower that they are putting their machines in position, getting ready to sweep Yankee Hotel. The tower then asks the snow sweepers to sweep another runway (Yankee Juliet) than previously agreed on. This involves a change in plans, and a break from the routine. This is obvious in several ways; she formulates a question, *asking* the snow sweepers if they can do this rather than telling them to do it. This means that she opts out of the institutional order of talk. She uses the polite "do you think that you can...", which gives the snow crew the theoretical possibility of declining to do so.

Furthermore, she does something that is rather unusual in the talk between the tower and the sweepers; she gives the reason for why a certain action should be carried out. She says that the reason why they should sweep another runway than previously decided upon is because they would need it later tonight for some reason. *The decision process in the tower is thus made more transparent to the sweeping group*; they are given reasons for decisions rather than just the decisions without a context.

Furthermore, the tower's use of "great" is a way to show gratitude towards the sweepers for being able to change their plans according to her wishes. There is no institutionally described way of showing appreciation and thankfulness; this is not regulated in the manual.

These two examples show the ways in which the sweeping group takes an active part in the decisions the tower makes about air traffic. The order of work was negotiated over the radio, and there was a discussion about what to do next. The tower was not simply given orders and instructions; they asked the sweeping group for permission and negotiated the best way of carrying out work. It can be concluded that the everyday practice is to some extent decentralized, in that the sweepers take an active part in the everyday decision-making on the airport.

Coordination within the sweeping group

In the following, we will look at the conversation within the sweeping group itself. We will see how the group use local knowledge, visual contact and radio talk in order to attend to highly local issues and problem on the runway.

In this case, there is a breach against the regulation stating that they should use channel one when on the runway. As soon as they leave this area the radios are switched to channel two. However, despite what the manual prescribes, the snow sweepers and other personnel sometimes use channel two when they are on the runway. This is seen in the following example, where the sweepers try to solve a problem with a machine. The sweepers all know that Peter is a novice. His vehicle is the last in the line of snow machines, but he cannot get it to run as fast as the others. Consequently, the distance between Peter and the rest of the group increases. This can of course be serious, since the group has to keep together and leave the runway by a certain time. Their talk about the machine is shown below:

Excerpt 5

PETER: u:h:: why doesn't he change gear now?#
(3.0)
SECOND SWEEPER: o you have the driver mounted?#
PETER: The driver is mounted#
 SECOND SWEEPER: >>I'm stepping on the gas and it's so heavy it hasn't been this heavy before?<<#
PETER: No, not like this it's on. I have the accelerator pressed to the floor but it only reaches fifteen hundred revs (0.5) and thirtythree kilometers#
THIRD SWEEPER: Check that the stop is really pushed#
(11.0)
PETER: omething happens if I push the stop with my hand (.) Then he got to:: thirtyfive at least#
THIRD SWEEPER: [inaudible] a bit hard. But he's coming#
PETER: it does .... # [deleted section]

The sweeping group is now about to exit the runway. When turning the corner, the lead sweeper turns around a looks out the window, to get a look at the vehicles lining up behind him. When he sees the large gap between Peter and the rest of the machines, he says to himself: "My God, is he that far behind!".

LEAD SWEEPER: Peter switch to two# (8.0) Peter switch to channel two#

Peter and the lead sweeper switch channels and discuss what to do with the malfunctioning machine. Peter says it "it's hairy." They decide that the vehicle should be taken back to the garage and replaced.

LEAD SWEEPER: yeah okay. I will exit here at Golf or something. [switches the radio back to channel one]

Peter starts with an open question about his machine "Why doesn't it change gear now?" This is not addressed to anybody in particular; rather it is a call for help to whoever can help him. The snow sweepers know that Peter is a novice, and the second driver in the group responds quickly to help him out. The lead sweeper has a special responsibility for the group to adapt his own speed so that no one falls behind. He gets a good look at the team when the group turns and exits from the runway. This local awareness, as well as their knowledge of Peter's lack of experience, makes him take action and switch channel It is likely that the switch is made because he knows that there has been too much to talk already and he wants to avoid further blocking channel one. Although this is against the manual, we observed several instances when the snow sweepers would switch to channel two on the runway to talk about these types of issues.

It is worth noting that the practice of switching channels on the runway is visible to the tower since the request to change to channel two is made on the channel that is overheard by the tower. The lead sweeper claimed that he had never been discouraged or ordered not to use channel two by the tower. Thus, there seemed to be a common understanding that they could shift to channel two if they had to perform extended conversations. This could however be a danger-ous way of pursuing co-ordination. If the tower had given the lead sweeper an urgent order, e.g. to leave the runway immediately, the lead sweeper would not hear it. However, the lead sweeper had developed a workaround to be able to receive these messages. The brake vehicle, with which the lead sweeper cooperated, was equipped with two radio receivers, and they were always listening to both channels. If it was within sight of the front sweeper he counted on the driver of the brake vehicle to warn him on channel two if the tower could not reach him at channel one. Thus, the institutional rules for the technical op-eration of the radio equipment were not in compliance with their actual needs, and they had therefore found other ways of collaboration to achieve safe ways of supporting coordination.

From these examples it is obvious that coordination within the snow crew is based on local, visual information obtained by looking out the windshield. Fur-thermore, we have seen how this information needs to be discussed over the ra-dio. These examples point to the highly local-dependent information the sweepers use in their work. Keeping an eye on the machine in front of them, letting others know if there is a problem and if so how it should be adjusted. Together they take great responsibility for the machines and for leaving the runways clear. In this work the radio proves important, so important that the sweepers break the rules for radio use on the runways.

Discussion

Coordination of air transport is currently under reconsideration in Northern Europe. Air traffic authorities and airline companies are exploring new principles and technologies to redesign air traffic control. New, innovative techniques are being developed that will not only support air traffic control in the tower, but also engage pilots and other vehicle operators in the coordination of activities. These systems are being considered as an alternative to radio talk. This paper considers the attempts of decentralizing coordination.

The work in the sweeping group that we have observed has been relatively unproblematic. Breakdowns occur in the system, but are resolved. However, the problem identified by the management and which initiated the design and introduction of the SnowCard system, still remains. There is an increase in traffic at the airport. Currently, they are in the process of building a third runway, something that is likely to intensify the risk of coordination breakdowns. If the goals behind the SnowCard system are to be met, that is increasing traffic capacity and safety, the design should be informed by an understanding of the current social practices.

The coordination of snow clearing can be understood as an ongoing interactionally negotiated practice. The tower and the snow clearers occupy different viewpoints in the system depending on their task and the situation. Coordination is then achieved through negotiations between different localities. There is not one single unit with control; the control is distributed over various people, and the decisions are consequently also distributed, although this goes against regulation. The snow sweepers and the tower have different perspectives in the system that the ground air traffic management comprises. This becomes evident in the topics discussed on radio, as well as in how they constantly would avoid the institutional formats for radio communication for various purposes.

We have found that the new system was of minor use for coordination. Instead the tower and the snow clearers used the radio communication system for coordination and negotiation of next actions. Radio talk, as well as visual sight, are still the most important tools to do the job. By examining radio talk-in-interaction between the snow crew and the tower, we have identified a set of important factors in radio talk. These are necessary to consider when designing alternatives, or additions, to talk, as the SnowCard does. Activities that were carried out in talk were:

- *Repairing misunderstandings.* When there had been a misunderstanding, based on e.g. a mishearing or differences in access to information, this was resolved through talk.
- *Negotiating the task-at-hand and intentions.* When there was a need to talk about what the next planned action was, both from the tower and the sweeping group, this was done through talk.
- *Talking about the work order and the order of talk.* Letting others know that they had done something that was believed to be inappropriate, or asking them the reasons for actions be stated.

These things were all found to be of great importance for the work and are difficult to accomplish within the institutional system. Further, conversational language was used to make it stand out from the institutional, thus stressing its extra
importance, and that there was something out of the ordinary to attend to. This
paper has also shown the many things that can be accomplished within a conversational mode. There is an interesting comparison with the talk on the radio and
the manual itself. When the manual wants to give extra emphasis to the fact that
unnecessary talk or "chatting" on the radio is not appropriate, the text actually
switches from institutional, neutral jargon, to more conversational and colloquial
language. This implies a need for opting out of the institutional mode in order to
mark the text as something that requires special attention, just like conversational
mode was used in the radio talk. In the light of this, the need for informal conversations on the radio seems even more evident.

Implications for design

One motivation behind this study was to evaluate the resources available to coordinate the snow maintenance at the airport. The resources included the old technology, namely the UHF-radio, and how it was used alongside the newly introduced technology, the SnowCard. We found that the new system was not widely
adopted by the snow crews.

The system is currently under consideration at other airports. Being the first
evaluation of this system, we find it important to identify a set of factors that
could influence a successful redesign of the system, or at least factors to influence
the design process within this new systems concept. We argue that:

- *A decentralized approach for developing technical support does fit with
  current practice.* However, the current attempt has not yet become an
  important enough tool for them.
- *In the current use of the system, there are two competing sources for
  visual information* – the SnowCard system and the view from the windshields. The system is not used. Perhaps the system will be used in a
  greater extent when most of the vehicles on the airport, as well as the
  planes, are visible on the screen. It could also be used if more information was given on the other vehicles than their positions. We suggest
  that it could be of use to display which channels other vehicles are using on the UHF-radio.
- *A system giving visual information cannot give the information needed
  about next action.* Information about the location of a vehicle is not
  enough. It is not possible from the SnowCard system as it is today to
  ascribe intention to the small dots that represents the snow vehicles.
  This is something that has to be negotiated through talk.

- Thus, *design for increasing situation awareness must go hand in hand with the introduction of better tools for supporting the necessary negotiation work.*
- We suggest *a design approach that integrates visual information in the system, rather than considering it as an alternative to the radio system.*

The main problem and the reason for the limited use of the SnowCard system by the snow crew we have studied, lies in the underlying assumptions about what the system sets out to do. The system is designed so that more information about the current situation can be obtained by simply looking at the screen. This implies giving the snow crew more information, thus decentralizing the decision-making by enabling the crew to make their own decisions about their work. However, the existing formal institutional rules do not support these types of decentralized decisions. We have seen in our fieldwork that the institutional order is frequently opted out of in order to carry out work. *This means that decentralized decision-making is not supported by the organization, as expressed in the manuals concerning snow clearance operations, but this is exactly what the SnowCard system sets out to support.* We believe that this is the key problem, and something that needs to be explicitly formulated and attended to in redesign.

Acknowledgments

First of all, we thank all the members of the snow crew at Arlanda airport. We would also like to thank Daniel Normark Vesterlind for pointing us towards the SnowCard system. For valuable comments which helped us improve the paper we wish to thank Paul Luff, as well as the anonymous reviewers. This project was part of the Mobile Informatics Program, funded by the Swedish Information Technology Institute (SITI).

References

Bellotti, V. and Bly, S., (1996) Walking Away from the Desktop Computer: Distributed Collaboration and Mobility in a Product Design Team, Proceedings of CSCW '96, (Cambridge MA USA, 1996), ACM Press

Bentley, J. A. Hughes, D. Randall, T. Rodden, P. Sawyer, D. Shapiro and I. Sommerville; (1992) Ethnographically-informed systems for air traffic control, Proceedings of CSCW '92, ACM Press

Dourish, P. and Belotti, V. (1992) Awareness and Coordination in Shared Workspaces, in Proceedings from CSCW '92 ACM Press

Dourish, P. and Bly, S. (1992) Portholes: Supporting Awareness in a Distributed Work Group, Proceedings of CHI '92, ACM Press

Gerson, E. and Leigh Star, S., (1984) Analyzing due process in the workplace, ACM transactions on office information systems, 4

Goodwin, C. and Goodwin, M.H., (1998) Seeing as situated activity: Formulating planes, in Cognition and Communication at Work, (eds.) Engeström, Y. And Middleton, D. Cambridge University Press

Heath, C. and Luff, P. (1992), Collaboration and Control - Crisis Management and Multimedia Technology in London Underground Line Control Rooms, Computer Supported Cooperative Work, Vol. 1 (1992), 69-94

Hughes, J., King, V. Rodden, T and Andersen, H., (1994) Moving Out from the Control Room: Ethnography in System Design, Proceedings of CSCW '94, Chapel Hill, NC, USA, ACM Press

Hughes, J. A., Randall, D. Shapiro, D., (1992) Faltering from Ethnography to Design, Proceedings of CSCW '92, ACM Press

Hutchins, E. (1993) Learning to Navigate, in S. Chaiklin and J. Lave (eds.) Understanding Practice: Perspectives on Activity and Context, Cambridge University Press, Cambridge

Hutchins, E., (1995) Cognition in the Wild, MIT Press

La Porte, T, (1988) The United States Air Traffic System: Increasing Reliability in the Midst of Rapid Growth, in The Development of Large Technical Systems, (eds.) Mayntz, R. And Hughes T.P. Frankfurt am Main: Campus Verlag.

Luff, P and Heath, C., (1998), Mobility in Collaboration, Proceedings of CSCW '98, Seattle, Washington USA, ACM Press

Luff, P. and Heath, C. (2000) Broadcast talk: Initiating Calls through a Computer-Mediated Technology, Working paper, Work Interaction and Technology Research Group, Management Centre, King's College, London.

Luftfartsverket, [Civil Aviation Administration] (1997), Radiokommunikation på flygplats (UHF) [Radio communication on airport (UHF)]

Pritchard, B and D Kalogjera (2000), On some features of conversation in maritime VHF communication, Selected Paper from the 7th IADA Conference 1999, Birmingham. eds Coulthard, M., J Cotterill and F Rock, Tübingen: Max Niemeyer Verlag.

Michael, M., (1996) Technologies and tantrums: Regulating hybrids in the case of 'road rage', Keynote speech at the Conference Regulating Identities (Queensland University of Technology, 1996) 2-4 October

Sanders, R.E, (2000) Conversational socializing on marine VHF radio: Adapting laughter and other practices to the technology in use, in Festschrift in honor of Robert Hopper.

Sanne, J. (1999) Creating Safety in Air Traffic Control, Arkivs förlag, Lund

SCAA, Swedish Civil Aviation Administration, VDLmode 4 (VHF Data Link for CNS Applications) in CNS/ATM, issue 1, 19991029

Schmidt, K. and Simone, C., (1996) Coordination Mechanisms: Towards a conceptual Foundation of CSCW Systems Design, Computer Supported Cooperative Work, 5

Suchman, L. (1987), Plans and Situated Action: The Problem of Human-Machine Communication, Cambridge, England: Cambridge University Press

Suchman, L. (1991) Centers of Coordination: A Case and Some Themes, in Discourse, Tools, and Reasoning: Essays on Situated Cognition, eds. Resnick, L.B., Säljö, R., Pontecorvo, C., Burge, B., Springer

Web address

Swedish Civil Aviation Administration, the SnowCard system http://blinder.lfv.se/ans/card/

W. Prinz, M. Jarke, Y. Rogers, K. Schmidt, and V. Wulf (eds.), *Proceedings of the Seventh European Conference on Computer-Supported Cooperative Work, 16-20 September 2001, Bonn, Germany*, pp. 399-418.
© 2001 Kluwer Academic Publishers. Printed in the Netherlands.

When Worlds Collide: Molecular Biology as Interdisciplinary Collaboration

Vicki O'Day, Annette Adler, Allan Kuchinsky, Anna Bouch
University of California, Santa Cruz, USA; Agilent Technologies, USA;
University College London, UK
*oday@calterra.com; [annette_adler, allan_kuchinsky]@agilent.com;
A.Bouch@cs.ucl.ac.uk*

Abstract. The field of molecular biology is in a remarkably rapid period of change, as the genome sequencing projects and new experimental technologies have generated an explosion of data. To analyze and draw insights from the vast amounts of information, biologists use a new generation of bioinformatics software tools, often working closely with mathematicians and computer scientists. There are elements of both *collision* and *convergence* in these interdisciplinary encounters. We conducted user studies with biologists engaged in investigating the molecular basis of disease. We describe several issues that arise in this collision/convergence of disciplines, drawing on the notion of *boundary objects in-the-making*. We provide recommendations on building technology for people whose work now sits at the crossroads of diverse and rapidly changing scientific fields.

Introduction

The field of molecular biology is in a remarkably rapid period of change. One notable characteristic of current genomics research is its increasing reliance on computational tools, including genomic databases (public and proprietary), online scientific literature, and data analysis software. This has led to immense interest and investment in bioinformatics information and tools. In addition to this proliferation of information and tools in the genomics research community at large, some molecular biologists are generating huge amounts of information in their own labs using a new technology called DNA microarrays. Microarrays allow biologists to simultaneously probe the activities of thousands of genes under diverse experimental conditions, which is useful for investigating relationships within and across families of genes. Microarray experiments can produce terabytes of data, and it is simply not possible to analyze these data without significant computational support. It is likely that even larger data sets will arise as data are shared among many academic and industrial labs, just as genomic and other databases arose from distributed efforts. One of the central themes of computer-supported cooperative work (CSCW) is the study of collaborative encounters, especially when new technologies are involved. We are interested here in a collaborative encounter between *disciplines*, as biologists and computational experts work together to solve hard biological problems. Interdisciplinary collaboration raises challenging issues for practitioners and for technology designers who wish to support their work.

Several years ago, a leader in the biotechnology industry declared that "biology is now an information science" (Williams, 1995). More recently, an article in the *New York Times* announced that " all science is computer science." (Johnson, 2001) These are provocative claims, and most biologists probably would not characterize the changes in their field in quite those terms. However, these statements do point to a current tension for molecular biologists. Information models are not new to biology, but the work of biologists is changing through its contact with informatics (and vice versa). On the one hand, biologists are clearly working on problems that emerge from biology; they want to identify genes and understand how they function in living organisms. On the other hand, it is increasingly necessary to address these problems using information visualization, statistics, and other techniques for manipulating large amounts of data. But these techniques do not come ready-made for biological applications. To provide effective computational support, computational experts have to understand biological questions and work with biologists to try out new forms of analysis, using real biological data. Biological systems have a different character than computational or physical systems. They are less well-behaved; exceptions are as common as rules. It is harder to make simplifying assumptions than it is in the physical and computational sciences. Computational experts have to adapt their approaches to the way living systems work.

What makes an interdisciplinary encounter difficult (and interesting) is that it involves different worlds, or different systems of meaning. People learn through their disciplines to formulate and solve problems in particular ways. They learn what *counts*—as a valid object of attention, a good method of analysis, or a reasonable solution. In CSCW, we are accustomed to thinking about people's different (and possibly competing) activities, responsibilities, locations, and work styles. But here we must also consider people's different ideas about what information *is* and what makes it reliable and meaningful.

We emphasize here the interdisciplinary collaborations between molecular biologists and what we call "computational experts," but each of these categories is diverse in itself. Molecular biologists work in different problem areas that shape their perspectives in particular ways. Computational experts include (at least) mathematicians, statisticians, and software developers, each with different backgrounds and skills. These fields converge in bioinformatics and computational biology and in industry terms such as "biocomputing," which are emblematic of the hybrid character of this work. However, at this time most practitioners are still either biologists or computational experts, but not both. We focus here on the challenge of collaborating across this significant disciplinary boundary, while keeping in mind the many differences within each group.

In some settings, biologists and computational experts work together directly on the analysis of experimental data, especially when the biologists are just beginning to use computational packages. Later, it is more common for biologists to encounter statistical methods and other computational techniques primarily through data analysis software. That is, the tools act as intermediaries between biologists and computational experts. Eventually, analytical techniques may become a kind of black box—something a biologist knows how to apply and need not understand in depth. But at this stage, biologists and computational experts must build on one another's knowledge and intuitions to develop workable methods for finding and interpreting patterns in biological data. Although the title of our paper refers only to worlds colliding, we see an interplay between collision and convergence in the new biology.

The central question addressed in this paper is: How should technology be designed for people whose work now sits at the crossroads of different disciplines? This is a situation in which the technology mediates between disciplines with different ways of looking at the world. What issues arise for participants in an interdisciplinary collaboration? How do people collaborate across disciplines when the ground is shifting on each side? To explore these questions, we discuss interdisciplinary encounters between biologists and computational experts. This discussion draws on a series of ethnographic interviews with research biologists and microarray designers. The discussion is lopsided in favor of biologists, since the issue of interdisciplinary collaboration emerged through a set of interviews with biologists which were originally meant to look at their particular technology uses and needs.

We find the notion of *boundary object* (Star & Griesemer, 1989, Bowker & Star, 2000) to be particularly helpful in thinking through the issues raised in this example. In our view, it is not a perfect fit for the objects we see migrating across community boundaries, but that makes it even more interesting—it adds to our understanding of the idea of boundary objects, as well as of the objects held in common by molecular biologists and computational experts. We use boundary objects in discussing three issues that arise in this interdisciplinary collaboration: contrasting biological and computational stories, contrasting notions of biological and statistical significance, and changing work practices. We end with a discussion of software design implications.

Method

Our group at Agilent is engaged in software research to support molecular biologists, with a particular focus on the problems involved in disease and drug discovery. To ground our group's software design projects in an understanding of users' needs, we conducted a series of ethnographic interviews with molecular biologists. Most of our interviews (about twenty) took place in a single laboratory at the (U.S.) National Institutes of Health (NIH), where biologists are investigating the molecular basis for different types of cancer. We also interviewed several biologists and computational experts in university labs and local biotechnology companies. In addition, we interviewed colleagues in our own company who were trained as molecular biologists and who now work as developers of our company's microarray technology.

We conducted our interviews in the biologists' labs. The interviews were open-ended and informal; we asked the scientists to explain to us how they formulated and carried out their research projects and what they were learning from them. In most cases, people turned to their computers and walked us through their data, showing us which software tools they used, how each tool fit into their analytic strategy, and how they interpreted the information presented in each tool. For the most part, we chose to talk with people who used microarrays in their experiments. Agilent makes microarray products (including arrays, scanners, and analysis software) and we were interested in how people handle the large volumes of data generated by microarrays.

Microarrays in Molecular Biology

Molecular biologists seek to identify and understand the relationships of genes, proteins, and pathways in living organisms. An increasingly important tool for research in molecular biology is the DNA microarray, or gene chip. Using microarrays, biologists shift from examining the way a single or a few genes change as cells move from state to state to simultaneously monitoring thousands of genes across different conditions. Microarrays are a new technology, and only a few labs have experience in using them (DeRisi et al, 1996). The NIH lab we visited (which is among the earliest microarray users) has been using microarrays for about four years. During this time, members of the lab have developed basic protocols for microarray use and established lab-wide software standards.

A microarray gene expression experiment starts with an array and a sample. The array is a glass slide on which thousands of *probes* have been deposited in a grid-like arrangement. Each probe consists of a small sequence of DNA that complements a particular gene from a particular organism. Many researchers at the NIH lab use an array with about 6000 probes that represent a cross-section of the 30,000 genes in the human genome.

To perform an array analysis, researchers collect samples of the biological materials whose genetic activity they want to study. For example, a sample might consist of tumor cells from cancer patients or cells from a particular kind of tissue. Then RNA is extracted from the sample; the RNA molecules are produced by active genes and are specific to those genes, so they indicate which genes are expressed or "turned on" in a cell. The RNA is used as a template for synthesizing a form of DNA called complementary DNA, or cDNA, which is used because it is more stable than RNA. This cDNA is in turn labeled with a fluorescent dye. Then a solution containing these labeled molecules is distributed over the slide containing the probes. If the sample contains cDNA that matches any of the probes, the cDNA will bind (or hybridize) to those spots on the array.

The slide is scanned and the amount of fluorescence is measured at each spot (a measurement which requires considerable data processing in itself). The different levels of fluorescence at different array locations give information about which genes are being expressed in the sample and at what levels. The brighter the fluorescence, the more cDNA has attached to the probe, so the more active the gene corresponding to that probe must be in that sample. Each time a sample is hybridized to an array, thousands of data points are generated. It is a common practice to include labeled reference material along with the sample, so each of the thousands of probes actually gives two data points—one for the experimental sample and one for the reference. Relative gene expression patterns are determined by comparing the expression levels in different experimental samples to the same reference sample.

Once the data have been generated, researchers use a variety of tools to look at them, including spreadsheets (for basic number-crunching), off-the-shelf database programs (to query the data along different dimensions), and special-purpose bioinformatics tools (for more complex algorithms to find patterns in the data). Each of these tools is a way of filtering the thousands of data points, to identify a small number of genes (usually fewer than a hundred) that seem to be interesting and worth looking at further. Then the biologists usually consult genomic databases (such as GenBank) and scientific literature databases (such as Medline) to see what is already known about these genes.

There are many different kinds of gene expression experiments that can be done using microarrays. Though we cannot characterize a typical experiment, we can give examples of the projects being done by researchers in the NIH lab. Several researchers are trying to find genetic markers for particular kinds of cancer. For example, certain cancers are quite rare and difficult to diagnose. By analyzing the gene expression activity associated with similar cancers, researchers hope to find a set of genes whose pattern of expression is unique to each cancer. They hope these unique genetic profiles could be used to develop diagnostic tests. Other researchers are trying to learn the functions of particular genes. They can modify a gene of interest in a cell line and then take snapshots of more general gene expression activity at several time intervals after the modification. They hope to figure out what the "downstream" effects of that gene are, to begin to piece together the biological pathways in which it participates. An important aspect of using microarrays is figuring out how to translate research questions into choices for arrays and samples in such a way that the data analysis will yield useful answers, in light of current data analysis approaches and tools.

There is a good deal of formal and informal collaboration among people working on related projects. Visitors and post-docs share lab space in very tight conditions—each person has only a few feet of lab bench and nearby desk space (with computer). People are aware of each other's projects, especially where there are overlapping interests in particular diseases, and they exchange information and advice about lab protocols and data interpretion. Most papers are co-authored by a long list of researchers.

There are two people in the NIH lab we visited who play a special role in supporting the molecular biologists in their microarray experiments. These people (one biochemist and one image processing expert) choose which software tools should be used in the lab, teach people how to use them, consult with people on data analysis for particular experiments, and write custom software when needed. This kind of contribution has been well-documented in the human-computer interaction literature (Mackay,1990, Gantt & Nardi, 1992, Williams, 1993). We draw attention to it here because it is a vitally important part of the interdisciplinary collaboration between biologists and computational experts—most of the biologists we interviewed emphasized that they could not have done their experiments without the help of their on-call consultants.

Boundary Objects In-the-Making

The biologists we interviewed had adopted a large number of computational resources, especially since they had begun using microarrays. Each person had assembled a working set of information tools and services to help them throughout the course of their research projects. Despite the biologists' adeptness in using their tools, it was clear from our conversations that there were aspects of these technologies that puzzled or bothered them at times, as we will describe in more detail in the following sections. There is something about the way these information tools work that seems a little askew—they don't quite fit the way biologists think about their world. We want to look more closely at this problem of fit, and we find the concept of *boundary object* helpful in thinking about the gaps left open by bioinformatics technologies.

Star uses boundary objects as a way to talk about objects that circulate among different communities of practice, taking on distinct local meanings and uses in each one (Star & Griesemer, 1989, Bowker & Star, 2000) (A *community of practice* is one in which people develop a sense of shared activities and membership through sustained participation (Lave & Wenger, 1991).) A boundary object retains some common structure and is recognizably the same object across communities, but it has "different meanings in different social worlds" (Bowker & Star, 2000, p. 297). In the examples of Bowker and Star, boundary objects travel well and facilitate collaboration across communities in part because their local differences don't have to be confronted or reconciled.

The mobility of objects such as software tools, algorithms, and data sets allows biologists and computational experts to cooperate on solving analytical problems in molecular biology. However, several questions arise: Do computational experts and biologists agree on what counts as important in data? If you translate biological data into computational data and perform mathematical operations on them to find patterns, are the results biologically meaningful? Are anomalies in one domain also anomalies in the other domain? How much common structure is retained, and to what extent do local differences of interpretation matter? The interdisciplinary collaboration would be more comfortable if analytical tools and data worked as boundary objects whose local interpretations were not called into question, but this is not quite the case.

Some features of this collaboration depart from the boundary object scenarios described by Bowker and Star. First, this is not a situation in which people in different communities of practice are focused on their own activities and problems. On the contrary, it is a more intimate collaboration, in which people from different disciplinary communities are trying to work together on a common problem. They must enter into each other's worlds, shift their own practices, and accommodate unfamiliar points of view. They have to achieve a kind of double vision, to see common objects both from their own disciplinary perspective and from the perspectives of their colleagues. Second, Bowker and Star point out that boundary objects arise over time in durable cooperative arrangements. However, the interdisciplinary encounter between biologists and computational experts is new and not yet stable. It is far from a durable cooperation, although it may grow into such a relationship over time.

It may be more useful to look at the objects in this interdisciplinary collaboration as boundary objects *in-the-making*—they are circulating across communities, but sometimes it is necessary to confront and reconcile their different local meanings. What we want to draw attention to here is that these unstable objects can still work to facilitate collaboration across communities—they give people common ground for discussion and negotiation.

The interdisciplinary collaboration we describe has features in common with several earlier projects in the CSCW literature. Bannon and Bødker discuss the issues of designing and using "common information spaces" (Bannon & Bødker, 1997). They include situations in which cooperative work is mediated by a database, since the person who records information in a database and the person who accesses that information try to understand each other's context. Bannon and Bødker point to the tensions and tradeoffs in creating common information spaces, and they draw attention to the importance of human mediators in helping people from different communities make use of common information. As we have mentioned, we also found that human mediators play key facilitator roles.

Van House, Butler, and Schiff describe a digital library project that involves sharing environmental planning data sets (mostly measurement data) on the web (Van House et al, 1998). They describe users' concerns about the ways data might be misused or misunderstood when it is dissociated from its original contexts and communities of expert practitioners. Harper reports on an ethnographic study of "missions" sent by the International Monetary Fund to member countries, during which economists gather and analyze data and prepare reports on national economies (Harper, 1997). His fascinating study shows how meetings between the visiting economists and their hosts help to make the numbers "count. " These meetings are a "social process that converts *speechless* numbers into ones that have a *voice*" (Harper, 1997, p. 363). Through conversation and negotiation, "raw numbers" are converted into meaningful and useful information. As in Harper's case, we must pay attention to whether and how numbers are adopted, not just how they are generated.

Each of these projects raises the important issue of trust and reliability when information objects travel across communities of practice. We emphasize the complexity of trust in the sections below, since it emerges as a central theme of the interdisciplinary collaboration between biologists and computational experts. We do not mean to imply that people are suspicious of each other, but rather that both biologists and computational experts are still trying to bring their problems and methods into alignment, so they can both feel confident of their results.

Comparing Stories

As we listened to molecular biologists talking about their research, we were struck by how often they described their activities in terms of *telling a story*. Each story is an interpretive framework—a way of making sense of experimental data and situating it in a context of earlier work. By looking at how these stories are put together, we can see some of the strangeness bioinformatics tools have for biologists. In this section, we revisit our account of microarray experiments to look at collisions and convergences in biological and computational stories.

Biological Stories

The stories told by molecular biologists usually focus on how genes and proteins interact with other genes and proteins in biological pathways (such as energy metabolism or cell growth). When genes are expressed, they encode proteins. In turn, proteins can catalyze biochemical reactions in the body, provide cell structure, transport nutrients, or regulate further gene expression. Molecular biologists explain biological phenomena by narrating the interrelationships of genes and proteins.

As we have discussed, microarray experiments yield data about the relative expression levels of genes under specific conditions, such as which genes are expressed in a set of breast tumor samples. Usually, the researchers in the NIH lab examine a series of samples using their arrays and cross-compare the results. The data live in huge spreadsheets, where each of the 6000 rows corresponds to one gene and each column corresponds to an experimental condition; it is not uncommon to have 20 to 40 experimental conditions. It is very challenging to see the traces of biological phenomena in this sea of numbers. People are looking for patterns, usually quite subtle, that imply interrelationships among the genes. They hope to infer a network of cause and effect relationships among genes—including the coordinated effects of multiple genes acting together—since such networks are the basis of biological pathways. Deciphering pathways is what most molecular biologists refer to when they speak of "putting together the story. "

Biological stories are told from diverse points of view. When biologists search the scientific literature for references to a gene they are investigating, they are most interested in what is known about the gene in a context similar to their own. But they are likely to come across references to quite different contexts, which tell a different story about the gene—in fact, the gene might have quite different functions across these contexts. For example, a prostate cancer researcher might find information about a gene of interest, but it is told from the perspective of a biologist studying liver function. Or two or more researchers may independently discover the same gene, but refer to it by different names. Since there is a pride of ownership involved in naming a gene, it is not easy to standardize gene names. Biologists have to be aware of the different aliases for a gene under study.

In general, biological stories need to accommodate multiple hypotheses and alternative explanations, which change as new data are obtained. Biologists use bioinformatics tools or literature searches to generate and check out their ideas, and they find it challenging to organize and manage the links between computational results and the biological stories they support.

Computational Stories

There is no way to analyse spreadsheet data in thousands of rows and a series of columns without some computational help. Biologists use bioinformatics tools to filter, sort, and find patterns. That is, they use tools that put together a *computational* story for those data.

One important character in a computational story is a *cluster*. The clustering algorithms used in bioinformatics tools work like document clustering—they reorganise a large set of elements into groups whose elements are somehow similar to one another. One row of a spreadsheet (the expression levels of a particular gene over a number of experimental conditions) can be thought of as an expression "profile" for one gene, and different gene profiles can be compared to see how similar they are, based on mathematical notions of similarity. Sets of genes with similar expression profiles are grouped together in clusters. In other words, the clustering algorithm surveys the numerical values of expression levels and looks for non-random correlations. If clusters have biological as well as mathematical meaning, then each cluster describes a group of genes that may be co-regulated, implying their involvement in the same biological pathway.

People often combine clustering with visual inspection. Gene expression levels are encoded into shades of red and green, and biologists look at array data that is mapped in this way to see if they can see patterns in the arrangement of colors. They can use clustering algorithms to reorder the data, to allow for new patterns to emerge through visual inspection.

Double Vision: Making Stories Converge

Although clustering tools are common for molecular biologists who use microarrays, we found that biologists are reluctant to trust the clusters identified by the tools. Biologists draw a sharp distinction between computation and biology and do not take for granted that meanings can be translated in a straightforward way from one domain to the other. Nor do they trust the findings they read in the scientific literature when these results are based on mathematical analyses that the paper's authors don't appear to understand.

Many of the biologists we interviewed try to adopt a mathematician's perspective, to look into the inner workings of the algorithms and convince themselves that each step makes sense from a biological perspective. This brings the biologists into contact with someone else's unfamiliar way of looking at things. Consider this biologist's description:

> I think we spend two thirds of the time thinking about the biology and a third thinking about this kind of logic which feeds into it eventually. Because it makes you—it determines whether or not you can believe what all these computer manipulations are telling you.

We are struck here by the alien quality of "this kind of logic." The computational logic "feeds into" the biology eventually, and there is no way to get to the biology except through this logic. Despite its strangeness, biologists have to work with it to make the different stories converge.

There is an ironic note to the labor-saving possibilities of bioinformatics analyses. Although in principle these tools reduce analytical effort by suggesting mathematical relationships that may be useful, biologists tend to run through extra analyses so the analyses will check up on each other. For example, they may run a clustering algorithm repeatedly, using different similarity measures to see if the sets of clusters that come up are consistent. If they get the same results from several different methods, they have some confidence that the results may be biologically significant. Of course, checking results and calibrating tools are always part of good scientific practice. But in this situation, biologists emphasized to us their uncertainty about how much cross-checking was enough—how much it would take to make the computational patterns biologically convincing.

We emphasize that microarrays are new, and both the biologists and the computational experts are unsure of how to bring their disciplinary strengths together. Both are learning, and both are nervous about the prospect of producing unreliable findings. A mathematically-derived set of clusters in gene expression data is a new kind of common object that emerges through interdisciplinary collaboration, belonging to both disciplines and not fully to one or the other. The analytical algorithms are themselves a topic of research, and they continue to be tested and revised with new sets of biological data. A computational expert at the lab, whose skills are very much appreciated by his biologist colleagues, talked about some of his doubts:

> When you run the program and see all those relationships, it tends to mean something but basically means nothing. So you don't want to make a big story out of nothing. You really want to make sure that everything goes smooth, as if there is a real story there. So that part of the abstraction is usually—we are all learning and trying to figure out...

For both computational experts and biologists, it is not enough to have a story that makes sense only in one perspective or the other. It is important for the stories to converge, since biologists rely on computational tools in sorting through their data. One of the biologists talked in similar terms when he described a conversation with some mathematicians about a new algorithm:

> One caveat they pointed out, this analysis is susceptible to meaninglessness. They showed us some data that just didn't correlate with anything—no clinical characteristics, no laboratory measurement, no demographic information, nothing. Instead their strongest association was with a particular date in the year, of all things. It turns out that Cluster A was done prior, statistically significant...So what happened? I'm willing to go that route, because they may have had some technical problems, we don't know. What we can do—we can then look at the genes and we want the genes to tell us..."

He wants to be able to trust the convergence between biological and computational features of the data (so the genes will be able to speak), but he is also realistic about the possibility of misalignment.

Stories as Boundary Objects

Stories are a kind of boundary object. As they travel across communities of practice, they are more or less successful in helping communities to collaborate with one another. They work to focus people's collective attention on something of common interest: an account of how genes seem to be related to one another. In the interdisciplinary encounters between biologists and computational experts, these stories are rather unstable—it is hard to be sure whether a particular story is a good one or not. As boundary objects in-the-making, stories about genes based on computational analysis are subject to scrutiny, and their different interpretations call for explanation. But even in these circumstances, the stories work to facilitate the collaborative analysis of experimental data across disciplines.

Stories are boundary objects between biologists, as well as across disciplines. They circulate through different biological contexts, and as people collaborate on data analysis, alternative stories come into play. As one post-doc said, "Most people in the lab analyze each other's data and recognize things. Because no two people had the same training." When biologists look at data, they look for familiar characters—genes they know well from other projects and other contexts. A gene that is quite unknown to one biologist may be an old friend to another. In general, biologists have to look through and understand other people's points of view (both biological and computational) to compose a good biological story. As one scientist at NIH put it, they try to develop a "consensus hallucination as to what the data is trying to indicate to us," pulling together the knowledge and ideas of people with diverse experience and expertise.

Comparing Biological and Statistical Significance

One of the central tensions that emerges in the interdisciplinary work of biologists and computational experts is how to decide which data are biologically significant. The discipline of statistics has developed mathematical methods for establishing significance in data analysis. Biologists use statistics, but they also rely on experimental know-how and a sense of what is biologically interesting and believable. Sometimes their approaches and criteria lead in different directions than those of computational experts.

Deciding what is significant is a way of organizing what can be seen. When data are labeled significant, they become more visible—they *count*. When data are labeled not significant, they become invisible and no longer receive attention.

Notions of significance are deeply embedded in many data analysis tools; this is not a concept that can be readily customized for different users. In this section, we discuss how molecular biologists grapple with differences between statistical and biological significance, as they try to tease apart the signal and noise generated in biological experiments.

Outliers and Anomalies

To make sure that only good data are presented to users, software tools often set high statistical cut-offs on measurement data (such as the level of signal intensity required to indicate the influence of a gene). However, biological phenomena are often subtle and may be lost when statistical cut-offs are too stringent. Statistical assessments of significance rely on looking at relatively few variables over large samples. But there are many dimensions of interest in biological array data, which may not all have the large number of measurements needed by traditional statistical methods. These data call for new kinds of analytical approaches from computational experts. Also, it is important to consider what constitutes a new finding: an effect that is slight but unexpected can be much more informative than an effect that is pronounced but already understood by biologists.

Many biologists talked about wanting to look around the edges of their tools' statistical cut-offs, to see what is "under the shadow." They want to see shades of gray, rather than just black and white. When they can't see past a statistical wall, it raises concerns about the integrity of the data analysis. It is especially difficult to figure out how to handle outliers—those bits of data that don't seem to line up with the rest. The problem is that there are different ways to account for the categorization of data as outliers. They might be effects of the mathematical algorithms—perhaps the algorithms rendered marginal some data that are worth paying attention to biologically. (An odd variation in the pattern might be just the thing to look at.) Or an anomalous piece of data might be the outcome of unintentional variations in the experimental set-up, such as a smudged slide. Or it might be just a sideline to the important biological story whose patterns are beginning to take shape in the data. In this case, biologists want to set it aside. Depending on the explanation, outliers are either *extra* data that can be safely discarded or *missing* data that should not be discarded. Of course, biologists don't know how to explain outliers unless they take a close look at them, which may be difficult with tools that make them hard to see. This is not a problem of biologists not understanding statistics; they do understand them. It is rather a difference in how to interpret and work with categories such as "outlier."

Here is how one biologist discussed outliers in his data set:

> So what defines that data set, and what our gut feeling about it was that I think it was nice that there were these overlaps of genes, and I think if you shrink the data set down too much where you have only one copy of the gene, if it shows up and it's out there in the middle of nowhere and there's nothing questionable around it, you don't know if it's a red herring or if it's just the

most important gene…That's why it should be looked at…How do you look at it? These are distributed here because they're meaningful and that's the reason they're here? Or were they distributed here as some type of statistical variation? I think that if a chip has multiple homologs [variants] for a certain gene, you start becoming more comfortable with these outliers.

The biologist is pointing here to the useful strategy of taking statistical significance into account in his experimental design. In particular, he finds that it works best if there are variants of the same gene on the array. When the sample is hybridized to the array, the expression levels for that gene should be about the same for each of the variants. If that turns out to be true, then the biologist can at least feel assured that the result is correct, even if it can't yet be explained biologically. Here is a description from another biologist along the same lines:

So as your sample size increases, the need to view the actual image [fluorescence data] decreases. But these experiments are only one of the two ways people are doing things. The other way people are doing things is they are taking one sample and doing it in triplicate and looking at the genes that change over that series of experiments, so in that case your N is somewhat smaller. Small is relative, whether it's small or not. What's too small?

In this case, the biologist describes a strategy of replicating sample runs rather than replicating genes on the array, but it's the same idea of building in redundancy. Yet even with redundant designs, it is still hard to know how much is enough.

Flexibility and Rigidity

Biologists in the NIH lab are also attuned to the material features of the microarray technology and how these might affect their statistical analyses. The microarray technology includes printers and scanners, and clogs or other problems can lead to a "dirty" hybridization, where one portion of the array is no good. Here, a biologist points out that analysis tools can't always cope with situations like this:

You can have non-specific hybridization going on across the whole slide, which was missed by the analytical measurement. What you can do is, you can look at the ratio outliers to see if they're uniformly distributed or non-uniformly distributed. The histogram and scatterplots will give you some idea also, but it's the whole picture, it's all the parts. And likewise you can also look for some dirty hyb. It could be confined to one quadrant or it could be the whole thing. If it's the whole thing, the statistics usually tell you, but if it's a portion of the array, the statistics sometimes don't pick it up.

In circumstances like this, it may be the biologist who can judge what is going on and the statistical tools that have limited information. In this case, the biologist wants to be able to tell the tool, rather than the other way around—for example, to mark off one quadrant as unsalvageable, while keeping the remaining three quadrants in the analysis. This is a complex scenario; in some circumstances, several different tools used in combination can elucidate the problem. However, sometimes the whole hybridization has to be thrown away.

Biologists in the NIH lab draw a contrast between biological and computational styles of thinking in terms of flexibility. In their view, statistics are unnecessarily rigid. As we watched people using their information tools, people offered a number of suggestions for how the tools could be made more usable. Most of the time, the suggestions had to do with loosening up restrictions and making hard-wired operations tailorable. What about letting the user adjust the angle that separates clusters, or allowing more cross-experiment comparisons?

Besides offering usability feedback, the biologists' comments reflected more generally on their sense that they wanted to steer the tools differently, as biologists. One person explained as he showed us an operation he wanted to do:

> So if I'm the biologist and I want to say: 'I think for this experiment, I think these spots are important and also these; only these things are not important so I want to draw a line like this. '

We notice in these comments how the biologist claims his authority to direct the tool. He says, "if I'm the biologist," because he wants to remind us that the biologist should be in charge. This same person named the central issue as one of interdisciplinary differences:

> Sometimes I find that the statistics thing, the hard statistics world, is not well applied to biology because we're not that rigid somehow. Because life is always very flexible. So it's really hard to say, "Cut-off is this." What about the red over there? So that's the thing we deal with constantly.

It is important to keep in mind that there are strengths in the statistical analysis tools, as well as uncomfortable mismatches. Biologists do want to let the statistics inform the biology, as well as the other way around—the analytical tools have capabilities they want to take advantage of. The design problem is to find a balance that works to suggest new directions and at the same time support biologists' ideas about what makes sense biologically.

Changing Work Practice

We have discussed the different stories and types of significance produced by biologists and computational experts as they work with data. In this section, we turn to the question of how microarray technology rearranges lab practice. Microarrays are a disruptive technology—they perturb the customary rhythms of the research projects in which they are used.

Molecular biologists in the NIH lab have experienced a change in the pace in their experimental work when they use microarrays. There is a difference in what people do and for how long. In particular, data analysis has assumed a much larger part of the picture, to a degree that was unexpected by the biologists.

Consider this account of a visiting biologist in the NIH lab, in answer to a question about how long she had been working on her project:

> Biologist: Oh yeah! Almost two years since I started doing the first hybs. I think maybe this case is a bit unusual because I had a very limited number of samples, and they're so precious I had to be sure that it was going to work, if I was going to do a hyb. I was actually working in [my home lab], and I just came here to do these hybs. We stupidly thought that I was going to do it really quickly and then just go back home. It didn't work that way. So I decided to come back—so there was actually a break, when I went home and stuff. And then we did this with fewer samples and started doing MDS [multi-dimensional scaling] plots and everything. We knew that we had to do more tumors, so I did them last—oh, around Christmas, I guess. But since then, and even meanwhile, when we didn't have that many samples, everybody was working on the data frames, looking at them in different ways. It's definitely the largest portion of the work, analyzing the data.

The project is not neatly divided into temporal phases. The biologist and her colleagues continue to explore the data produced in early hybridizations while she looks for more samples to use in later hybridizations. The insights they get from these plots and clusters suggest new things to try with the next sets of data. For this biologist, the work of "analyzing the data" seems to encompass more and more of the project.

We are interested in how people experience these changes. One of the biologists in the NIH lab described data analysis as a kind of "downtime":

> I guess one consequence of working out there on the edge—there's a lot of downtime in the sense that—what do I mean by downtime. You know, when you're used to working at the bench 8, 10 hours a day, there's no waiting at the bench. Things happen, there's a protocol, there's a script you have to follow. In some cases with this data analysis, we're waiting for it. You know, it's a process, and we're all willing participants. I'm a biologist, a human geneticist by degree, and actively involved in the bioinformatics and the data analysis, and that's where we want to go.

There is considerable ambivalence in this biologist's story of what it feels like to be working out on the edge. The time away from the bench is unstructured (there's no protocol or script to follow), and he feels it as *downtime*, a time when things are *not* happening, rather than a busy and productive time. This particular biologist is notable for the breadth of his tool set. But more options lead to less certainty about which paths or protocols he should follow, and some of the analysis options take a very long time to run. The biologist is convinced of the utility of microarrays and plans to continue using them in future projects. Microarrays, with their huge data sets and attendant data analysis tools, are "where we want to go." But microarrays also interfere with the usual protocols for lab work and experimentation, and biologists do not yet have stable new protocols that capture the particular rhythms of microarray work.

It is not just the introduction of microarray technology that produces uncertainty in lab practice. There are continued changes in technologies and experimental methods (such as protein and tissue arrays), so biologists must repeatedly adjust their practices. Also, biologists sense that their data may have a short shelf life, depending on changes in tools and instrumentation. When tools change, old data may no longer be analyzable. Comparison is at the heart of data analysis: As we have seen, biologists compare one set of tumors to another, or normal cells to tumor cells, or cells at one moment to cells at another moment. Cross-experiment comparisons are made possible when each experiment is first compared to a common reference of some kind. But when the instrumentation changes, this throws up a barrier between past and future experiments—the reference changes too, and data can no longer be compared. New software can lead to the same problem, if data formats change.

Computational approaches change the kinds of research questions people ask in molecular biology. The rapid updates to computational technologies increase the sense of urgency people feel in designing experiments to address their new questions. We have offered only a brief discussion of changing work practices here, but our interviews suggest that this would be a fruitful area to explore through extended observations of lab practice.

Implications for Software Technology

In this paper we have described the work of molecular biologists and some of the current changes in their science and practice. These are turbulent times for molecular biologists: As new understandings and new experimental approaches emerge, new questions and new ways of considering data emerge too. Microarrays in particular offer potential for great insight, but they do so by generating phenomenal amounts of data. These changes have led biologists to a collaboration with computational experts (statisticians, mathematicians, and computer scientists) to help in interpreting the resulting mountains of data. We have characterized this collaboration in two ways. It is a *collision*, in light of the felt impact of new methods of analysis and new colleagues who have quite different ways of making sense of data. It is also a *convergence*, as biologists and their analytical allies strive for a shared understanding that shapes the new biology.

We have described how people from each discipline bring their own interpretative frame to the data and negotiate to find a mutually understandable and workable perspective—a "consensus hallucination." At the end of the day, people in biological and computational disciplines try to produce biological understanding by bringing their distinctive interpretive frames together. But as we have discussed, it is likely that there will be an ongoing need for negotiation between disciplines. It is not the case that biologists can simply learn how to run the numbers; the numbers and ways to run them continue to be problematic as biologists ask new questions and encounter new forms of data. Similarly, mathematicians and computer scientists are challenged to develop new analytical methods to deal with the flexibility and multi-dimensionality of living systems. Biologists and computational experts need to continue their collaboration.

This collaboration is largely mediated through software. Software plays a central role in representations of data, analytical tools, and databases of genomic information and research publications. There is currently a proliferation of new tools. People are trying out a variety of approaches, from natural language analysis of scientific literature to machine learning and probabilistic reasoning over data sets. In this environment, we have to assume that collaborative capabilities must coexist comfortably with many different analytical tools and databases. Support for rapid updates, user customization, and mix-and-match tool strategies is needed. Drawing on our understanding of the difficulties experienced by biologists working with computational experts, we offer several recommendations for software to support their collaboration.

Support exploratory thinking for groups. When biologists work with computational tools, they try out different ideas—changing parameters to see how clusters shift, going out to the gene databases to see what information comes up about some genes that appear in an interesting pattern, using a different visualization technique to see what new relationships it highlights. This is an exploratory process, and it is easy to lose track of the trail one has followed and the links that have emerged along the way to developing a biological story. It would be useful to have explicit support for the earliest phases of observing relationships and developing hypotheses from array data. This support might look like design rationale tools (e.g., Conklin & Begeman, 1988, Moran & Carroll, 1996), but the kind of software we envision would emphasize the short-term capture of emergent lines of thinking, rather than long-term archives. The idea is to capture a developing understanding in a lightweight way—to help people remember (for now) that this gene should be explored further or that cluster looks familiar from another context. Annotations of both data and actions (across diverse tools) would be useful for this purpose.

Take advantage of local experience. In addition to helping a small group to track its own developing ideas, it would be useful if people could piggyback on the ongoing activities of larger groups, such as those sharing a lab or a particular research focus. As people find that certain articles or gene database entries are more relevant for their purposes than others, they need ways to make those more salient to those around them and to their own computational environments. Previous work on adaptive indexing and collaborative filtering of large databases in light of their patterns of use among groups (e.g., Furnas, 1985, Maes, 1995) might be fruitfully reapplied in this domain.

Support drill-downability. Array data span many layers of representation. As the data are visualized and manipulated using data anlysis tools, it is often the case that one layer of representation obscures others. For example, after image processing software has resolved the locations and magnitudes of spots on a slide, spot data are usually replaced by numeric expression levels. There are sideways layers too—a multi-dimensional scaling program shows one view, and a dendogram shows alternative relationships among the same data points. Different perspectives are built into these views. When people in an interdisciplinary collaboration are trying to achieve the kind of double vision we have described, they need to juxtapose multiple views and see how they relate to one another—flexibly drilling down and across layers of representation to build a bigger picture and see how layers (and perspectives) link up. There are analogies here to coordinated multiple view systems, such as Spotfire (Schneiderman, 1999). Supporting navigation through multiple views is one way of handing more control over to the biologists who use computational tools, to enhance their ability to apply their own intuitions while working with computational algorithms.

Acknowledgements

We thank all of the scientists who generously allowed us to visit their labs, peer at their data, and learn about their work. We also thank our management at Agilent for their support, and we thank Robert Ach, Mike Bittner, Patricia Collins, Bonnie Nardi, and several anonymous reviewers for their helpful feedback on this paper.

References

Bannon, L. & Bødker, S. (1997). 'Constructing common information spaces', *J. Hughes et al. (eds.), Proceedings of the Fifth European Conference on Computer Supported Cooperative Work*, Kluwer Academic Publishers, pp. 81-96.

Bowker, G.C. & Star, S.L. (2000). *Sorting Things Out: Classification and its Consequences.* MIT Press, Cambridge, Massachusetts.

Conklin, J. & Begeman, M. L. (1988). 'gIBIS: A Hypertext Tool for Exploratory Policy Discussion', *ACM Transactions on Office Information Systems*, vol. 6, no. 4, pp. 303-331.

DeRisi J., Penland L., Brown P.O., Bittner M.L., Meltzer, P.S., Ray M., Chen Y., Su Y.A., Trent J.M. (1996). 'Use of a cDNA microarray to analyse gene expression patterns in human cancer', *Nature Genetics*, 14, pp. 457-460.

Furnas, G. (1985). 'Experience with an adaptive indexing scheme', *Proceedings of ACM CHI '85 Conference on Human Factors in Computing Systems*, pp. 131-135.

Gantt, M. & Nardi, B.A. (1992). 'Gardeners and gurus: patterns of cooperation among CAD users', *Proceedings of the Conference on Human Factors in Computing Systems (CHI '92)*, pp. 107-117.

Harper, R.H.R. (1997). 'Gatherers of information: the mission process at the International Monetary Fund', *J. Hughes et al. (eds.), Proceedings of the Fifth European Conference on Computer Supported Cooperative Work*, Kluwer Academic Publishers, pp. 361-376.

Lave, J. & Wenger, E. (1991). *Situated Learning*, Cambridge University Press, Cambridge, England.

Mackay, W.E. (1990). 'Patterns of sharing customizable software', *Proceedings of the Conference on Computer-Supported Cooperative Work*, Los Angeles, California.

Maes, P. (1995). 'Social information filtering: algorithms for automating "word of mouth"', *Proceedings of ACM CHI '95 Conference on Human Factors in Computing Systems*, pp. 210-217.

Moran, T.P. & Carroll, J.M. (Eds.) (1996). *Design Rationale: Concepts, Techniques, and Use.* Hillsdale, NJ: Lawrence Erlbaum Associates.

Schneiderman, B. (1999). 'Dynamic queries, starfield displays, and the path to spotfire', <http://www.cs.umd.edu/hcil/spotfire>.

Star, S.L. & Griesemer, J. (1989). 'Institutional ecology, translations, and boundary objects: amateurs and professionals in Berkeley's Museum of Vertebrate Zoology, 1907-39', *Social Studies of Science*, 1, pp. 387-420.

Van House, N.A., Butler, M.H., & Schiff, L.R. (1998). 'Cooperative knowledge work and practices of trust: sharing environmental planning data sets', *Proceedings of the Conference on Computer-Supported Cooperative Work*, Seattle, Washington, pp. 335-343.

Williams, M.G. & Begg, V. (1993). 'Translation in participatory design: lessons from a workshop', *Proceedings of the Conference on Human Factors in Computing Systems—Adjunct Proceedings (ACM INTERCHI '93)*, pp. 55-56.

Williams, N. (1995). 'Europe opens institute to deal with gene data deluge', *Science*, v. 269 (Aug. 4 '95), p. 630.

Johnson, George (2001). 'In Silica Fertilization; All Science is Computer Science', *New York Times*, March 25, 2001.

Index of Authors